T0330261

Rules for the Global Economy

Rules for the Global Economy

Horst Siebert

Princeton University Press
Princeton and Oxford

ISBN: 978-0-691-13336-2 (alk. paper)

Library of Congress Control Number: 2009924886

British Library Cataloging-in-Publication Data is available

This book has been composed in Times using TEX
Typeset and copyedited by T&T Productions Ltd, London
Printed on acid-free paper ∞

press.princeton.edu

Printed in the United States of America

10 9 8 7 6 5 4 3 2 1

Contents

Foreword

When Horst Siebert started work on his pathbreaking book, more than a decade ago, the world economy was running smoothly. The dot.com bubble was still expanding. The attack of 9/11 was over the horizon. China had already entered its growth spurt, pulling much of Asia into years of prosperity. And five fat years of American prosperity were around the corner.

In fact, before the Great Crash of 2008, an informed observer might well have asked, "Why worry about new rules for the global economy? Didn't we survive the dot.com burst and al-Qaeda? Don't we already have the best of possible worlds with Anglo-Saxon capitalism and the Washington consensus?" Indeed, during George W. Bush's first months as president, a few commentators, exemplified by Alan Meltzer, went so far as to advocate early retirement for the International Monetary Fund and the World Bank. The least regulation was the best regulation.

Then Bear Stearns collapsed, followed by Lehman Brothers, AIG, Washington Mutual, Wachovia, the Royal Bank of Scotland, and the near-death of Citigroup, UBS, Lloyds, Barclays, and industrial giants with the stature of General Motors. Elite opinion turned almost 180 degrees. The demand for new modes of governance became an outright clamor.

Here is where Siebert's book enters center stage. In the wake of the crisis, British Prime Minister Gordon Brown and French President Nicholas Sarkozy called for a top-down overhaul of the Bretton Woods system. Evidently, they had not absorbed the lessons distilled by Siebert in his new book. Even in a crisis, all major parties must benefit if new rules are to be agreed. Washington and Tokyo saw little to be gained from putting the World Trade Organization, the World Bank, and the International Monetary Fund in a blender to create brand new institutions. Others, such as Beijing and New Delhi, could only see a payoff if the new institutions gave them a larger voice, and thus awarded Britain, France, and other established powers a smaller voice. This was not to be.

The G20 Summit Communiqué, forged in London early in April 2009, recognizes Siebert's realities. Instead of a grand redesign, the Communiqué called for smaller but focused regulatory upgrading that would benefit all players: less leverage in the banks, better surveillance of financial institutions that might pose a systemic risk, regular monitoring and reporting of new protection, and much more. Officials who are tasked with translating these G20 aspirations into new rules will greatly benefit from Siebert's sound analysis. The rest of us can use Siebert as a guide to distinguish between rules that genuinely answer the needs of our new era and fluffy wisps in the sky.

Gary Clyde Hufbauer
Reginald Jones Senior Fellow
Peterson Institute for International Economics

Preface

In this book, I analyze the institutional arrangements that deal with global economic issues. The principal question to which my study tries to give an answer may be put in the following way. Under which conditions do international rules come into existence? That is to say, under which circumstances do national approaches prove no longer sufficient to solve economic problems, so that sovereign states are prepared to cede part of their sovereignty to international rule systems? And, finally, do international rules contribute to an improvement in the human condition?

My answer will highlight how rules, and among them international arrangements, find their raison d'être in human experience. Unfortunately, the kinds of world events that lead to the establishment of institutions are mostly negative experiences, such as historical disasters, internal civil turmoil, and wars, all of which inflict severe hardship on people. Rules evolve in order to prevent human hardship. They are the result of pathological learning.

Disastrous harm and hardship can be interpreted as costs in economic terms. Resources unnecessarily employed for quarrels and disruptions could be used in production to generate a higher income for people, thus also allowing an improved standard of living. Such an unneeded use of resources represents opportunity costs, i.e., the costs of a forgone opportunity. We can also address them as pointless transaction costs, where transaction costs are defined as resources used in human exchange. If rules can prevent civil wars or wars between countries, they reduce such costs and allow benefits thanks to the fact that people can gain from mutual exchange. Likewise, benefits accrue from the reduction of border-crossing negative externalities, for instance, acid rain, and also from preventing one nation's opportunistic behavior to the detriment of another in the international division of labor. The reduction of transaction costs can therefore explain many rules, especially within economy-related institutional arrangements. We therefore speak of a transaction-costs approach or of an experience approach to rules.

International economic rules represent norms of behavior for governments, firms, and citizens and they embody a form of self-commitment: within such a system, states limit their national governments' choice of actions in the future. Behind any rule system we can therefore detect a "negative catalogue," i.e., a series of restraints imposed on the national governments' behavior. These constraints protect the international division of labor against the conflicting interests of national governments. The states' self-commitment also works as a shelter against the power of protectionist groups in national economies.

Wide-reaching rules become especially important in a globalizing world economy in which economic interdependence between nation states is intensifying. Similarly, as the development of property rights and other rules have followed the increase in the scarcity of goods in the history of humankind, the global rule system has to go along with the stronger interdependence between countries.

In the economic sphere, rules concern many areas, most importantly the international division of labor in the trade of goods and services as well as competition policy (both relevant for the global product markets); the flow of capital, the diffusion of technology, and the migration of people, including labor and human capital (all three areas relevant for international factor markets); the protection of the global environment (relevant as a restraint on markets); and the stability of the monetary–financial system (relevant for the global currency and financial markets). This book studies the conditions allowing international arrangements to come into existence, for instance, the requirement that they generate visible and direct benefits for its members as well as an increase in benefits over time. I will also discuss different institutional arrangements for rule systems applying to different economic areas, for instance, those where direct benefits for a country fail to arise, as in the case of global environmental goods. In this area, rules can have the effect of reducing global warming, but this benefit may be perceived as merely indirect, while abatement costs and losses in the achievement level of economic policy goals represent direct costs, borne by the signatories of an agreement. The book also analyzes the role of stabilizing and destabilizing mechanisms in these areas, such as generalizing an agreement through the most-favored-nation clause, bargaining procedures applying reciprocity of concessions, and the concept of single undertaking.

The transaction-costs approach has the advantage that it does not need a rosy concept of world welfare to motivate such rules. Such welfare might be easily, yet arbitrarily, determined by a politburo, by a dictator, by political leaders or parties that hierarchically impose how people should behave, or by some other organization. However, it would be impossible to define this welfare within the context of free societies, given the different preferences held by their individuals. Nor can we indulge in the Orwellian dream of a social planner designing such an order in a technocratic way, one who, supposedly, has all the necessary information to plan and enforce a rule system from the top down. The transaction-costs approach does not start from the preferences of a subgroup of society either, for instance, the ideas of some NGOs, shared by their supporters but not necessarily accepted outside the group by other members of society. It is not a collectivist approach. On the contrary, under the transaction-costs approach, the benefit of rules is assessed according to the concept of reduced costs, and these costs can be defined in a decentralized way by individuals according to their own individual preferences and by nation states according to their goals. Thus, this approach is in line with the Hayekian view of economic reality and with the subsidiarity principle.

In chapter I, following the Freiburg School of German economics, I develop a concept of the world economic order, adopting a Hayekian approach where rules find their reason in the lowering of transaction costs. The taxonomy of mechanisms which reduce transaction costs encompasses decentralization of the economic decisions, reliance on markets, property rights, the principle of territoriality, lowering uncertainty in transactions, cooperative behavior among states, internalization of negative externalities among states, and global public goods.

Chapter II studies how the forces of globalization affect the different areas of the international rule system: the trade of goods and services, competition and anti-trust policy, international factor flows (capital, technology, and labor), the internalization of border-crossing negative externalities, global environmental protection, the stability of the monetary–financial system, and human rights.

Chapter III focuses on how rules are established. This encompasses a rich institutional experience such as institutional competition, decentralizing economic decisions, securing gains from cooperation, principles of bargaining for cooperation gains, the requirement that countries enjoy direct benefits, and trade externalities in bargaining. Establishing rules to prevent negative spillovers between countries is more complex. This applies especially in the case of global public goods where direct national benefits are only remote and where burden-sharing is needed. The chapter also looks at cases in which multilateral rules are not accepted and respected.

Chapter IV studies the mechanisms that stabilize international rule systems. Among them are positive mechanisms by which cooperation gains are multilateralized, for instance, the "most-favored-nation" clause in the trade order, side payments, and self-enforcing contracts. Agreed-upon restraints, sanctions, and dispute settlement are further instruments. A major issue in the order of the international division of labor is whether the practice of waivers destabilizes the multilateral system and which roles bilateralism and regionalism will play. Mechanisms to internalize negative externalities are another approach where international law and international courts have an important function. In this context, European integration can be thought of as a laboratory experiment for the world economy. I also look at the relationship between rules and power.

Chapter V is centered on issues concerning rules for international product markets. Among these issues are unsolved GATT problems such as market access, anti-dumping, subsidies (especially in agriculture), and arrangements for the service sector. The chapter also discusses the institutional setup of the WTO and its decision-making framework, as well as its relationship with international competition policy.

Chapter VI studies arrangements for border-crossing factor movements, i.e., rules dealing with international factor markets. These include agreements on the flows of capital such as the Agreement on Trade-Related Investment Measures of GATT, while an attempt of the OECD to establish a detailed agreement on foreign direct investment failed. The issue has resurged with the fear of foreign infiltration through sovereign wealth funds. Global rules for technology flows, which have to make sure that the whole world can benefit from progress in technological knowledge, include property rights such as patent conventions and the TRIPS agreement. Rules for migration are one of the toughest areas of the international order. Immigration remains a national policy arena. Moreover, a "pecking order" between the different forms of interdependence—trade, capital, technology flows, and migration—is discussed.

Chapter VII analyzes institutional arrangements for the global environment. I start by considering that the environment can be employed for two competing uses: as a public good, e.g., the global atmosphere, and as a private good, e.g., as a sink for carbon emissions. I then discuss the problems that institutional arrangements must solve in order to protect global environmental media, how environment-related goals can be determined, and which criteria can be used for allocating emission rights and the costs of reducing pollution. The Kyoto Protocol and a potential follow-up are discussed.

Preventing monetary–financial instability and currency crises is the topic of chapters VIII and IX. Since money is not neutral, such crises have a severe impact on the real economy, in the worst cases slashing real national GDP by one-fifth to one-third. While national institutional arrangements for monetary policy are well established, international rules for monetary and financial stability are only slowly evolving. As the severe crisis that hit the banking industry in 2008 shows, false incentives creep into the system and pathological learning happens from time to time. Rules should encompass many elements: rules for financial soundness, among them standards for behavior that banks set for themselves, safety nets established by the industry and regulatory standards such as balance sheet truth and efficient supervision, all aiming at a solid banking system. The ideal mixture between these elements is an open question because asymmetric information between the regulator and regulated banks exists and because the regulator cannot possibly know *ex ante* all future "states of nature." In the past, regulation has often failed; this is demonstrated once more by the lessons from the subprime crisis. Chapter VIII studies the origins of the 2008 crisis and looks at the necessary elements of an international rule system as well as potential flaws.

Chapter IX focuses on how currency crises can be prevented. This is the mission of the IMF, an explicitly international organization. However, the IMF finds itself in an orientation crisis. It faces several dilemmas, among them that *ex post* assistance and conditionality is loaded with moral hazard and makes the IMF appear a detested taskmaster, so that governments walk away from it. In this situation, the issue is how the IMF can be refocused. Looking for new tasks such as regulations to prevent currency distortions may be a questionable avenue. Adjusting the Bretton Woods Quotas to the new international conditions is more promising. An additional issue is establishing procedures for decision-making.

Chapter X—on ethical norms, human rights, fairness, and legitimacy—discusses the restraining role of such aspects in the definition of international rules that we observe. An alternative approach would be normative. It would consist in starting axiomatically from philosophical principles, such as fairness, and deriving international rules from these principles. This is quite different from voluntary rules that evolve in a bottom-up process. In such a normative approach, a major topic is the identification of criteria to define fairness, such as the golden rule, the Kantian imperative, or the Rawls criterion. It is crucial to assess whether the human condition is improved and whether a rule system is sustainable. Equality of results versus equality of initial conditions and social standards are further aspects in the discussion. Rules need legitimacy, but the term "legitimacy" has a vague meaning in political science and outside of specific value systems.

Chapter XI discusses the interdependence of orders, the structure of the rule system and the division of labor among orders (the so-called institutional fit). It analyzes suborders within a major order, and it focuses on the relations between their goals, on the rank order of rules, on their spatial dimension, and on the universality of some rules. The consistency or the inconsistency of suborders is a major issue. Of special interest is the consistency between the international environmental order and the international trade order. The chapter also describes the institutional setup for the world economy and surveys the elements of an institutional order, looks at examples of important multilateral treaties, and reviews the most significant global political forums, regional integrations, and international organizations.

In the final chapter, I look at the major challenges facing the rule system in the future. The issue is how the rule system can accommodate trends such as population growth, emerging markets and their integration into the international division of labor, increasing energy scarcity with rising prices, and global warming. Unforeseeable events—such as financial crises, border-crossing mass migration, and terrorism—represent special risks for the world economy's rule system. Also a major source of instability may come from geopolitical shifts due to new equilibria and from the political hazards this process may entail.

With this book, I have no intention of advocating a world government. Values are too diverse, cultures too dissimilar, religions too far apart, preferences too different, historic conditions too varied, and ways of life too distinct to entertain this idea. Moreover, variety is an important asset for our problem-solving nature. For these reasons, advocating a world government would be naive. If interest groups captured such a global institutional arrangement, the consequences would be disastrous, because the possibility of a plurality of solutions would be lost. The power accruing to those in charge would be an incredible temptation for those taking the decisions; and those in command would quickly develop a taste for extending their power. It is therefore impossible to legitimize such a world government.

I conceived this book as the companion to my other work *The World Economy: A Global Analysis*. It draws from my research and teaching experience at the Universities of Mannheim, Konstanz, and Kiel in Germany and from the research I undertook when I headed the Kiel Institute for the World Economy during the period

1989–2003. Since 2004 in the spring semesters I have been teaching a course on the world economy at the Bologna Center of the Johns Hopkins University's Paul H. Nitze School of Advanced International Studies.

I am grateful to many who have criticized the manuscript in its different stages and, of course, to all those who have influenced my thoughts at the universities where I have taught, especially at the Kiel Institute for the World Economy. Specifically, I discussed the section on approaches to rules in political science in chapter I with Marco Cesa and Erik Jones; Richard Pomfret provided comments to chapter IV; Ron Steenblik recommended changes in the text on subsidies and Henning Klodt on the section on competition policy (both in chapter V); Rolf Langhammer and Mike Plummer criticized chapter VI, in which I also discussed sovereign wealth funds with Herbert Grubel; I owe comments and suggestions on the section on financial markets to Inga Bartsch, Anthony Elson, Guenter Franke, Jan Pieter Krahnen, Sara Konoe, Mike Plummer, Stephan Kohns, Joachim Scheide, and Ingo Walter; I received suggestions from Erik Jones and Walter Suntinger with respect to chapter X; and I discussed the trade-environment nexus with Gary Clyde Hufbauer. I am deeply indebted to my student research assistants, both at the Bologna Center and at the Kiel Institute for the World Economy, who helped in tracking down information, looking for data, assisting in preparing tables and figures, and also criticizing the manuscript at several points in its development. Criticism and comments were provided by Steffen Elstner (chapters II, VI, and VII), Thomas Seidner (chapters III and IV), Eduard Eyckelberg (chapters V and IX), Philipp Mengeringhaus (chapters VI, IX, and X), and Doina Cerbotary (chapters I–IV). I also appreciate research support from Anke Dodenhof and Paula Nagler. Lorenzo Erroi read everything except chapters VIII and IX and improved the English considerably. Jonathan Vogan also read several chapters and suggested improvements. Last but not least I want to thank my editor at Princeton University Press, Richard Baggaley, for his ongoing encouragement, three anonymous reviewers, and also the copy editor and typesetter Rowan Dennison from T&T Productions Ltd.

I am also grateful to the Rockefeller Foundation, which made it possible for me to work for one month in the enchanting environment of the Villa Serbelloni in Bellagio and to conceive the book. I also acknowledge the support of the Heinz-Nixdorf-Foundation.

The bulk of the manuscript was finished in June 2008; some parts were later extended. Chapter VIII was finally completed on November 30, 2008. Further minor changes were introduced while the book was in production.

Rules for the Global Economy

I

The Concept of a World Economic Order

Institutional arrangements—including informal norms of behavior, laws and property rights for the use of land, and natural resources and the environment—represent a set of rules and procedures which humankind has introduced for the governance of society and the economy. These arrangements draw from historical experience, originating mostly from past mistakes, that is, learning the hard way from errors and false approaches. In a broader sense, institutions—not to be confused with organizations—both reflect and help establish the way things are done within a society.

In the domain of economics, institutional arrangements assign the benefits and opportunity costs of an economic decision to individuals or social subunits. Common examples of these subunits are individual households consuming goods, supplying labor, and generating savings; firms producing and investing; the private sector; and the government and its different layers (Siebert 1996a). By assigning benefits and opportunity costs, institutional arrangements define the incentives for the economic agents. These incentives in turn determine the performance of the economy, for instance its growth and employment; they also impose restraints that an economy and its members have to observe, representing a complex system of incentives and restraints. Rules take the place of ad hoc solutions and discretion (Kydland and Prescott 1977).

On a global scale, rules refer to the institutional arrangements among states. In specific areas and to a certain extent, sovereign states cede sovereignty. This leads to the establishment of a multilateral rule system, binding sovereign states and their citizens. In the economic sphere, the institutional setup affects all aspects of international interaction and interdependence, including the allocation of goods and resources, the flow of capital, the diffusion of technology, the mobility of labor and human capital, and global environmental scarcity. This system of rules refers not only to the international interaction and interdependence on the real side of the economy, but also to international relations on the monetary side. Using the word "order" in the tradition of the German Freiburg School (see Eucken 1940, p. 238), we can speak of a world economic order.

Like norms within a nation state, rules for a world order can be based on ethical grounds. A theologian or a philosopher may attempt to build a rule system in a constructionist "top-down" process—starting from one or more basic ethical axioms, originating in religious values, natural laws, or philosophical principles, such as the Kantian categorical imperative. From these principles specific and concrete implications may be derived for the behavior of economic agents. Such a constructionist approach, however, is not likely to succeed in deriving precise rules for economic decisions. In fact, even the same ethical principles allow a wide range of behavioral patterns within given situations.

Reduced Transaction Costs as a Measure of Welfare Gains

I will therefore adopt a different approach. This approach starts from the observation that the emergence of rules is the result of learning from experience rather than theoretical documentation. Most importantly, negative experiences that inflict severe hardship on people—historical disasters—become the underlying origin of a new rule. Rules arise from the attempt to prevent human tragedies in the future. Without rules, in the words of Thomas Hobbes (1651, chapter 13, p. 89) life would indeed be "solitary, poore, nasty, brutish and short." Without rules, humankind would be mired in anarchy and engaged in a Hobbesian war of all against all.

Disastrous harm and hardship can be interpreted in terms of transaction costs. In a narrow sense, transaction costs are defined as resources used in human exchange, as understood in the interpretation of Coase (1937, 1960). Costs mean opportunity costs, i.e., the costs of an opportunity forgone: when a resource is used for one purpose, this implies relinquishing its use for another purpose. Opportunity costs represent the welfare lost when someone is no longer able to use a resource for a forgone alternative. A good example of high transaction costs comes from a barter economy where people repudiate the use of money, as happened during the transformation of the Soviet Union in the 1990s and in Germany after World War II. Because of the loss of confidence in money, resources had to be used to barter rather than to meet other basic needs, for instance within the production process. Consequently, transaction costs can go together with hardship and human tragedy. I adopt this broad interpretation when I speak of transaction costs. Examples are wars between nations, internal turmoil, for instance civil wars, border-crossing negative externalities, for instance acid rain, and also opportunistic behavior of one nation to the detriment of another in the international division of labor. The reduction of transaction costs can therefore explain many rules, especially within economic institutional arrangements. We thus speak of a transaction-costs approach or of an experience approach to rules.

There are many ways of reducing transaction costs: lowering transportation costs, reducing market segmentations, decreasing uncertainty due to all sorts of distortions and disruptions, for instance those arising from internal or cross-border political turmoil and from internalization of the negative effects of one nation's actions on another, i.e., internalization of negative externalities. According to this approach, the rules for the world economy evolved following a bottom-up process of learning from experience, starting from subsidiary national rules. Whenever the severe international transaction costs of national arrangements became apparent—because new interdependencies arose or because the unexpected opportunity costs of existing sets of rules revealed themselves—new institutions evolved.

Ethical norms and values act as a de facto restraint on such rules: they limit the rule space that can be established nationally and globally. If ethical values differ markedly between nations, the reach of global rules is inevitably limited. For instance, if the values of a specific social group imply the destruction of other groups as their core aim, global rules cannot be established. This outcome becomes evident in the case of the Islamic terrorists' creed and the Nazi ideology. When values in different nations and cultures start to diverge significantly, an international rule system may fall apart. If ethical values are instead universal, there is more scope for an international institutional arrangement.

I will introduce ethical norms such as fairness or the Kantian categorical imperative at a later stage. We will then see how far the transaction-costs approach takes us in explaining the international order and what role ethical norms play in restraining the rule space.

Ethical principles may be interpreted as being completely independent from economic institutional arrangements. However, any given institutional setup influences human interaction and is essential to create or prevent new economic options. Economic activities and interdependencies may in turn affect ethical values, for instance by showing the implications of behavior and the opportunity costs of norms. From this point of view, ethical principles are not completely autonomous of institutional arrangements. With the long-run impact of ethical norms being revealed by reality, the institutional arrangement reflects, at least to some extent, the experience drawn from the implementation of such norms.

There is another link between ethical norms and institutional arrangements: as societies and economies have become more complex, rules have taken the place of ethical norms. For instance, archaic societies and non-Western civilizations steer environmental allocation and the use of nature by internalized ethical norms— witness as an example American Indians—whereas the complex organization of industrialized countries devise legal approaches to environmental scarcity (Siebert 2008b).

The transaction-costs approach has the advantage that it does not motivate rules by means of a rosy concept of the welfare of the world. Such a concept might be imposed on the whim of a politburo, a dictator, or some other organization, yet it would not represent what people want within the context of free societies given the different preferences of their individuals. Nor can we rely on having a social planner design such an order in a technocratic sense, one who (supposedly) has all the necessary information to plan and enforce such a rule system from the top down.

This would be the case within a Trotskyist–Leninist approach, as political leaders or political parties hierarchically specify how people should behave. The transaction-costs approach does not start from the preferences of a subgroup of society either, for instance the ideas of some NGOs, which might be shared by their supporters but not accepted outside the group by other members of society. In contrast, under the transaction-costs approach, the benefit of rules is assessed according to the concept of reduced costs, and these costs can be defined in a decentralized way by individuals according to their preferences and by nation states according to their goals.

This approach differs from the anarchy described in Leviathan as the defining characteristic state of nature where life is "nasty, brutish and short" (Brennan and Buchanan 1985, p. ix). Given the Orwellian consequences which developed from Hobbes's ideas over time—last but not least in their Marxist realization—the centralization of decisions per se cannot become the guideline for viable solutions. The goal of avoiding market failures cannot come at the cost of worse policy failures. Besides, economists should not define market failures against the background of an abstract theoretical model detached from reality, as sometimes happens (Brennan and Buchanan 1985, p. 13).

When rules serve to reduce transaction costs, a crucial question is whether they are actually capable of achieving this goal. What rules should we then look for? One problem is to take into account the long-run impact of a rule system, i.e., to study which institutional arrangement performs better than others. Internationally, comparing the experience of different countries is therefore vital. Another important problem is that we do not have *ex ante* all the information necessary to forecast how a rule system will perform. This is the Hayekian issue of "pretense of knowledge" (Hayek 1975a), since the output of rule systems only evolves over time (Brennan and Buchanan 1985, p. 14). Another precondition is that all the opportunity costs of a rule system have to be taken into consideration. Finally, such systems should not serve to establish power, unless power is legitimate. As a corollary, individual liberty must represent a value that the system cannot relinquish.

We also need an understanding of the procedure according to which transaction costs are detected and assessed, since this is vital for the emergence of rules within a society. In the transaction-costs approach, the reduction of transaction costs comes to light either thanks to a market process revealing lower costs or through explicit political mechanisms aggregating the preferences of an entire society. This means that the transaction-costs approach assumes a competitive process, an open society, and democratic structures. Under these conditions, if a country accepts a rule, it is because the country itself finds it advantageous, unless it is coerced to obey the rule. By agreeing on rules voluntarily, the cost reductions are revealed implicitly. If, however, monopolies or the political power of specific groups locks in economic transactions, the scope for reducing transaction costs through new rules is limited or nonexistent. An example of this phenomenon comes from distortions between countries, for instance when there is no common agreement on free-market access and when regulations or subsidies protecting domestic producers prevent market access.

The transaction-costs concept is in line with a contractarian approach in the sense of constitutional political economy (Buchanan 1975; Brennan and Buchanan 1985, p. 21). It is also in line with the property-rights approach. The constitutional approach, with the distinction of outcomes generated within defined rules and by the rules themselves, may be interpreted as a positive science trying to determine which rule system fits the best given goals. In that interpretation, the constitutional approach is seen to be functional. Brennan and Buchanan interpret constitutionalism from a contractarian viewpoint in a normative sense, starting from the presupposition that the "individual is the unique unit of consciousness from which all evaluations begin" (Brennan and Buchanan 1985, p. 21), the individual being the only source of value. Starting from this presupposition, with all persons treated as morally equivalent, it is possible to derive a contractarian explanation of the social order (Buchanan and Tullock 1962; Buchanan 1975). Such an order prevents the "nasty, brutish and slavish" way of living, as depicted in Hobbes's Leviathan. From this point of view, the social order does not have to rely on romantic ideas as would be the case if some "natural harmony" among persons had to play a role in the elimination of all conflicts in the absence of rules.

The concept of opportunity cost varies with preference shifts over time. A case in point is that opportunity costs for future generations may become more relevant within the utility functions of individuals or within the goal functions of governments, as for instance with respect to environmental degradation in Europe since the 1970s. When it comes to such shifts, NGOs and new political parties such as the Greens in Europe could be a forerunner or prime mover of those values which will eventually make their way into society. This is especially relevant since preference shifts often occur together with generational changes, i.e., as new young cohorts enter the population. According to this interpretation, social subgroups can indeed play a role in determining the political preferences of society. Another example is that the utility function of individuals begins to include argument variables that extend to a wider space than the nation state, thus including phenomena in other countries. The tsunami that hit Thailand and other parts of Southeast Asia in December 2004, for instance, provoked widespread concern.

The gains for individual countries accepting a given rule need not be identical. Some countries may derive a larger gain from the rule system than others. Take the case of preventing a war through a rule system: in that case, it is difficult to determine whether the benefits of such a rule system are identical to all countries. It is, however, more important to have an effective rule preventing wars than to discuss who gains most. Yet, if the benefits of a rule system are visibly one-sided or if they diverge significantly, the stability of a rule system will most likely be thrown into question.

Admittedly, the approach described here is rather functional and rationalist, being founded as it is on historical experience, or as Voltaire put it "la raison la plus forte est toujours la meilleure." It corresponds to approaches discussed during the Enlightenment, for instance by Immanuel Kant. For many people and for many NGOs, the transaction-costs approach may not seem compassionate enough, neither showing sufficient empathy nor displaying "a heart and a soul." But this claim is questionable. It is more important to have a reliable rule system than to be at the mercy of the bloomy feelings and deeply felt intentions of many do-gooders. Good intentions alone are not enough to establish a viable international order.

Lowering Transaction Costs through International Institutional Rules

International rules, representing norms of behavior for governments, firms, and citizens, reduce transaction costs through several mechanisms. We offer the following taxonomy.

First, the practice of decentralizing economic decisions, made possible by a framework of rules, represents a method for lowering transaction costs. This practice can be interpreted as an informal agreement, corresponding to the subsidiarity principle, applied to the different layers of national governments in federal states; but it is also relevant for the institutional setup of regional integrations, such as the European Union, to say nothing of several other multilateral arrangements. Decentralization draws from past experience; the devolution of decision-making to peripheral actors has proved, in many areas, more efficient than its centralization, one reason being that at the lower levels of organizations information is more readily available and preferences can be expressed more easily. As a matter of fact, explaining rules through the lowering of transaction costs is implicitly based on the concept of decentralized decisions.

Second, relying on markets is a specific form and an essential way of decentralizing decisions and implementing the subsidiarity principle. Markets represent an institutional mechanism that aligns the production of private goods with the consumers' willingness to pay, determines consumption, saving, and investment from individual choices, and allocates scarce resources toward competing uses. The core function of markets is to signal the benefits and opportunity costs of economic decisions to individual agents. Markets express economic constraints and indicate scarcity in the form of prices to economic agents—a function increasingly important within a globalized world. Thus, global resource constraints are denoted by scarcity prices. Within this frame, new demand (from emerging countries) can drive out the "old" demand (from developed economies) in a peaceful way.[1]

---

[1] For instance, China's share of world imports is 46% for iron ore, 36% for cotton, 23% for copper ore, 21% for pulp and paper, 20% for rubber, and 6.2% for crude oil. For comparison, China's share of world output was 5% (data for 2005). In 1993 China did not need oil imports.

How efficient can markets be in allocating resources? An answer to this question could be observed after the transition of property rights from the large oil companies (the so-called Seven Sisters) to the resource countries, i.e., the oil-rich countries, before the first oil crisis in 1973. In this case, spot and futures markets replaced a hierarchical allocation system, which depended on the Seven Sisters and on their vertical integration encompassing both upstream and downstream activities. Before this change, the Seven Sisters controlled oil exploration and oil production (upstream activities) as well as refining, transportation, and distribution (downstream activities). Concession contracts, often valid for a period of 50–70 years, allowed oil companies to exploit their oil fields and provided access to the undiscovered oil deposits of the resource countries. When the extraction rights shifted to the resource countries, the vertical integration of these enterprises was broken up; spot markets (for example, in Rotterdam) and forward markets replaced vertical integration. Moreover, long-term resource contracts between governments—the result of political negotiations—became unattractive as soon as spot and futures markets for crude oil had developed. Note that a firm can be interpreted as a network of explicit and implicit contracts, combining different production factors. Following institutional economics, we can also describe a firm as an organizational unit with lower transaction costs than those of the market: a transaction takes place within a firm if the transaction costs within the firm are lower than in the market. If the market allows lower transaction costs, a transaction is done through it. Thus, the level of the transaction costs determines the dividing line between firms and the market.

The reduction of market segmentation is an important vehicle for reducing transaction costs. Over time, new options for reducing market segmentation arise: this is the case of technological progress in transportation, new property rights in network industries, and institutional harmonization, as it takes place through regional integration processes.

Third, property rights represent a crucial condition for decentralization and for reducing transaction costs. A property right can be defined as a set of rules specifying the use of scarce resources and goods (Furubotn and Pejovich 1972). The set of rules includes obligations and rights; laws may codify these rules, or they may be institutionalized by other mechanisms such as social norms together with a pattern of sanctions.

The definition of property rights covers a wide range of specific uses. Dales (1968) distinguishes four types of property rights. A first category comprises exclusive property rights, covering the right of use—notably the right of sale and the right of disposal—and even the right to destroy the good or resource. However, exclusive ownership does not mean absolute ownership: a set of restraints protects other individuals or maintains economic assets. According to national regulations, for instance, a homeowner may not destroy his house. Zoning rules and criminal law are additional examples of restrictions on exclusive property rights. A second type of property right is status or functional ownership, referring to a set of rights accorded to some individuals but not to others. In this case the right to use an object or to receive a service is very often not transferable. Examples of this type of right include access to some services restricted to party officials within communist countries, licenses to notarize documents, and, during the Middle Ages, the right of admission into a guild. A third class includes the right to use a collective good such as a highway or to have access to a school or to a public good (such as health protection against contagion) for a specific purpose. A fourth class of property rights encompasses common-property resources such as the commons; they represent de facto a nonproperty because virtually no exclusion is defined.

Property rights constitute a mechanism aimed at reducing the occurrence and the scale of social conflicts. Accepting property rights means that people give up brute force, while, without such rights, people would resort to violence and dash out each other's brains. This holds for individuals within a society, but it also applies to nations engaged in international relations—the dimension which we will be looking at most closely.

In the past, common properties or free-access goods and resources have become private properties. An example of such an evolution comes from jurisdiction over the seas. The high sea was "*res nullius*" (i.e., nobody's property) when Hugo Grotius lived in the sixteenth century. Since then, however, we have established rules for how we use the seas: from the eighteenth century up to the mid-twentieth century, the territorial waters where a sovereign state had complete jurisdiction extended to three nautical miles. At the end of the twentieth century, this zone grew to twelve nautical miles (UN Convention on the Law of the Sea negotiated during 1973–82, entering into force in 1994). In a contiguous zone, up to 24 nautical miles beyond the 12-mile range of territorial waters, a coastal nation can prevent infringement of its customs, fiscal, immigration, or sanitary laws and regulations. In addition, countries enjoy the control of all economic resources—including fishing, mining, oil exploration, and control over pollution of these resources—over an exclusive economic zone that extends for 200 nautical miles. Thus, a coastal country has a differentiated control of its coastal waters.

The property-rights approach enables us to pose some very basic questions of economics: how should property rights be defined in order for the economic system to generate "optimal" results? Note that the meaning of "optimal" may be manifold and respond to quite a few criteria such as freedom of the individual and correct incentives to produce, invest, find new technologies, search for new resources, and supply the resources that an agent owns (for example, capital, labor, and raw materials). We should also ask ourselves whether property rights can be defined in such a way that externalities are internalized.

A crucial issue in property rights involves the right to use land: property rights assign the use of land to those having a title to it. The same happens, implicitly, with the land of an entire country. Historically, the principle of territoriality—mandating the respect of the territorial integrity of other countries—can be interpreted as a national property right, preventing war as a means to conquer space. Territoriality is therefore an international principle by which nation states agree on respecting each other's autonomy—in my interpretation, each other's property rights. This gives a state the legal authority to exercise jurisdiction within its borders, but not beyond them. Most importantly, territoriality protects a nation's right to decide on the use of its resources and the organization of its economy and its political system.[2] In that sense, a nation can be understood as a "resource machine," allocating resources and the power to decide on their use.

Territoriality has its limits in international public law, especially in the violation of its principles. Figures like Slobodan Milosevic and Adolf Hitler cannot be allowed to motivate their decisions by the principle of territoriality. Thus, the principle of territoriality does not (and cannot) cover the violation of "natural" law and human rights.

Territoriality is also overcome by international agreements, for instance by ceding sovereignty to a supraregional level in regional integrations (like the EU) or in international treaties (like the Kyoto Protocol). The principle of territoriality also loses importance if the utility functions of individuals include more and more argument variables depending on other countries. Courts such as the International Court of Justice at The Hague serve to implement these agreements and to solve disputes (see chapter IV).

Fourth, international rules reduce uncertainty in transactions. Many factors contribute to such uncertainty, for instance the opportunistic behavior of national governments. This also applies to market participants while fulfilling contracts, for example in the interpretation of contracts. Rules replace ad hoc negotiations between governments in the case of disputes. If rules do not exist, ad hoc negotiations are needed to solve disputes over the behavior of governments; likewise they are necessary when private market participants fulfill their contracts, for instance to prevent cheating, finagling, and double-dealing. Uncertainty is likely to arise when states of nature change, so that contingent contracts are imperfect. Thus, reliability and certainty of an international institutional framework represents a de facto public good, enhancing the welfare of nations.

Fifth, international rules set limits on the strategic behavior of national governments. This refers to governments enjoying political or market power which might use policy instruments to increase the national gains coming from the international division of labor, thus penalizing other countries. Within this context, international rules ease potential conflicts between different national interests. Countries that find their own advantage negatively affected by the strategic behavior of others are bound to object to such rules. Once again, international institutional arrangements end up playing the role of public goods.

---

[2] See Langewiesche (2007), who explicitly mentions power resources, "the access to culture," and the distribution of "what has been commonly produced" (author's translation).

Table I.1.   Welfare levels with cooperative and noncooperative behavior.

		Foreign country	
		Cooperative strategy	Noncooperative strategy
Domestic country	Cooperative strategy	I $(27, 27^*)$	III $(10, 30^*)$
	Noncooperative strategy policy	II $(30, 10^*)$	IV $(12, 12^*)$

Sixth, an international rule system represents a form of self-commitment: states within such a system limit the future choices of their national governments. Behind any rule system we can therefore detect a "negative catalogue," i.e., a series of restraints imposed on the behavior of national governments. These constraints protect the international division of labor against the conflicting interests of national governments. The self-commitment of states also works as a shelter against the power of protectionist groups in national economies. It helps against political cycles, such as a government's protectionist leaning before a national election, in the hope that protectionism will attract votes. It also shields against the shift of political preferences in a country, for instance when a government comes into power with completely different inclinations.

Seventh, a rule system can lead to cooperative behavior among states, which in turn makes it possible to increase the total benefits coming to all countries from the international division of labor (while the distribution of the additional benefits is another story). Without cooperative behavior, countries find themselves caught in a prisoner's dilemma, unable as they are to reduce their protectionist measures or to capitalize on potential gains. The structure of a single game is illustrated in table I.1, where we assume that benefits can be measured in utility units, or utils. If countries cooperate, they can enjoy benefits of 27 utils each (case I). If they dominate the solution, individually they can improve their results (cases II and III). In the case of noncooperation, they both have lower benefits (case IV). For a fuller explanation see figure III.2 and table III.1. Only some sort of agreement, convention, or rule system can exclude an undesirable payoff to the players (Brennan and Buchanan 1985, chapter 2; Barrett 2005). Cooperative behavior is more likely to occur in repeated games, in which economic agents have to deal with each other over time. Rules are then embedded into a relational contract (MacNeil 1978). As a result, transaction costs would be higher with noncooperative behavior.

Eighth, rules can internalize negative externalities between states (negative spillovers) and thus reduce transaction costs. Negative externalities represent forms of interdependency between economic activities that escape market mechanisms rather than following nonmarket systems such as natural or "technological" systems. For instance, national economic activities are interdependent due to border-crossing groundwaters or river systems, atmospheric systems, or the biochain. Contagion in a currency crisis facilitated by our communication, social, or "psychological" systems is another example of economic interdependency. In a broader interpretation, a war started by one country can be considered as an extreme form of negative externality. It is hoped that rules may be able to prevent this "superexternality." As with negative externalities, positive externalities such as the supply of biodiversity by a country can be internalized.

Ninth, global public goods require specific rules in order to reduce transaction costs. Public goods are those goods that are consumed in equal amounts by all (Samuelson 1954). There is no rivalry in consumption and, technically, users cannot be excluded. A public good should not be confounded with a meritorious good, i.e., with a good that is judged to be worthy to be supplied by a group, a political party, or a country. In our context, public goods have a global dimension; Earth's atmosphere in the case of global warming or the depletion of the ozone layer, for instance, represent public goods. Other examples are smallpox eradication or asteroid deflection. Such goods can be interpreted as a special case of negative externalities, but public goods are an important case in their own right in the taxonomy of interdependencies. Decentralized market decisions cannot determine the quantity of a public good we want to have; this process would indeed lead to an under-provision of the public good, while transaction costs would be too high. Instead, the optimal provision of a public good must be determined by the aggregation of the countries' preferences in a bargaining solution between states. Institutional arrangements are needed in order to establish the desired quantity of the public good, i.e., to aggregate national preferences. Put differently, an international agreement is needed on how much deterioration in the quality of the public good is acceptable, for instance how much global warming can be tolerated. Agreement is also needed on how the costs of the desired quality of the public good are allocated to individual countries and how free-rider behavior can be prevented.

Note that global institutional arrangements such as the trade order are sometimes considered to have the property of a public good, although they must not be used in equal amounts by all and consequently do not satisfy the definition of public goods. Also note that global public goods in the strict sense represent only one of the nine aspects in the taxonomy of international rules. It would be too narrow an approach if the lowering of transaction costs was only discussed under this heading.

The last two cases are in line with the concept that transactions should be done in organizational units where they have the lowest transaction costs. The firm gets the first shot if transaction costs there are lower than in the market (see above). Allocations that can be accomplished through markets at lower transaction costs than in firms should be done there. What cannot be allocated through markets— externalities and public goods—must be dealt with by the political process, usually in the national political process. Finally, when transaction costs can be reduced by shifting transactions beyond the nation state, then multilateral arrangements come into play.

This taxonomy encompasses nine categories within each of which which it is possible to reduce transaction costs. One may interpret these cases as failures of national markets, leading to too high transaction costs. The international rule system can then be viewed as a correction of subsidiary national rules and of national market failures. Similarly, multilateral rules appear as an expression of the subsidiarity principle: only when national rules lead to undesirable results with high transaction costs are multilateral rules auspicious. However, the definition of market failures cannot come from theoretical models which do not fully reflect economic reality. Nor can such a definition come from flawed models. For instance, the hypothesis of a downward-sloping Philipps curve relating the inflation rate and the unemployment rate may lead to the policy conclusion to expand aggregate demand: the opposing hypothesis—that the Philipps curve varies together with institutional conditions and that it is not downward sloping if agents have rational expectations—does not suggest a policy failure in this sense. It is also well-known that the correction of market failure by bargaining and cooperation is not free from policy failure. Only if the costs of policy failure are lower than the benefits of correcting market failure will transaction costs be reduced.

Note that the taxonomy presented here is quite different from the theory of fiscal federalism. The latter applies when communality is relevant as a common interest, for instance in the form of some national identity in culture and language and where usually at least a weak institutional arrangement exists. The conditions for fiscal federalism, as presented by Ahearne and Eichengreen (2007)—namely similarity of tastes and economies of scale—appear to me somewhat narrow and misleading. In any case, they do not give sufficient reasons for multilateral arrangements. Note that the similarity of tastes should not be confused with the utility function including phenomena in other nation states. It would seem that the concept of economies of scale is too narrow to apply to existing organizational units.

A Hierarchy of Rules

The rule system is a complex network. Most rules have a spatial dimension: some are local, others are regional, while a good number of them are national; some apply to regional integrations or pertain to border-crossing interdependencies; finally, various rules relate to global phenomena. In our interpretation, rules follow the subsidiarity principle: they are relevant for the organizational layer, for instance households, firms, and organizational strata of governments, where they can best fulfill their function. Thus, local rules make sure that information on problems is easily available at the local level and that the preferences of local people can be straightforwardly expressed. Therefore, it is possible to decentralize quite a few rules. When spillovers occur, the dimension of rules needs a larger scope. Rule systems therefore have a vertical structure: with globalization and increasing interdependencies, institutional arrangements become more global.

In contrast to this vertical structure according to the subsidiarity principle, some rules are universal. This characteristic applies to ethical norms, religious values, and principles of natural law. Such universal rules cut through the network of hierarchical rules. Thus, the rule system becomes a complex matrix containing many dimensions: it is defined over space; together with its spatial connotation comes its vertical structure; it applies to different walks of life, which also have their own spatial dimension; and it contains universal rules.

The Process of Ceding Sovereignty

Historically, a long process in ceding sovereignty from nation states to multilateral arrangements has taken place, with many accomplishments but also many setbacks. The progressive devolution of national decisions has been accompanied by poor historical experiences as well as by the occurrence and appearance of unprecedented interdependencies. An example is the increased awareness of environmental degradation in recent decades, affecting not only national environmental systems but also global systems such as the atmosphere. Another example is the disintegration of the world economy experienced during the 1930s and World War II, which in turn led to the establishment of GATT, the IMF, and the World Bank.

The transaction-costs approach to rule setting relies on rules set by voluntary decisions since these are expected to bring advantages. Historically, rule systems have been strongly influenced by a hegemon as was the case with the Bretton Woods institutions after World War II, strongly affected by the United States. At other times, the rule system was imposed by the dominant power as in the case of *Pax Britannica* or *Pax Romana*. Often, such rule systems collapsed together with the dominant power. Then, new rule systems had to be invented. This is the moment when the transaction-costs approach once again in demand. Consequently, in a long-run historical analysis, the transaction-costs approach holds.

There is a rich practice of ceding rules within the European Union, where the process of giving up sovereignty has been going on for nearly sixty years, having started with the European Coal and Steel Community in 1951. The original group of six members has now grown to twenty-seven, through four consecutive steps: enlargement to the north, south, to the neutral states, and to the east. The ceding of sovereignty also included the devolution of policy instruments, as was the case with the establishment of the single market and monetary union as well as with giving up the control of national borders. The process of ceding sovereignty embraces many other mechanisms. For instance, constitutional court judges from all EU countries gather informally to discuss inconsistencies between national constitutions and the European treaties.

As it concerns the extent to which the establishment and implementation of rules are ceded, we can distinguish between unconditional delegation to a supranational agent, supervised delegation, and coordination (Coeuré and Pisani-Ferry 2007, p. 29). Unconditional delegation is unusual. The monetary policy in the euro area and EU competition policy are examples of unconditional delegation, where the agents have full authority to take decisions (although the EU member states remain masters of the EU treaty). The term "unconditional delegation" better fits processes taking place within nation states. Supervised delegation is equally unusual on the international stage. Again in the EU, trade policy may be used as an illustration, as a committee of trade officials nominated by the member states monitors the negotiation process (Coeuré and Pisani-Ferry 2007, p. 30). Coordination means instead that states cooperate in taking into account existing conditions and the instruments chosen elsewhere as well as the interests of other countries. Note that international rules may be either formal or informal. When they are formal, they imply obligations, even though they are not enforceable in a hierarchical legal system (Hoekman and Kostecki 2001, p. 25). Such obligations may in turn result from a mediating convention between signing parties, or they may crystallize into an international organization whose members are themselves states, as in the case of the World Trade Organization (WTO).

As for the ceded rules, they apply to different areas (see the following chapter). At the same time, the process of relinquishing rules can take place with different degrees of intensities. For instance, Stiglitz and Charlton (2005, p. 133) distinguish a descending order of transparency-enhancing obligations on firms and countries, cooperation between jurisdictions, and the establishment of enforceable international rules.

A Political Order as a Precondition

A necessary frame of reference for the transaction-costs approach is some measure of international political stability, i.e., a political order in which rules are respected. At the same time, the rule system may in turn contribute to political stability, thereby initiating a virtuous circle in the long run. Such a rule system can come from a hegemon, provided that the hegemon is not selfish. It can also stem from a group of nations or from *all* nations, a pluralistic approach fitting a multipolar world. This will be our frame of reference.

The political order, however, does not always represent a stable equilibrium. Imperial or ideological dominance, political supremacy, and strategic behavior have the potential to harm existing international rules.

As a warning, the experience of Communist regimes and of National Socialism in Germany remind us that rules, even when agreed upon within a country and between countries, may be fragile. Dictators may rise to power, governments or political systems may become authoritarian, populists may seduce people, and institutions may fall into the hands of lunatics while political preferences may vary over time. Historical experience tells us that the transaction-costs approach is not immune from ideological and religious groups, which may want to destroy other ethnic groups or peoples sharing different religious beliefs. Nor is such an approach hedged from terrorism. We, and especially those generations that have not seen a war in Europe in the last sixty years, cannot be sure whether rules will not be reneged upon, forgotten, or thrown into the dustbin of history. Unfortunately, humankind has a short memory. Sometimes, it seems as if we are only one generation away from the Stone Age. A partial consolation comes from knowing that the more integrated all countries in the world order become, the smaller the possibility of overthrowing the rule system. Consequently, the international community has a strong interest in preventing a country from deviating from such a system.

Historically, shifts in the balance of power have coincided with periods of disruption of the international rules. A case in point is the rise of Germany after its unification in 1871 and the two world wars that ensued, to a large extent as a consequence of the shift in the balance of power between European nations. A case for the future will be the shift of power in the coming decades from the United States to China. In order to defuse the disruptive potential of such shifts, it is essential to have a rule system that is able to accommodate the rising powers and include effective forms of mediation that can be used.

International Rules: A Brief History of Ideas

Philosophers have been studying international rules for a long time. The Enlightenment especially saw many proposals looking into the issue of how rules can be found. Common features are the principle of rationality and the analysis of how such a rule system may function.

In his *Leviathan*, Hobbes (1651) developed the idea of "war of all against all" ("*bellum omium contra omnes*") with the often quoted words "*homo homoni lupus*" ("man is a wolf to man"). Man in his natural state cannot help but defend himself in any way possible when threatened with death. Self-defense against violent death is Hobbes's highest human priority. Since men have a self-interested and materialistic desire to end war, Hobbes argued in favor of a social contract: "the passions that incline men to peace are fear of death, desire of such things as are necessary to commodious living, and a hope by their industry to obtain them" (xiii, 14). Much of the book constitutes a demonstration of the necessity of a strong central authority— an absolute sovereign or a Leviathan—to avoid the evil of discord and civil war. Any abuse of power perpetrated by this authority has to be accepted as the price of peace, since an absolute sovereign ensures the enforcement of the contracts.

In his *Theory of Moral Sentiments*, Adam Smith (1759), one of the founders of economics, explained rules by a combination of sentiment and experience. As stated in the opening sentence of his book, moral sentiments, called sympathy by Smith, are feelings or emotions of approval, disapproval, gratitude, or resentment:

> How selfish soever man may be supposed, there are evidently some principles in his nature, which interest him in the fortune of others, and render their happiness necessary to him, though he derives nothing from it except the pleasure of seeing it.
>
> Smith 1759, p. 1

Sympathy means "having feelings in common with another person", or putting oneself in someone else's shoes. By observing the behavior of others and by feeling or expressing approval or disapproval, rules are revealed.

> Our continual observations upon the conduct of others, insensibly lead us to form for ourselves certain general rules concerning what is fit and proper either to be done or to be avoided. Some of their actions shock all our natural sentiments. . . . We thus naturally lay down to ourselves a general rule, that all such actions are to be avoided, as tending to render us odious, contemptible, or punishable, the objects of all those sentiments for which we have the greatest dread and aversion.
>
> Ibid., p. 265

Thus, it is the experience of which actions are approved or disapproved that leads to a general rule. These general rules are universally acknowledged and appealed to as standards of judgment. They determine the laws and institutions, Smith's term for rules (also see his *Wealth of Nations* (Smith 1776, Book I, chapter 8)). Unlike Hobbes, Smith assigns positive effects to human interactions, allowing gains from the division of labor.

In contrast to Smith, Immanuel Kant provides a rationalistic foundation of international rules. Reason becomes the basis for any rule, for instance of an institutional arrangement to prevent war:

> Nonetheless, from the throne of its moral legislative power, reason absolutely condemns war as a means of determining the right and makes seeking the state of peace a matter of unmitigated duty. But without a contract among nations, peace can be neither inaugurated nor guaranteed. A league of a special sort must therefore be established, one that we can call a league of peace (*foedus pacificum*), which will be distinguished from a treaty of peace (*pactum pacis*) because the latter seeks merely to stop one war, while the former seeks to end all wars forever.
>
> Kant 1795, p. 117

Karl Marx (1867) proposed a system of rules for organizing a society based on the public ownership of the means of production. Meanwhile, especially in Europe, we have gained experience with Marxist societies and economies. Communist economies were centrally planned, and nearly all sectors of the economy were nationalized. Private ownership was minimized. Individuals were deprived of economic and political freedom, access to information was limited, and freedom of expression prohibited. One political party controlled all political processes and all educational and cultural activities. The organization of society followed the principles of constructive rationalism with the communist ideology as the underlying approach. Self-correcting mechanisms were lacking, the consequences of which were detailed in Aleksandr Solzhenitsyn's *Gulag Archipelago*, cost many millions of lives. Residents found themselves walled in. Although the system clearly failed and citizens ran away from it when the iron curtain fell, the disaster of its historical performance is fading in the perceptions of the young and Marxist principles are receiving attention again within the intellectual circles of Europe and elsewhere.

Two other immoral orientations that had a devastating impact on the world and on the international institutional arrangement were National Socialism in Germany and Fascism in Italy. Again, power was centralized, political freedom and democracy abolished, and one party gathered all the power. Decisions were taken by the führer and by his immediate entourage appealing to nationalistic emotions. The laws of the state and social behavior were brought in line—all ending in a terrible world war.

The experience of Communism and National Socialism in Germany gave birth to a new generation of social philosophers, whose intention was to understand whether such aberrations were the inherently necessary consequence of poor institutional arrangements. They also tried to identify conditions that would prevent the recurrence of such anomalies and tried to look for principles on which superior rules could be based.

Germany's Freiburg School, most prominently Walter Eucken, developed the concept of competitive order and its constituting principles: open markets—nowadays the most important ingredient of the concept of contestable markets—are a prerequisite for competition. Private ownership is both a guarantee of individual liberty and an incentive to minimize costs and reveal true economic information. Freedom of contract is conducive to competition. Liability ensures that social costs are internalized. The constancy of economic policy helps prevent a misallocation of resources over time, and price-level stability is a sine qua non for the price mechanism to operate. All this feeds into the competitive order which for Eucken represented the fundamental principle for organizing an economy. The ordoliberals took the view that the competitive order is instrumental in allowing individual liberties. Decentralization permits individual choice and provides options. How the institutional setup affects the behavior of the individuals and firms was a central issue for the ordoliberal thinkers of the Freiburg School—to think in terms of an order, i.e., in terms of incentives, was a central demand of the ordoliberals. Their thinking became the foundation of Germany's concept of social market economy.

Karl Popper (1945) developed his concept of the open society, countering a closed society in which inheritance, tradition, party membership, and status decide on an individual's options while measures and hierarchies cement social structures, limit entry, and restrain vertical income and social mobility. According to Popper (2003), society should be open "in which individuals are confronted with personal decisions" (p. 186), "in which institutions leave . . . room for personal responsibility" (p. 185), and "which sets free the critical powers of man" (p. xvii). This concept of a free society implies "competition for status among its members" (p. 186).

Hayek (1944, 1971, 1973) conceived the concept of a "spontaneous order" evolving from the interaction of a multitude of decentralized agents. Many rules and institutions have evolved in a historical process and have been refined by selection. The institutional arrangements for the different spheres of human life—economic, political, educational, cultural, and religious—are partially separate. They are so complex that it is impossible for any individual to know all the facts which are relevant to the functioning of such rules. The rules are not "designed" nor can they be "designed" by a social planner. Rather, they "emerge" spontaneously from a seemingly complex network of interactions among agents with limited knowledge. Instead of constructive rationalism "from above," rules and institutional arrangements are the outcome of evolutionary rationalism. The subsidiarity principle is part of the institutional arrangement. Self-correcting mechanisms for amending errors and improving malfunctioning are essential, while market prices are important information signals to bring about adjustment to changed conditions. Governments must create a legal framework—including laws of property, contract, and tort—which allow the market order to function.

Balance of Power and Some Concepts in Political Science

My approach explaining the emergence of rules through learning from experience and the reduction of transaction costs differs from some that have been used in political science, where institutional arrangements are explained by the balance of power in the sense of the classical realists or the concept of realpolitik. This approach is in line with such ideas as a state-and-sovereignty-based order as we know it from the Westphalian peace (Hurrell 2007), but also from the analysis of wars or understanding the situation of the post-Cold-War system and hegemonic stability. Such approaches have also been labeled state-centric realism (Gilpin 1987, 2001). Collective security can be considered to be an issue under such conditions that has to be resolved in the self-interest of states. Without a hegemon, state-based pluralism can be viewed as playing a fundamental role in international institutional arrangements.

Yet another view is to look at major changes in the world economic system and to trace their impact on the international rule system (Gilpin 1987), i.e., how an economically integrated world economy has affected the international rule system (Frieden 2006). Another approach is to analyze changes in value and in ethical views and their effect on the rule system. I take up this issue in chapter X, where I discuss the restraints of the international rule system that arise from human rights, demands for fairness, and the issue of legitimacy. Within the context of changing values, political scientists study the changes that take place in international society and the challenges that derive from globalization (Hurrell 2007). State solidarity may be an outcome of this thinking.

Last but not least, one may return to the balance-of-power approach and look at the impact of impending geoeconomic and geopolitical shifts such as the rise of emerging markets on the world's institutional arrangement. I take up this theme in the final chapter.

II

Globalization and Its Impact on the International Rule System

Global rules become especially important in a globalizing world economy in which the economic interdependence between nation states is intensifying. Similarly, as the development of property rights and other rules have followed increases in scarcity throughout history, the global rule system has to reflect the stronger interdependence between countries.

The Forces of Globalization

Globalization is a process in which the segmentation of national markets is reduced and economies become more open and interdependent. Catalysts for the globalization process are as follows: falling transport and communication costs in the past seventy years; the technological revolution in information technology and the rise of the World Wide Web; the reduction of political tensions following the end of the Cold War; regional efforts toward integration, for example in Europe; the strengthening of multilateral trade agreements especially in the 1990s; the radical policy shift in the former centrally planned economies of Central and Eastern Europe after the fall of the iron curtain; the opening of China; a changed orientation of political elites in many developing countries away from communist ideology; the crumpling of apartheid in South Africa; the change in the political strategies of developing and newly industrialized countries with regard to development and foreign trade; and the deregulation of important sectors in developed countries including the privatization of state-owned enterprises, which also comprises the introduction of new property rights for networks, for instance power lines, thereby exposing previous natural monopolies to competition (Siebert 2007e, chapter 1).

We can distinguish eight different channels of interdependence. In the first channel, the exchange of goods and services intensifies in the world's product markets, national economies become more open (as measured by their export share in GDP), market segmentation fades, and economic distance shrinks. For instance, the export share of Japan (exports of goods and services relative to GDP) has risen from 13.5% in 1980 to 16.1% in 2006; the same share for Germany has increased from 26.4%

in 1980 to 45.0% (also in 2006), while the share of the Netherlands has risen from
54.3% in 1980 to 71.7% (2005). In contrast, the share of the United States has
not changed substantially (from 10.1% to 11.1% in 2006). For newly industrialized countries, the increase in openness is quite pronounced: Korea's export share
has moved from 32.7% in 1980 to 43.2% in 2006, that of Mexico from 10.7% to
31.9% in 2006 (IMF 2007c). Finally, for developing countries such as China and
India expansion of exports has been a major driver of economic growth. In the world
economy, the share of total merchandise exports to world GDP has risen from 18.4%
in 1980 to 23.3% in 2005.

Services present a puzzle. They now account for about 70% of value added in
industrialized and postindustrialized economies. About two-thirds of world output
consists of services. Oddly, the international division of labor does not reflect this
phenomenon; the share of trade in services now makes up only about 20% of total
trade, up only two percentage points since 1977, if one relies on World Development
Indicators (World Bank 2007). The share of services in total exports is admittedly
higher for some countries, accounting for 29% of U.S. exports (2004) and even more
for the United Kingdom (35%), quite probably due to financial services. In contrast,
services represent 15% of French and 13% of German exports. Looking at world
service exports as a share of world GDP, it has risen from 3.5% in 1980 to 5.4% in
2005, increasing at a lower speed than the trade in merchandise exports. While it
is true that a large part of services in world GDP is nontradable, it can be expected
that a growing number of services, for instance electronic banking, health services
for patients prepared to cross borders to get treatment, or distance learning services,
will become more tradable. Note also that a measurement problem may exist for
the trade in services. Macroeconomic accounting does not fully include intrafirm
trade of the multinationals, among which there is the trade in services (Hufbauer
and Stephenson 2007).

As a consequence of increased openness, structural changes are taking place.
Countries participating in the international division of labor specialize in the production of those products for which they enjoy a comparative advantage. Exports
influence production, investment, employment, GDP, and sectoral structure, thus
leading to the growth of national income and usually also to an increase in GDP per
capita. This increase attracts more imports, stimulating the exports of other countries. Thus, thanks to their growth, developing countries come to represent a market
for the products of industrial countries, and vice versa. This volume effect magnifies
the gains from trade. New information technologies allow the reorganization of production processes and the fragmentation of production, i.e., to slice up the vertical
value-added chain and to change locations.

Structural change is brought about through the change in relative prices. According to Jevons's law, arbitrage leads to a globally uniform price for a particular product
in the long run after adjustment has taken place. Price effects are also relevant for
important inputs such as minerals and energy. They direct resources to the best use,

Table II.1.   Increase in intrasector trade.[a]

	1961	1971	1981	1991	2001	2005
United States	0.46	0.52	0.49	0.67	0.66	0.60
Japan	0.24[b]	0.27	0.19	0.33	0.37	0.46
Germany	0.41	0.57	0.60	0.75	0.74	0.73

[a]Grubel–Lloyd index, at the two-digit level, calculated as an average for all sectors. Includes only sectors where data are available for the whole period. It is defined as

$$\text{GL} = \frac{\sum_i [(\text{Ex}_i + \text{Im}_i) - |\text{Ex}_i - \text{Im}_i|]}{\sum_i (\text{Ex}_i + \text{Im}_i)}.$$

[b]1962.
Source: OECD (2007); author's calculations.

i.e., where they have the highest productivity, and decide among competing uses. Developing countries, for instance China, automatically push up the price for inputs such as oil.

Not only will the reduction of market segmentation strengthen the commodity arbitrage between different supply conditions in the traditional sense of intersector trade, as explained by the Heckscher–Ohlin model, it will also allow for different product preferences of consumers to come into play and for economies of scale in production to be exploited. In this respect, intrasector trade, i.e., the trade of similar goods, has gained in significance. The tendency toward intrasector trade is supported by the fragmentation of production, by intrafirm trade, and by the increasingly global orientation of firms. Intrasector trade has risen considerably for the developed countries, where it now represents the overwhelming part of trade. The high income level is one reason for the love for product variety; economies of scale are the other factor. Intrasector trade is measured by the Grubel–Lloyd index (table II.1). It is zero for a sector if the sector is a pure import sector ($\text{Im}_i = 0$) or a pure export sector ($\text{Ex}_i = 0$). It is zero for the whole economy if all sectors have intersector trade. It is 1 if the export value of a sector corresponds to its import value. Intrasector trade is most pronounced for Germany, where the Grubel–Lloyd index of intrasector trade on the Standard Industrial Classification (SIC) two-digit level increased from 0.41 in 1961 to 0.73 in 2005. For the United States, the index rose from 0.46 in 1961 to 0.60 in 2005; for Japan, it increased from 0.24 in 1962 to 0.46, also in 2005.

In contrast to the implications of the Heckscher–Ohlin model, where the import-competing sector has to shrink while the export sector expands, in intrasector trade all sectors can increase output simultaneously, albeit in different varieties of products. This means that employment in a sector does not have to decline when intrasector trade takes place.

The real effective exchange rate—i.e., the relative price of currencies—is another price vehicle for adjustment, as it enables the restoration of equilibrium when disequilibria in the balance of payments arise. It is defined as the trade-weighted nominal bilateral exchange rate, corrected for the price levels of the countries trading with each other. The reason that the price levels enter the picture is that a nominal exchange rate does not alone determine exports and imports. If a currency devalues in nominal terms, exports may not increase if inflation is higher than abroad. In the case of two countries, the real exchange rate represents the relative price of exportables versus importables. For instance, for the dollar–euro areas, the real effective exchange rate formula is $e_R = eP^\$ / P_\euro$, where e is the nominal exchange rate €/$, $P^\$$ is the price level in the United States, and $P_\euro$ is the price level in the euro area.[1] Alternatively, the real exchange rate is defined as the relative price of tradables versus nontradables, $e_R = eP_{NT}/P_{NT}$, where P_T is the price of tradables (in U.S. dollars) and P_{NT} is the price of nontradables in euros. A real depreciation increases the incentive to produce more exportables or tradables and fewer import-competing goods or nontradables; a deficit in the current account declines. A real appreciation has the opposite effect of reducing the production of tradables and stimulating the production of nontradables (Siebert 2007e, chapter 6).

The second channel of independence encompasses the interlinking of the countries' macroeconomies in terms of economic growth and, of course, business cycles. This link operates through trade both on the demand and on the supply side, and also through price changes, including the exchange rate, and through changes in expectations (see below). A strongly growing economy like that of the United States, which produces more than one fourth of world output, stimulates exports of other countries thanks to its imports. By increasing the production of export goods of other countries, a boom in the United States usually leads to a business cycle upswing elsewhere, for instance in export-oriented countries like Japan and Germany.

In a third channel, involving global factor markets, the factors of production—capital, technology, and high-skilled labor—have become more mobile internationally. Foreign direct investment, including greenfield investment and the acquisition of firms, grows faster than trade, while the expansion of world trade has outstripped the increase of world production, all variables being measured in real terms. World GDP augmented at an average real growth rate of 3% per year during the period 1973–2006, whereas the world trade volume grew by an annual average of 5%, as measured by the volume of the world's merchandise exports. In the same period, foreign direct investment rose by 12% per year in real terms although its rates of change were extremely volatile and susceptible to the business cycle and to political shocks; the sharp fall after the boom in 2000 and in the aftermath of September 11,

---

[1] The dimension of the exchange rate is $Q/Q^* = (\euro/\$)(\$/Q^*)/(\euro/Q)$, where Q denotes exports from the euro area and Q^* stands for U.S. exports.

2001 demonstrates this tendency (Siebert 2007e, figure 1.5).[2] With foreign direct investment accounting for 12.2% of total world investment in the period 2000–5 (having peaked at 22.3% in the boom year of 2000), real capital flows have become an important factor in the international division of labor, even compared with the world's export-to-GDP ratio of 26.9% in 2005 (when World Development Indicator data are used). Industrial economies attract three fourths of the world's foreign direct investment, measured as inflows (1991–2006).

The implication of increased capital mobility is that capital now has a strong exit option. As a result, multinational firms have built up a portfolio of production sites in order to optimize their production and investment activities. When capital leaves a country, the country's factor abundance and also its production potential decline. Conversely, the country's production potential on receiving a capital inflow is enhanced. The same effect also holds when whole firms move out.

Technology has become more mobile, too: it is increasingly traded in markets as well as exchanged and diffused within the network of multinational firms (*International Herald Tribune*, October 3, 2005). The technology balance, part of the overall balance of payments, represents an indicator of technology trade. It includes payments for licenses and patents and the purchase of technologies and technological support. For instance, the technology balance of the United States (0.25% of GDP) and Japan (0.23%) are positive, whereas Korea's is negative (−0.32%; data for 2004 (OECD 2006)).

When a technology transfer takes place, its impact depends on whether exclusive ownership titles are defined. If so, the country to which the technology is transferred can use it exclusively; in other cases, the same technology may be used simultaneously in both the sending and the receiving country.

At the same time, labor markets are becoming substantially more global for people with good qualifications. Human capital, especially in the realms of research and management, has become more mobile. Countries compete for it. For those with fewer skills, however, labor markets remain largely nationally segmented, despite existing pressure for migration. This is not to imply that there is no international competition between workplaces for less qualified labor, only that interdependence here has an indirect effect, for instance via trade flows and capital mobility.

A fourth, increasingly relevant, channel concerns the environmental interdependencies which take place in the form of externalities. Externalities can be defined as interdependencies between economic activities within the context of natural environmental and other nonmarket systems. Pollutants, for instance, move from one country to another through river systems and via the atmosphere. A special case of externalities involves global environmental systems, such as Earth's atmosphere,

---

[2] In the calculation of real growth rates, nominal foreign direct investment flows were corrected by the U.S. Capital Equipment Producer Price Index.

currently endangered by global warming and by the depletion of the ozone layer. The potential loss of biodiversity is yet another case of an externality.

In a fifth channel, namely financial markets determining the price of assets, portfolio capital has become extremely mobile. In fact, portfolio capital can react to new data instantaneously; it can now move around the world from one financial market to another at the push of a button. Besides stock and bond markets, currency markets and money markets are also interlinked internationally. Demand for and supply of currencies—determining the exchange rates for national or regional monies—reflect not only trade and capital flows, for instance in the case of foreign direct investment and equity, but also the exchange of bonds, international bank loans, and short-term portfolio flows. Expectations are a vital factor so that portfolio flows may dissociate themselves from the real side of the economy. When expectations change, reversals in capital flow become possible. It is estimated that the world currency markets move the volume of world trade in about five days. In 2007, the daily average turnover on the foreign exchange market, adjusted for double counting, amounted to US$3.2 trillion (Bank for International Settlements 2007). It has doubled since 1998. In 1986, the average gross turnover was US$209 million per day. Note, however, that only four central banks reported their data in 1986, while fifty-four banks collaborated for the 2007 estimate.

The sixth channel involves communication flows. Information can now flow freely through the media and the World Wide Web between nearly all countries, so that a "CNN effect" or a "demonstration effect" takes place. People are informed on what is happening elsewhere in the world and they observe which policies are undertaken abroad: consequently, changes in the psychological mood or in expectations in one place affect other countries or regions, as happens, for instance, within the business cycle or when a contagion effect kicks in during a financial crisis.

In a seventh channel, the utility function of people now extends beyond the national territory. Due to information flows, personal contacts, and tourism, variables reflecting phenomena that happen abroad are now included in the utility function of individuals. An example is the willingness of people in Europe and the United States to donate money in the case of the Southeast Asian tsunami at the end of 2004. Similar dynamics underlie regional integrations: in the European Union, for instance, a transnational European identity is slowly developing and overcoming the purely national interests of member states.

The eighth and last channel encompasses those interdependencies which prevail in the political arena, since the policy instruments chosen in one country may have negative or positive effects on other economies. Within the framework of intensified interdependence, political interdependence in the use of policy instruments increases. Governments may therefore be willing to cooperate on specific issues, and they may opt for a regional integration or multilateral arrangement.

The forces of globalization flowing through these channels have to be contrasted with some factors that oppose the process of globalization. Each national economy still retains a large sector not directly exposed to the international division of labor: the sector of nontradables whose output is not internationally traded. In this sector, national consumption must equal national production. Globalization directly affects only the sector of tradable goods, i.e., the export sector and the domestic sector of import substitutes; the impact on the sector of nontradables is rather indirect. In large countries or regions like the United States, Japan, or the European Union, the nontradable sector is still very strong. It amounts to about three fourths or more of GDP if for simplicity we use the export and import shares in order to calculate the sector of nontradables. In smaller open countries, this sector is admittedly far less important. Moreover, a large portion of the factors of production, especially low-skilled labor, is still immobile.

Furthermore, segmentation exists with respect to information and the institutional setup varies between countries. These factors may explain the "home bias" observed in financial markets. In addition, the preferences of households and entrepreneurs tend to differ; countries have dissimilar aggregated political preferences, diverging cultural identities, diverse legal systems, and political processes that are sometimes poles apart. Different countries may often find themselves at different stages of their political cycles. What is more important, political demands for redistribution and social protection may put the brakes on the process of globalization. Also, internalizing environmental costs may lead to rising transaction costs, especially transportation costs as the prices for fossil fuels increase. On top of which, the fear of global terrorism increases uncertainty, thus negatively affecting international trade and investment flows. It may also lead to an increase in regulations, limiting personal freedom and the freedom to trade and invest. Finally, a protectionist backlash at the political level cannot be ruled out.

How Does Globalization Affect the Rule System?

Together with intensified interdependence in the world economy comes the need for global rules. In this section we will develop the analysis of this two-way bond along different lines.

In the spirit of the transaction-costs approach, one can rely on an evolutionary process in which market participants, when necessary, can interact with each other to find new rules. To let decentralized markets take care of the increased number of links and to see how markets respond constitutes a first answer to globalization. For instance, standardization undertaken by the business community may provide efficiency gains, and institutional competition—as a discovery process—will serve to identify and develop the most promising institutional arrangements.

Since the potential gains from the international division of labor will increase with the widening of markets, countries may be more tempted to behave even more opportunistically and strategically in order to reap higher rewards. For instance, they may increasingly resort to helping their firms gain strategic positions through subsidies, thus permitting rent creation or rent shifting. Arguably, then, the need for rules increases together with the widening of markets. Moreover, this widening and the reduction of market segmentation allows larger cooperation gains which cannot be obtained if countries are caught in a prisoner's dilemma. Also, globalization puts pressure on import-competing sectors to adjust by reducing output and employment in the absence of innovation. This gives rise to protectionist demands. Furthermore, the social models of several countries, for instance in continental Europe, may be in question, not only due to globalization but also to the aging of their populations. All this may induce politicians to obstruct the international division of labor. This outlook calls for the strengthening of the WTO rule system in order to prevent the strategic use of subsidies and reduce the risk of protectionism.

The higher potential gains from trade in a globalized world induces countries to enter into bilateral agreements which seem easier to reach than multilateral arrangements. At the same time, the general trend toward regional integrations, which exceed the depth of trade arrangements in many areas, for instance in the free movement of people or in monetary policy, leads to a dichotomy between the bilateral and regional approaches on the one hand and a multilateral rule system on the other. How to integrate these two approaches remains an unresolved issue.

In spite of the relative constancy in the share of services in international trade over the last two decades, the trend toward a service economy and even a knowledge economy may have its impact on the international division of labor. Moreover, the new communication technology is likely to benefit border-crossing services. The WTO rule system for trade in services should reflect this development in the years to come. Consequently, the stronger the tertiarization process (i.e., the structural shift toward services) becomes in both industrialized and developing countries and the more the share of services in GDP increases, the more important rules for international trade in services should turn out to be.

Wider markets can go hand in hand with the growth of firms, either through internal expansion or through mergers and acquisitions. These developments may bring about more contestable markets, but they may also give firms the opportunity to achieve a monopolistic position and to behave accordingly, for instance in a specific market segment. Competition policy is therefore needed. EU countries, attempting to create a single market, were prepared to hand competition policy over to the European level and transatlantic cooperation is taking place in this area. However, rules for an international competition policy have not yet been established.

The strong increase in foreign direct investment represents an opportunity to raise the benefits coming from an improved international allocation of capital. Whereas locational competition stresses the exit option of capital and its negative impact on productivity if capital leaves a country, the discussion in some industrial countries is more concerned with an unwanted infiltration of foreign capital through sovereign wealth funds. Once again, an international investment code is still to be found.

Integrating the developing countries into the international division of labor represents an opportunity to reduce the pressure toward migration. With rising income made possible by trade, the incentive to migrate is reduced. In that sense, trade is a substitute for migration. The same dynamics apply to capital flowing toward developing countries. However, pressure toward migration remains stark whenever incomes per capita differ strongly. There is a pressing need to understand whether a rule system for migration is needed and, if so, what it should look like. It is also important to study the interdependence between a rule system for migration and that applying to trade and capital flows.

With cross-border externalities increasing and the threat of deterioration of global public goods such as the depletion of the ozone layer and global warming becoming more relevant, more sovereignty will have to be ceded in order to internalize social costs. This development becomes possible as people become more aware of global public goods. A more global orientation of people, i.e., an extension of their utility functions to include phenomena in other countries and parts of the world, assists this process. The rule system must in turn be extended in order to include these phenomena.

With financial markets becoming more globalized, the impact of financial risk may affect more countries and systemic risk may increase. It is argued that new financial products allow better risk sharing and risk shifting. If this hypothesis holds, financial markets will become more efficient. However, larger markets may also accumulate risk. The introduction of the euro, for instance, was expected to reduce exchange-rate volatility. Unfortunately, the euro turned out to be quite volatile in the medium term. Thus, over several years, large upswings and downswings relative to the U.S. dollar have taken place. It has also become apparent that new financial products may add to the systemic risk of the financial system. Hedge funds and structured investment vehicles, or conduits, have exposed the financial system to new risks and forced the central banks to provide additional liquidity to keep the system functioning. Especially in the fall of 2007, the supplementary liquidity was in conflict with the central banks' objective of keeping the price level stable. Financial crises, including currency crises, cannot be ruled out for the future. It is therefore paramount to think about a rule system that can prevent financial instability.

With reduced economic segmentation, the benefits from political cooperation are likely to increase. Political cooperation is the companion of economic cooperation through rules. It can be its forerunner and facilitate the understanding necessary to cede sovereignty, a crucial step toward the implementation of new rules. Political cooperation may also be the consequence of gains from economic cooperation and economic rules. These processes are influenced by geopolitical conditions and geopolitical shifts. The Cold War, with its countervailing threats exchanged between the Soviet empire and the North Atlantic Alliance, may have been the reason why a new war could be prevented and only regional wars broke out. Also, the end of the Cold War reduced the necessity to cede sovereignty within geopolitical blocs.

The decline of a hegemon, the establishment of a multipolar world, and the shift of power from the United States to China, from the West to Asia will all have an impact on the rule system.

Areas of an International Economic Order

The international rule system encompasses several issues: the international division of labor in the trade of goods and services, the relationship between regional integration and multilateral rules, competition policy, capital flows, technology flows, migration, border-crossing negative externalities (and border-crossing positive spillovers), the global environment as a public good, and the stability of the monetary–financial system. At the same time, the issue of human rights extends to all of these areas.

In the trade of goods and services, the rule system has the function of allowing countries to exploit potential cooperation gains, of preventing the opportunistic behavior of one state to the detriment of other states, and of avoiding protectionism. Here, the World Trade Organization (WTO) and its predecessor, the General Agreement on Tariffs and Trade (GATT), represent rules systems which have proved successful over the last sixty years. However, some major problems concerning this issue are still unresolved, most notably the access of developing countries to agricultural markets and to those markets where antidumping policies of industrial countries play a role, for instance textiles; market access of industrial countries to developing countries; and the setting of rules for the service sector. Another organization, the World Bank, is not the expression of a rule system but has as its target the promotion of economic development and the consequent enabling of developing countries to participate in the international division of labor. In extending credits, then, the World Bank plays a rule-setting role.

With respect to the relationship between regional integrations and multilateral rules, it is important that regional integrations, and especially bilateral and other selective free trade areas, do not become a stumbling block for the multilateral order.

As for the channel of macroeconomic interdependence, the chances for international macroeconomic cooperation to succeed are slim for several reasons. Concerning economic growth, it is in the interests of each country to choose institutional rules that promise a high GDP growth rate, the environment and other conditions allowing. At the same time, past experience suggests that the Keynesian concept of smoothing expenditures over the business cycle (beyond automatic stabilizers) has failed: whereas in a national context an expansion of expenditures often takes place during recessions, curtailing such expenditures during a boom is not a common practice. Indeed, the political process does not abide by an intertemporal restraint over the business cycle. Most importantly, the political cycle follows its own mechanics:

winning an election often becomes an overwhelming priority to which the management of expenditures is subordinated. Internationally, additional difficulties hamper cooperation in this area. Countries may find themselves in different phases of the business cycle (not all business cycles are synchronized internationally), conditions between countries may differ, and political cycles diverge. The only relevant precedent of international macroeconomic cooperation we have so far is the Growth and Stability Pact in the euro area. The Pact introduced coordination by restraint, in the sense that it excludes an excessive budget deficit in order to shield the European Central Bank against pressure due to an increase in governmental debt (on exchange-rate coordination, see chapter IX).

Global cooperation is also lacking in the area of competition and antitrust policy, i.e., the control of excessive market power in the world market. So far, we have witnessed an established tradition of competition policy in Europe and the United States, with cooperation between the respective authorities on both sides of the Atlantic. In essence, a multilateral approach aimed at preventing global monopolies would be desirable. This, however, would conflict with the interests of nation states and with their policies of rent creation by means of national champions. One question which remains open is what a multilateral arrangement should look like.

In the area of international factor flows—migration and flows of capital and technology—the rule system should encourage an optimal allocation of the factors of production. This, in turn, requires tackling issues such as how a country can attract factors of production in order to stimulate its economic development, and which incentives would allow the world to enjoy a constant stream of new technologies. The answers to these questions hinge upon the criteria used to define optimality, and they vary for the different factors of production.

As for the channel constituted by border-crossing negative externalities, the role of the rule system consists in reducing such externalities by internalizing social costs. A relevant example comes from the management of environmental problems: instead of applying the polluter-pays principle, the victim-pays principle may be adopted, with the pollutee delivering side payments to the polluter.

In global environmental protection, the function of a rule system is to prevent the deterioration of global public goods such as Earth's atmosphere and to minimize the negative impact of global warming. Many international agreements related to environmental issues are already in place, such as the United Nations Framework Convention on Climate Change and the Kyoto Protocol.

With respect to the stability of the monetary–financial system, prudent standards such as those on monetary–financial stability developed through the Financial Stability Forum are instrumental in preventing financial and currency crises. In addition, the IMF can be viewed as an institutional arrangement that attempts to prevent financial crises from developing into a systemic crisis. At the same time, the IMF also aims to improve those institutional arrangements that hedge countries against such currency crises. Finally, the IMF helps countries caught in a currency crisis by providing fresh capital.

With respect to human rights, it is usually thought that the arrangements for allocation—the world markets for goods, services, and factors of production—require an ethical framework. Some ethical norms can be considered to be universal, being based on common philosophical principles such as the Kantian categorical imperative, on common religious doctrines, or on natural law. Other norms are specific to particular religions or cultures limited to given regions of the world. In addition, humanity attempts to implement norms through organizational means such as the International Labor Organization, seeking to promote internationally recognized labor rights, and courts such as the International Court of Justice at The Hague and the European Court of Human Rights, attempting to enforce a framework of human rights.

III
How Rules Are Established

Institutional rules have emerged in several ways: by learning from experience and searching explicitly for lower transaction costs; by relying on competition between institutions; by agreeing on markets as a mechanism of allocation; by trying to secure cooperation gains; by internalizing border-crossing externalities; and by dealing with global public goods.

Learning from Negative Experience and Searching for Lower Transaction Costs

One way to explain the emergence of rules is to interpret them as the result of learning from experience. Most importantly, rules often spring from a negative experience that inflicts severe hardship on people. They are established *ex post*, after the negative experience has occurred. In these cases, they may be regarded as the outcome of pathological learning, and their function is to prevent human tragedies in the future.

A historical case of a negative experience serving as a starting point for new rules is the principle "cujus regio, ejus religio" ("whose realm, his religion") introduced by the Peace of Westphalia signed in Münster, Germany, in 1648. The rule came to life at the end of the Thirty Years' War, which had drawn the European continent into a religious conflict between Catholics and Protestants. According to this new principle, the religion of the ruling prince or king determined the religion of his subjects. In this way, religious wars could be prevented. Similarly, the disintegration of the world economy in the 1930s and World War II led to the establishment of today's most important global rule systems: GATT and its successor, the WTO, aimed at fostering trade relationships among nations, and the IMF, devoted to the maintenance of monetary–financial stability. The World Bank, also established after World War II, does not match the strict interpretation of rules adopted throughout this book. However, this organization plays a pivotal role in enabling developing countries to participate in the international division of labor, i.e., to accept the rule system for trade.

Not only disasters, but also a milder negative experience may be at the origin of rules. This is the case when existing procedures are deemed inadequate, too costly, or in any case, open to considerable improvement. When dissatisfied with a given situation, people actively search for new rules. Unlike the *ex post* approach following a devastating experience, an *ex ante* pattern of action emerges. A significant example of this dynamics is the evolution of the GATT into the WTO, i.e., the advancement into a better, more comprehensive institutional setup. Also, the imminent dangers of global warming may encourage people to engage actively in the change of the rule system.

In any case, it is difficult to draw the line between an *ex post* approach in response to a negative experience and an active and explicit *ex ante* search effort. Rules may evolve through a slow process in which *ex post* and *ex ante* are barely distinguishable. An example from the distant past is the acceptance of a good—for instance, shells or precious metals—as a unit of value and as a means of payment. The acceptance of such a rule, marking the invention of money, can be considered as an essential technological innovation. Another historical illustration of a major organizational improvement is the invention of a freight bourse for transatlantic shipping in the nineteenth century, improving the allocation of the existing shipping capacity. Further examples abound: staking land claims eventually established a procedure through which the claims were respected, for instance through titles; merchants agree on procedures and standards for their products or for accounting; industries concur on standards of measurement. A further example is that e-mail addresses are offered by private companies (GMX, Yahoo, Google, Microsoft, etc.), and the internet domains on which they work are assigned and supervised by the group of organizations that goes under the banner of the "Internet Society" (see ICANN below).

In all the above cases, the decentralized agreement of economic agents on "how things must be done" is pivotal to the particular development of international rules. This process does not necessarily involve the government, even if the rules are international. Implicitly agreeing on markets for allocating goods and resources may very well be a decision of private agents without governments coming in. In a different venue, governments may agree on international procedures for using natural resources. Thus, the Kyoto Protocol introduced the possibility of establishing markets for CO_2 licenses in the European Union.

All these arrangements can generate benefits for individuals and countries and lower transaction costs. Take two countries I and II whose transaction costs fall after the introduction of a rule, and where, for the sake of argument, the rule may have different degrees, i.e., a different intensity meaning more precision or greater comprehensiveness (figure III.1). Since we are interested in the welfare of a country, we consider the total transaction costs of each country. In the area of the two curves where total transaction costs fall for both countries, both countries are interested in having a more comprehensive rule. When the transaction costs of one country start to rise while the costs of the other are still falling, there are gains for both as long as the fall in costs for one country outweighs the increase for the other. In this case, total transaction costs for both countries keep decreasing. Then, one country may

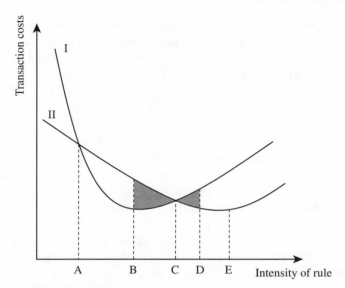

Figure III.1.   Falling transaction costs and intensity of rule.

be willing to share part of its gains with the other country, and both may end up agreeing on the rule.

In figure III.1, the intensity of the rule at point A (where the two transaction-costs curves cross) is not optimal, since to the right of A the transaction-costs curves for both countries continue to fall. Both countries gain until point B, where country I reaches its lowest cost. From B to C and even beyond C, there are gains for both countries together if the cost reduction in country II outweighs the cost increase in country I. Let point D represent the lowest point of the total cost curve. In the area between B and D, both countries can negotiate on the rule.

Under more realistic conditions, aspects other than compensation may lead to an agreement on rules. For instance, a country may accept a rule even if its intensity is already on the rising branch of the transaction-costs curve. A country is likely to do so if it expects a downward shift in its transaction-costs curve in the future, or if it has an advantage from a package of rules, so that lower gains or even losses from one rule are offset by greater benefits coming from the agreement of other rules.

Institutional Competition

A specific pathway leading to new rules is institutional competition, in which established national rules stand side by side and compete with one another. The market decisions of economic agents, as well as political decisions, highlight over time which rules produce unsatisfactory results and which perform best. Such competition leads to what, in Hayek's words (1968), might be called a discovery process.

Competing for mobile factors puts pressure on countries to find new solutions, for instance by implementing new institutional arrangements or by exploring new technological horizons. Such competition stimulates the imagination and intensifies the search for solutions. Moreover, in this view, the technological or institutional solutions employed in different locations can be explicitly compared. Indeed, seeing positive or negative examples coming from elsewhere may encourage a country to improve its actual performance. Thus, the analysis of "best practices," or "benchmarking," represents an explicit attempt made by firms and politicians to learn how things are done elsewhere, for instance in subunits of multinationals, in the organization of different firms, or in the policy approaches adopted by different governments. As Mark Twain once remarked, "few things are harder to put up with than the annoyance of a good example." Institutional competition can become a useful mechanism to control the efficiency of governments. In a globalizing world, where any remarkable event anywhere in the world is likely to be picked up by the media, this demonstration effect is intensified. In contrast to an explicit search, in which rules are established *ex ante* and follow an evolutionary process, they are established *ex post*.

This institutional competition method encompasses taxation, regulations of product and factor markets, delineation of the private sector versus the public sector, and the organization of the state. It also includes economic policy concepts and philosophies such as central planning versus the market approach.

Results of institutional competition are, for instance, the arrangements that a country chooses for its corporate governance, its rules for the banking sector, accounting rules, business and other taxes, the setup of the labor market, arrangements for social security, welfare, and environmental regulation. Interdependence among national regulation systems stems from the fact that people and factors of production can avoid national regulations by moving to a region or country where rules are more favorable. Most importantly, capital enjoys an exit option and can be relocated wherever the institutional conditions are most encouraging. Similarly, labor and citizens can move between countries (Siebert 2006a).

A key example of global institutional competition between economic policy concepts is the contest between the economic philosophies applied from 1950 to about 1985 in Latin America (import substitution) and Asia (export diversification). Eventually, Latin America had to give up its strategy. Also relevant is the hidden rivalry between China and the former Soviet Union from the 1960s to the late 1980s. A historically outstanding case was the contest between communist central planning in Central and Eastern Europe and the market economies of the West before the fall of the Iron Curtain. In this Tiebout competition (Tiebout 1956), the citizens of Central and Eastern Europe eventually voted with their feet and the communist systems finally collapsed as the East Germans fled from the Eastern Bloc on August 19, 1989. They made their way to the West through Sopron, in Hungary, whose borders with Austria were no longer sealed. In the future, we will see institutional competition between the Chinese model of organizing the economy and society, the Anglo-Saxon approach, and the continental European paradigm.

Institutional competition, however, does not apply to the case of border-crossing externalities and global public goods. It also does not allow countries to overcome a prisoner's dilemma in order to enjoy benefits from cooperation gains. This is the same as saying that institutional competition is limited whenever a multilateral rule system has the property of a public good. An example is the WTO. Besides these clear points, when rules are needed to keep transaction costs low, a major concern is that institutional competition may degenerate into a race to the bottom. For instance, it is feared that business taxes in a country may be reduced if other countries lower their tax rates for businesses or that the protection of a nation's environmental quality may decrease if other countries place a low value on their environment. Although the answer to these fears is a complex one, the choice of a national policy instrument is derived from cost–benefit calculations. Thus, if citizens attach a high value to environmental protection and if this preference is expressed in their voting behavior, the political process will make environmental protection more likely. Admittedly, if a goal conflict exists between environmental protection and keeping capital and jobs at home, a loose approach to the environment elsewhere will increase the opportunity costs of environmental protection. However, if the citizens of a country have a strong preference for environmental protection, this will outweigh the higher opportunity costs in terms of goal losses in other areas. If the reasons for regulation are sufficiently tailored to the preference function of the country's citizens, then regulations will be upheld. With respect to infrastructure and business taxation, for instance, firms remain willing to pay taxes if sufficiently attractive public goods are supplied. Moreover, the state can adjust the financing of its location factors, for example by introducing user charges for infrastructure such as roads, ports, and airports. Additionally, it is possible to privatize parts of a publicly owned infrastructure in order to set its scarcity price. Alternatively, the government can switch to benefit taxation, which means that taxes are equivalent to the benefits received by users and not to their ability to pay. For all these reasons, it is not correct to argue that cost–benefit analysis will lead to the conclusion that the environment need not be protected at all (Siebert 2006a).

In evaluating institutional competition, we must note that it is natural for governments to strive for intergovernmental cooperation and institutional harmonization if this strengthens their position at home, for instance with respect to taxation. Often, to form a cartel of institutional rules, restraining the mobility of factors of production and of residents makes the life of governments much easier. Care should be taken that this does not happen, although clear distinction must be drawn between this occurrence and cases when an international public good is at stake. There is also the risk that standardization, while able to lower transaction costs, will be used to define an important economic position by firms or countries to the detriment of other standards. In this case, standardization becomes a weapon in the hands of a technological hegemon and represents a trade barrier.

Institutional Competition in the European Union

The European Union has a rich experience in institutional competition and rule setting. It can be considered a laboratory for global governance from which the world can learn. The EU has made the principle of mutual recognition an important element of its integration policy. Since it proved impossible to harmonize *ex ante* the different legal systems—among them, the logically constructed French law based on Roman law; the German law, with its own tradition; and the pragmatic British common law, or case law—it was thought best to let the legal systems stand side by side, mutually recognizing the rules of each nation. The pathbreaking Cassis de Dijon verdict of the European Court of Justice in 1979 ruled that a product legally brought to market in one of the member countries of the EU was automatically admitted into the markets of all other EU countries. The verdict dealt with Cassis de Dijon, a Burgundy fruit liqueur, widely used in France, in popular aperitifs such as kir royale (with champagne), kir cardinal (with red wine or rosé), and kir bourgeois (or kir ordinaire with white wine). Before the ruling, Cassis de Dijon could legally be imported into Germany but could not be marketed there. German regulation, the monopoly law on spirits (*Branntweinmonopolgesetz*) of 1922, required fruit liqueurs to have an alcohol content of at least 32%; Cassis de Dijon, with its 17% alcohol-per-volume content was verboten.

The verdict of the European Court of Justice established the country-of-origin principle according to which the rules of the country of origin, i.e., the home country, and not the rules of the country of destination are to be applied in a transaction. This principle holds not only for products, allowing, for instance, the export of Belgian beer to Germany even if it is not brewed in accordance with the German beer Purity Law of 1516, but also applies to services, allowing a British bank product to be marketed in Germany or a company incorporated according to Irish law to operate plants on the continent. Following this principle, the different national regulations are de facto mutually recognized and can coexist. The principle of respecting the home rule has proven to be a pathbreaking decision, opening up national regulations to institutional competition in Europe. Only in cases in which products are hazardous or damaging to health, safety, or the environment does the principle not apply (Article 30 of the EC Treaty).

The EU has seen institutional competition with respect to policy concepts, too. Witness the debate in the 1960s on the French concept of *planification*—a combination of the government's objectives and markets, especially with respect to investment—and the German philosophy of the social market economy. According to the French approach, the national government attempted to plan and determine the investment decisions of firms; this was alleviated by the fact that major sectors of the economy were in the hands of the government and major government-owned banks supplied the financing.

Agreeing on Markets in order to Decentralize Economic Decisions

Another viable path toward reducing transaction costs is to accept markets as an institutional arrangement for the allocation of a specific group of goods, namely private goods. For these goods, market participants have no interest in not revealing their true willingness to pay—a condition that is not satisfied for public goods (see chapter VII). As a consequence, economic decisions for private goods are decentralized. Individual households and firms enjoy the benefits of their decisions in terms of utility and profits, but they also carry the opportunity costs of these decisions. In this way, benefits and opportunity costs of economic decisions are devolved upon the individual units of society. Given a framework for markets, economic decisions occur more or less automatically, independently of governments and political activity. They are depoliticized. Governments only intervene in order to define the institutional setting for such markets. Thus, markets represent a decentralized mechanism for coordinating human actions.

In the world economy, markets allocate the gains from trade to countries, providing incentives for a country to specialize in those areas of production that generate gains from trade for them. In this process, markets also allocate scarce goods and resources to the use involving the highest reward. Markets therefore represent an instrument that selects the best use for scarce resources among competing options. This becomes all the more important in a world economy where the strong economic growth of developing countries boosts the competition for resources. The demand of the newcomers (developing countries) drives out the demand of the incumbents (industrialized countries). This occurs as a good or a resource becomes more scarce and its price rises.

There are several concerns with markets. A first concern is that markets can lead to monopoly power. In such a case, one agent can dominate demand or supply and influence prices. Supply monopolies may be organized either horizontally, extending over one product and its substitutes, or vertically, comprising several stages of production within backward or forward linkages. One consequence of the possible emergence of monopolies is the necessity of competition policy in the market approach. Another approach is the correct definition of property rights so that monopolies disappear. In the case of networks such as power or telephone lines, natural monopolies were long considered virtually inevitable. However, with new property rights for networks, i.e., the right of transmission, such natural monopolies disappeared. In the oil industry, spot and futures markets replaced the vertical integration or hierarchies after extraction rights passed to the resource countries in the 1970s (see chapter II). Nevertheless, the correct definition of property rights will not be sufficient to undo monopolies. Competition policy is also needed. Indeed, the major difficulty consists in organizing an international competition policy.

A second concern relates to the observation that monopolistic positions do not arise only because the private sector tries to attain them. Governments may as well try to influence market results strategically, and pay subsidies in order to allow their firms to establish themselves early in the market (rent creation) or to enable them to conquer favorable market positions and thereby shift rents from other countries to national champions (rent shifting). Therefore, rules on subsidies to prevent distortions are needed. Such rules should also stop strategic trade policy. Since an undervaluation of a currency represents a general subsidy to the export sectors, rules to avoid undervaluation are required.

A third concern is that information is not evenly spread on both sides of the market: information asymmetries often occur. This means that one side of the market may enjoy information advantages. Moreover, information on aspects such as product quality is often incomplete and collecting information can involve high costs. The answer to this problem is twofold. It is in the self-interest of each market participant to obtain as much information as possible. In addition, competition among the sellers will be an incentive to improve the information provided by the market.

A fourth concern is whether markets are fair. The advantage of markets is that they are efficient, making sure that resources are used where they yield the best results, that goods are produced with least costs, and that new products are developed. Efficient, however, is not necessarily synonymous with fair: the ensuing income distribution may be thought of as unjust. It would be unrealistic to expect markets to bring equality of results for all participants. Indeed, the international rule system affects the international distribution of income and also the distribution of benefits (see below). Nationally, one answer is to change the income distribution through a tax-transfer mechanism; internationally, however, this approach is not viable because the right to tax rests with the nation state. A more realistic approach is to seek improved starting conditions. In this way, an institution such as the World Bank can help developing countries so that they can enjoy the gains from trade.

A fifth concern is that markets produce results which are not politically acceptable. This discomfort, for instance, has become a prevalent attitude in countries like France. Until the 1970s, France adhered to *planification*. Meanwhile, it had become somewhat taciturn about *planification* itself. In the same spirit of governmental influence, France relied on long-term contracts for crude oil in the two oil crises of the 1970s, during which, as a resource importer, it negotiated directly with resource-exporting countries, thereby attempting to reduce resource uncertainty. These contracts specified oil quantities to be supplied by the resource countries and prices to be paid by the resource importer. As soon as spot and futures markets for crude oil developed in the late 1970s and early 1980s, supply and price risks were considerably reduced, so that long-term contracts lost their attractiveness. Another nonmarket approach comes from the communist countries, where the pre-1989 COMECON introduced a centrally planned international division of labor "from above," obviously under the strong influence of the Soviet Union. Instead of letting markets decide which goods to produce in which country, this decision was made politically. The Hungarians produced autobuses, the Czechs streetcars, and the East Germans wagons for the Trans-Siberian Railroad. It is apparent that this system failed.

A sixth concern is market failures. One such failure occurs when markets simply do not exist. For instance, capital markets may not have enough temporal depth to cover intertemporal risks. The solution here consists in establishing markets where possible. However, one problem is that real markets are often evaluated against the background of perfect and ideal models that cannot encompass all aspects of economic reality. A more important failure occurs when monopolies come into being through an endogenous market process or cartels are formed, so that market processes end up being distorted. This is exactly the point at which competition policy must come to the fore. Another major market failure takes place when technological externalities prevail and public goods are involved. In the case of externalities, the discrepancy between social and private costs has to be reduced. In the case of public goods the willingness to pay cannot be aggregated via the market. In both cases, institutional rules are required (see below).

Securing Gains from Cooperation

Cooperation gains are possible in cases where mutual benefits are feasible within a positive-sum game. An important case in point is the international division of labor, from which all participants can gain. Nevertheless, a country may behave strategically (or opportunistically) in international affairs in order to maximize its benefit by reducing the benefit for others. For instance, a dominant country can levy an import duty or intervene in other ways in order to maximize its benefits, even if this means that the gains of the other country will decrease. Another case is strategic trade policy through subsidies.

Consider a two-country case in which the free-trade solution generates as an outcome benefits of 27 utility units to each country relative to autarky; I assume that "utils" represent a measure of benefits for both countries. Point I $(27, 27^*)$ in figure III.2 is the free-trade solution, where the first number refers to the home country and where an asterisk denotes the foreign country. Now assume that the home country can push up its trade benefit to a value of 30 and reduce the foreign country's benefit to 10 by means of strategic measures: point II $(30, 10^*)$ in figure III.2 denotes the home country's gains from trade relative to autarky. Alternatively, the foreign country can raise an optimal tariff in order to increase its gains from trade, a move which in turn causes a decrease in terms of domestic gains from trade: point III with the bundle $(10, 30^*)$ denotes the corresponding outcome. Alternatively, in an initial situation IV $(12, 12^*)$ both countries are implementing a tariff policy. Finally, in the extreme case in which both countries push protectionist measures to their maximum they find themselves in the autarky situation, where the gains from trade are zero at the origin $(0, 0^*)$.

Starting from an initial position with some trade (point IV), the area above point IV up to the curve II–I–III defines the area of potential trade benefits for both countries. Both can therefore benefit from the transition to free trade. If they cooperate, they can achieve outcome I, where the two of them reach a maximum welfare of 54 utility units. For simplicity, we assume that utility units can be aggregated.

Agreement is needed on how to distribute the total benefit. Such an agreement can take place by accepting free trade, namely by means of decentralization via markets and by simply accepting the distribution of total benefits that results from markets. In this case, the two countries then maximize their benefits. However, in the case of noncooperative behavior, they cannot reach the optimal situation I. Each country wants to realize its favorite position with larger individual gains (II or III), but the total utility is then lower with 40 utility units. Such a situation is not sustainable, unless one of the two countries can enforce its own conditions. If one of the countries does not dominate, both remain in situation IV, in which noncooperative behavior of both countries prevails. Each country chooses its strategy believing it is the best one possible; each expects that it will have greater benefits in a situation different from point I. This is a typical prisoner's dilemma. It represents a noncooperative equilibrium (Nash equilibrium).

The situation considered above corresponds to a one-shot game with four possible outcomes. In table III.1, the players' payoff matrix illustrates the gains from trade for both players. The first row and the first column indicate cooperative behavior, from which both countries get the highest joint benefits (entry I). Entry II indicates instead a cooperative strategy by the foreign country following the dominating domestic country. Entry III characterizes a situation in which the domestic country is cooperative. Entry IV indicates the case in which both countries do not cooperate. The situation can also be described in the following terms: there is a potential for cooperation gains out there, but the countries are unable to find it. In principle, a positive-sum game is possible. The key question is how to unearth it and how to implement it. Note that the game presented here is a single-round game. In a repeated game with many periods, the reputation of the two players comes into play, making a cooperative solution more likely.

World gains resulting from lower tariffs have been estimated empirically. For example, Brown et al. (2003) calculate in an applied general-equilibrium model that a complete removal of all tariffs and other barriers would increase world GNP by US$2.1 trillion, thus boosting the GNP of all economies by a significant rate, for

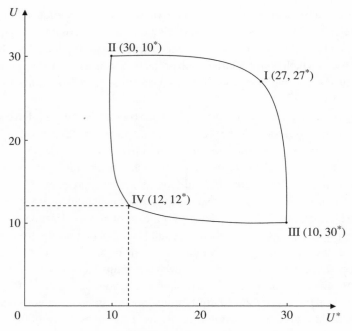

Figure III.2. Trade benefits area.

Table III.1. The prisoner's dilemma:
welfare levels with cooperative and noncooperative behavior.

			Foreign country		
			Cooperative strategy (free trade)		Noncooperative strategy (tariff policy)
Domestic country {	Cooperative strategy (free trade)	I	$(27, 27^*)$	III	$(10, 30^*)$
	Noncooperative strategy (tariff policy)	II	$(30, 10^*)$	IV	$(12, 12^*)$

instance by 5.5% for the United States, by 6.3% for Europe, by 7.75% for China, and even by 16.4% for the Philippines.

A solution proposed by economists to avoid of such an impasse is the Pareto criterion. According to this approach, a rule system is efficient if it makes all countries better off without making a single country worse off. The gains may be redistributed to ensure all countries are better off (Kaldor criterion).

An important issue is the positional difference between who gains most (absolute gains) and who gains relatively more (relative gains). This is a sensitive question. In principle, it is possible to supplement a rule system by redistribution measures.

However, to explicitly introduce redistribution between countries gives rise to many debates, for instance on how to determine the benefits of individual countries relative to the situation before the introduction of the rule. This makes it nearly impossible to implement a system redistributing the countries' benefits. It is therefore extremely helpful for the development of a rule system that each country can enjoy direct benefits (see below), that benefits accrue to all countries, and that they are not excessively disproportionate (see below). In this case, the topic of relative benefits moves to the background. This seems to apply in the trade area.

Trade Externalities in Bargaining

A different way to analyze the relationships between countries is the concept of externalities, defined as interdependence between economic activities. We distinguish between market externalities and technological externalities.

According to Scitovsky (1954), a market externality exists between economic agents via prices and incomes, i.e., through the market mechanism. For instance, a price increase for crude oil in one country leads to a price hike in another country. Such a pecuniary externality not only reflects market interdependence between producers of different countries and between consumers, but also between governments inasmuch as their budgets are affected when prices change elsewhere.

Conversely, a technological externality is defined as interdependence between the volume structure of different production functions, i.e., the argument variables, and also different utility functions (Siebert 2008b, p. 7). Such externalities run through technological systems such as the atmosphere, as in the case of acid rain, or through groundwater structures or river systems, as in the case of upstream and downstream interlinkage. Usually such technological externalities involve at least two private units, for instance private firms, and they may occur within a national jurisdiction. Technological externalities merge into public goods whose spatial dimension can be either national or global. Thus, environmental quality in one country may be affected by the pollutants present in the environment of another country. This is typical of negative border-crossing technological externalities. As a limit to this case, we have public goods extending to many countries or global public goods.

Interpreting technological externalities as interdependencies between the public goods of different countries or regions opens up a more general interpretation of technological externalities. Then our interpretation includes such phenomena as the interlinkage of financial stability in different countries or of the financial systems of different countries insofar as a country's financial stability can be interpreted as a public good. In this case, the financial system itself becomes the technological system through which externalities run. Another example is the accumulation of pollutants in a biochain. Yet another example is the spread of news through a global information system, setting contagion-like dynamics in motion. Admittedly, such a case cannot easily be distinguished from the price mechanism.

This wide interpretation of externalities can be applied to all institutional arrangements whose efficiency or other properties can be interpreted as those of a public good. In a similar context, technological externalities can be seen as arising from bargaining games. They then run through the system as defined by the bargaining context, through which interdependencies exist between the policy instrument adopted by one country and the benefits from a game accruing to another country. These can be called policy instrument externalities, since a country's policy instrument affects the welfare of another country in terms of the international division of labor.

An example of such a policy instrument externality is the concept of a terms-of-trade externality, according to which a unilateral action of a government causes a decline of benefits for another country or group of countries (Bagwell and Staiger 1998, 2002). This effect can be interpreted as a technological externality, because the interdependence is not occurring directly through the market mechanism but rather due to a policy instrument and to the interplay of different governments within a bargaining game. The reach and scope of all governments' decisions are therefore interlinked. Another way of looking at the same phenomenon is by noting that the reduction of transaction costs in a country as shown in figure III.2 depends on the actions taken in other countries.

In such a Nash negotiation game, governments, which are eager to improve their terms of trade, can adopt policy instruments such as tariffs that penalize other parties. Such a game becomes reality whenever exporters lobby for better terms of trade and manage to outbid protected import-competing industries. In such a political economy model, governments do not maximize trade utility as in the offer-curve theory but maximize their preferences for better terms of trade.

This Nash equilibrium prisoner's dilemma over tariffs can be transformed if each government trusts the other to lower tariffs, so that demand increases for the exports of both. By adopting the appropriate instruments, the prisoner's dilemma can be turned into a positive-sum game (Barrett 2005). Small countries will gain more than large ones from such rules. Since they are price takers on the world market, they cannot influence the terms of trade. Only large countries have the option to influence their terms of trade. The GATT's principles of reciprocity and nondiscrimination work as simple rules that help governments implement efficient trade agreements; such rules are instrumental in order to bargain lower tariffs than those set unilaterally, thereby protecting the economies from inefficiencies (see below).

A word of caution concerning the concept of policy-instrument externality is in order: our analysis does not mean that the adoption of *any* policy instrument gives rise to an externality. In fact, such an interpretation would run the risk of justifying government cartels even when there are no cooperation gains. It would allow governments to play against their citizens. Institutional competition would then be impossible. Policy instrument externalities can only be interpreted in the context of a bargaining game, namely a rule system, presenting the properties of a public good.

Principles of Bargaining for Cooperation Gains in Trade

Given such conditions, there needs to be an understanding between countries that cooperation gains exist and that it pays to introduce rules in order to prevent strategic behavior. Thus, a rational analysis by the participants may highlight the positive prospect of gains that can be reaped by all participants even if the degree of gains differs. We can also state that countries are well aware of terms-of-trade externalities. A large body of institutional experience relates to the international division of labor, especially trade.

Several principles and mechanisms are instrumental in establishing an international rule system: the principle of equal opportunity, the principle of nondiscrimination, reciprocity of concessions, equivalence of national treatment, and the principle of mutual recognition.

The principle of equal opportunity means that each country should be able to play according to the same rules. Tariffs and other obstacles to the international division of labor, including national regulations, hamper equal opportunity. Liberalization can be viewed as a method through which equal opportunity is obtained. Distortions, for instance through subsidies for agriculture in the industrial countries, violate the principle of equal opportunity.

Nondiscrimination in the rule system, in turn, can be interpreted as an expression of the principle of equal opportunity, or, similarly, as a method not to violate such principle. Nondiscrimination is a necessary but not sufficient condition for equal opportunity. In the world trade order, trade policy measures should not discriminate against countries; all countries should be treated equally. In particular, there must be no discrimination between domestic and foreign products. The reach and significance of such a principle is explained very well by Thailand's cigarette case, examined by GATT in 1990. Thailand had raised a tariff on imported cigarettes, referring to health policy reasons, but without taxing cigarettes manufactured domestically. In the Thailand cigarette case, the GATT ruled that it is consistent with the world trade order for a country to take measures for health reasons (Article XX); however, no difference can be made between domestic and imported cigarettes; no discrimination against imports is allowed.

Calls against discrimination differ from the desire for a level playing field. It is the core of the international division of labor to exploit differences in preferences and endowments, be they related to labor, capital, or technology. Only in this way are gains between countries possible. Endowment conditions are given by nature, but they are also acquired through a country's effort: in accumulating a capital stock through investments, building human capital through education, and improving technologies through invention and innovation. For these reasons, asking for a level playing field cannot mean that countries should not exploit differences in endowment and preferences.

Reciprocity of concessions is an often-used procedure to obtain common rules. The *do ut des* ("I give, so that you may give") of concession seems to appeal to the idea of fairness, loosely defined. This approach eases the multifacet bargaining situation where one country yields a position in one area while the other country concedes in another area. The negative impact of a concession often falls on a specific group, whereas the benefits are widespread. This quid pro quo procedure is an old principle, corresponding to basic rules for barter trade in archaic societies (see chapter X; Mauss 1923/24).

Reciprocity of concessions has been used in trade negotiations through reciprocal tariff concessions in the trade of goods, requiring that the tariff cuts by one country be matched by equivalent reductions in another country. In other words, one country offers a concession in one area if another country does the same in a different sector. The procedure of mutual concessions is crucial during liberalization rounds. It is also highly relevant for the issues of market access and cutback in distortions, for instance subsidies. This approach has been formalized in the rule system for trade by a bilateral demand–supply system. Only when a country is the principal supplier of another country, i.e., when it provides the bulk of its imports to its trading partner, can a government ask for concessions involving a specific product (principal supplier rule). Curiously, the concept of reciprocity is used despite its being rooted in a mercantilist philosophy largely inconsistent with the free international division of labor. According to the free-trade-for-one theorem, a country can gain from free trade even if other countries are protectionist, although it gains less. Only if such protectionism is too strong will the open country be confined to autarky and gain nothing. In terms of political economy, the export sector's gains from trade help to compensate losers in the import-competing sector, also assisting in selling the idea of free trade politically (Hoekman and Kostecki 2001, p. 32). Moreover, it may be politically easier to agree with a foreign country on a tariff reduction than it would be to agree on the redistribution of the gains from trade among different social groups back at home. Reciprocity of concessions is a way of addressing the terms-of-trade externality.

National treatment works as a strong antidote to discrimination. It requires that a foreign good—once it has satisfied whatever border measures apply—should be subject to the same taxes and charges that apply to domestic goods, and to the same regulation. In other words, it should be treated no less favorably than a domestic product (see chapter V). In cross-border services and in the location of foreign firms, the rule of national treatment establishes the option for nonnationals to do business in a foreign country. It can be seen as a form of nondiscrimination as it allows equal opportunity in the specific areas of services and foreign direct investment.

Figure III.3. Continuum of principles and procedures.

Finally, mutual recognition represents a far-reaching guiding principle for the acceptance of other countries' rule systems. This can mean different things. With respect to the production of traded products, the rules of the country of origin, not of the importing country, apply to imports. The country-of-origin rule takes precedence over the country-of-destination principle (see below). With respect to services, the home rule of a service provider applies in the country importing the service. In reality, the principle of mutual recognition entails much more than simply allowing the equivalence of national treatment or granting a concession. All the principles discussed so far can be arranged in a continuum of intensity of impact (figure III.3).

Preventing Negative Spillovers

Besides exploiting cooperation gains, an international rule system must limit negative spillovers between countries. This is the case when negative externalities prevail, i.e., when the decisions in one country negatively affect the welfare in another country. One of the most prominent examples is acid rain.

One modus operandi to prevent excessive disturbances between nation states is to respect the other country's territory and not to intervene in its affairs. Territoriality is an old principle of diplomacy; it was already applied, at least partly, by the Congress of Vienna in 1815 in order to rearrange the political landscape of Europe. Territoriality is an essential principle for keeping transaction costs low and, although it relates more closely to war and foreign policy, it is also crucial for economic relations. States respect the autonomy and legal authority of other states; we can also say that states accept each other's property rights.

When states cede sovereignty to a supraregional level (like the EU) or agree to international treaties like the Kyoto Protocol, they stop acting according to the principle of territoriality. By the same token, territoriality is restrained by international public law, especially in the case of violations of basic principles. Most specifically, the violation of "natural" law and human rights is not covered by the principle of territoriality. Another exemption to the territorial principle applies in the case of national defense.

Dealing with Global Public Goods

Global public goods having a global dimension in space—such as the ozone layer and Earth's atmosphere—cannot be allocated by means of competitive processes.

For instance, because of greenhouse gases, the concept of competition between countries cannot be used in global warming to determine the optimal quantity or quality of the environmental media at stake. International institutional arrangements of the bargaining process are therefore needed in order to aggregate the countries' political preferences, to allocate the costs of abatement to individual countries, to find the least-cost solution for the abatement of pollutants, and to prevent free riding. Often benefits appear to be only indirect or remote, for instance in fighting global warming, whereas costs affect the individual country directly. Instead of cooperation gains with each country enjoying benefits, burden sharing is the approach used with the sharing giving rise to controversial debates. As will become apparent throughout the book, it is a complex issue to establish rules for global public goods (chapter VII). Another example of a public good to which a competition-based approach does not apply is internal security; due to organized crime and terrorism, threats to security have a global dimension.

If public goods only have a national dimension—that is to say, if they do not satisfy the property of a global public good—then they can be exposed to competition between countries. Note that merit goods, judged meritorious by some groups or even according to the aggregated preferences of society, are not public goods.

When Multilateral Rules Are Not Accepted and Respected

Multilateral rules to reduce transaction costs do not always emerge. A country may think that the costs of joining an agreement outweigh its benefits and that the downside of narrowing its options is too significant. For example, the United States has not entered into several multilateral agreements. It signed the 1982 Law of the Sea Convention, having 155 members, but Congress has not ratified the agreement because important U.S. firms think it will curb their ability to exploit the deep sea bed (chapter IV). The United States signed the Kyoto Protocol, but again has not ratified it. This issue is also relevant for the post-Bali process of finding a new institutional arrangement against global warming when the participation of India and China is at stake (chapter VII).

A further issue is that countries may prefer to enter into regional agreements such as the EU instead of ceding sovereignty to multilateral rule systems. At heart is the debate between regionalism and multilateralism (chapter IV). Moreover, countries have taken recourse to bilateral agreements, which are easier to conclude, since only two sides have to agree on rules. Thus, countries have entered into thousands of double-tax treaties (over 2,600) and bilateral investment treaties (over 2,500) because both parties value the fiscal certainty, the investment stability, and the flow of capital.

Not all multilateral agreements in which nation states cede sovereignty are constructive for the world economy. Coalitions of countries may form a cartel in order to limit competition and to exploit a quasimonopolistic position as in the case of OPEC.

Last but not least, countries have walked away from international agreements in the past. For instance, Argentina repaid IMF loans amounting to US$9.8 billion in 2005 and simply walked away from the IMF. Along similar lines, Asian economies are accumulating international reserves in order not to depend on the conditionality conditions of the IMF. In 1970, the United States gave up its role as an anchor currency so that the Bretton Woods system collapsed. As discussed in chapter II, in the case of internal turmoil and in the case of war, rules are forgotten and broken. Then, rules that had developed over hundreds and thousands of years are annihilated.

IV

How Rules Are Stabilized

International rule systems contain mechanisms that play a stabilizing role in the institutional arrangement. Such mechanisms are needed in order to prevent countries from defecting from agreed-upon procedures and to induce them to abide by multilateral rules. They become particularly necessary when the real world is in flux, i.e., when the conditions to which the rules apply change quickly and markedly. The richest experience of this is available in the WTO, but the issue extends to other areas such as global public goods. The questions to ask are: how do these mechanisms function and how can they be improved?

Positive Mechanisms

Compared with negative constraints such as banning discrimination, positive mechanisms play a vanguard role as they include a constructive motivation, strengthen the institutional arrangements and help expand the rule system. In the world trading order, one such mechanism is the "most-favored-nation" clause, representing a positive manifestation of the principle of nondiscrimination which rules out differential treatment. The obligation toward a general, positive and unconditional most-favored treatment, included in Article I of the GATT treaty, implies that a tariff reduction granted to one country has to be granted to all countries ("favor one, favor all"). In this way, bilateral tariff reductions are made multilateral. The "most-favored-nation" clause is not conditional; most specifically, it does not depend on reciprocity. While the nondiscrimination principle is a negative mechanism prohibiting discriminatory behavior, the most-favored-nation principle is a positive mechanism, strengthening free trade.

An essential condition for an international economic order is that it should generate visible and direct benefits for each of its members. For each country, the advantages of membership must exceed the advantages of nonmembership. Visible and direct benefits should attract the support of the private sector; they should also induce the approval of NGOs. These developments would in turn restrain national interest groups. (On legitimacy see chapter X.)

Another crucial stabilizing condition is that each country should expect an increase in visible and direct benefits in the future. It then pays to stick to the rules, because there will be a reward later on. Future direct benefits reinforce the repeated game nature of the rule system and give stability to the system. The individual country's cost–benefit calculations should not shift asymmetrically over time, in the sense that the net advantage for each country should increase and in no case worsen. If this condition is not fulfilled, there will be an incentive to renege on the contract. With hindsight, the institutional arrangement for the world trade order has been attractive for the world community. Indeed, it has been successful in raising the interest in ownership of its members by increasing its membership from 23 in 1947, when the GATT was founded, to 153 in the WTO in July 2008, by opening markets in eight tariff rounds[1] and also by extending the rule system beyond trade. Important countries that are not yet members are Algeria, Iran, Kazakhstan, and Russia.

Compared with the trade order, institutional arrangements in other areas face less favorable conditions in generating visible and direct benefits. Thus, global environmental protection signals a restraint and only generates the benefit of a global public good, whose advantages are diffused and less direct than those from trade.[2] Environmental policy for global public environmental systems is about burden sharing and allocating the costs of abatement and emission prevention. In a similar way, IMF policy imposes an often detested conditionality for countries involved in a currency crisis; the IMF is then experienced as a restraint.

To interpret a rule system extending to several areas (the WTO covers trade in commodities, services, and investment) as a single undertaking increases the incentive to accept rules in a specific area even if a country dislikes these specific rules. This is because rules of different areas are packaged and are thus subject to "linkage": the loss brought about by one rule is offset by the expected advantage in other areas. The single undertaking also enables participants to develop the rule system further whenever new issues in the international division of labor have to be dealt with. The approach of "packaging" is also helpful in focusing the bargaining process when a liberalization round is being concluded.

In the past, plurilateral agreements, introduced in the Tokyo Round, allowed a subset of GATT members to sign contracts for specific areas, for instance the Agreement on Civil Aircraft and the Agreement on Government Procurement. Such a procedure, though facilitating a contract among at least some GATT members, represents an à la carte approach and entails the risk of fragmentation of the multilateral trading system (on waivers, see below).

In spite of the advantages of a single undertaking, the "offsetting" between the advantages of suborders should not be carried too far. If in the course of time the advantages of countries shift asymmetrically in the individual suborders, a fragile structure of acceptance could collapse like a house of cards. To avoid domino

---

[1] The Doha Round was not concluded until February 2009.

[2] By the same token, competition policy limits the maneuvering space of large firms; competition policy requires the insight of governments insofar as the control of excessive market power benefits the consumer.

effects, the suborders should basically legitimize themselves autonomously instead of accepting them conditionally.

Acceptance of rules is essential. Besides visible and direct benefits, rule making with the "one country one vote" principle as in the WTO with consensus and even unanimity ensures that a country's preferences will not be overruled. In principle, any of the WTO's 153 members can exercise a veto, since all decisions must be made by consensus. In practice, however, only a handful of countries have the economic clout to stand in the way of a deal. China, for example, announced in November 2007 that it would veto a WTO compromise for liberalizing global commerce in manufactured goods that failed to shield Chinese industries from competition (see below).

Additional crucial measures are those aimed at making sure that nations will keep their promise. They have to commit themselves by credibly excluding or promising future actions. Here the key word is "credibility"; the other players should not expect that a commitment will be broken. This aspect has been analyzed for national monetary policy (Kydland and Prescott 1977). One approach to ensure credibility is shifting the countries' policy instruments to a higher decision-making level, as happened in the European Union. Another avenue is that countries lock themselves into an agreement, for example by putting up capital for operating a rule system (as in the case of the IMF) or by contributing to the operating costs of an arrangement on a regular basis. Other mechanisms are relevant when public goods are involved (see Barrett 2005, chapter 6). Yet a further approach is to bind tariffs, a specific commitment to agree on the reduction of tariffs. A country that wants to raise the bound tariff has to negotiate with the countries most concerned, and it has to compensate the trading partners' loss of trade. Thus, to bind tariffs means hardening a country's promise by creating opportunity costs for noncompliance. In this way, the results of liberalization rounds are "chiseled in stone"; countries cannot easily walk away from agreements once they have been reached. However, not all commitments hold. In the worst cases, countries may simply disregard their commitment. Witness the United States abandoning the gold standard in 1933 (Barro 1986) and its walking away from the Bretton Woods System in 1971. Another important strategy is to make commitments enforceable, for instance through sanctions and a dispute settlement mechanism whose verdicts can be implemented.

Taking advantage of mutual recognition within a well-defined multilateral approach may strengthen the institutional setup. This step decentralizes rule-finding processes and makes the discovery of new rules more or less automatic. Thus, the world trade order aims at accepting the production standards of the exporting country (country-of-origin principle). If each country applied its own product standards to its imports (country-of-destination principle), the world would be mired in economic chaos. However, in order to protect its citizens' health and life and to conserve natural resources, a country may take its own measures (Article XX of the GATT

Treaty), provided that they are nondiscriminatory. Note that the approach of mutual recognition leads to institutional competition.

Nondiscrimination requires that if restrictions to market entry are applied, regulations through production permits, facility permits and product norms must not favor domestic producers and domestic goods. The same applies to taxation: identical measures should be applied as to similar domestic and foreign goods (see the Thailand cigarette case above). In order to compare international and domestic products, the concept of like products is essential (Article III: 4 GATT). Nondiscrimination should also satisfy the condition that policy instruments respect the proportionality principle; measures justified by Article XX must accordingly satisfy the condition of necessity: their implementation should occur only when environmental policy aims or the protection of natural resources could not be achieved otherwise. Usually, however, these aims are better achieved through specific environmental policy measures rather than through trade policy (see below).

A major issue in determining the potential harm to health and the environment is whether the similarity of products should be defined from the demand side or from the production side. The similarity of products should be defined from the demand side, for example in terms of possible harmful effects, for instance in the case of toxic goods, and not from the production side. However, this means, in principle, that the method of production in another country is not restrained. In the Mexican–American tuna fish–dolphin case (1991), the method of fishing which does not sufficiently protect dolphins was accepted in the WTO ruling. This means that the country-of-origin principle was used.

However, we have a different verdict of the Appellate Body in the shrimp–turtle case (India and others versus the United States), decided in 1998 (WTO 2007b). The bottom line of this ruling is that trade policy instruments can be used to enforce environmental standards even in other nations. At the heart of the case were the sea turtles being killed in shrimp trawl nets by other Indian trawlers. The United States wanted to prohibit the importing of shrimps from countries which do not require shrimp boats to be equipped with turtle-excluding devices. The United States argued that their trade measure was covered by Article XX of the GATT, exempting WTO members from their trade obligations in order to protect human, animal, and plant life. While the United States lost the case, it only lost it because it discriminated, since it did not give other countries enough time to modify their fishing methods. In 2000, the Appellate Body rejected Malaysia's complaint and accepted the revised U.S. guidelines, maintaining that programs implemented by other members should be "comparable in effectiveness" (Hufbauer and Kim 2008). Unlike the tuna–dolphin case, the country-of-origin principle was not applied. While the reasoning correctly stipulates that measures must be necessary in the sense that environmental policy aims or the protection of natural resources could not be achieved otherwise, it also implies that a country (the United States) can implement its environmental targets in other countries. If this principle is generally accepted and subject to a wide interpretation, a country can project its environmental goals onto other countries in contrast to the territoriality principle. With countries usually following a different environmental policy, confusion in the international division of labor is likely (see chapters IV and IX).

As a precondition for the positive mechanisms discussed so far, it is self evident that clarity of the rules and transparency on what is happening in other countries represent vital prerequisites. International rules imply ceding national sovereignty, thus making it necessary to specify the exact conditions under which the international rule system takes precedence over the nation state's prerogatives. A country also needs information on whether other states abide by the rules agreed upon. Witness the Trade Policy Reviews of the WTO.

Side Payments

One incentive to attract countries to a rule system and to keep them interested is side payments. Such side payments can help establish preconditions so that a country can join a rule system and stick to it. For instance, the European Union has been using and still uses structural funds in order to allow countries to catch up by means of a quicker development. Thus, Ireland has annually received 5.0% of its GDP in the period 1990–2000 from the EU's structural fund in order to be able to increase its GDP per capita, with transfers down to 2.5% in 2000; its GDP per capita is now at 128% of the EU15 level (2005). Development aid can be interpreted as a side payment to make it possible for developing countries to participate in the international division of labor and join the WTO. Credits from the IMF to a country in a currency crisis can also be regarded as side payment.

In contrast to positive-sum games in which all participants can gain, burden sharing in the case of global public goods represents a different matter. In such a setting, a common goal is shared by many, often to differing degrees, and it can only be achieved if the actors share the costs of reaching the goals. With respect to the opportunity costs of reaching the goal, we have a negative-sum game; albeit some or even all countries may benefit indirectly from the common goal. An example is the reduction of CO_2 emissions as a solution to global warming. In this case, side payments can be used as an incentive to get countries interested in a rule system.

Side payments may also take place in the form of technology transfers. Thus, the Clean Development Mechanism of the Kyoto Protocol applies to projects in developing countries, undertaken by the firms of developed countries: the firms receive a credit for their abatement which they may sell on the market for CO_2 emission rights (see chapter VII).

Self-Enforcing Contracts

When international treaties deal with free-rider behavior and quickly varying problems rather than with relatively stable issue patterns and direct benefits, as in the international division of labor, self-enforcing contracts constitute an appropriate instrument. One aspect of the situation is that the country's benefits are indirect, that burden-sharing is an issue, and that information on future states of the world is not perfect. A case in point concerns international environmental problems, when countries have to bear the costs of abatement and burden sharing is likely to be judged differently over time. In this case, a self-enforcing contract must contain mechanisms that stabilize it and make sure that the contract is honored as the states of nature change (see chapter VII). Most importantly, the contract should hold even if the internal situation of signatories changes. Possible instruments include fines for deviating countries, a membership fee or initial capital endowment put up by individual members, side payments such as transfers to members in economic trouble and sanctions. Self-enforcing contracts have been especially proposed for environmental treaties.

Restraints and Sanctions

An alternative to positive mechanisms for stabilizing a rule system is to impose bans and to "forbid," i.e., use negative rules. Such constraints are agreed upon *ex ante* and are part of international agreements. The principle of nondiscrimination in the trade order represents such a restraint. Other restraints apply to environmental issues as in the case for the ban on fluorocarbons and restrictions to the trade in ivory. Further restraints relate to macroeconomic aspects. Two examples: the conditionality stipulations of the IMF in case of a country's currency crisis and the limits forbidding budget deficits in excess of 3% of national GDP within the Growth and Stability Pact of the European Monetary Union. Necessary conditions for a successful ban are the possibility of monitoring any deviating behavior effectively and the ability to apply fines, withdrawal of benefits, or other types of sanctions.

Sanctions in an international environment can take different forms: banning exports of military weapons; outlawing the export of strategic products, for example components for military weapons; prohibiting the export of investment goods essential for the development of a country; blocking intermediate inputs for production; and preventing the export of luxury consumption goods, thus disturbing the political elite. As a very last measure, bans on the export of consumption goods may be applied, with a direct impact on the basket of day-to-day goods available to the general population. The level of sanctions is determined *ex post*, when the deviating behavior of a country becomes apparent. They impose a cost on a country and therefore constitute an incentive to accept the rules. Hopefully, sanctions are anticipated by the agents and thus steer the agents' behavior *ex ante*. Sanctions are used in such issues as ethnic conflicts, human rights violations, narcotics smuggling and nuclear proliferation (Hufbauer et al. 2007).

Sanctions can be imposed by international agreements as well as by single states or groups of states. For instance, retaliation—a form of sanction—is allowed in the WTO if it represents the result of rulings by the WTO itself within the dispute settlement procedure. Similarly, the UN Security Council can impose sanctions. Prior to 1990, the UN Security Council approved just two mandatory sanctions: against the white minority regime in Rhodesia (today's Zimbabwe) and against South Africa (in the form of an arms embargo; other antiapartheid actions were voluntary). From 1990 to 2007, the Council mandated sanctions against eleven states: Iraq, the former Yugoslavia, Libya, Haiti, Somalia, Liberia, the UNITA faction in Angola, Rwanda, Sierra Leone, North Korea, and Iran. Out of fifty new sanction cases launched in the 1990s, twenty-four of these were launched by the United States in cooperation with other nations. Twelve of these were launched by the United States unilaterally (Elliott and Hufbauer 1999).

The end of the Cold War altered the political chessboard determining sanctions. New centers of influence able to influence sanctions have grown besides Washington, like Beijing, Moscow, or Brussels. Nongovernmental organizations (NGOs) also came to hold more sway, bringing about a relative shift in the targets of sanctions. In addition, U.S. private business actors have been increasingly vocal in their objections to sanctions. Such objections are now politically acceptable, whereas this would not have been the case during the Cold War.

The increase in the use of sanctions by the UN has provoked concern in two areas: the humanitarian impact of comprehensive sanctions on women, children, and the elderly (as in Iraq) and the costs of enforcing sanctions for frontline states, such as the Balkan neighbors of the former Republic of Yugoslavia during the Bosnian conflict. Both concerns have contributed to growing opposition against the imposition of broad sanctions and have stirred interest in targeted sanctions (in particular, freezing the personal assets of political, military, and economic leaders in rogue states); the goal is to find a way to enhance the effectiveness of sanctions, while also making them less blunt in their effects (Elliott et al. 1999). According to Elliott (2006), sanctions are more likely to be effective when goals are limited and clearly defined, the target is small and vulnerable, and when sanctions are imposed quickly and decisively. Following Hufbauer, Schott, Elliott, and Egg, roughly 25% of sanctions can be considered successful, where "success" is meant as the achievement, at least in part, of the sanctions' objective and their effective contribution to a positive outcome.

Globalization has played an important role in reducing the effectiveness of uni-lateral sanctions. In fact, since target countries are now increasingly engaged in international markets, they are now better positioned to bypass sanctions by shift-ing their trade and financial flows. This, however, does not imply that multilateral sanctions are instead an easy panacea: international cooperation is often costly to generate, it creates delays and the potential for competing objectives as, for example, in the case of the UN Security Council Resolution No. 1737. This resolution against Iran's nuclear program in December 2006 was passed only after two months of intense negotiations and several amendments to please the Russians and Chinese (Elliott 2006).

Blockades undertaken in times of peace are a specific form of sanctions. They have mostly been used in exceptional circumstances. Historical examples are the Soviet land blockade of Berlin in 1948–49, the selective United States "quarantine," i.e. the blockade during the Cuban missile crisis in 1962, and the NATO blockade of Yugoslavia (1993–96).

Dispute Settlement Mechanism

A dispute settlement mechanism is instrumental in solving conflicts that arise in the interpretation and implementation of rules. To some extent, it may also help develop a rule system further when the rules have to be applied to borderline cases. Such a mechanism must be objective and fair. It should not be dominated by the largest economies. Moreover, large countries should accept the rulings reached in the settlement procedure.

A major example is the WTO's dispute settling mechanism, agreed upon in the Uruguay Round. Within this institutional arrangement, the General Council—including all the members of the WTO—meets as the Dispute Settlement Body (DSB). The procedure works by "negative consensus": once parties have been unsuccessful in resolving their dispute through consultation, the General Council establishes a Panel, unless the General Council decides by consensus not to allow the establishment of a Panel. This procedure implies a high degree of automation. Members nominate the panelists serving the Dispute Settlement Body; the approval of the disputants is needed for the composition of each panel. The steps of the procedure include an Appellate procedure (figure IV.1). The DSB can adopt the Appellate Report, unless it is rejected unanimously. The appellate review is limited to three months. The DSB then monitors whether recommendations are implemented. If an offending party fails to adopt corrective measures within a reasonable period of time, a compensation has to be negotiated. In the case of nonimplementation, the DSB has the authority to allow retaliatory countermeasures. Time limits are set for each step. The total time lapse from the start of the settlement consultations until the adoption of the Final Report by the DSB is one year without appeal, or one year and three months in case of appeal.

Retaliation involves raising tariffs against the respondent. These tariffs can take various forms. For instance, a "carousel approach" is permitted in which tariffs are raised on a different set of imports every six months. In exceptional cases when

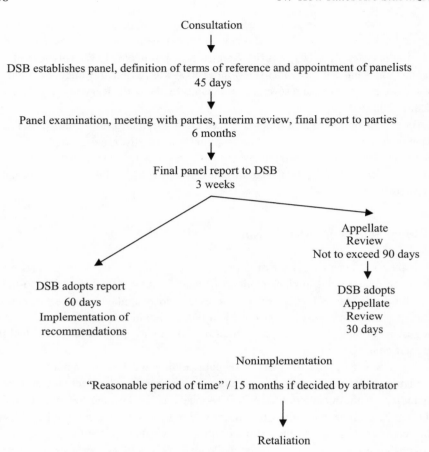

Consultation

↓

DSB establishes panel, definition of terms of reference and appointment of panelists
45 days

↓

Panel examination, meeting with parties, interim review, final report to parties
6 months

↓

Final panel report to DSB
3 weeks

DSB adopts report
60 days
Implementation of
recommendations

Appellate
Review
Not to exceed 90 days

↓

DSB adopts
Appellate
Review
30 days

Nonimplementation

"Reasonable period of time" / 15 months if decided by arbitrator

↓

Retaliation

Figure IV.1.   Stages in the dispute settlement process.
Source: WTO home page (WTO 2007d).

the claimant does not import much from the respondent, cross-retaliation is permitted. This may extend to the application of retaliatory measures of TRIPS on the respondent's products.

In the period 1995–2006, 356 cases were brought for settlement, of which 142 were presented by developing countries, 84 by the United States, and 76 by the EU. Addressees of the complaints were the United States (97 cases) and the EU (58 cases); China received 8 complaints. The overwhelming number of complaints from developing countries came from Latin America, mostly on agricultural issues. Other issues involved were dumping, the steel sector, and intellectual property rights. No complaint came from African countries. As a result of the generally good compliance record of members, there have been only six WTO cases to date where retaliation has been requested and authorized, and only four where retaliatory measures have actually been imposed (Wilson 2006). This mechanism represents quite an improvement compared with the settlement procedures in the GATT era.

A major decision by the WTO Dispute Settlement Body came in 2005, when Brazil and Thailand won the cotton case against the United States, after demonstrating that U.S. subsidies to American cotton farmers did damage to Brazil. In the equally important sugar case, it was decided in 2005 that the EU must change its sugar regime. These outcomes reveal that developed nations—in particular the United States and the EU—now have less leeway to inflict unilateral retribution upon other nations over trade disputes. Developing nations are potentially more able to defend their case. However, some developing countries have serious problems with the dispute settlement procedure, because the costs of bringing a case can be prohibitively high while the developing nations' ability to inflict retaliation on developed countries is limited. Therefore, it has been suggested that developing countries receive administrative support from the WTO and that smaller nations should be allowed to band together in applying retaliatory measures. Moreover, developing countries tend to tackle specific issues only, without playing a role on precedent setting cases; as a consequence, they have minimal opportunity to shape the system to their advantage. Finally, developing nations fear retaliation by stronger nations outside the boundaries of the WTO.

Another example of dispute settlement, albeit with fewer teeth, is the one devoted to disputes in the fruition of the sea. This mechanism is laid down in Part XV of the UN Convention on the Law of the Sea, currently including 155 members. The convention requires the parties to settle their disputes over the interpretation or application of the Convention by peaceful means, as indicated in the Charter of the United Nations. However, if parties to a dispute fail to reach a settlement by peaceful means of their own choice, they are obliged to resort to the compulsory dispute settlement procedures entailing binding decisions, subject to limitations and exceptions contained in the Convention. The mechanism established by the Convention provides four alternative institutions for the settlement of disputes: the International Tribunal for the Law of the Sea (see below), the International Court of Justice, an arbitral tribunal constituted in accordance with Annex VII (Arbitration) to the Convention, and a special arbitral tribunal constituted in accordance with Annex VIII (Special Arbitration). A State Party is free to choose one or more of these means. However, if the parties to a dispute have not accepted the same settlement procedure, the dispute may only be submitted to arbitration in accordance with Annex VII.

Other organizations have dispute settlement tools at their disposal, but these institutions follow different rules, and many mechanisms are weaker than those of the WTO. The UN Security Council can impose sanctions, but they are determined through a political bargaining process: they do not follow a dispute settlement procedure according to preestablished rules. Enforcement of sanctions is equally difficult. The IMF's conditionality stipulations are strict, yet they vary on a country-by-country basis. The World Bank only has weak rules for the suspension of foreign aid payments and of project financing development. Conventions have even weaker teeth.

Besides a formal dispute settlement mechanism, conflicts between states can be handled more informally by international arbitration panels which states set up on an ad hoc basis or which are incorporated into international treaties involving individual states or the international community at large. Nations submit themselves to the verdict of such panels. Relevant examples are the commissions handling disputes over borders or violations of a state's sovereignty. Arbitration is similar to the dispute settlement mechanism, albeit its structure is less formal. A more official mechanism is instead found in the international courts, such as the International Court of Justice, the International Criminal Court, the International Maritime Court, and the European Court of Human Rights (see below).

Waivers: A Stabilizing or Destabilizing Mechanism?

A major issue in the international rule system is whether exceptions to the rules agreed upon should be granted. At the core of this problem stands the question of whether waivers stabilize the rule system or destabilize it, and whether regionalism helps a multilateral order or leads away from it.

As in private contracts, international institutional rules include a force majeure clause for unexpected and unusual situations, such as abnormal states of nature, in which the rules do not apply. These safety valves allow countries to sign an international treaty and cede sovereignty, while remaining able to respond autonomously to abnormal situations by means of their own policy instruments. Safety valves are different from waivers or opt-out clauses in that the former do not relate to temporary exceptional situations but rather to long-term structural issues (see below). With respect to unexpected states of nature representing abnormal situations, a rule system may easily fall apart if it is too strict and rigid. If, on the contrary, it is flexible, it may nevertheless be too soft, not providing a reliable guide for the behavior of governments and economic agents. In the WTO, countervailing duties can be imposed on subsidized imports and antidumping duties can be put on imports that are sold at a price lower than the domestic one. By the same token, an industry seriously harmed by foreign imports can be protected. Actions can also be taken in case of serious balance-of-payments problems (see chapter V).

A highly controversial issue is whether a waiver to a rule system—that is, an exception related to a specific problem (for instance, national public health or the environment), or specific sectors (agriculture) or an opt-out clause for a specific rule (as those often adopted by the European Union)—stabilizes or rather destabilizes the institutional arrangement. Arguably, exceptions to one or some of the rules of an international rule system may allow countries to join a multilateral arrangement if they do not accept the regulation devised for a specific area. From this point of view, a waiver helps the acceptance of an international order. However, it is evident that a waiver contradicts the concept of a single undertaking. Opposite positions, pro-single undertaking and pro waivers, cannot hold simultaneously.

In order to cast some light onto this debate, we must address four different questions regarding the impact of waivers on an international rule system. First, is the rule for which the exemption is granted a contradiction to the international rule system, i.e., is the waiver inconsistent with the international rule system? Second, is the rule for which the exemption is granted essential for the international rule system or is it peripheral? A peripheral rule is not at the core of the rule system, i.e., the rule system can exist without this specific rule. Such a peripheral waiver may be acceptable. Third, is the rule for which the exemption is granted an add-on through which the current existing rule system may be further developed in the future, without being essential for the actual rule system? An add-on may become an essential part of the rule system only in the future. In this case, the exemption may be acceptable. Fourth, if an exemption is granted, even if it is essential, will the waiver start or allow a process by which eventually the rule system is improved in the long run?

In terms of practical experience, we can address these issues through the experience of the European Union. The core target of the European Union is to establish a single market granting four kinds of freedoms: the free movement of goods, of capital, of services and of people (including labor). In these essential areas, no exemption can be made. Apparently, interim solutions for a limited period do not violate this condition. An example of such measures is the temporary restriction of the free movement of labor for the new members in Central and Eastern Europe, which joined the EU in 2004. Admittedly, some of these freedoms are not easily accepted by all EU members. A blatant example of such reluctance is the service directive, restricting the free mobility of service personnel and, consequently, of services across the European Union. In less essential areas, such as border controls on persons within the EU and monetary policy, some EU members can go further ahead than others in ceding sovereignty. In such areas, the European Union has applied the philosophy of "variable geography," or "two speeds," allowing member countries to pioneer integration areas in which not all the members want to engage.

In the world trade order, a waiver for health reasons and environmental protection (Article XX of GATT) can create issues of delineation that, in theory, can jeopardize the trade order itself. By and large, this waiver applies to all countries and has proven acceptable. A new issue is that of standards for internalizing environmental costs. An unresolved old issue is the waiver for agriculture, obtained by the United States in 1955, which became an invitation for the EU to start its own agricultural policy. By using a set of protectionist measures, the waiver severely hurts the developing countries and has discouraged their cooperation to the Doha Round. A similar argument applies to the Short Term Arrangement on Cotton Textiles introduced in 1961 during the Dillon Round. It took nearly fifty years to discontinue it.

Regionalism versus Multilateralism

Whereas the experience of a waiver inside the European Union is positive in peripheral areas, it is not clear whether a waiver allowing a deviation from the international trade order in favor of regional integrations and bilateral agreements will strengthen or weaken the order itself. The waiver for the trade order is defined in three provisions: in Article XXIV of the GATT Treaty, allowing customs unions and free-trade areas ("the provisions of this Agreement shall not prevent, as between the territories of contracting parties, the formation of a customs union or of a free-trade area"); in Article V of GATS, allowing service agreements; and in the enabling clause for developing countries, allowing preferential treatment.

The four most important regional integrations are the European Union, NAFTA (North American Free Trade Agreement), AFTA (Asian Free Trade Area), and Mercosur. Besides these major regional integrations, many bilateral free-trade areas involving only two states as well as selective free-trade areas among several countries have gained importance; they now by far outnumber regional integrations. These bilateral or selective free-trade areas do not necessarily include geographically neighboring states as in regional integrations; indeed, they can embrace countries that are as far apart as Singapore and the United States. Meanwhile, some 368 regional trade agreements had been notified to the GATT/WTO up to December 2006. Of these, 292 were notified under Article XXIV of the GATT 1947 or GATT 1994, 22 under the Enabling Clause, and 54 under Article V of the GATS. At that same date, 215 agreements were in force. Including regional trade agreements which are in force but have not been notified, those signed but not yet in force, those currently being negotiated and those at the proposal stage, a figure of close to 400 agreements is likely to be implemented by 2010 (WTO home page, July 18, 2007). Of these agreements, less than 10% are customs unions. In comparison, the GATT received 124 notifications of regional trade agreements in the period 1948–94. However, the simple counting of regional trade agreements may overstate their spreading because the cumulative WTO counts do not exclude already abrogated agreements. For example, the 65 regional trade agreements between the EU and its new member states, which joined in 2004, are still included in the WTO figure although they have lost their relevance (Pomfret 2007). Nevertheless, compared with earlier decades, the last fifteen years have seen a steep increase in the figures of regional trade agreements.

The key issue is: will these waivers prove to be building blocks for the multilateral trade order, permitting liberalizations between countries and in regions, where they could not be achieved multilaterally? Or will they rather prove to be stumbling blocks, eventually leading to the erosion and even the collapse of the multilateral order for the international division of labor?

Whereas a condition for economic integration—customs unions and free-trade agreements—is that they shall not impose on third countries more restrictions than before their establishment, the waiver of Article XXIV of the GATT Treaty clearly contradicts the principle of nondiscrimination: it excludes outsiders. The "most-favored-nation" clause, a principle at the core of the WTO, is not applied. Regional liberalizations are not multilateralized. And, of course, the waiver also contradicts the WTO's single-undertaking nature. Politically, the United States and the EU as major players have used the waiver to build up their own hub-and-spoke system, extending favors to the members of their network, as in the case of free-trade arrangements between the EU and, among others, the EFTA countries, Croatia, Morocco, Turkey, Israel, Egypt, Syria, Mexico, and Chile. Furthermore, the EU has de facto included in its trade network many developing countries through a set of preferential agreements, most importantly with seventy-five developing economies in Africa, the Pacific, and the Caribbean—the APC countries—through the Lomé Convention. The EU and the United States has thus built a set of concentric rings around themselves.

There are manifold reasons why regional integrations are nevertheless accepted in the international trade order. Whereas there is no doubt that regional integrations divert trade, trade creation is expected to dominate over trade diversion in the long run, not only for the members of a regional integration but also for the world economy as a whole. In fact, a regional integration will stimulate not only the economic activity of its members, but also of third party countries with dynamic effects through growth. Moreover, regional integrations extend in different forms to other countries and, if successful, attract additional members over time. Again, the European Union is a fitting example of regional integration attracting outsiders so much that it has expanded from six to twenty-seven members. In addition, many expect that within a regional integration free trade can extend more easily to services and investment flows, with market access becoming easier. Observers also hope that some of the rules will eventually be generalized in a multilateral order. The Kemp–Wan existence theorem (Kemp and Wan 1976) identifies conditions under which a customs union is Pareto optimal for all its members. Most importantly, a regional integration can develop deeper forms of interaction than a multilateral, worldwide approach: the European Union is a case in point. From a practical point of view, we can observe that it is simply impossible to ban a deeper approach of regional integration in which countries cede national sovereignty, and to prevent a whole continent such as Europe from establishing a common economic, and to some extent political union. Seen under this light, regional integrations may prove to be a vehicle to organize a multipolar world. Thus, regional governance is justified as a means to reach global governance.

Despite these advantages, the waivers for regional integrations dent the importance of the WTO. Indeed, such integrations reduce the interest in strengthening the WTO. For instance, the WTO most-favored-nation tariffs of the EU apply to only nine countries of the world, albeit including the United States and Japan as important markets (WTO 2004b). Whenever countries only agree on the reduction of trade impediments on a regional or bilateral basis, the ensuing agreements take the place of a multilateral order: it is much easier to conclude regional deals than multilateral arrangements. This holds most specifically for bilateral agreements: coordinating an agreement between only two states is understandably easier than reaching a consensus on a complex arrangement among 153 WTO members. The same is true for free-trade agreements involving only a few countries. The consequence is that countries are less willing to invest political energy in highly complex negotiations as the Doha Round. The institutional arrangement then becomes fragmented and looks like a spaghetti bowl—a term first used by Bhagwati (1995). It turns out to be easier for politically powerful countries and regions with leverage to get their way, while it will be more difficult for smaller countries to obtain institutional rules taking their concerns into account. Other bilateral agreements, for instance on foreign direct investment, intensify this tendency.

A way out of this conundrum is to require more openness for customs unions, free-trade areas and preferential agreements. This concept of "open regionalism" means that members of a regional integration should voluntarily decide to keep the integration open in specific areas, such as trade, services, market access, and possibly regulation. Other countries are invited to join and to implement the rules of such regional integrations. They can choose to adopt one, some, or even all rules of integration. This calls for part or all of the rules of regional integration to remain open to multilateralization. An important aspect is that "best practices" in regionalism should be applied in order to bridge the gap between the multilateral approach and the regional approach (Plummer 2007). This implies a comprehensive coverage of goods and services, a low level of rules of origin, WTO-consistent customs procedures, intellectual property protection, and minimal technical barriers. Since regional integrations represent a deeper form of integration, multilateralization does not have to apply to all forms of integration. Countries outside the regional integration will realistically only apply some of the rules in the international division of labor, not all of them. Deeper forms of integration such as monetary union or abolishing border controls remain specific to a regional integration without being multilateralized. Using this approach to get out of the conundrum will not ease the negative impact of bilateral arrangements on the world trade order.

Destabilization by Large Players

Another threat to the multilateral system is that large countries and regional blocs tend to behave strategically. Thus, the United States introduced the "Omnibus Trade and Competitiveness Act" (Super 301) in 1988, creating the legal possibility of retaliating in the event of trade restricting measures by other countries. Similarly, the European Union developed its "Trade Defense Instrument" in 1994. Moreover, both blocs have established their hub-and-spokes systems around themselves. Although both blocs must respect the WTO rules, they can use their economic power to defend their interest, for instance in antidumping cases. There is therefore the risk that they defy the international institutional arrangement. Furthermore, an Asian bloc around China is likely to evolve in the future. Whenever these blocks pursue an aggressive trade policy, they endanger the multilateral system.

A Transatlantic Free Trade Area and a WTO-Plus

TAFTA, a Transatlantic Free Trade Area, represents a concept to integrate the United States, or possibly the whole of NAFTA, and the EU in a common economic area. Both regions are interlinked through reciprocal trade, accounting for about 20% of each other's total trade in goods, and almost 40% of their trade in services. In addition, they represent for each other the most important source and destination of foreign direct investment, accounting for about half of each other's foreign direct investment flows as well the exchange of stocks (Sapir 2007, p. 5). In trade itself, however, the obstacles between both regions have been reduced to a very low level, so that further reductions do not promise great additional gains. Moreover, lower trade barriers in the agricultural sector seem far from becoming a reality. In energy and environmental policy, the policy concepts diverge considerably (Siebert 2005b). In contrast, transatlantic cooperation is more promising when it comes to standard-and-rule setting. The existing Transatlantic Business Dialogue, supplemented by the EU–U.S. Regulatory Cooperation Forum, represents a meeting place for business leaders and government officials, where they can attempt to reduce transaction costs by setting common standards and by working toward mutual recognition. This bargaining forum can be useful for business, the financial sector, market access, and competition policy. With the transatlantic region representing about 60% of world output, such cooperation might well become a trendsetter for international rules. At the same time, it would exert some significant leverage in establishing global rules. A necessary condition, however, is nondiscrimination: transatlantic cooperation must remain an open club. Indeed, openness for other regions and major players would help defuse the impression that a western club wants to determine the rules of the game in its favor, excluding new players in the international division of labor such as Brazil, China, and India.

A tricky issue is whether or not a subset of WTO members should be allowed to resolve new problems autonomously. These countries could commit themselves to realize attempted results of the WTO rounds more quickly than planned, liberalize more than agreed and employ the permitted exceptions less often. Such a WTO-Plus, two-speed world integration could advance the integration process in the world economy. This also holds for dovetailing various regional blocs by establishing a free-trade zone between such blocks. This mechanism, however, conflicts with the single undertaking nature of WTO and the concept of "packaging" advantages in different areas. It is most important that a WTO-Plus is an open club which does not limit entry. It also must be guaranteed that such a coalition is not interpreted as de facto excluding other countries. The workability of such an approach also depends on the given situation. Thus, if we go back to after World War II, it seemed reasonable that a coalition of countries, even if small, started international organizations. In areas other than trade, for instance in environmental treaties, coalitions of a group of countries are an acceptable method to start an agreement.

Mechanisms to Internalize Negative Externalities

Border-crossing negative externalities — linking countries through technological systems such as groundwater conditions or an atmospheric setting—distort market allocation and the competitive process. Cross-border pollution, for instance acid rain, is an example of such negative externalities. Gains are possible in the case of cooperation aimed at internalizing these externalities. This requires the internalization of their social costs. The polluter-pays principle, where the polluter, for instance the upwind country, carries the abatement costs to cut emissions is unlikely to be applied, since the polluter is in a strong bargaining position. Therefore, the victim-pays principle is the more typical solution: the pollutee pays compensation in order to induce the polluter to undertake abatement. The cost arrangement will then depend on other types of interdependencies, whose benefits may make countries more willing to take over the costs of abatement. For instance, the bargaining position of the polluter within the European Union is weaker, because EU member states are interlinked in many ways and compromising in one area brings benefits in other fields.

Negative spillovers go beyond negative environmental externalities. Thus, an upstream country may use the water of a river that is also exploited by its downstream neighbor. It may even change the direction of a river. Last but not least, hostilities and warfare fall into this category.

Cooperation is necessary in the case of externalities running through technological systems. In the case of policy instrument externalities in the context of a rule system representing a public good, the benefits from cooperation must outweigh the costs of living with the externality. Otherwise, one has to live with the externality. This principle requires some qualification. Care must be taken that policy instrument externalities are only interpreted in the context of a rule system as a public good that can be reached in a bargaining game. A policy instrument externality cannot mean that *any* policy instrument generates an externality.

An important specification is that the costs of cooperation should not involve costs for reducing competition between countries. If they do, such costs represent long-run opportunity costs because innovative pressure is taken out of the system. Then, the opportunity costs of reducing competition represent part of the costs for finding a solution, so that the costs of reducing competition should be included into a cost–benefit analysis. The gains from cooperation must more than compensate for the costs of reducing competition. Correcting externalities running through technological systems usually applies to allocation; therefore, normally, competition between countries does not decrease. However, solutions may be chosen that reduce competition, thus having a distorting impact on the market position of firms and countries.

Unlike technological externalities, pecuniary externalities constitute interdependencies between market variables such as prices and incomes, running through the market mechanism, as already explained above. Such market interdependencies are desired, and, in principle, they give no justification for cooperation.[3] Cooperation between governments in the case of market externalities always implies that competition is reduced.

As an additional aspect, market failures may become relevant in this context. Competition between governments involves the functioning of many markets, especially goods and labor markets. Ideally, these markets function well. If market failures exist, national and international policy failures have to be distinguished: national failures have to be resolved at the national level, while international market failures require cooperation. The costs of international policy failures should not outweigh the costs of market failures.

Cooperation loses its legitimacy if governments undertake it for the single purpose of retaining their power. Indeed, this type of cooperation is nothing but collusion between governments. Take the case of when governments cooperate to limit the exit option of residents, for instance by detaining a country's inhabitants behind walls. This limits freedom and runs counter to an open society in the spirit of Popper (1945).

In contrast to negative externalities, positive spillovers represent a beneficial interdependence. A case in point is the equatorial rainforest in Brazil, which creates such positive spillovers by allowing biodiversity. In these cases, the country generating the positive externality should receive compensation.

International Law and International Courts

International law consists of rules and principles, governing the relations and dealings among nations. It includes the basic, classic concepts of law in national legal systems: status, property, obligation, and tort (or delict). It also includes substantive law, procedure, process, and remedies. International Law is rooted in acceptance by the nation states which constitute the system. On the one hand, customary law and conventional law are primary sources of international law. Customary international law results when states follow certain practices generally and consistently out of a sense of legal obligation. Recently, the customary law found its codification in the

---

[3] Sometimes, the term "pecuniary externality" is used rather loosely to justify government intervention. Compare, for instance, Stiglitz (2008). See chapter VIII.

Vienna Convention on the Law of Treaties, which came into force in 1980. On the other hand, conventional international law derives from international agreements, and may take any form upon which the contracting parties agree. Agreements may be made with respect to any matter, unless they conflict with the rules of international law, which in turn incorporates basic standards of international conduct as well as the obligations of each member state under the Charter of the United Nations. International agreements themselves constitute a law for the parties involved: they may also lead to the creation of customary international law, insofar as they are meant to foster general adherence, and are in fact widely accepted.

General principles common to the systems of national law represent a secondary source of international law. There are situations in which neither conventional nor customary international law can be applied. In this case, a general principle common to the major legal systems of the world may be invoked as a rule of international law, insofar as it seems appropriate for international claims. International law imposes certain duties upon the nations with respect to individuals. Thus, it is a violation of international law to treat an alien in a manner which does not satisfy the international standard of justice.

International organizations play an increasingly important role in the relationships between nations. The United Nations, the most influential among international organizations, was created on June 26, 1945. The declared purposes of the United Nations are to maintain peace and security, to develop friendly relations among nations, to achieve international cooperation for the solution of international problems, and to be a center in harmonizing the actions of nations and in allowing the attainment of their common ends. The Charter of the United Nations has been adhered to by virtually all states. Even the few remaining nonmember states have acquiesced to the principles it established.

International courts represent an institutional arrangement to resolve disputes between states. In that function, courts are similar to the dispute settlement mechanism of the WTO, albeit in a less formalized way, and usually with little or nearly no power to implement a verdict.

The International Court of Justice is the main legal organ of the UN. It was established with the UN Charter in 1945 and has its seat in The Hague, Netherlands. Its role is to resolve disputes between states. Whereas UN membership automatically subjects a state to the jurisdiction of the Court, the Court may entertain a case only in specific circumstances, for instance when some states conclude a specific agreement to submit the dispute to the court, if both states have signed appropriate clauses in international treaties (there are about 300 of them) or if they have signed a declaration to accept the jurisdiction of the court as sixty-seven states have done so far. A specific environmental chamber was established in 1993. The implementation of a verdict is in the hand of the UN Security Council. In its most famous case, Nicaragua versus United States of America (1986), the court judged the United States to have violated international law by supporting the contra guerrillas and by mining Nicaragua's harbors, and ordered them to pay reparations.

The International Tribunal for the Law of the Sea, based in Hamburg, deals with disputes regulated in the 1982 UN Convention on the Law of the Sea. The Convention currently has 155 members ("States Parties"); the United States has not ratified the convention but the agreement has become customary law. The convention establishes a comprehensive legal framework to regulate all ocean space, its uses, and its resources. It contains, among other things, provisions relating to the territorial sea, the contiguous zone, the continental shelf, the exclusive economic zone (see chapter I), and the high seas. It also regulates the protection and preservation of the marine environment, marine scientific research, and the development and transfer of marine technology. One of the most important parts of the Convention concerns the exploration and exploitation of the resources located on ocean floor and its subsoil, an issue beyond the limits of national jurisdiction.

Unlike these international courts, the European Court of Justice, established by the EU member states, has more teeth. It has the power to interpret international European treaties, including the latest basic treaty of 2007 (not in force after the no-vote in Ireland in 2008). The Court's decisions are binding. Whereas the European Court of Justice cannot create "original" law, which is the prerogative of the European Council, i.e., the council of heads of state, the Court has an important function in interpreting law. More specifically, it can clarify whether national law is inconsistent with rules pertaining to the EU, for instance with respect to the four freedoms of the single market. Thus, the Court can influence the rules.

The European Court of Justice consists of the Court of Justice, the Court of First Instance and the Civil Service Tribunal. Among other competences, the Court of First Instance has jurisdiction to hear direct actions brought by natural or legal persons against Community institutions, actions brought by member states against the Commission, and actions brought by member states against the Council in the field of state aid or "dumping." Appeals on points of law can only be brought before the Court of Justice against judgments and orders issued by the Court of First Instance. If the appeal is admissible and well founded, the Court of Justice can invalidate the judgment of the Court of First Instance. Where the state of the proceedings so permits, the Court may itself decide the case. Otherwise, the Court must refer the case back to the Court of First Instance, which is bound by the decision given on the appeal.

In order to ensure the effective and uniform application of Community legislation and to prevent divergent interpretations, the national courts may, and sometimes must, refer to the Court of Justice and ask it to clarify a point concerning the interpretation of Community law. The Court of Justice's reply is not merely an opinion, but takes the form of a judgment or reasoned order. The national court to which such judgment refers is, in deciding the dispute before it, bound by the interpretation given. Likewise, the Court of Justice's judgment binds other national courts before which the same problem is raised.

In addition, "actions for failure to fulfill obligations" enable the Court of Justice to determine whether a member state has fulfilled its obligations under Community law. Before bringing the case before the Court of Justice, the Commission conducts a preliminary procedure in which the member state is given the opportunity to reply to the complaints against it. If that procedure does not result in the member state's termination of its failure, an action for infringement of Community law may be brought before the Court of Justice. Either the Commission—as, in practice, is usually the case—or a member state can bring the action. If the Court finds that the charged state has not fulfilled its obligation, the state must bring the failure to an end without delay. If, after further action is brought by the Commission, the Court of Justice finds that the concerned member state has not complied with its judgment, it may impose on it a fixed or periodic financial penalty. With regard to "actions for annulment," the Court of Justice has exclusive jurisdiction over these types of actions when a member state brings them against the European Parliament and/or against the Council (apart from Council measures concerning state aid, dumping and implementing powers) and when one Community institution brings such action against another.

An unresolved problem exists when the European Court of Justice and national constitutional courts rule differently over the same issue. A related question is whether the EU needs a competence court that can decide where the competence lies for specific policy questions—i.e., which competence lies with the different decision-making layers within the EU, including the competence of the European Court of Justice relative to the national constitutional courts. The dynamic interpretation of aspects of European integration by the European Court of Justice, and also in developing further EU law actively, quite in contrast to its role, often creating a fait accompli, demonstrate that the Court neither respects nor protects the subsidiarity principle, as Herzog and Gerken (2008) point out. Herzog is the past president of Germany and was previously president of the German Constitutional Court.

Other international courts, such as the International Criminal Court and The European Court of Human Rights, address specific issues involving crime and human rights (see chapter X).

Lessons from European Integration

The European Union can be considered as a laboratory experiment for the devolution of sovereignty by nation states. In a process which has lasted for nearly sixty years, the countries of Europe have gotten ready to shift a sizable amount of their sovereignty to the EU level. The European Coal and Steel Community of the Six in 1951 represented a starting point for the decade-long building of a common market for all products, which now includes—after several enlargements—twenty-seven members. Through the mixture of a customs union, a monetary union and elements of a political union, many policy decisions have shifted to the European level. The list includes trade policy, competition policy, and subsidy control as essential elements of a single market. The four freedoms granting the free flow of goods, services, capital, and people represent the cornerstones of a single market. The principle of mutual recognition allows different legal settings to coexist and compete with each other. Lately, the Union's powers in judicial cooperation, the free movement of persons, foreign policy, and public health have been strengthened. The political aspects of integration, namely a common European citizenship, a common foreign and security policy, and bolstering internal security are also on the agenda.

Fiscal federalism as explained by Olson (1969) can elucidate part of the European development. However, I find similarity of tastes as used by Ahearne and Eichengreen (2007) a misleading concept for understanding what is happening in Europe. In fact, preferences in Europe are far from being similar; they are diverse. I therefore find my approach of utility functions starting to include phenomena in other countries more convincing than the similarity of tastes approach. It is not as strong as similarity of tastes. The other argument put forward in favor of fiscal federalism is economies of scale. This is similar to the lowering of transaction costs, which I have used to include negative experience and negative externalities, covering the experience of World War II, and to explain under which conditions communality of interest prevails over national sovereignty.

Admittedly, both the concept of lowering transaction costs and of economies of scale can be exploited by a power-seeking European Commission to enhance its own influence. Then, an intensified form of integration is judged from the perspective of how the EU can play a more important role in the world (Sapir 2007). While it is legitimate to ask this question, we are concerned here with a more global view. With respect to the increase in regional power, some European proponents of fiscal federalism see a trade-off between economies of scale and heterogeneity of preferences. Their point is that a single EU member state cannot enforce its preferences internationally since it does not have the necessary power to do so. If countries unite in the EU they become more efficient at delivering. Efficiency requires unity. But how is efficiency in delivering something to be defined? What is to be delivered? Can we speak of efficiency in delivering even if a country dislikes what is to be delivered? Apparently, in this approach preferences cannot diverge too much. This brings back the argument of similarity of political tastes as a prerequisite for integration. However, this argument is utterly power-centered; it attempts to meet the interests of the EU Commission and of members of the European or even Brussels political establishment. Consequently, this approach seems somewhat imperialistic vis-à-vis the member states. Finally, it is neither an integral nor a necessary element of fiscal federalism.

Decision making in the EU represents a complex matrix of centralization and of upward devolution of national sovereignty. Decisions lie with the EU Commission, the European Council (of heads of states)—requiring unanimity or a qualified majority—and the member states. Trade policy, competition policy, and the control of state subsidies are completely centralized and in the hands of the Commission. Monetary policy in the euro area of fifteen member states is also completely centralized and depoliticized (2008). Monetary policy and competition policy have been delegated to independent agents, the ECB and the Competition Authority. The ECB is checked by public opinion (Coeuré and Pisani-Ferry 2007, p. 29); however, the term "unconditional delegation" is not appropriate since the member states remain the masters of the treaty. The negotiation process regarding trade in goods is monitored by supervised delegation through the 133 Committee (Coeuré and Pisani-Ferry 2007, p. 30), made up of trade officials nominated by the member states. Agricultural policy, the single market, international agreements, regional and cohesion funds, and financial assistance in crises are decisions resting with the European Council and requiring qualified majority. The responsibility for environmental issues, consumer protection, and cross-border movement of labor is a responsibility shared between both the commission and single nation states: on these areas, the EU Commission exerts a relevant influence by means of its directives. Direct taxation and indirect taxation (except for minimum indirect tax rates) require unanimity. This also holds for immigration rules for non-EU citizens with, however, some influence from the EU Commission. Policies at the national level include: taxation; wage policy in those countries where wages are not determined by the markets, i.e., where they are negotiated by the social partners; the organization of the health sector; education and culture; and the social security systems, including pensions as well as health and unemployment insurance.

Mechanisms Stabilizing Institutional Arrangements for Global Public Goods

These issues can best be discussed with respect to international CO_2 agreements. This will be done in chapter VII.

Rules and Their Effect on Power

We have interpreted rules as the result of a bargaining process under the constraint of long-run institutional competition. Consequently, bargaining power is an important element in the rule setting process.

Who Sets the Rules?

Large countries tend to have more sway in establishing the rule system. Diplomatic experience and strategic behavior influence the bargaining process. A hegemon can control the rules to some extent. If he is benevolent, he will take care that the system is efficient in the long run. Past performance in certain areas, for instance the success of an economic approach, adds to the credibility of a bargaining position. Technological leadership is instrumental in setting standards and rules. If power leads to the mere imposition of rules, as it was in the case of Soviet Russia with respect to its satellites, then the rule system may eventually fail due to the loss of dynamics in institutional competition, as the case of the COMECON showed.

Rules are influenced by lobbying with the aim of influencing the rules to the favor of groups, for instance industry. Such rent seeking can cause severe distortions if the national rules are set in favor of a group and if the national rules set the standard for international arrangements. With the influence of the United States and of the European Union on international rules, it pays to lobby in order to influence the rule setting in these regions of the world. Thus, with a larger relevance of international rules, the risk of capture of these rules by social groups rises. This is a strong argument for institutional competition and subsidiarity in order to make sure that humankind employs a variety of institutional approaches and the "best practice" can be found. Besides, the internalization of rules involves the risk that power is established that is hard to be controlled. Note that it is not only industry which seeks to lobby for rules; the same applies to NGOs.

In a multipolar world, it is impossible to impose rules: state actors must agree upon them voluntarily. Regional integrations can exercise their influence. Since the EU has a much richer experience with a deeper integration than any other regional integration, it may well set the standard for rules that will be acceptable in other parts of the world. The EU is therefore likely to become an international rule setter, one reason being that the world is looking for a non-American option. Within this tendency, however, a major risk for the world economy is the adaptation of EU rules if those are far from efficiency-oriented from a global perspective. In fact, the EU institutional arrangements tend to be tailored to national interests, such as strategic trade policy (as in the French approach) and to weak political systems (as in the case of Italy), and they are customized to be equity-oriented as in many continental European countries, including Germany. This trend might lead to a loss of competitiveness (as in the case of the real appreciation of Italy in the 2000s), which in turn might drive the EU as a whole along more protectionist pathways.

The Effect on Power

Rules reduce transaction costs and they should usually benefit all parties involved. However, rules do not only decide on the size and the distribution of benefits, they can also decide on power. For instance, standardization can lower transaction costs. In the best case scenario, the bodies dealing with standardization reach an agreement on necessary standards and then allow each interested party to shape these standards and work with them. In the worst-case scenario, however, standards become a weapon to shield an economic advantage, for instance by specifying market entry conditions. This also holds for other policy areas. Thus, property rights and rule systems influence market structure. Witness, for example, the property rights of the major oil companies prior to the first oil crisis in the 1970s.

With respect to power, rule systems based on a "one member one vote" principle theoretically grant equal power to each member. This is especially the case when the decision-making process follows the principle of consent or requires strict unanimity. In some rule systems, different decision-making rules are applied in order to make decisions effectively (see chapter XI).

Rules, as they evolve from reducing transaction costs, counterbalance the Hobbesian paradigm that might creates right. This holds for international relations in power politics, trade policy, investment agreements, environmental policy, and other fields.

Rules restrain power, at least as long as a relatively powerful state believes that the benefits of adhering to the rule system outweigh its costs. In recent years, for instance, the United States has become increasingly worried that the UN excessively constrains its power to pursue its strategic interests.

Rule systems existing at a certain moment in time reflect the distribution of power at the time the rules were set up. If the power constellation changes substantially over time, some members, ascending in power, may want to amend the system; while at the same time, other members may prefer to keep it unchanged, fearing a loss of influence and power.

V
Rules for International Product Markets

The international division of labor is the area that has seen the most important advance in the international rule system. It is in this area that quite a bit of experience has been collected. The purpose of GATT/WTO is to prevent distortions in international product markets, such as those caused by a country's strategic behavior in the trade of goods and international services. The basic principle is that differences in endowments and in preferences between countries are accepted as the starting point for the international division of labor. Moreover, institutional arrangements in the field of competition policy try to prevent firms from establishing market-dominating positions, thus undermining the benefits of globalization.

Liberalization of Trade

The core purpose of GATT/WTO is to reduce trade barriers in order to allow all countries to benefit from the international division of labor. The rule system for the international product and service market holds this goal as its main reference point. Consequently, all nations should abstain from raising existing tariffs or levying new ones. Quantitative restrictions and other nontariff barriers are also forbidden. More generally, countries should open their markets completely, banning all protectionist measures from their trade policies.

After World War II, as the world economy sought new institutional arrangements, the U.S. Congress blocked the creation of an International Trade Organization. In its place, a less ambitious General Agreement on Tariffs and Trade (GATT) was negotiated. The new institution started with twenty-three member states in 1948. In 1995, GATT eventually evolved into the WTO, the World Trade Organization. While the GATT's institutional setup was limited to a multilateral treaty among contracting parties, the WTO represents a full-blown international organization, with states as its members. The WTO now includes 153 members; some important nations, such as Russia (so far) still remain outside the system. The WTO administers the trade agreements, contracted by its members. Besides GATT and its numerous issue-specific agreements, such as those on regulating antidumping and subsidies, the WTO also monitors the General Agreement on Trade in Services (GATS) and the Agreement on Trade-Related Aspects of Intellectual Property Rights (TRIPS). In accordance with the single undertaking, agreements represent multilateral rules, applying to all WTO members. This holds, for instance, to the agreement in agriculture, in spite of the deviation from the principle of free markets. Another type of agreement only covers a subset of products. For example, the information technology agreement was concluded by thirty-nine countries in 1997.

Despite the temptation of strategic behavior in the international division of labor, nation states have succeeded in concluding a multilateral agreement concerning trade for a variety of reasons. First of all, the memories of two world wars and the disintegration of the world economy in the 1930s worked as the driving force behind the search for a new set of rules, one that could prevent similar disasters and increase the level of international prosperity. Second, the experience of the pre-World War I period made intellectuals and politicians confident that institutional arrangements, as a way out of the prisoner's dilemma, would allow welfare gains for all nations. By the same token, a tariff war is by no means advantageous for any single country. Third, it must be noted that an agreement on rules is not a solitary event: it is rather part of a broader sequence of agreements. The repetition of the game within an infinite time horizon multiplies the gains again and again. As a result, cooperation can indeed grant optimal payoffs. Moreover, in a repeated game, countries care about their reputation which then works as an incentive toward compliance, as the reputation as a "cheater" in the international system would offset the short-term temptation not to cooperate. Finally, the uncertainty over future gains from new negotiations can lead to a less aggressive, more cooperative behavior.

The world trade order has several roles to play (Hoekman and Mavroidis 2007). It can be viewed as a negative catalogue listing the instruments not to be used. Thus, it protects the international division of labor against the behavior of national governments (Tumlir 1983). It subjects nations to a multilateral discipline. They cede sovereignty and give up policy instruments or limit their use, for instance with regard to binding tariffs. Moreover, the rule system shelters national governments from the power of protectionist groups within individual economies, as it imposes restrictions on industry associations, sector-specific interests and trade unions and shields the political process against these groups (Tumlir 1979a,b). The WTO has been likened to a mast to which—like Odysseus—governments can tie themselves to escape the siren-like calls of domestic interest groups and even, to some extent, of their voters (Hoekman and Kostecki 2001). At the same time it contains positive mechanisms that extend liberalization.

A set of mechanisms and principles are crucial for the stabilization of the rule system. Among them are the nondiscrimination principle, the most-favored-nation clause, the reciprocity of concessions, bound tariffs and single undertaking, and the important procedure of dispute settlement (see chapter IV). Besides these aspects, vital WTO instruments spring from a coherent interpretation of the term "like products," the national treatment principle, the Trade Policy Review Mechanism, from accepting new members and from exceptions when the rules do not apply.

The principle of nondiscrimination presupposes the comparability of those products for which a definition of discrimination can be given. Article I, section 1 of the GATT Treaty on the general most-favored-nation treatment stipulates that privileges granted "to any product originating in or destined for any other country shall be accorded immediately and unconditionally to the like product originating in or destined for the territories of all other contracting parties."

Apparently, the similarity of products is an important aspect of trade rules. Along similar lines, we can draw a distinction between country-of-origin rules and country-of-destination rules with respect to traded goods. The country-of-origin principle applies to the traded good of the rule in force in the country of origin, i.e., where it is produced, whereas the country-of-destination principle enables the importing country to set the domestic standard as the yardstick for its imports. If the country-of-destination principle were applied in the international division of labor, the subsequent use of a hodgepodge of diverging standards would represent a serious barrier to trade. Moreover, such regulations can easily fall hostage to domestic interest groups. The aim of GATT and the WTO has therefore been to reduce the role of the country-of-destination principle. The regulations for the production of all goods should be left to the discretion of the country of origin. The different regulations of all countries of origin should have equal standing within a framework of mutual competition. In other words, the goal of the world trade order is that countries mutually accept the regulations of the country of origin for product quality and production processes, in order to minimize transaction costs. In this way, competition between rules can thrive. This institutional competition has far-reaching implications; national regulations are harmonized *ex post*.

Only in precisely demarcated cases, for example, when the issue of public health protection is involved, should the country of destination and its standards take precedence over the norms of the country of origin (GATT Article XX). Even then, the measures adopted should imply neither discrimination nor protection (GATT Articles I and III). A new issue arises from the tendency of the Dispute Settlement Body to allow importing countries to apply their environmental standards to the production of imported goods in their countries of origin (see below).

Beside the most-favored-nation clause, the national treatment of goods is another strong principle working against discrimination. Indeed, the dismantling of tariff and nontariff barriers only covers one aspect of market access. National treatment is an additional requirement once a good has satisfied whatever border measures can apply. This principle requires that a foreign good should be treated no less favorably than a domestic product. More specifically, a foreign good should be subject to the same internal (indirect) taxes and charges that apply to a "like" or directly competitive domestic good (Article III: 2 GATT). Also, the same laws and regulations should apply to like products (Article III: 4 GATT).

Transparency is an important ingredient of the international order. In particular, concepts such as the most-favored-nation clause and national treatment imply the necessity that nations be informed on how rules are implemented in other countries. This is the reason why all trade laws are published. WTO members must also provide a consolidated notification each year, in which they inform other WTO members on changes in their laws and regulations. Regular meetings and numerous committees enhance information. The Trade Policy Review Mechanism scrutinizes the trade policy of each member state on a regular basis. The frequency of each country's review varies together with the country's share of trade. This review tries to ensure the transparency of the members' trade policies by means of regular monitoring, to improve the quality of public and intergovernmental debate on these issues and to assess the effects of given policies on the world trading system. As a result, the Mechanism is expected to instill discipline into the trade policy of member states. On the basis of this information, countries can bring complaints if rules are breached by a member of the WTO, especially if the nondiscrimination principle is violated and if some policy measure is used to prevent a country from garnering the full benefit of a WTO agreement (nonviolation complaints).

The WTO is an open club; membership is open to any state or separate customs territory. In the long run, the optimal size of the WTO is the world as a whole, because only then will all potential benefits of the international division of labor be exploited. There is, however, one important condition for the extension of membership. The system of rules should not be weakened, but rather strengthened when a new member enters. Therefore, new members must have a track record, demonstrating that they have already been following the basic WTO philosophy for some time. Moreover, economic conditions in the new candidate countries must be such that the country is fit to survive in the world market. A candidate must bind its tariffs, nowadays usually set at about double the tariff rate of the OECD countries. It must also be prepared to liberalize market access. Also required is the removal of WTO-inconsistent measures. The country also has to accept the WTO rule system as a single undertaking. Accession negotiations are held between the acceding government and all WTO members having an interest in improving their access to the new member's market. This includes market access for services. A working party examines the application. As of July 2008, thirty states are applying for membership, among them Russia. The acceding country takes on the role of a *demandeur*, and negotiations usually take a long time: the negotiations with China, a member since 2001, took fifteen years. Accession must be approved by a two-thirds majority of the council (see below).

Four exemptions from the WTO rules perform the function of safety valves (see chapter IV). First, countervailing duties can be imposed on subsidized imports. Second, antidumping duties can be imposed on imports, sold at a price below the one charged in the country of origin. Note that Article VI, allowing antidumping and countervailing duties, is superseded by the GATT 1994 Agreement on Antidumping and the Agreement on Subsidies and Countervailing Measures. Third, an industry that is seriously harmed by foreign imports can be protected, even if there is no dumping and if subsidies are not applied. Fourth, actions can be taken in the case of serious balance-of-payments problems. Note that the WTO cannot possibly resolve the issue of distribution between nation states. Introducing distributional constraints into the international division of labor would make the world order ineffective. Such issues, including the alleviation of poverty, have to be resolved in other ways.

Unresolved GATT Problems

The eight liberalization rounds which have taken place since the foundation of the GATT in 1948 prove that the path of liberalization has worked well in the past. This is true for all of the following negotiation rounds: the Geneva Round (1947); the Annecy Round (1949); the Torquay Round (1950–51); the Geneva Round (1955–56); and the Dillon Round (1960–61). All five rounds were on tariff cuts: the Kennedy Round (1963–67, establishing an antidumping code); the Tokyo Round (1973–79, spawning a new antidumping code and a code on subsidies); and the Uruguay Round (1986–94, concerning rules on services and intellectual property and dispute settlement). The Uruguay Round was the last one to be concluded successfully more than a decade ago. In contrast, the Seattle Round failed in 2000. The Doha Round, started in 2001, is stalling. The later negotiation rounds took longer to be completed as it proved increasingly difficult to reach a positive outcome.

The main unresolved issues in the trade order are the improvement of market access, antidumping rules, restraint on subsidies, environmental standards, and the role of large players.

Market Access

Free market access is not yet fully established. Agriculture is still subject to tariffs and quantitative restrictions. For the EU, agricultural protection remains high, with tariff rates at 15.1% in 2006 against a nonagricultural tariff average of 3.9%. In the textile sector, it took five decades to eliminate the waiver. Moreover, the Doha Round failed insofar as developed economies proved unwilling to completely open their product markets, especially in agriculture, a crucial step in order to eradicate the plague of poverty in the developing countries, the vital goal of development economics. At the same time, developing countries were not prepared to open their markets to the industrial products of developed countries. In any case, it would not be sufficient for market access that governments give up their tariff and nontariff instruments, with which they can directly hamper trade flows as they reach their borders. Another necessary condition is indeed that national regulations do not restrict access for goods and firms, i.e., that the principle of national treatment is implemented for all products. Therefore, barriers resulting from national legislative and informal practices effectively limiting access to markets should be dismantled. These barriers include policy measures in the broadest sense, such as licensing procedures for economic activities, facilities and products, technical standards, arrangements for public procurement, and interlocking ties between firms (as with Keiretsu in Japan), all resulting in the exclusion of outsiders.

Antidumping

Antidumping measures or countervailing duties, though defensible within the framework of strictly theoretical models, can easily degenerate into a severe impediment for trade and thus come to represent a form of "administered" protection. These measures are defined by national legislation, but can fall captive of national interest groups; they can therefore correspond to a way around bound tariffs and otherwise forbidden quantitative restraints. Even when antidumping measures or countervailing duties are not actually applied, the threat of using them entails a degree of uncertainty which may itself induce trading partners to adopt the "appropriate" export behavior. In economic categories, contingent protection represents effective protection. Antidumping is used by the EU and serves as an important protectionist device of U.S. trade policy. American law permits the levying of countervailing duties in order to raise the price of a subsidized imported good when the U.S. International Trade Commission determines that material damage is caused to American producers. An antidumping duty may be imposed if the Commission finds that a good is being sold at less than its fair value or below its cost. The task of the WTO will be to contain the protectionist impact of this approach (Messerlin 2001). The definition of standards to be respected by national antidumping laws is necessary.

Subsidies

While tariffs and quantitative restraints have progressively lost their importance as forms of protection, governments are still tempted to use subsidies in order to lower their producers' production costs, thus establishing an artificial price advantage and distorting the international division of labor. Both export subsidies and subsidies for import-competing products are responsible for this distortion. Subsidies prevent market access. The Global Subsidy Initiative, based in Geneva, estimates total specific subsidies in the world at US$1 trillion. Not all of them affect trade. A country's subsidies take market shares away from other countries and usually lead to political demands for retaliation. Thus, their effect resembles those of protectionist measures. Often, the distorting effect is felt in areas where it was not expected. For instance, subsidizing biofuels competes with the production of foods and artificially drives up world prices of foodstuffs.

Reasons that are given for subsidies are the goal of autarky and independence from foreign supplies, the willingness to conquer international markets, and the call for social protection. Increasingly, subsidies are now introduced in order to protect the environment and encourage energy saving, as in the case of windmills, the cogeneration of heat, and biofuels. Subsidies are regularly given without considering their opportunity costs. Hence, they may not reach their goal and may sometimes have adverse effects, for instance when agricultural subsidies cause overproduction, water pollution, and deterioration of the soil. Subsidies are often justified by appealing to equity considerations. This argument is regularly used for agriculture. Subsidies of European agricultural policy, for instance, are allegedly aimed at protecting the small family farm. However, empirical studies indicate that an overwhelming share of these subsidies—some observers say up to 80%—end up in the hands of large, well-to-do agricultural producers and agribusiness (Oxfam International 2006). Furthermore, the interpretation of equity in national terms is ethically questionable within a global economy. As people in rich countries become increasingly aware of the global context, it becomes harder to convince voters that equity and social protection can be defined solely within national borders. A case in point is subsidies for biofuels in industrial countries, being introduced with the intention of becoming less oil dependent and to reduce CO_2 emissions. It now becomes evident that biofuels come at extremely high costs, estimated at US$300–1,000 per ton of CO_2 equivalent (Global Subsidies Initiative 2007; Siebert 2008a). What is even more damaging: subsidies for biofuels drive out food production and are one reason for the food price increase in the years 2007 and 2008. Finally, it is simply inconsistent and unfair to praise the benefits of competition and open markets for the international division of labor and then to shut the exports of developing countries off from the agricultural markets of the rich countries.

Some subsidies have a negative environmental impact and distort trade at the same time. Examples are: coal subsidies (for instance in Germany) that subsidize an energy source generating CO_2 emissions; subsidies for tobacco production in conflict with human health; subsidies to agricultural production implying the use of chemicals or intensive land use, and subsides for the fishing industry. In these cases, nations can benefit from reducing the subsidies. It should be in the self-interest of individual countries to reduce them. A "double dividend" may exist if two distortions are reduced at the same time. Here the packaging of benefits can best be achieved. Multilateral subsidy reduction can help countries to go ahead with this type of distortion reduction.

The WTO Agreement on Subsidies and Countervailing Measures, concluded in 1994 as part of the Uruguay Round, defines the following constituent elements of a subsidy: (i) it is a financial contribution; (ii) it is provided by a government or a public body; and (iii) it confers a benefit. The agreement also defines the concept of "specificity": a specific subsidy is industry-specific or export-specific, being granted to a specific firm or group. Specific subsidies can either be domestic or export subsidies. Only specific subsidies are subject to multilateral disciplines or to countervailing measures. Specific subsidies are further classified as prohibited or actionable.

Prohibited subsidies are simply forbidden. These are subsidies that require recipients to meet certain export targets or to use domestic goods instead of imported goods. Such subsidies are prohibited under Article 3 of the Agreement on Subsidies and Countervailing Measures because they are ipso facto trade-distorting and harm the trade opportunities of other members. They are product-specific or industry-specific and come in the form of direct transfers, tax reductions for specific industries and tax rebates for exports. Prohibited subsidies can be challenged in the WTO dispute settlement procedure which handles them by following an accelerated timetable. If the dispute settlement procedure confirms that the subsidy is prohibited, it must be immediately withdrawn. Otherwise, the complaining country can take countermeasures. If domestic producers are harmed by imports of subsidized products, a country can impose countervailing duty.

Actionable subsidies are those which have adverse effects on the interests of a WTO member. This includes all domestic support measures judged to distort production. Adverse effects include injury or threat thereof to a domestic industry, nullification or impairment of tariff concessions, or serious prejudice to the country's export interests. The agreement defines three types of damage that subsidies can cause. One country's subsidies can hurt the domestic industry of an importing country. They can hurt rival exporters from another country when the two compete in a third country's markets. Additionally, domestic subsidies in one country can hurt exporters as they try to compete in the subsidizing country's domestic market. Remedial procedures start with consultations and then move to dispute settlement or the imposition of countervailing duties by the affected importing country. The complaining country has to prove that the subsidy has an adverse effect on its interests. Otherwise, the subsidy is permitted. If the Dispute Settlement Body rules that a country's subsidy does have an adverse effect, then the country must either withdraw it or take measures offsetting its adverse effect. If domestic producers are hurt by imports of subsidized products, the imposition of a countervailing duty is allowed.

Permitted are nonspecific subsidies, i.e., subsidies not aimed at a specific recipient or industry. Examples are the financing of education or infrastructure. The Uruguay agreement originally also contained a category of nonactionable specific subsidies. In this category, specific subsidies to research and development were nonactionable if they did not exceed 75% of the costs of industrial research or 50% of the costs of precompetitive development activity. Furthermore, specific subsidies to disadvantaged regions, promoting regional development, and specific subsidies that supported the adaptation of existing facilities to new environmental requirements were also allowed. This category existed for five years, ending on December 31, 1999. It was not extended because of lack of consensus. The disciplines set out in the agreement only apply to specific subsidies. They can be domestic or export subsidies.

In the GATT's traffic light terminology, this classification of subsidies reads as "red box" (prohibited), "amber box" (actionable: slow down, i.e., reduce the subsidies), and "green box" (permitted). Boxes used for agriculture are somewhat different.

Important sectors such as agriculture and the aviation industry still enjoy special treatment, either explicitly or implicitly. Whereas, in principle, the 1994 subsidy agreement applies to both industrial products and agricultural goods, subsidies for the latter were exempt from challenge under the Agriculture Agreement's "peace clause." This clause, however, expired at the end of 2003. Since then dispute settlement for agricultural subsidies has become more frequent, as the cotton and the sugar cases in 2005 demonstrated. In agriculture, things are complicated. As in the nonagricultural sectors, the WTO uses different boxes. There is no red box, although domestic support exceeding the reduction commitment levels in the amber box is prohibited. The amber box contains all domestic support measures judged to distort production and trade (with some exceptions). Article 6 of the Agriculture Agreement defines these measures of the amber box as all domestic support measures except those in the blue and green boxes. They include measures to support prices or subsidies directly related to production quantities. Subsidies in the amber box should be reduced, although a level of minimal support is allowed: 5% of agricultural production for developed countries, 10% for developing countries. These are the so-called "de minimis" levels. The 30 WTO members whose subsidies were above the "de minimis" levels at the beginning of the post-Uruguay Round reform period committed themselves to reduce these subsidies. The reduction commitments are expressed in terms of a "total Aggregate Measurement of Support" (AMS) where all support for specified products together with nonspecific product supports are expressed as a single figure.

There is a blue box for domestic support tied to programs that limit production. Given their limits, these subsidies are less trade distorting than open-end forms of support. The blue box represents an "amber box with conditions"—conditions designed to reduce distortion. At present, there are no limits to spending on blue box subsidies.

The agricultural green box includes subsidies that do not distort trade or that only cause minimal distortion. They must be government-funded (not by charging consumers higher prices) and must not involve price support. Usually, these subsidies tend to be programs that are not targeted at particular products and they include direct income support for farmers decoupled from current production levels or prices. They also include environmental protection and regional development programs. "Green box" subsidies are therefore allowed without limits. The different categories of subsidies, both in the agricultural as in the nonagricultural sector, are summarized in table V.1.

In the current Doha negotiations, some countries want to keep the blue box as it is, because they see it as a crucial means of moving away from distorting amber box subsidies without causing too much hardship. Others would like to set limits

Table V.1. Subsidy rules

	General rules		Rules for agriculture
Red box (Prohibited)	Subsidies intended to stimulate exports or the use of domestic goods		No red box Subsidies must be reduced according to an agreed schedule
Amber box (Actionable)	Specific subsidies that cause adverse effects on the interest of other WTO members		Trade-distorting support (should be reduced to "de minimis" levels)
		Blue box	Subsidies to farmers when the farmers are required to limit production (Amber box with conditions)
Green box	Nonspecific subsidies		Non-trade-distorting subsidies or subsidies with minimal impact

or reduction commitments, and some of them advocate moving these supports into the amber box.

In the future, strategic trade theory could become more appealing for national policymakers and provide a rationale for subsidizing promising sectors, albeit on the basis of rather restrictive and naive economic models. We may soon see a new tide of interventionist policies in some OECD countries as a reaction to globalization, especially in France and the United States. This may lead to political demands for retaliation.

In the context of strategic trade policy, another unresolved problem of the world trade order is the implicit or explicit undervaluation of a currency, used as a means to stimulate domestic production and exports. A case in point is the discussion of the Chinese renminbi. An undervaluation has a positive effect on exports and restrains imports; it can keep an economy "under steam" and may be seen as easing structural change. However, it has major drawbacks: it represents a distortion in favor of old industries, thus hindering structural and sectoral change to new sectors; it keeps real income of labor lower than necessary as it reduces the international purchasing power; it keeps domestic consumption low; and it also exposes a country to inflationary pressure, increasing the instability of the monetary–financial system. Internationally, undervaluation increases the risk of retaliation. Admittedly, the increase in the price level over time will eventually eat up the positive effects of a nominal undervaluation (see chapter IX).

Internationally, a hopeful signal in the context of subsidy control comes from two decisions by the WTO Dispute Settlement Body—namely, the cotton case, decided in favor of Brazil and against the United States, and the sugar case, decided in favor of countries producing sugar cane and against the EU's sugar regime (see chapter IV). Also, the case of U.S. Foreign Sales Corporation, decided in 2000, reined in special concessions for U.S. corporations.

Undoubtedly, the existing subsidy code needs further development in order to prevent subsidy competition between governments. In the European Union, experience on the limits of state aid has been collected; the single market of twenty-seven countries requires that competition is not distorted artificially between the member countries through governmental subsidies.

Environmental Standards

The waiver of Article XX of GATT to protect health and the environment, when necessary, by trade policy instruments, may represent a major issue in the future. When GATT was introduced, environmental issues were not a matter of concern. It is evident that Article XX allows countries to apply measures against imports that endanger the health of its citizens, for instance when toxic material is part of imported consumption goods. Also, imported goods have to respect the domestic standards of use. This applies to consumption and investment goods alike, for instance with imported machines. Moreover, the Kantian categorical imperative requires that countries do not export their toxic waste to be deposited in other countries without taking into account the long-run environmental damage there.

As for other imports, the WTO is aware of the trade-environment nexus; witness the establishment of the Committee on Trade and Environment in 1995. We have taken the position that, if the environment is a national factor of endowment, national environmental scarcity should be treated similarly to other national factors of endowment such as labor abundance and capital abundance. According to this view, trade policy instruments should not be used to impose a country's environmental preferences on other countries. This is in line with the tuna fish–dolphin case (1991) and the country-of-origin principle. However, in the shrimp–turtle case, decided in 1998 and in 2000 by the WTO, the application of domestic performance standards to the imports of other countries was accepted. Two other cases, decided by WTO dispute settlement, the U.S. gasoline case of 1996 and the Brazil retreated tyres case of 2007 point in the same direction to introduce green aspects to the WTO (Hufbauer and Kim 2008).

The case of global warming is different from national environmental endowment, since we have a mixture of a public good and a private good. The world's climate represents a global public good; however, it can be used as a sink, with both roles competing (see chapter VII). The environment as a receptacle of greenhouse gases represents a private good, for which property rights can be defined; for instance emission limits can be set for individual polluters. As a matter of principle, a country should not apply environmental standards extraterritorially to other countries.

However, since countries may use different environmental policy instruments such as taxes or performance standards domestically, when attempting to provide solutions to a global problem, their competitiveness will be affected. As a practical problem, it seems unlikely that countries will agree on similar or comparable policy instruments to reduce global warming. In order to prevent a hodgepodge of diverging environmental standards applying to imports, it is proposed that the WTO introduces a "green space" in which different national performance standards are allowed for the production of carbon intensive goods. Measures included in this "green space" would not be subject to challenges in the WTO's dispute settlement procedure. Hufbauer and Kim (2008) discuss a code approach on trade-related greenhouse emission control measures for carbon intensive products; that is to say, a TRECM that would be part of the WTO rule system besides TRIMs and TRIPS. This would include a definition of greenhouse gas control measures, the requirement of equal treatment of imported and domestic products and provisions for different environmental policy approaches such as carbon taxes and cap-and-trade approaches. Comparability of approaches would be a major issue. Subsidies for biofuels could be included. This approach is intended to avoid the interruption of the trade liberalization while at the same time giving countries the option to use different environmental policy instruments.

It is questionable how such an approach would fit into a Kyoto-like environmental agreement which might be reached in Copenhagen in 2009 or after, which allocates emission reduction obligations to the different regions of the world. Such an agreement would define what individual countries have to do in terms of emission reductions. Assume emission certificates are used. Then, the prices for these certificates express environmental scarcity of a specific country, as agreed upon internationally. By international agreement, the global public good has then been transformed into a national endowment. Consequently, it must be treated similarly to national endowment. To apply national performance to imports would then mean dealing with global warming twice. Note, however, prices paid for emission certificates should not be rebated when a product is exported.

Moreover, such an attempt is not without risk: it introduces another waiver into the WTO; it deviates from the principle of exploiting differences in endowment and preferences in the international division of labor. Rather, it stems from the philosophy of a level playing field; starting from the premise that a country can impose its standards on other countries—a rather imperialistic perspective. In spite of a code it will bring many problems in detail, for instance in establishing comparability of environmental policies.[1]

---

[1] If one adopts the strategy of imposing standards to other countries, it may well be that a "social space" in the WTO is demanded as well. The only argument against such a demand is that global warming represents a public good, whereas social standards are merit goods.

The Role of Large Players

Another unresolved problem is to what extent large players and customs unions will accept the WTO set of rules when this conflicts with their national interests. A case in point is whether WTO sanctions, obtained by small countries, can actually be implemented against larger trading partners, such as the United States or the EU. Examples are the verdict obtained by Brazil against the United States in the cotton case, and the verdict received by Thailand, Australia, and Brazil in the sugar case against the EU, both in 2005. These countries can use trade sanctions which will hurt themselves. Among the measures they can take, it is debated whether they can invalidate intellectual property rights of larger countries such as the United States. In any case, retaliations are not in the spirit of the WTO. It would be preferable to multilateralize the titles countries obtain in verdicts, for instance by making them transferable through auctions. This issue will become increasingly relevant with the rise of China.

The five unresolved areas of the trade order—market access, antidumping, subsidies, environmental standards, and large players—represent fields in which institutional improvements are needed. Another major open question in the world trade order is whether regionalism and bilateralism will destroy the multilateral order (see chapter IV). Besides these issues, specific conflicts exist between countries. Among these are the United States/EU dispute on beef hormones, the treatment of genetically modified food and the EU's banana regime. Thus, the 1998 WTO ruling in favor of the United States and against the EU ban on the import of hormone-treated beef was interpreted by many as an intrusion of WTO law into the cultural traditions and basic food habits of peoples. Last but not least, the WTO has developed rules mainly for produced goods; however, the institutional arrangements are sparse for energy such as crude oil and natural gas. Thus, the WTO has no lever to forbid or impede resource cartels such as OPEC. Resource countries are not willing to cede sovereignty.

Rules for Services

Three special arrangements of the WTO extend the multilateral arrangement beyond the product market, defined in a narrow sense. The General Agreement on Trade in Services (GATS) expands the concept of the international division of labor to services (see below). Two further arrangements look at trade related aspects in investment and in intellectual property rights. The Agreement on Trade-Related Investment Measures (TRIMs) prohibits measures that represent obstacles to investment if investment is related to trade. The Agreement on Trade-Related Intellectual Property Rights (TRIPS) deals with violations of intellectual property rights through trade (on both see chapter V).

The increasing integration of the world economy changes the conditions for the trade in services. The width and diversity of services becomes apparent by the WTO classification list, including twelve main categories (and some 166 subcategories): These encompass business services (professional services like legal services, computer services, research and development services, real estate services, rental/leasing, other business services including advertising), communication services (including telecommunication services, audio-visual services such as motion picture production and distribution, radio and television services), construction, distribution services, educational services, environmental services, financial services (insurance, banking services and related services), health-related and social services (hospital services), tourism and travel-related services, recreational, cultural and sporting services, transport services (maritime transport, air transport, rail transport, road transport), and other services (not included in the above classification).

A major distinction of service categories runs between border-crossing and domestic services. This distinction is analogous to the one between tradable and nontradable goods. Applying these categories, another differentiation, namely between "person-disembodied" and "person-embodied" services, becomes relevant (Bhagwati 1984). Disembodied services, like detail engineering, developing computer programs and software, as well as accounting data processing, are not "embodied" in people by the time these services cross the border. They do not require business partners to meet locally to carry out the service. For the international trading order, these services are not too different from the exchange of tangible goods. Similarly, as commodities are carried by the transport system via borders, disembodied services cross national borders by means of communication media. They represent cross-border supply.

This approach leads to a more systematic and theoretical classification of services according to four different modes of supply: a service like an international telephone call or the processing of accounting data may actually cross a border as discussed above ("cross-border supply"); consumers or firms of one country may use the service in another country ("consumption abroad"); a service may be supplied in another country ("commercial presence"); or alternatively individuals may travel to supply their service in another country ("presence of natural persons").

In all four modes, gains from services are similar to those from the trade of goods. This is obvious for cross-border supply, where the analogy with the trade of goods is evident. There is a potential for gains in the other modes of service provision as well, i.e., in cross-border movements of the consumer, in the establishment of a commercial presence within a market and in the temporary movement of the service provider himself. In addition, services represent an important input for manufacturing and for merchandise trade. Consequently, high input prices for services imply a distortion to the detriment of manufacturing. High input prices then come to represent an effective protection for imported inputs that may be needed for exports, such as IT imports. Moreover, they hinder the exploitation of gains from trade in the manufacturing sector of developing countries.

In order to reap the benefits from the international division of labor in the service sector, a similar rule system as in the trade of goods is needed. In particular, border-crossing disembodied services should be treated like commodities. As a consequence, markets must be open for them just as they must be for traded commodities. In the case of person-embodied services (consumption abroad, commercial presence, presence of natural persons), nondiscrimination can be obtained through national treatment, i.e., by applying to foreigners the same treatment applied to nationals. Foreign suppliers must therefore be treated in the same way as domestic suppliers. Yet this principle is still much weaker than the norms applied in the trade of products. In the trade of services, the country-of-origin principle has not been fully accepted so far. The European Union represents a positive exception; there, at least in principle, the free movement of services represents one of the four freedoms on which the single market is based; moreover, mutual recognition is in line with the 1979 Cassis de Dijon verdict of the European Court of Justice. By the same token, the home rule principle has been applied to the EU's banking industry. However, even in the European Union the acceptance of the country-of-origin principle has encountered significant obstacles, in particular after the eastern enlargement. This is especially true for natural persons crossing borders in order to provide a service. In this case, EU member states have introduced several barriers, one of them being the requirement that workers hired by a firm in the country where the service is provided be paid the local wage.

The General Agreement on Trade and Services (GATS), which came into force in 1995, applies to all modes of supply. It holds for all services, with the exception of those supplied in the exercise of governmental authority and of air transport services. All WTO members are at the same time members of GATS, having as its core principles the requirement of nondiscrimination and the most-favored-nation obligation. National treatment and a market access obligation are specific commitments. GATS establishes a framework for the notification of existing rules, ensuring the increased transparency of relevant rules and regulations and attempting to promote progressive liberalization through successive rounds of negotiations.

In contrast to GATT, however, GATS does not provide a general liberalization for trade in services. Each WTO member is required to voluntarily schedule its commitments and to notify them accordingly. Commitments are undertaken with respect to each of the four different modes of service supply. A schedule of specific commitments is required, identifying the services for which the WTO member guarantees market access and national treatment, together with the specification of any limitations that may be attached. Most schedules consist of both sectoral and horizontal sections. The sector-specific sections contain entries that apply only to a particular service. The horizontal section, instead, contains entries that apply across all sectors subsequently listed in the schedule. Horizontal limitations often refer to a particular mode of supply, notably commercial presence and the presence of natural persons. It is, admittedly, quite difficult to define precise commitments with respect to such diverse interdependencies between some 160-odd types of services exchanged in the world economy, because a single measure of segmentation such as tariffs does not exist. A difficulty also arises because commitments are voluntary.

In principle, countries were free to schedule their commitments, i.e., to notify which commitments they were prepared to make once GATS had become effective. The majority of current commitments came into force on January 1, 1995, together with the WTO as a whole. Nearly all the commitments for services were of a stand-still nature; that is, not to become more restrictive than was already the case for selected sectors. Moreover, commitments vary considerably among countries. New commitments have since been scheduled by participants in extended negotiations and by new members that have joined the WTO.

There is no subsidy discipline for services. Examples of subsidies for services are: a governmental bail-out clause in favor of a specific bank group (as in the case of German savings banks); privileged access for domestic banks and insurance companies; privileged access to governmental procurement; privileged risk treatment as the government takes over certain risks for domestic suppliers; a privilege accorded to domestic firms in their covering costs, for instance fuel costs for airlines or airport costs; preferential tax treatment, as for tourism; and privileges accorded to domestic transportation in terms of road costs for cars, economic opportunities for domestic railroads and national airlines. It seems difficult to define common standards for subsidies for services along the distinction into the four different modes of supply of services.

The GATS contains specific exemptions. For instance, the Annex on Financial Services entitles members, regardless of other provisions of the GATS, to take measures for prudential reasons, including for the protection of investors, depositors, policy holders or persons to whom a fiduciary duty is owed by a financial service supplier, or to ensure the integrity and stability of the financial system.

All things considered, then, GATS is indeed a much weaker institutional arrangement than GATT is. In principle, the WTO dispute settlement is responsible for disputes concerning GATS. However, given much weaker rules, this mechanism is also much weaker.

Since not all services-related negotiations could be concluded within the time frame of the Uruguay Round in January 2000, the GATS contains what is called a "built in" agenda, namely a work program for additional negotiations. Since 2000, over 140 WTO members governments have been engaged in negotiations aimed at further liberalization of the global services market. At the sectoral level, negotiations on basic telecommunications (among all WTO members) and in the area of financial services (signed by fifty-six WTO members and a total of seventy countries) were successfully concluded in 1997.

As a result of the Hong Kong Declaration adopted in December 2005, plurilateral negotiations started on many services sectors. Markets are yet to be opened in many respects: barriers discriminating against foreigners or nondiscriminatory barriers erected by means of competition policy will have to be torn down; the product coverage must be extended. So far, there are exemptions to the most-favored-nation treatment: in the future, the conditionality of the most-favored-nation clause prevalent in services should instead be replaced by an unconditional use. National treatment as a central principle only applies to services where a country has made a specific commitment; exemptions are allowed. Moreover, the present approach is focused on finding agreements for specific services. This sector-by-sector approach raises the risk that sector-specific aspects will dominate over a more balanced across-the-board negotiation, with the result that the export interests of the economy as a whole are not sufficiently harnessed in order to dismantle barriers of trade.

The Institutional Setup of the WTO and Its Decision-Making Mechanism

The WTO is an international organization based on a multilateral agreement. The ministerial conference, the central decision-making body, is responsible for general issues and for carrying out the general functions of the WTO; it meets at least once every two years (figure V.1). The WTO is managed by the General Council, which meets several times a year in the Geneva headquarters. About 70% of the WTO members take part in the meetings of the General Council, usually the delegations that are represented in Geneva. Additionally, the General Council meets as the Dispute Settlement Body and Trade Policy Review Body. At a more specific level, three subsidiary councils are assigned to the issues of Trade in Goods, Trade-Related Aspects of Intellectual Property Rights (TRIPS), and Trade in Services. Furthermore, various specialized committees, working groups, and working parties operate in several areas such as trade and environment, development, and regional trade agreements. The Trade Negotiation Committee, which works under the authority of the WTO Council, and its subsidiaries are in charge of the negotiations mandated by the Doha Declaration. In principle, all members can participate in all councils or committees. However, there are some exceptions; for example, not all members signed the agreements within the activities of the Plurilateral Committee.

The decision-making process of the WTO is sluggish and clumsy. The WTO has not succeeded in dismantling the protection of agriculture in the developed countries and in establishing market access in this area for developing countries. Similarly, it has neither managed to improve the developed countries' market access for industrial goods to developing countries, nor to liberalize newly developed services as in the IT sector. It has not been strong enough to initiate changes in the rule system that could stimulate new developments and breakthroughs; rather, it

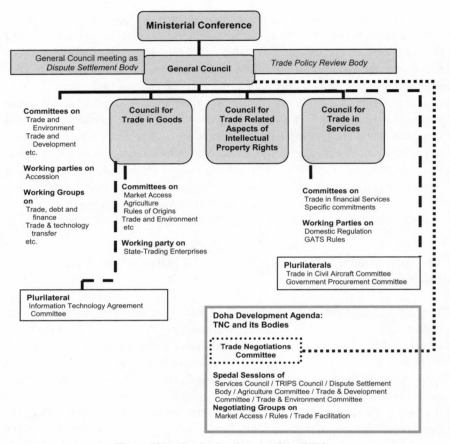

Figure V.1.   Institutional setup of the WTO.
I acknowledge the WTO for permission to reprint quotations.

has endorsed developments only once they were already established. The tendency toward regional integrations and toward bilateral trade agreements has taken momentum away from the WTO in concluding new liberalization rounds. A blatant example of such a slowdown is the stagnation of the Doha Round that started in 2001 and was far from being concluded as of June 2008.

Unlike the IMF, where the quota and consequently the country's voting share has to be adjusted to the changing economic weight of countries as in the case of China, the consensus approach of the WTO allows the accommodation of structural economic shifts and geopolitical changes in the world economy. Thus, a newcomer to the club like China has to accept the existing rules of the game, but can eventually make its influence felt within the given institutional arrangement.

The World Trade Organization is not only about respecting rules but also about making them. In developing the rule system further, globalization represents a chal-

Table V.2. WTO voting rules.

Issue	Voting rule
Amendment concerning general principles	Unanimity
Interpretation of the provisions of the WTO and waivers of WTO discipline	Three-fourth's majority
Amendments to the WTO relating to issues other than general principles; accession	Two-third's majority
Themes not specified otherwise	Consensus

lenge to the international order. It accentuates the difference between the impact of structural change, experienced by the "man in the street," and its impact on the general rule system necessary to initiate long-term adjustment, for instance to the rise of emerging markets. Globalization requires structural change in all countries in order to enjoy the benefits of international trade. Even if we do not apply the Heckscher–Ohlin model (which predicts that the import-competing sectors in the developed countries will have to shrink), but rather adopt the intrasector trade model (where exchange occurs within a sector and where this sector does not necessarily have to contract), it is reasonable to predict that a supply shock due to a dramatic increase in the labor supply would affect the terms of trade for traditional or low-skilled labor in developed countries. This development exerts pressure on this type of labor, forcing it to adjust by improving its human capital. Without such structural adjustment, the benefits of globalization cannot be fully exploited. Globalization is therefore viewed by some as an economic threat, associated for instance with an increase in the uncertainty of jobs. Under such conditions, new rules for a globalized world are difficult to come by. A more intense exchange involves even the political risk of a backlash of protectionism if structural change is not mastered wisely in the nation states, especially in the developed countries. Protectionism brings the risk that well-established rules are given up.

An additional issue is more psychological. People need identification; they want a local mayor and feel safer when the responsibility for decision making rests with institutions they are closer to, such as regional or national government. But globalized rules are rather general in order to include many different cases. This is a similar problem as experienced within the European Union, where such concerns translate into the issue discussed under the term "distance from Brussels," and more generally under the expression "democratic void." This is why we pleaded in favor of the subsidiarity principle, making sure that important decisions are taken locally.

However, where it is necessary to reduce transaction costs, new rules have to be developed at a higher level.

The Role of the World Bank

In contrast to the World Trade Organization and the International Monetary Fund (to be discussed later), the World Bank, while being an international organization, does not represent the international expression of a system of rules. Its task is to promote economic development by providing loans and knowledge to developing countries with the stated goal of reducing poverty. Its mission is to reduce poverty and to push poorer countries and their inhabitants along the path of sustainable development, including the achievement of the UN Millennium Development Goals. It thus makes it possible for developing countries to participate in the international division of labor. Only when it extends credits is it rule setting.

The World Bank is an internationally supported bank helping countries develop a friendly environment for investment, job creation and sustainable economic growth. The core idea is that investing in and empowering the poor would enable them to participate in development. Originally, the World Bank was established in 1944 as the Bank for Reconstruction and Development. Its mission consisted of assisting the rebuilding of Europe after World War II. The focus of its mission later shifted to developing countries, when the International Development Association was created in 1960. There are two constituent parts of the World Bank: the International Bank for Reconstruction and Development, lending primarily to "middle-income countries" at interest rates which reflect a small mark-up over its own (AAA-rated) borrowings from capital markets, and the International Development Association, providing low-or-no-interest loans and grants to low income countries with little or no access to international credit markets.

International Competition Policy

An essential element of any market economy is that markets should not be exposed to the market power of single firms. Companies have a natural propensity to strive for a market-dominating position and, if possible, to exploit such a position by preventing competition and by setting prices to the disadvantage of buyers. If the behavior of firms remains unchecked by competition or antitrust policies, this kind of market failure can surface as an endogenous outcome of the market economy. To control the misuse of market power and to prevent firms from achieving monopolistic positions is therefore a crucial ingredient of market economies, as requested, for instance, by the German ordoliberals (Eucken 1940). Now that monopolistic behavior can turn international and firms can reach an even more powerful position than would be the case nationally, the challenge of competition policy moves from a national to an international dimension. In other words, competition policy can no longer be oriented toward national issues alone. Globalization changes the nature of competition policy. Besides globalization, new technologies, allowing, for instance, vertical forms of concentration in the IT industry through bundling, require new solutions in competition policy as the Microsoft case shows.

Competition policy relies on different philosophies in different regions of the world, and its approaches have changed over time. In Europe, where Germany introduced a competition law in 1957 which then became the model for the EU competition policy concerning the single market, the market-structure approach was, and still is, dominant. In this way of thinking, the decisive criterion is whether a firm has gained such a large market share that it can influence the market to its advantage. The underlying idea is that structure determines performance. The most important instruments of competition policy are to forbid mergers and acquisitions, to prohibit the misuse of pricing power and, if necessary, to break up monopolies. In the EU, an independent EU agency is vested with the power of competition policy in the single market; smaller cases and those of purely national interest remain in the hands of national competition authorities. In the United States, due to the influence of the Chicago school, competition policy has relied more on the concept of contestable markets, where the essential criterion is the intensity of competition. In this approach, the threat of market entry of a newcomer is an important element. In Japan, the Fair Trade Commission, established in 1947, followed a traditional approach to regulation before the 1990s that was not in line with modern principles of competition policy. One of the principal targets has been to prevent bid-rigging. Reforms have been undertaken in this decade. All of these approaches forbid cartels. The concept of competition policy has attracted interest internationally, with the number of competition authorities increasing from 31 in 1989 to 117 in 2008 (Bertrand and Ivaldi 2007, p. 160; American Trade Commission 2008).

Globalization makes markets more contestable, and in this sense free trade is the best competition policy. When market barriers disappear globally and markets widen, firms are exposed to more intense international competition. Therefore, all measures that improve market access support competition. But since firms will try to create positions of dominance in the global markets, competition policy cannot simply rely on markets becoming more open.

Traditionally, the territoriality principle meant that a country applied its domestic laws only to domestic companies. But in a quickly integrating international economy, such an approach was unrealistic even before the talk about globalization started. Thus, the EU's competition policy had to address the issue of the anticompetitive behavior of firms early on, incorporated outside the EU. The first step of this approach has been to consider European affiliates of foreign companies and their parent companies as an economic unit, i.e., as if the foreign parent company were acting within the EU. This means that decisions of the European competition agency can directly involve the foreign parent company. This concept of "unity" as a group of firms can be considered an interpretation or even an extension of the territoriality principle. Second, the extraterritoriality principle is applied to the anticompetitive behavior of foreign firms, whose effects are felt within the EU, even though these firms are not actually present inside the EU. Thus, in the 1969 Dyestuff case of price collusion among British and Swedish firms, eventually decided by the European Court of Justice in 1972, the European competition agency imposed fines even though the United Kingdom and Sweden were not EU members at that time (Klodt 2005, p. 47). In the Wood Pulp case on price collusion, the European Court of Justice upheld in 1988 that the EU competition agency was justified in claiming violation, since the violation only depended on the effects of the action and not on the location of the firms (Bertrand and Ivaldi 2007). This is known as the implementation doctrine (in Europe) or the effects doctrine (in the United States). The effects doctrine was borne in 1945 in the Alcoa decision of the United States Supreme Court which banned a price cartel formed in Switzerland for the U.S. market.

With the effects doctrine accepted as a basic element of competition policy, a major stumbling block in the application of the extraterritoriality principle will arise if, in the future, countries follow the policy of promoting national champions, a problem not only for competition policy, but also for trade policy. In no case should competition policy be oriented to the advantage of domestic firms or home-based multinationals; it should not be used to permit firms to build up or exploit monopolistic positions internationally. Competition policy should also oppose business practices aimed at reducing global competition. It should prevent the exploitation of market power and help improve the contestability of the world product markets.

It is evident that competition authorities of different countries can come to divergent conclusions with respect to anticompetitive behavior if they follow different philosophies. Moreover, given the increasing number of competition authorities, the likelihood of contradicting decisions being made by different authorities increases. To avoid this problem, some type of cooperation between authorities must take place. As one answer, bilateral agreements have evolved, in which countries agree on notification of anticompetitive practices elsewhere (when noticed by the authorities involved in the agreement) and on consultation. In addition, negative comity and positive comity represent two other mechanisms, aimed at extending the extraterritorial application of antitrust decisions; however, these mechanisms are not binding (Bertrand and Ivaldi 2007, p. 165). Negative comity means that an authority commits itself to consider the consequences of its actions on the authorities of other countries. Positive comity is a stronger concept, and it draws a distinction between a requesting party and a requested party. The authorities of the requesting party may ask the competition authorities of the requested party to investigate and, if warranted, to amend anticompetitive behavior in accordance with the requested party's competition laws (Article III, 1998 Agreement between the European Communities and the United States on the Application of the Principles of Positive Comity in the Implementation of their Competition Laws). This means that a country faced with a foreign firm's noncompetitive behavior can request that the authorities of the firm's country of origin remedy such noncompetition in accordance with its own competition law.

Bilateral cooperation between the EU and the United States began in 1995, including notification of cases, exchange of information and negative and positive comity, though nonbinding. However, such cooperation does not guarantee congruent decisions if the authorities apply different principles and if they represent different national interests. Thus, a conflict of interest arises between competition policy and industrial policy. Countries can in fact attempt to promote "national champions" (and Europe can endorse European champions); implement strategic trade policies, in order to create monopolistic positions; or shift rents from other countries toward national champions. In the past, transatlantic relations stumbled onto several similar cases. The merger of Boeing and McDonnell Douglas, for instance, was approved by the Federal Trade Commission while it clearly had an impact on the international market structure, affecting Airbus. The EU authorities could not prevent the merger, the main reason being the fear of a major trade conflict with the United States. The EU only obtained the acceptance of some minor conditions in 1997 (Klodt 2005, p. 53). On the contrary, the intended merger of General Electric and Honeywell was approved by the U.S. antitrust authority, but it was stopped by the competition policy of the EU in 2001. In yet another example of divergent interests and decisions, namely the Microsoft case, the EU laid heavy fines (497 million euros) on Microsoft, arguing that Microsoft had abused its dominant position by not providing interoperability information to its competitors. The European Court of Justice upheld this decision in 2007.

An attempt made by the EU in the 1990s to include a multilateral competition policy in the WTO and to add Trade-Related Antitrust Principles (TRAPS) to the world trade order has failed (Klodt 2005). GATT and the WTO have the task of reducing market barriers between countries and to improve market access for firms in the markets for both goods and services. This makes competition policy easier, because open markets are also more contestable. What is then needed is a less strict antitrust policy. In this sense, the trade order and competition policy are interrelated. Linking the two areas is also the fact that mergers and acquisitions distorting competition also distort trade. Thus, strategic trade policy—fostering national champions—represents a serious drawback for both institutional arrangements and the philosophy behind them; both aspects relate to the international product market. Of course, the WTO's dispute settlement procedure would be a welcome institutional arrangement for an international competition policy. In addition, the international economic order would be strengthened by a simple, easy-to-understand structure with separate institutional rules for the world's product markets—for border-crossing factor flows, for global environmental media, and for international financial stability. These are some of the reasons why the Havana Charter of 1948, the original draft sketching an economic frame of reference for the international product market after World War II, included competition policy in its Articles 46 and 50. The Charter, however, was not ratified by the U.S. Congress. In any case, the world trade order has undergone its own historic development, generating a path bound to shape the next steps of its institutional progress. An important consequence is that, besides all common features, competition policy means more than simply opening markets, so that its policy tools need to be quite different from the WTO's trade policy instruments. Competition policy must be able to forbid cartels, to prevent mergers and acquisitions if they threaten to create a dominating position, and to ban the misuse of price fixing and price collusion, including cartels. Furthermore, the argument that the international product market is the key issue is not a sufficient reason to assign competition policy to the WTO; the same argument also holds for environmental allocation.

An alternative approach is to look for multilateral agreements in the field of competition policy outside the WTO. An important example is competition policy within the European Union. Another is the International Competition Network, founded in 2001, and representing an informal multilateral cooperation framework which includes the United States and the EU as major players. It has now attracted more than eighty jurisdictions from OECD and non-OECD countries in addition to international organizations such as the OECD, the United Nations Conference on Trade and Development (UNCTAD), and the WTO (Hoekman et al. 2005; Bertrand and Ivaldi 2007). This framework seeks to cooperate on a voluntary basis, to share information and to reduce conflict, representing a rather soft way of coordination. The International Competition Network does not exercise any rule-making function. When the network reaches consensus on recommendations or "best practices," arising from the exchange of ideas, individual competition authorities decide whether and how to implement them through unilateral, bilateral, or multilateral arrangements, as is deemed appropriate. Such an arrangement may lead to less conflicting, universally accepted rules at some point in the future.

Competition policy still has to answer some relevant questions: should countries rely on the recognition of mutual competencies, i.e., should institutional rules be mutually recognized? Should international competition law ("hard law") be harmonized? Should a country harmed by another country's competition and antitrust policy have the right to obtain changes in the objectionable policy or not? Should an International Competition Agency be established and granted the right to file a complaint in the courts of the country where anticompetitive behavior occurs? Should a party hit by the anticompetitive practices of a foreign-based firm or by the competition policies of an authority of a foreign country have a right to bring its case before an international court or an international competition authority, empowered to enforce competition rules (Scherer 1994)?

Presently, it is not foreseeable that a more binding multilevel rule system of competition policy will be established which can effectively restrict the misuse of monopolistic market positions and discourage competition-limiting mergers. Such an arrangement could include some basic common principles of competition policy as minimum rules and a dispute settlement procedure. Alternatively, an international court whose verdicts would be binding could be agreed upon. Such a rule system might, for instance, act as an interface between the major product markets of the EU, the United States, and Japan. This arrangement would then come to represent a competition policy club (Klodt 2005). It should be open to new members. Surely such a system could only include less formal rules than those adopted within the EU. However, as long as economic conditions differ widely between countries of the world and as long as fundamental variations in legal systems exist, as in the case of Anglo-Saxon and continental European law, one size cannot fit all. The concept of fiscal federalism rather suggests that competition law should be tailored according to the political, cultural, and historical environment of each country. A world cartel office or a global competition authority remains beyond our imagination. Most importantly, it is most likely to prove inefficient.

VI
Rules for Border-Crossing Factor Movements

Whether rules for international factor movements are necessary depends on which role border-crossing factor mobility plays in the international division of labor. It can be argued that the need for rules increases together with the mobility of factors, unless factor mobility can be considered to be a normal affair that can be left to the market. Factor movements include capital flows as well as the relocation of firms, the flow of technology, and the migration of people. These movements are driven by different economic opportunities for factors in different countries, i.e., different rates of returns to capital and technology and different real wages for labor. Such differences stem from cross-country divergence in factor endowment, production possibilities and demand conditions. Factor movements then take place if these differences overcompensate the costs and risks associated with factor mobility.

Factor endowment is not a given constant. Countries can accumulate factors of production, for instance by building up their capital stock, developing their technology, increasing their workforce and improving their human capital. They can also try to attract mobile factors by adopting appropriate institutional arrangements, taxes, and infrastructure in the widest sense, including the education system and the universities. Consequently, countries engage in locational competition for mobile capital, technological knowledge, and qualified labor.

Rules for Capital Movements

Similarly to rules for trade, rules for capital flows play the role of allowing benefits for the world economy as well as for countries which export and import capital. In the world economy, these benefits are possible when capital can move across the borders to its most efficient use. Hence, world GDP will rise.

Countries' Benefits from Capital Flows

A capital-exporting country can secure a higher income by investing abroad rather than at home, if marginal capital productivity, F_K, is larger abroad, $F_K^* > F_K$ (an asterisk denoting the foreign country), or if the real interest rate in the world capital market (r^W) is higher than productivity at home, $r^W > F_K$. Moreover, capital exports allow consumption smoothing over time. For instance, a society facing an aging population can invest abroad today in order to enjoy a higher income in old age. At the same time, the capital-importing country enjoys the benefit of accumulating capital earlier than would be possible by means of its own savings, i.e., $F_K^* > r^W$. The country can therefore produce more. Its labor is equipped with more capital so that labor productivity increases. For instance, the United States imported capital in the nineteenth century in order to build up its capital stock; today China and other emerging countries enjoy an advantage from foreign direct investment. In addition, consumption smoothing in a capital-importing country can prevent the impact of a severe economic downturn or a natural disaster. These arguments resemble those that apply to the gains from trade. Capital flows exploit differences in countries' characteristics, such as age structure of the population, savings behavior, investment opportunities and risk profiles. Moreover, capital flows bring about technology transfer and can increase the competitiveness of the capital-importing country.

In contrast to this theoretical picture, international border-crossing capital flows only amount to less than one-tenth of world gross investment, the overwhelming part coming from national savings. This is due to the fact that capital markets are segmented by institutional arrangements. Nevertheless, individual countries may succeed in financing up to 50% of their gross investment in specific periods, for instance Hungary in 1995 (Siebert 2007e). Institutional conditions also hinder foreign capital from reaching a country. According to the Lucas paradox, the marginal product of capital in India was supposed to have been fifty-eight times higher than in the United States (in 1998), yet the flow of capital did not correspond to this difference (Lucas 1990).

When we speak of rules for capital flows, we mean the rules affecting *real* capital flows, i.e., of the allocation of savings and foreign direct investment, and not portfolio flows. Portfolio flows require their own rules. Admittedly, real capital flows and portfolio flows are interrelated; for instance bonds and credits may pave the way for foreign direct investment. But the main goal of the rules for portfolio flows is granting financial stability (see chapter VIII).

Competing for the Mobile Capital

To shelter the benefits from capital flows, rules regulating them should be based on a competitive order. According to this paradigm, it is reasonable that countries compete for the mobile capital through tax and institutional competition and try to become more attractive for mobile capital (see chapter III; Siebert 2006a).[1] Govern-

---

[1] Krugman's statement (1994, p. 41) that competitiveness is "a largely meaningless concept" is a serious misjudgment of the profession.

ments can influence the attractiveness of a location by improving or extending the supply of public goods, by providing infrastructure in the fields of transportation and education, by improving soft location factors, by means of taxation, and by introducing institutional regulations. Their task is to find an optimal mix of policy instruments in their cost–benefit calculus of locational competition. A large part of the competition among locations takes place in the form of institutional competition within the regulatory framework, determining the way things must be done in a society. These institutional rules can be formal norms, such as constitutional requirements, modes of collective bargaining or the procedure of licensing firms, production processes and products, as well as informal aspects involving noncodified, habitual behavior. Locational competition can then be interpreted as a useful mechanism to control the efficiency of governments and as a discovery device in the sense of Hayek (1968): competing for mobile factors puts pressure on countries to find new solutions, be they new institutional arrangements or new technological horizons. Competition stimulates the imagination and intensifies the effort to find solutions. Moreover, in this view, the technological or institutional solutions employed in different locations can be explicitly compared. Seeing positive or negative examples from elsewhere may encourage a country to do better. One aspect is that countries can mimic approaches already used successfully elsewhere. This is why "benchmarking" has become a key concept in the reform programs of several continental states in Europe. Note, however, that the benchmarking strategy does not entail the search for new institutional frontiers.

To ban capital invested in a country as well as domestic savings from leaving a country has severe negative consequences and provides false incentives in the long run. National income and the income of capital owners will be reduced. The country forgoes the option of consumption smoothing. Residents are less motivated to save and accumulate capital. They also experience an incentive toward capital flight, which may take place concealed in the form of underinvoicing their exports while receiving shadow side payments from their export partners. Foreign direct investment is less inclined to flow in according to the economic law that an exit constraint from the market also represents an entry constraint. If the risk of expropriation or the risk of a severe increase in business taxes is anticipated, foreign direct investment is unlikely to be forthcoming.[2] Moreover, uncertainty for investment may cause uncertainty in trade. Each country should therefore structure its institutional framework for saving and investment in such a way that domestic capital wants to stay and foreign capital wants to enter. To this end, states must provide secure property rights, avoid uncertainty about expropriation and increases in corporate taxes, and develop a tax system and a general economic framework that make the country less risky and more attractive for foreign direct investments.

---

[2] In the case of Chile, severe entry conditions even for portfolio capital requiring a non-interest-bearing deposit of 30% had a negative effect on the inflow of equity capital and had to be given up. Malaysia's entry constraints of 1998 for portfolio capital could only be used temporarily.

It may be argued that it is the host country's own responsibility and concern to enhance its attractiveness, and that this is not a matter for international rules. However, it is helpful to have an investment code in order to minimize disruptions in the international division of labor. For instance, countries may impose performance requirements for foreign direct investments such as local content rules. Or, they may change the rules of taxation and other regulations after foreign investment has entered the country, so that firms face a holdup problem. A crucial aspect is that investment uncertainty should not spill over to trade. In order to prevent a negative externality from investment flows to trade, an institutional rule for Trade-Related Investment Measures (TRIMs) is needed.

Trade-Related Investment Measures

The TRIMs agreement, in effect since 1995, prevents countries from making the approval of investment conditional on compliance with laws or administrative regulations that favor domestic products. It addresses trade-related investment measures that violate Article III (National Treatment) or Article XI (general elimination of quantitative restrictions) of GATT. Violations are not clearly defined, but rather are explained by means of an illustrative list. Once notified to the WTO, existing obstacles must be eliminated during a transition period. New WTO members agree to eliminate existing obstacles. Note that the Enabling Clause gives developing countries some flexibility. Nevertheless, sometimes even the original ASEAN countries still use performance requirements with respect to their FDI. GATS includes the establishment of a firm in a foreign country as a mode of supply. This provision can be developed further and significant commitments can be made on the basis of this provision.

TRIMs is not sufficient to improve capital mobility. In addition, rules should allow the repatriation of capital and profits and make foreign direct investments more secure for the sending country. These rules should extend beyond trade-related investment measures and can make a country more reliable, for instance by protecting foreign direct investments against expropriation in the case of a change in government. A two-speed approach might prove useful for the development of an investment code, with the OECD countries going ahead and the WTO following. In any case, an investment code should be administered eventually by the WTO. Up to now, the WTO has not made progress beyond TRIMs.

An attempt by the OECD to establish a Multilateral Agreement on Investment (MAI) among twenty-nine OECD countries, liberalizing investment flows and including a most-favored-nation clause as well as a dispute settlement procedure failed in 1998 after France decided to abandon the negotiations (Hoekman and Saggi 1999). The main concern was that the agreement would have weakened the countries' authority to pursue regulatory policies vis-à-vis foreign firms. The real issue, however, was that foreign firms would have been granted compensation. Actually, bilateral agreements are in place between high-income countries and developing countries, dealing with the issue of foreign direct investment. Moreover, regional integrations such as the EU and NAFTA have developed their own rules for foreign direct investment which may eventually set standards for international real capital flows. As in other areas of the international division of labor, bilateral investment treaties take the place of multilateral arrangements. It is estimated that their number amounts to more than 2,500.

Private Equity and Hedge Funds

A major concern relating to foreign direct investment is the fear of foreign infiltration or even foreign domination. Some fear that foreign economic interests rather than domestic economic interests may play the decisive role. This concern casts doubt upon the economic benefits of free international capital markets. Meanwhile, capital markets are integrated globally; in the euro area and also in the European Union, deepening the capital market is a deliberate aim of integration. For instance, in the major thirty German stock companies listed on the Frankfurt stock exchange (DAX companies) with widespread and dispersed ownership, the majority is now owned by foreign stock holders, not only from the euro area. After all, this brings advantages to the firms, such as the access to foreign capital—making them more independent from national financing constraints—and the possible exposure to foreign technology. Thus, firms can become more competitive. These benefits outweigh, at least in part, the risk that foreign investors, for instance the Chinese, will siphon off technological knowledge. However, concerns about foreign infiltration usually attract public attention. For instance, opposition against American foreign direct investment ran high in the late 1960s in France (Servan-Schreiber 1967), but has remained more or less a permanent concern.

Another worry is that private equity and hedge funds have shortsighted interests. They buy up firms, restructure them and sell them again in order to make a profit. If they succeed in exploiting the restructuring potential, their action represents an efficiency gain for the economy. It cannot be ruled out that private equity and hedge funds load up the firms they bought with credits and manage to find buyers for the credit-loaded firms in the market, for instance in a merger hype. Admittedly, this represents a degeneration of the market process. However, the price to pay in order to prevent such deterioration is to close a country off from foreign equity and foreign direct investment. The fact that credits to equity funds and hedge funds given by banks must show up in the balance sheets of these banks, where they should be consolidated, is a different story; this issue relates to financial stability. A related major concern is that foreign capital drives out labor by requiring a more efficient organization. In the long run, however, jobs are sustainable only if matched with a sufficient amount of capital. If not, workers will not be equipped with new capital and new technology. Then jobs will not persist. Therefore, capital mobility does not go against labor in the long run. In conclusion, private foreign direct investors should receive equal treatment to domestic investors.

Sovereign Wealth Funds

Another key concern is that foreign political interests can come into conflict with national political interests, and may eventually clash with national policy. This is a relevant question when foreign state-controlled agencies, namely sovereign wealth funds, act as foreign investors. Such wealth funds do not represent a matter of concern if they follow pure economic interests, for instance, when a country just wants to reinvest its current account surpluses, such as its oil surpluses. It does not make sense to limit surplus countries to accumulate currency reserves or to channel the reserves into the international liquidity of the banking system. Of course, prudence is required; remember that the debt crisis of the developing countries in the 1980s was the result of petrodollar recycling in the financial markets. Moreover, sovereign wealth funds do not present a problem if they seek to optimize their returns on accumulated assets and spread their risks. They are also less of a concern when they invest in bonds and other portfolio capital instead of buying equity or investing directly in firms. And they do not represent a major problem if they strictly follow the target of consumption smoothing when investing in real estate and equity.

However, it is realistic to take into consideration the fact that foreign governments have political interests beyond the economic domain. Then the issue becomes trickier. State agencies can be instrumentalized by strategic foreign policy interests and a country may get into the position of being held to ransom by sovereign wealth funds and their governments. If this is the case, even bonds may be used opportunistically. For instance, right-wing Japanese politicians in the late 1980s and early 1990s were in favor of using the country's stock of U.S. bonds as a policy weapon; a similar threat is frequently heard (although not officially, so far) in Chinese political circles. Indeed, foreign policy conflicts between states may interfere with the economic situation and may threaten the sovereignty of a nation state. Therefore, rules for foreign direct investments by state-controlled agencies are desirable in areas where national sovereignty is at stake.

In order to determine where rules are needed (and where they are acceptable) it is important to know the size and the type of state-controlled foreign direct investors. Sovereign wealth funds or gold sovereigns were estimated to hold assets of US$3 trillion in 2007, mainly coming from the international reserves of oil countries and Asian economies (table VI.1). Estimates put the assets of sovereign wealth funds in 2012 at US$10 trillion; in the financial crisis of 2008, some assets have melted away.

About three-fourths of all sovereign fund assets belong to oil countries, above all in the Middle East (US$1.6 trillion), Brunei, and Norway (US$0.3 trillion). Australia's fund, too, is future oriented; this also holds for Temasek Holdings, which

Table VI.1.   Sovereign wealth funds and assets (March 2007).

Country	Fund	Assets ($bn)	Inception (year)
UAE	ADIA	875	1976
Singapore	GIC	330	1981
Saudi Arabia	Saudi Arabian funds of various types	433	N.a.
Norway	Government Pension Fund: Global	300	1990
China	State Foreign Exchange Investment Corporation and Central Huijin[a]	300	2007
Singapore	Temasek Holdings	1,340	1974
Kuwait	Kuwait Investment Authority	264	1953
Australia	Australian Future Fund	40	2004
U.S. (Alaska)	Alaska Permanent Fund Corporation	40	1976
Russia	Stabilization Fund	30	2008
Brunei	Brunei Investment Agency	30	1983
South Korea	Korea Investment Corporation	30	2005

[a]Not yet finalized.
Source: Morgan Stanley (2007); Sovereign Wealth Funds Institute (2008).

manages the Singapore government's direct investment, both locally and overseas; this is commercially oriented. It is most likely that all these funds have an overwhelming interest in economic returns. The same partly applies to the new fund of US$300 billion, started by China in 2007, although its focus will be on the acquisition of technology and access to natural resources as well. Russia's stabilization fund only accounts for US$30 billion; other data indicate higher values. Admittedly, government-controlled Russian firms can also act as foreign direct investors.

Rules to defend national sovereignty should not be a catchall for protectionism against foreign direct investment. Such rules should be restricted to specific areas. These areas include national security,[3] in particular military equipment, and energy; national security justifies more restrictions than energy. In the energy sector itself, production, transportation networks, i.e., electricity and gas networks, and distribution facilities have to be distinguished, again justifying different degrees of control. Telecommunications, where competition prevails, definitely need significantly less protection; monopolistic behavior can be checked by competition policy. Infrastructures such as railroads, sea ports, and major national airports are already partly controlled by governmental authorities anyway. In the energy area, not all foreign direct investment of sovereign funds should be disallowed. For instance,

---

[3] As an example, consider the U.S. Foreign Investment and National Security Act of 2007, which sets up the process by which the United States government reviews and consequently approves or disallows "covered transactions." These transactions involve U.S. companies acquired by foreign entities. In the reviewing process, it must be decided whether the transaction involves a threat to national security (Adams and Reese, LLL 2007).

cross-foreign direct investment between the European Union and Russia—i.e., EU investment in Russia's upstream activities and Russian foreign direct investment in the EU's downstream activities—may well represent a solution of mutual interest. Also, conditions can be set to limit the political influence of foreign direct investment, for instance in the energy sector, to capital ownership without operational influence, one example being nonvoting shares. Moreover, strategic economic behavior of foreign direct investment can be controlled by policy instruments such as competition policy and regulation, for instance network or banking regulation.

It is important that limits to foreign direct investment do not extend to sectors beyond those mentioned. They should not apply to sectors where domestic players simply seek economic protection against foreign competitors in the capital market. This means that policy instruments encompassing all the sectors of the economy should not be used. For instance, national governments should not introduce a regulation whereby they arrogate the general right to license foreign sovereign funds to engage in buying up domestic firms. Nor should governments retain a general right to be informed of all foreign direct investments by sovereign wealth funds, notwithstanding which sector is concerned. Political risks would be reduced if sovereign wealth funds invested through intermediary asset managers interested in risk management, as in the case of pension funds (Summers 2007).

France has set up its own defensive sovereign wealth fund in November 2008, endowed with 20 billion euros. It is intended to come to the help of national champions by acquiring part of their shares, i.e., partly nationalizing them as was done with some banks in the financial crisis in 2008. The Sarkozy plan to set up national defensive funds in the European countries runs counter to the concept of the international division of labor. It entails the risk that such protective measures will spill over to the trade system, with similar consequences as the disintegration of the world economy that were experienced in the 1930s after the Great Depression.

An international rule system for foreign direct investment of sovereign wealth funds should limit itself to a few sectors and should avoid including many sectors that simply seek protection. Bilateral reciprocity, i.e., to open up only those sectors that are also opened up abroad, is too weak an approach to be used as a foundation for an international rule system. In the EU, decision makers should take care that a general rule in this area does not follow the French doctrine of state intervention and the reluctance of Italy and Spain to open their markets to foreign direct investment. It is in the interest of sovereign wealth funds to prevent obstacles to their foreign direct investment. In this spirit, an international working group, representing twenty-six sovereign wealth funds, has developed guidelines for the October 2008 meeting for the IMF's policy-setting committee: the Santiago Principles.

An institution for arbitration devoted to investor–state dispute settlement is the International Center for the Settlement of Investment Disputes, which is part of the World Bank Group. It has 155 members.

Rules for Technology

Global rules for the area of technology have to make sure that all countries and the world as a whole can benefit from technological knowledge. This means that the rules have to define sufficient incentives so that new technological knowledge is produced as invention and applied as innovation. Such an arrangement is crucial, since modern economies can no longer be described only as industrial economies and service economies, but also as knowledge economies, namely economies where knowledge plays an important role for growth. In such an environment, it is essential to extend the technological frontier of the world and of individual countries. This emerging phenomenon for the world economy raises the question as to whether new rules are needed that allow countries to reap benefits from this new development. A question also arises as to whether the knowledge economy needs different rules from those which apply to the industrial society.

Knowledge, including technological knowledge, can have different properties: it can be a private good, available only to an individual or to an individual organization, for instance a firm, or it may be a public good that can be used in equal amounts by all. Instead of a public good we may also speak of a free access good, since knowledge may be used differently by different individuals. Examples of a private good are information available to one person only, an individual invention, or an investment by a firm on the basis of a specific technology. Examples of knowledge as a public good are the results of basic research, for instance of university research institutes, where the understanding is that such knowledge should be available to all researchers worldwide. The lines between knowledge as a private and as a public good are not clear-cut. Thus, states may attempt to design their diffusion process from basic knowledge to applied knowledge such that the basic knowledge remains within their national borders, specifically within their enterprise sector. In contrast, the results of basic research may be patentable so that they become private goods. Private firms may undertake basic research as a precondition to find inventions that they can apply in innovations, keeping the results to themselves.

Besides intrinsic motivation—for instance, the motivation of a scientist to become famous or to improve the conditions of humankind—the core of the incentive issue in decentralized economies is which incentive the rule system provides for the individual inventor to find a new technology and for an innovating firm to invest in a new technology. The inventor is rewarded with the intellectual property right to his invention; the firm is protected against imitation if it has obtained the property right to a new technological idea from the inventor or through its own research.

Property rights usually belong to individuals, firms, and, possibly, public corporations such as universities, but not to states. Property rights are usually territorial in nature, defined by national laws, and subject to national enforcement. They relate to all sorts of intellectual property: patents, copyright and associated rights, industrial design, the layout designs of integrated circuits, trademarks, and geographical indications (like appellations of origin). They represent exclusive rights given to the creator over the use of his or her creation for a limited period of time. The owner of a patent, copyright, or other form of intellectual property right is given the right to prevent others from using his inventions, designs, or other creations—and to use that right to negotiate payment in return for others wanting to use his invention, i.e., issuing a license.

Patents cover inventions. Most of the values of high-technology products, including new medicines, lies in the amount of invention, innovation, research, design, and testing involved. Patents must be available for both products and processes, in almost all fields of technology. If a patent is issued for a production process, then the right must extend to the product directly obtained from the process. Copyright and associated rights are granted to authors of literary and artistic work and performers, producers of phonograms, and broadcasting organizations. Thus, books, paintings, and films are protected by copyright. Industrial design rights offer property protection for the visual design of objects. Industrial design is supposed to improve the aesthetics and usability of products for marketing, brand development, and sales purposes. Layout design rights shield the layout of semiconductors and integrated circuits. Trademarks extend to brand names and product logos, being used to uniquely identify the source of a product or service. Geographical indications such as "champagne," "scotch," and "gorgonzola" cheese are place-names that identify a product's special characteristics, which are the result of the product's origins.

These intellectual property rights differ markedly from the ownership of assets, for instance stocks and bonds, and from the ownership of physical capital such as machines, enterprises, and land. These traditional property rights have an unlimited duration. In contrast, institutional rules in the area of technology cannot be granted for an unlimited time, since this would allow the owner of the property right to have a monopolistic market position and to exploit the demand side of the market. This interest conflicts with the need to secure user rights for new technological knowledge, lest there would be an insufficient incentive for potential inventors to search for new technologies. There would also be a weak motivation for an innovator to acquire the patent and adopt the new technological knowledge within an investment. National patent systems as well as international arrangements have to balance the two diverging interests. Aspects that represent guidelines to find an answer to this issue for the different types of property rights are: the lengths of the product life cycles, the time frame of research and development phases, and the extent to which a monopolistic position can arise and other market participants can be damaged.

Patents are usually granted for twenty years. Copyrights for many works are determined by the life of the author plus either fifty or seventy years in most of the world. In the United States, new works are protected for seventy years after the death of the author and ninety-five years for firms after publication or 120 years after creation, whichever endpoint is earlier (Copyright Term Extension Act). Producers of sound recordings have the right to prevent the unauthorized reproduction of recordings for a period of fifty years. Industrial designs and layout designs of integrated circuits are protected for at least ten years (according to TRIPS). In the IT industry, product life is short with a half-life of a year and less. Nevertheless, computer software is protected under the Bern Convention as literary works and copyright is extended to computerized data bases (see below). Another aspect of copyright is the provision of rental rights, allowing the authors of computer programs (as of sound recordings) the right to authorize or prohibit their commercial rental to the public. Semiconductors are protected under the layout designs of integrated circuits protection (for at least ten years).

Other types of property right, such as trademarks and geographical indications, do not protect knowledge as a good. Their aim is to allow product differentiation and to provide information to the consumer. Although these measures may serve protectionist vested interests in international trade, it is impractical to let protection run out. Trademarks are diluted when the use of similar or identical trademarks in other noncompeting areas robs them of their original capacity. Geographical indications usually hold for a long time unless the identity of the product is watered down.

Conventions

Economists could sit down at a drawing board and develop a rule system for the global economy, looking for the ideal incentive structure fitting such a system, as they focus on the crucial goal of extending the technological frontier of individual countries and of the world. Instead of such a constructionist top-down approach, it is more promising to study how national intellectual property rights have been established and how elements of a global system have developed in a Hayekian way, namely from below. Patents represent the most important case.

In a world where many national patent systems are in place, national procedures are likely to diverge. Under such conditions, an individual inventor has to apply for a patent at each national patent office, following the national procedures in each country separately. Since extraterritoriality does not apply to patent law, the inventor has to seek protection for his invention in all countries if he wants to be protected. He has to procure patents in all these countries. In addition, an innovator does not have the certainty of exclusive use. Again, a patent is only guaranteed within a country. A series of international conventions ease this problem.

The Paris Convention (1883) established the very important right of priority in the area of patents and industrial design. According to the Convention, the filing date of the first application applies as the actual filing date for later applications in other national systems. The Bern Convention of September 1886, amended several times until 1979, protects literary and artistic work. The Rome Convention, signed in 1961, protects performers, producers of phonograms, and broadcasting organizations. The

Patent Cooperation Treaty, concluded in 1970 and in force since 1978, makes it possible to streamline certain procedures of a patent application. The treaty counts 137 members as of July 2007 (among them are all the members of the European Patent Convention). In this context, the World Intellectual Property Organization, with its administrative arm, the International Bureau, seated in Geneva, was founded in 1967 and came into force in 1970; it turned into a specialized agency of the UN in 1974. It supervises the enforcement of such treaties as the Paris and Bern conventions and its function is to promote intellectual property protection. The Patent Cooperation Treaty allows the centralization of the procedures of a patent application. The applicant only needs to file a single patent application, in which he designates all the countries in which patent protection is sought. The World Intellectual Property Organization collects and controls the patent application. The organization then appoints one of the major patent offices in the world, usually the U.S. Patent and Trademark Office, the European Patent Office, or the Japanese Patent Office, as the international search authority which has to perform the literature search. The International Bureau then prepares a report, which has the role of an opinion and is not binding. After a successful search, the applicant can continue the procedure at the national offices of the countries he designated. He has up to thirty months for this. In spite of this easing of the procedure, the national examiners apply their own country's national standards for patentability.

The European Patent Convention, concluded in 1973, established the European Patent Organization and the European Patent Office. It provides a unique application procedure for individual inventors and firms seeking patent protection for up to thirty-four countries. An applicant files a single European patent application and designates the countries in Europe in which he wants to have patent protection. The European Patent Office performs a novelty search and prepares a search report. This procedure must be performed only once, regardless of how many countries were designated. The Examining Division then determines the patentability of the invention. If a European patent is granted, the applicant enjoys the same rights in all designated countries as would have been granted in the case of separate national applications. Non-EU members, too, can be party to the European Patent Convention. Consequently, a European patent effectively grants its owner national patents in every country that is party to the European Patent Convention (or those countries the owner designated). Once a European Patent has been granted, anyone has the right to oppose it within nine months after grant. If the patent is then found to be invalid, it is revoked in all countries simultaneously. After these nine months, the patent can only be revoked separately in each country in which it was granted. In particular, a European patent can only be declared invalid by a court in one country for that specific country. This means that someone wanting to invalidate a European patent that was granted in eighteen countries must start eighteen separate court proceedings. Note that Europe does not have an equivalent of the United States Court of Appeals for the Federal Circuit, which means that in principle every country can rule differently on patent matters, although some restrictions apply.

These patent conventions show that, historically, institutional rules tend to converge to some extent toward some common principles and mutual recognition. Also, one or several dominating models may take the lead.

An alternative to formal conventions such as international treaties are corporations in the special form of nonprofit public benefit corporations. ICANN (Internet Corporation for Assigned Names and Numbers) is an example of such a corporation. It is responsible for the global coordination of the Internet's system of unique identifiers. These include domain names (like org, museum, and country codes like uk) as well as the addresses used in a variety of Internet protocols. Computers use these identifiers to reach each other over the Internet. Careful management of these resources is vital to the web's functioning, so ICANN's global stakeholders meet regularly to develop policies to ensure the Internet's ongoing security and stability.

Trade-Related Aspects of Intellectual Property Rights

In spite of these efforts to streamline patent rules internationally, differences in national intellectual property rights have represented a source of recurrent friction in international trade; creators of intellectual property and firms using intellectual property in innovations were not protected. The situation created a major distortion in the international division of labor. The WTO's TRIPS agreement (Trade-Related Aspects of Intellectual Property Rights), introduced after the Uruguay Round in 1995, is an attempt to narrow the gaps in the countries' intellectual property rights, and to establish minimum levels of protection that each government has to grant to the intellectual property of fellow WTO members. In substance, patent protection is to be provided for at least twenty years for nearly all inventions, including processes and products. This provision implies harmonization to the standards of industrial countries. Members may choose to allow more protection above these minimum standards as long as this does not contravene the provisions of the agreement. They can also determine the method they want to use. WTO members must also comply with the main conventions of the World Intellectual Property Organization. This is why TRIPS is sometimes called "Bern and Paris Plus." Besides minimum standards of protection, enforcement of intellectual property rights and WTO dispute settlement on these rules are the main ingredients of the arrangement.

The TRIPS agreement starts from the basic principles of the trading system, namely nondiscrimination, national treatment (treating one's own nationals and foreigners equally), and most-favored-nation treatment (equal treatment for nationals of all trading partners in the WTO). The TRIPS agreement follows an additional important principle: intellectual property protection should contribute to technical innovation and to the transfer of technology.

The TRIPS agreement is integrated into the WTO. TRIPS is steered by the TRIPS Council, which comprises all WTO members. The council is responsible for monitoring the operation of the agreement, for instance how members comply with their obligation. Countries must notify their own domestic laws to the TRIPS council. TRIPS being part of the WTO, the WTO's dispute settlement system is now available when trade disputes over intellectual property rights arise. This is a major improvement compared with GATT, where no specific agreement on intellectual property rights existed except for some principles having indirect consequences on such rights. TRIPS requires WTO member governments to ensure that intellectual property rights are enforced under their laws, and that the penalties for infringement are harsh enough to deter further violations. The agreement describes in some detail how enforcement should be handled, including rules for obtaining evidence, provisional measures, injunctions, damages, and other penalties. Wilful trademark counterfeiting or copyright piracy on a commercial scale should be considered criminal offences. Governments should make sure that intellectual property rights owners can receive the assistance of customs authorities to prevent imports of counterfeit and pirated goods.

The agreement contains provisions for specific areas. Thus, it ensures that computer programs will be protected as literary works under the Bern Convention; it also protects databases as copyright and expands international copyright rules to cover rental rights. The agreement defines what types of signs are eligible for protection as trademarks. It protects integrated circuit designs ("topographies"); the basis for this in the TRIPS agreement is the Washington Treaty on Intellectual Property in Respect of Integrated Circuits, under the authority of the World Intellectual Property Organization.

The TRIPS agreement allows certain exceptions. Among them is the compulsory licensing and government use of a patent without the authorization of its owner under certain conditions, such as a patent owner abusing his rights, for example by failing to supply the product on the market. Then, a government can issue compulsory licenses, allowing a competitor to produce the product or use the licensed process. Members are also allowed to exclude some types of plant and animal inventions from patenting in their countries, namely to exclude from patentability "plants and animals other than micro-organisms, and essentially biological processes for the production of plants or animals other than nonbiological and microbiological processes." Plant varieties, however, must be protectable by patents or by a special system such as the breeder's rights provided in the conventions of the International Union for the Protection of New Varieties of Plants.

National technology policy is affected by the international subsidy code. In this code, limits should be set for industry-specific research subsidies in order to prevent international distortions though subsidies. In contrast, there is no need for controlling the improvement of the general conditions for research and development, for example, when countries introduce more favorable tax conditions for research and development, innovation, investment, and entrepreneurial activity, as well as when they organize basic research and foster technology transfer in order to boost their international competitiveness.

Developing Countries and Intellectual Property Rights

It is heavily debated whether poverty- and disease-stricken developing countries should enjoy preferential access to advanced technology and products. The issue is not a general privilege for all advanced technology and for all advanced products but a limited right to use medicine against major illnesses at lower costs, for instance against malaria or HIV. This is the issue of technology transfer. In principle, flexibility clauses such as compulsory licensing are written into the TRIPS agreement, but there is uncertainty with respect to their interpretation.

WTO ministers agreed at the Doha Ministerial Conference in November 2001 that the TRIPS agreement does not and should not prevent members from taking measures to protect public health. They agreed to extend exemptions on pharmaceutical patent protection for the least developed countries until 2016. Developing countries have until 2016 to ensure that their laws and practices conform to the TRIPS for pharmaceutical patents. A waiver allowing countries that are unable to produce pharmaceuticals domestically to import patented drugs made under compulsory licensing was approved on August 30, 2003.

Moreover, the TRIPS agreement includes a number of provisions on technology transfer which developing countries value as an important part of the bargain to protect intellectual property rights. For example, the agreement requires developed countries' governments to provide incentives for their companies to transfer technology to the least developed countries. Another issue is the diffusion of new abatement technology, which helps reduce emissions at the most efficient spot. In this case, it is in the direct self-interest of developed countries to spread the technology in order to reduce abatement costs.

Still, beside waivers it is to some extent unclear what the general guidelines in this debate are. One answer is that firms must provide products at a low or zero price to developing countries, especially when it comes to pharmaceuticals. Then firms would act according to the principle of social responsibility, but outside the market. A different answer is that supporting developing countries is a political issue of development aid and that it is the role of governments in the developed countries and not of firms to finance aid, including medical aid.

It is debated whether developing countries have an interest in choosing lower standards compared with developed countries. If this holds, it is argued that TRIPS requires the developing countries to harmonize the standards upward (Panagariya 1999). Therefore, some observers point out that TRIPS is not beneficial for developing countries and should not be included in the WTO. Some even claim that the WTO has turned "into a glorified collection agency" (Bhagwati 2005). My position is that the rule system for technology is a determinant of the technological frontier of the world. Lower standards would reduce the incentive to shift the global technological frontier outward (see also Maskus 2000). The world would experience a lower technological performance if lower standards were chosen.

Rules for Migration

Rules for the migration of people have the role of allowing an increase in welfare for individuals, for the world economy, and for individual countries. The structure of the problem is similar to that of capital movements. Migrants gain by moving to a place where they have higher labor productivity. The world gains from labor moving to places where its use is most efficient. The welfare gains with respect to individual countries vary. The country receiving workers enjoys an increase in its GDP; capital income there rises whereas immigration reduces the initial wage rate. The country of emigration experiences a decline of GDP; capital income there declines whereas the wage rate increases due to higher labor scarcity. Usually the country of emigration loses the most valuable and dynamic people, i.e., its human capital, including scientists and entrepreneurs who are necessary for its development. Note that the impact on real factor prices also comes about through trade, as countries specialize in the production and export of labor-intensive and capital-intensive goods.

Except for freedom migration (fleeing from political suppression) and famine migration (due to the risk of starvation), the movement of people is driven by income differences. The migrant applies an intertemporal utility- or income-maximizing approach. He deliberately or subconsciously maximizes the present value of utility or income for the remaining years of his life or for a chosen period. If the present value of income is higher at the new location relative to the old one, he will move. The migrant is likely to consider other variables such as the risk of becoming unemployed, either at the new or the old location. Moreover, the "option value of waiting" enters the picture. If a potential migrant expects the situation at his old location to worsen over time, the option value of waiting is negative and there is a greater incentive to migrate. If he expects the situation at his old location to improve, the option value of waiting is positive and the incentive to migrate is accordingly lower. Thus, the option value corrects the income difference. Thresholds in income differences also play a role: only a sizable income difference can stimulate migration. This rule applies independently of whether migration is demand-driven (as a consequence of a demand stimulus coming from the country of immigration) or supply-driven (as a consequence of an excess supply of labor in the country of emigration). It also holds for welfare migration, when the migrant compares market income and unemployment at home with welfare payments at his new location.

The right of individuals to leave a country, the so-called exit option, can be interpreted as an important element within a liberal order. Individuals should not be "walled in." From the perspective of political freedom, the exit right for people is more basic than the exit option for capital. Every individual should have the right to leave, given living conditions which he or she finds unacceptable. All countries should accept the exit option of people as a basic principle. A credible right to exit represents a limit on the actions of governments. It is an integral part of locational competition, providing a way for people to express their preferences by voting "with their feet" in the sense of Tiebout (1956) and Hirschman (1970). To some extent, and in extreme cases, competition between locations may even be seen as an instrument to implicitly control governments. This indeed happens when people vote with their feet, as when some 600 East Germans stormed the Hungarian border at Sopran on August 19, 1989, and Hungary did nothing to prevent them. In such cases, systems can collapse as communism did. Thus, competition among locations can also be seen as an important political mechanism to shelter freedom. Furthermore, competition between states reduces the opportunity of interest groups to rent-seek and thus raises efficiency.

Besides an outright political ban on emigration, governments can use other instruments to prevent people from emigrating. One is not to allow emigrants to take their valuables with them or to receive compensation for their land property, because of either political harassment or lacking markets. Another is to use tax obligations in order to prevent people from leaving. In principle, the citizens of a state must fulfill their tax duties when they take their residence abroad. However, tax duties must not be used as a device to keep potential migrants from leaving. Emigrants should not be discriminated against. Double-taxation treaties or multilateral agreements could ease these problems. In any case, the freedom of the individual should be given priority to the tax claims of the state. A related issue is that an individual has benefited in human capital formation from his home country. Again, the emigrant should not be discriminated against. With respect to student fees, a problem of discrimination arises if only the emigrants have to pay for their former education or if they have to pay back credits from banks or governmental support whereas domestic students remaining in the country do not have to pay. The issue of human capital formation can be dealt with by international (private) law.

The exit option does not, however, imply an entry option, i.e., the right to migrate into a country. One reason is feasibility. Even if a country might be willing to accept and welcome all the migrants of the world, it usually could not, if only for lack of space. Another reason is experience. Historically, land was overtaken by invaders who did not respect the property right of indigenous inhabitants. Conquests usually were the method through which migration took place. To respect the principle of territoriality can be understood as a way to prevent such brutal migrations. Territoriality allows a nation state to define the rights of the insiders, specifying the extent to which migrants can freely enter. States define their identity by setting their own immigration policy. It is hard to imagine that a democracy will define its immigration law against the majority of the voters. This means that the majority must accept immigration (Hillman 1994). In this sense, countries can be interpreted as a club with limited membership.

In this context, property rights to use land are relevant for immigration. They assign land use to those who hold the title. Thanks to the functioning land markets, immigrants can buy out the incumbents as owners of land over time. With the territoriality principle, the nation state and its citizens can also be thought of as owning the land and defining the conditions under which immigrants can live on this land. This creates difficult ethical questions. Such issues can be more easily resolved if potential countries of immigration are sufficiently open—beyond their duty to accept the politically persecuted. It is also helpful if regional integrations such as the European Union guarantee freedom of movement within their territory, although the EU is spatially limited from an international economic perspective.

The European Union has established the freedom of movement of people as one of the four freedoms upon which the single market rests. This means that a citizen of an EU member state has, in principle, the right to establish residence in any member state. In practice, the member states can ask for special conditions. Thus, welfare migration within the EU is prohibited, i.e., moving for instance from unemployment in one EU country in order to reap higher welfare benefits in another EU country. Nonnationals can receive welfare payments only under certain conditions, for instance if they have already established their residence in a country for some time. The freedom of movement of non-EU asylum seekers is limited within the European Union. Moreover, the freedom of movement for Europeans is limited, as the EU service directive shows.

A Pecking Order between Trade, Capital Flows, and Migration

An important aspect for rules in the realm of factor movements is that the rates of returns to factors are interrelated and that factor movements themselves are related to trade. The interdependence between the movements of different factors depends on whether they are complements to or substitutes for each other. In addition, the interdependence of factor movements with trade depends on whether factor movements are a complement to or a substitute for trade.

Factor movements represent a complement to trade if factor flows follow trade and if trade follows factor flows. For instance, an existing or a potential comparative export advantage of a country for a specific good attracts capital, technology, and people, i.e., factor flows follow trade. In contrast, trade can also follow migration. For example, after people have migrated, their consumption pattern in the immigration country may continue to include goods of their previous country, leading to imports to their new country of residence. By the same token, foreign capital invested in a country may increase the country's production and export potential, thereby determining an improvement in comparative advantage and an increase in exports. Last but not least, factor movements are complementary to each other, as is the case when capital flows are followed by the migration of people, i.e., if capital attracted to a country induces labor to follow in order to equip machines and provide services. Normally, such complementarities do not represent a policy concern; they are usually taken care of by market forces.[4]

The most interesting aspect of interdependence from a policy point of view is that trade and factor flows are substitutes and that some types of factor flows are also substitutes among themselves. The starting point for our analysis is that the international division of labor exploits differences in endowment through trade and factor flows. Demand for products is disperse and the production of a good tends to be concentrated in space, although not necessarily in one area alone. Consequently, a large part of the arbitrage in space must take the form of trade in goods. The reduction of transportation costs per unit of good exchanged has opened more scope for trade. Factor flows, however, take place when spatial arbitrage is worthwhile for factors of production, for instance when new spaces are opened up to settlement (as with the United States in the seventeenth and eighteenth centuries) or are unlocked for capital (as with China after the Deng Xiaoping reforms). Then, it pays to move a unit of a factor, for instance capital. With respect to labor, migration costs include the psychic costs of leaving the native environment.

The decision making on the different forms of interaction can be thought of as a three-stage hierarchical assessment. First, does it pay to move a good? Second, does it pay to move capital, and do capital flows make it unprofitable to move goods? Third, does it pay to migrate, and does this make it unprofitable to move capital or goods? In this hierarchical decision structure, the third criterion dominates the second, and the second dominates the first. The idea of a hierarchical decision structure is a description of the market process and of the choices of all the market participants.

For the relationship between factors themselves, the interdependence of factors due to the production function is relevant. When factors are substitutes, the factor price frontier indicates which combinations of real factor prices are available, given a specific production function and the technology it includes. In a two-factor model with capital and labor, if the price of one factor is given, the maximum possible price of the other factor is determined by the production function.

These considerations on the substitutability of different forms of interaction imply a pecking order between trade and factor flows, where the arbitrage of goods has an economic advantage over factor flows. This is consistent with a view taking into account the policy goal of keeping adjustment costs for people low.

In such a pecking order, trade can be viewed as the prime mechanism of adjustment. It deserves this high ranking as it reduces the need for the migration of people,

---

[4] Complementarities of factors have been discussed as a policy problem in regional economics when factors complementary to each other leave a region and, consequently, complementarities magnify the decline of a region.

raising real income in the country of potential emigration through the expansion of the export sector and through lower costs for import goods. The rates of returns to factors depend on the extent to which such differences in the rates of return can be leveled out by trade flows. In the exchange of goods, outsourcing is an important channel through which exports in other countries are stimulated, employment there is enhanced, and wage income improves. Historically, trade has been the traditional instrument to generate economic benefits. It often enjoys priority over other mechanisms of adjustment.

Capital and technology flows come in as the second mechanism of adjustment. When capital and technology flow toward people, the necessity for people in low-income countries to emigrate becomes less compelling. Thus, offshoring plays a similar role to outsourcing with respect to trade, as both open new options for developing countries. The policy approach is to "bring jobs to the people instead of bringing people to the jobs."

Migration as a mechanism of adjustment only comes in third. It generates benefits, but the migrant is burdened with relevant psychic costs. These costs can be prevented by trade and capital as well as technology flows. This view assumes that the benefits stemming from the forms of adjustment can be compared with a three-stage hierarchical process of market decisions. The approach requires that migration does not outperform trade and capital flows in generating benefits. Then, migration would be preferable.

A special case in the relationship between trade and migration has been discussed in international economics under the heading of an "integrated world market equilibrium." Trade can be viewed as a means to arbitrage away differences in factor endowments, because common product and relative factor prices are established through arbitrage in equilibrium. With given production functions, this may not be possible for all endowments: the endowments of different countries can be so diverse that factors of production cannot be fully utilized in trade.[5] If this is the case, capital flows or migrations are necessary to obtain maximum gains and to arbitrage away endowment differences. The ranking of the three forms of exchange also hinges on value judgments. If migration is thought to have a value in itself, for instance in order to mold a multicultural society, the merits of migration cannot be evaluated relative to the other forms of factor movements.

The pecking order of forms of interdependence can also be interpreted as a sequential process going on in time. At a first stage, countries export goods, while at a second stage these exports attract capital and technology. If in such a scenario education is brought to the people, at a third stage the labor pool attracts additional capital and technology which then represent a further basis for exports. This third stage may also occur simultaneously to the second. In a different scenario, the migration of

---

[5] In this case, in technical terms, the endowment point lies outside the parallelogram that defines the set of possible equilibria (Dixit and Norman 1980).

people at a first stage is followed by the inflow of capital and technology in a second stage, which then establishes a basis for exports.

As a consequence of this pecking order, it is recommendable to strengthen the rules for trade, so that people do not have to migrate and do not have to incur psychic costs. This corresponds to the strategy "let them export, then people can stay." As a second strategy, it is recommendable to strengthen the rules for capital and technology flows since these decrease the need for migration. This approach corresponds to the strategy of bringing capital and technology to the people.

VII
Rules for the Global Environment

Whereas a rich institutional experience exists for the international trade order includ-ing factor markets, an international rule system for the global environment has not yet developed. In this domain, we have a problem that is quite different from those involving the international division of labor. In trade, all countries can benefit indi-vidually from the acceptance of common rules. Each of them enjoys gains from trade. A country like China can expect that its benefit from trade will grow over time together with its internal development; with world economic growth, an individual country's gains will grow as well. Trade lifts all boats. The environment, however, is a different story. Take global warming. Each country incurs costs to prevent car-bon dioxide (CO_2) emissions. Yet the benefits of an improved global atmosphere are spread and not noticeable for an individual country, with the exception of a few specific cases (for instance for countries close to or even below sea level). Moreover, countries can engage in free riding. By comparing the rule systems for these two areas, we can see how difficult it is to develop an institutional arrangement for the global environment.

National rules for the environment and nature have attracted great interest in the past fifty years. Since the early 1970s, increasing awareness of environmental disruption, especially in Europe and there most pronouncedly in Germany, has given prominence to institutional arrangements for the use of environmental media. In addition, the two oil crises of the 1970s and the stark rise of the oil price since 2005 have drawn attention to the property rights of natural resources. Last but not least, the discussion of the greenhouse effect in the natural sciences has shed light on environmental degradation. In the following, I look at changes in the international institutional arrangement, being aware that introducing the environment as a scarce good into the paradigm of economics encompasses a comprehensive adjustment of society going beyond the specific aspects discussed in this chapter (Siebert 2008b).

Private versus Public Goods

With respect to international rules for the environment, the decisive questions are whether the goods or resources are private or public and whether they are national or global.

Private goods are characterized by the fact that rivalry in consumption prevails and that the exclusion principle applies. The pair of shoes I use is no longer available for you. Consequently, property rights can be defined fitting this type of goods. Usually, these property rights are defined nationally. Typical examples of private goods are natural resources such as minerals and crude oil extracted from deposits in the ground. Of course, the fact that national private property rights exist for such resources does not mean that these property rights have no international implications. As a matter of fact, the nature of property rights impacts on the international division of labor. The relevant example is the shift of property rights for oil in the 1960s.

Private goods may be scarce goods, but there are other categories of goods. There may be no demand, and therefore no price, for goods such as the sand in the Sahara desert. These are therefore free goods. Alternatively, property rights may not have been defined yet for a given good, so that it remains a free-access good or a common property good, as with the commons in the Middle Ages. Moreover, property rights may not be adequately defined because the good generates externalities or has the characteristics of a public good.

In contrast to private goods, public goods must be consumed in equal amounts by all; the exclusion principle does not apply. Typical examples are internal and external security, the lighthouse that can be used by all the fishermen of a region (possibly financed by the fishermen's association), or environmental quality, for instance air quality.

To explain the difference between private and public goods, we use the demand curves for the two goods representing the willingness to pay. Let us consider two countries I and II. In figure VII.1(a), the willingness to pay for a private good is determined by aggregating the demand curves I and II horizontally. The resulting total demand curve I + II then represents the horizontally aggregated demand curve for a private good of both countries. Now consider the public good "environmental quality." Since the public good must be consumed in equal amounts by all, the curves I and II indicating the willingness of the two countries to pay for the global environment are aggregated vertically (figure VII.1(b)). Note that the willingness to pay for environmental quality of country I differs from that of country II. The aggregated curves I + II denote the aggregated willingness to pay for the public good.

Environmental Quality: Public Good with Private Properties

For economists, the environment is indeed a scarce resource, but it is different from a pair of shoes that China exports to the United States in exchange for computer software. The environment has two different functions: take the global atmosphere of the planet Earth. It provides the air we breathe and produces the climate we enjoy. The air we breathe is different from a pair of shoes, which is used by only one person.

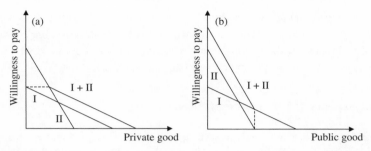

Figure VII.1.   Aggregation of willingness to pay for private and public goods.

Table VII.1.   Characteristic of goods, resources, and property rights.

		Type of property right	
		National	Global
Type of good or resource	Private	1. Private goods/resources with national property rights	3. Private goods with inter- national property rights
	Public	2. National environ- mental media	4. Global environ- mental media

The climate is consumed in equal amounts by all; it is a public good. However, the global atmosphere has a second function besides representing a public good. It receives CO_2 emissions and other greenhouse gases, originating from heating homes or driving cars. In this capacity, it is a receptacle for waste. From this perspective, the environment is a private good. We can limit the amount of waste dumped in the atmosphere, for instance by a specific polluter. This means that we can define property rights for using the environment as a receptacle of waste, and that these property rights are rivalrous. The environment is therefore characterized by two different functions, and these two functions compete with each other. Note that the term public good does not mean that the good is provided by the government.

So far, our analysis has shown that a good or resource can be private or public in nature. As an additional characteristic, the property rights for goods can be defined either nationally or globally (table VII.1). The definition of property rights depends on the spatial dimension of the good. This results in the following classification of goods. In a first category, many goods, such as a pair of shoes, are private goods and the exclusion principle applies (item 1 in table VII.1). Then property rights are national. We do not have a need for global rules of private goods. The subsidiarity principle requires that institutional rules for private goods are national or possibly even subnational. In a second category, public goods having a national dimension in space have nationally defined property rights, as in the case of national river systems (item 2 in table VII.1). For some private goods, a third category is needed, for instance international property rights in the case of patents or software (item 3). In a fourth category, public goods have a global dimension; they then require global property rights, including some coordination between national property rights (item 4). Border-crossing externalities are close to this category.

Global Aspects of Environmental Use

In order to structure our analysis, we distinguish between global environmental media[1] with a spatial dimension extending to the Earth as a whole, border-crossing environmental media, and national environmental media.

Global Environmental Media

Global environmental goods, i.e., public goods with a worldwide spatial dimension such as the Earth's atmosphere, require the agreement of all countries as to what amount and what quality of these public goods should be supplied. How much of a public good we want to have cannot be determined by decentralized market decisions; there would then be an underprovision of the public good. Instead, the optimal provision must be determined by the aggregation of the countries' preferences in a bargaining solution. Institutional arrangements are needed for the process of establishing the desired quantity of the public good, i.e., for aggregating national preferences. To put it differently, an international agreement is needed on the extent to which a deterioration in the quality of the public good is acceptable (for instance how much global warming we want to tolerate). Agreement is also needed on how the costs of the desired quality of the public good are allocated to individual countries and how free riding can be prevented. Any solution represents a de facto international allocation of emission rights. Once these issues are resolved, the market mechanism can be used to allocate the scarce resource to the different users.

Border-Crossing Environmental Media

When the spatial dimension of the environment extends to two or more states, pollutants are transported from one country to the other, for instance through river systems or through atmospheric conditions. Examples are acid rain in Europe and the transport of potash from the mines in the Alsace, France, through the river Rhine, affecting drinking water quality in downstream Netherlands. In such cases, negotiations have to lead to abatement activities in the upstream country. Often, the victim-pays principle is used, i.e., the pollutee offers a bribe to the polluter in order to induce him to adopt more environmentally friendly behavior. If countries have joint interests in other policy areas, as is the case in the European Union, it is easier to find a solution that prevents free-rider behavior.

---

[1] Soil, water, air, biota (plants and animals), or any other parts of the environment that can contain contaminants.

The Environment as a National Endowment

If the environment is an immobile national endowment factor, the diverging degrees of scarcity for environmental goods in different countries can be expressed by different prices of environmental services. This is relevant when the absorptive and regenerative capacities of national environments vary, when a high population density makes it more difficult to spatially separate residential and recreational areas from environmentally degrading transport and production activities and when the preferences of countries for environmental quality differ. Signaling different national environmental scarcities by means of different national prices does not require an international rule system; pricing can be left to national policies. A market economy approach to environmental policy, which taxes emissions nationally or establishes prices for environmental services through national emission licenses, is consistent with an institutional framework for the international division of labor. The more successfully the environment is integrated into the scarcity prices of individual countries, i.e., the more successfully welfare can be defined by taking the environment into consideration, the better environmental policies can be incorporated into the international trade order.

If prices for national environmental use are not (or cannot be) applied and if countries employ other measures such as administrative approaches, emission norms, or product standards in order to protect their citizens' health and life and to conserve natural resources (Article XX of the GATT Treaty), those measures must be nondiscriminatory. Nondiscrimination requires that in the case of market entry restrictions, regulations through production permits, facility permits, and product norms must not give preference to domestic producers and domestic goods. Thus, it should not be permissible, for example, with the aim of reducing health hazards as in the Thailand cigarette case (1990), to restrict the import of goods or to tax them unless the same measures are simultaneously applied to like domestic goods. However, the WTO Dispute Settlement Mechanism has concluded that it is permissible to use policy instruments to protect the environment in other countries (see the shrimp–turtle case in chapter IV). It is debated whether this may require some WTO rules for carbon-intensive products (Hufbauer and Kim 2008).

Problems to Be Resolved in Institutional Arrangements to Protect Global Environmental Media

A whole set of problems have to be resolved in setting up an international rule system to protect global environmental media. It is, indeed, a complex matter to reach an international consensus on the allocation of global environmental media.

How to Determine the Goal to Be Obtained

A major issue is how to find agreement on the extent to which deterioration in the quality of the global public good is acceptable, for instance how much global warming should be tolerated. Countries contribute different volumes of greenhouse gases to global emissions; they have undertaken dissimilar efforts to avoid emissions in the past; they apply production processes entailing diverging emission intensities; they rely on transportation systems whose volumes of emissions differ. The cost functions for the abatement of emissions, too, differ from one country to another. From the countries' own viewpoints, the marginal costs of abatement include different target losses; countries have different preferences with respect to environmental protection; they are also at different stages of their development; they have different per capita incomes and, consequently, a different willingness to pay; they may be affected differently by improvements in the condition of the global environment; for instance, countries below sea level will be harmed most by a rise in the sea level. Also, some countries have large resource deposits whose use is crucial for their economic development, as in the case of China and its large coal reserves. Under these conditions, it is difficult to agree upon a common target.

Least-Cost Environmental Protection

As soon as an agreement on the tolerable level of global warming or on the necessary volume of emission reduction is reached, it is required that the target is arrived at with the lowest opportunity costs in terms of resources used. This means that the target has to be attained in an efficient way. If not, resources would be wasted. The theoretical approach is to determine the marginal global benefit of abatement (in terms of global damage prevented) and the marginal global cost of abatement. Both marginal benefit and marginal costs require an aggregation of the benefits and costs of all countries.

In a simplified, static, two-country model, an efficient solution can be found if countries jointly maximize their aggregated benefit instead of maximizing their individual benefits. Let B_1 and B_2 denote the benefit of the two countries, and let R_1 and R_2 represent resources used to reduce emissions in the two countries, with R standing for the resources of both countries. C_1 and C_2 indicate abatement costs in the two countries. Then we have the joint maximization problem:

$$\text{Max } U = B_1(R) + B_2(R) - C_1(R_1) - C_2(R_2) \quad \text{s.t. } (R_1) + (R_2) - R.$$

Maximizing the Lagrangian function

$$L = B_1(R) + B_2(R) - C_1(R_1) - C_2(R_2) + \lambda[(R_1) + (R_2) - R]$$

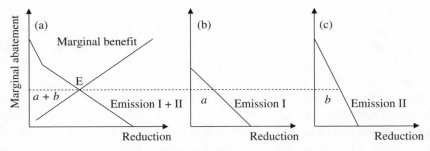

Figure VII.2. Efficient emission reduction

yields

$$\frac{\partial L}{\partial R} = B_1' + B_2' - \lambda = 0,$$

$$\frac{\partial L}{\partial R_1} = -C_1' + \lambda = 0,$$

$$\frac{\partial L}{\partial R_2} = -C_2' + \lambda = 0.$$

Consequently, we have as a result

$$B_1' + B_2' = C_1' = C_2'.$$

The condition requires that the marginal benefits of both countries are aggregated and that the aggregated marginal benefit is equal to the marginal reduction costs in both countries (which must in turn be equal). This implies that both countries together obtain the maximum amount of benefits and that abatement occurs where it is most efficient. An alternative to aggregating benefits is to rely on scientists and to accept their evaluation on the necessary emission reduction. Once the solution is determined, the world market can play to determine the price for emissions. Such a price per unit of CO_2 emission ensures that emissions are avoided or reduced at the most efficient spot in the world. This condition is portrayed in figure VII.2. Figure VII.2(a) describes aggregated marginal benefit and aggregated marginal abatement cost in the two countries, with point E as the equilibrium point. The two other figures represent emission abatement costs in the individual countries I and II. Note that the emission abatement costs are aggregated horizontally, i.e., the distance a (from figure VII.2(b)) plus the distance b (from figure VII.2(c)) yields $a + b$ (in figure VII.2(a)). In contrast, the marginal benefit curve has been aggregated vertically (see figure VII.1).

This is a simplified approach that interprets the allocation problem from a static point of view. A more detailed analysis leads to a more complex maximization problem: benefits have to be defined for a time period, for instance several decades. Due to the time preference, future benefits have to be discounted; the choice of the time preference or discount rate is a major issue since future benefits have a smaller present value. Moreover, a more complex approach has to model that pollutants are accumulated over time and that they are, in part, absorbed by nature. Irreversibility in these processes and fixed costs in the abatement function may aggravate the problem; economic growth and technological progress may make it easier for future generations to find solutions.

In order to implement a solution, agreement is needed on many crucial factors: the scientific model establishing a link between CO_2 emissions and global warming; the total number of CO_2 emissions that are tolerated as an indicator for the goal of reducing the likelihood of global warming; the actual initial level of CO_2 emissions; a base year or base period; the current and future contribution of the countries to the total number of emissions; the time available to implement the solution; the time-path of global emission reduction, for instance by a certain percentage per year (and alternatively, the time available to reduce the given stock of pollutants); the policy instruments to be used in order to achieve the desired goal; and the allocation of emission reduction obligations to different countries, which is equivalent to how the emission rights are allocated to countries if a cap-and-trade approach is used. When all these questions are answered in the spirit of the efficiency approach, the marginal benefit of emission reduction (in terms of global warming prevented per unit of CO_2 emission) and marginal costs of abatement are identical. Then it is possible to use prices for CO_2 emissions to stimulate prevention and abatement and to steer production, investment, and consumption.

Unfortunately, the economist's approach of aggregating the benefits and costs does not currently find political support, even though it shows how to use the environment with a minimum of global economic costs or, as one can also put it, at a minimum of environmental losses. The economists' solution requires that countries consider the use of the environment as an allocation problem, where environmental scarcity is the crucial guide to the solution. It implies a long-run equilibrium where a developing country would use the same amount of resources per unit of CO_2 emission abatement as a developed country. All countries pay the same price for using the global environment as a receptacle of CO_2 emissions. In this capacity, the environment is treated like energy, for instance oil, for which developing countries pay the same price per unit.

Criteria for Allocating the Costs of Reduction and Emission Rights

In a short-hand version, this method is also labeled as the cap-and-trade approach, in which a cap is established for the total volume of emissions and where emission rights can be traded. It is crucial to determine how the total quantity of emissions is allocated to the emission obligations of individual countries. This means deciding on the distribution of emission rights for countries. These emission rights determine future costs of abatement and the development potential of a country, especially the development potential from its own resource deposits. Emission rights can be interpreted as representing rents which decide on the income distribution between countries.

A case in point is China, which possesses huge coal reserves that are an important factor influencing its development potential in the future. The time profile of emission rights influences its economic growth, representing opportunity costs in terms of lower growth rates. It is therefore a major question whether and how a country such as China can be incentivized to join an international arrangement.

Historical Baselines

According to the historical approach, the level of emissions at a specific date or reference period is used as a starting point from which emission reductions for individual countries are defined. This version of the cap-and-trade approach starts from the premise that all countries have the same right to use the atmosphere as a receptacle of emissions. It respects the sovereignty of nation states, accepts the historical emissions as a datum and applies a practice similar to those used in the extension of territorial waters and economic zones in coastal waters. It is comparable with staking land claims as experienced when humans first settled in new territories. It can be interpreted as an expression of realpolitik. Once an agreement on the total quantity of emissions has been reached, in a given situation a price per unit of emissions will evolve. This price reflects environmental scarcity in the actual situation. It corresponds to the polluter-pays principle when only the flow of emissions, for instance per year, is taken into consideration.

This method can easily be used if all countries have similar economic conditions. Different previous successful efforts by single countries to reduce emissions can be accommodated in this approach. This has been applied in the EU's emissions trading arrangement. This approach, however, is unlikely to be implemented on a global scale because developing countries—latecomers in the use of the environment due to their economic development—feel disadvantaged.

Another version of the historical approach consists in looking at the emissions accumulated by a country over time, i.e., at their stock of pollutants rather than their annual emission flows. After all, the industrialized countries have created the current existing actual stock of pollutants, for instance the carbon stock, in the environmental system. The stock of pollutants is calculated as accumulated emissions over time, minus the normal diminution of pollutants in the natural system, i.e., it relates to the net anthropogenic increase of the stock of pollutants. The stock of pollutants has to be broken down to individual countries. This approach corresponds to the polluter-pays principle with respect to the accumulated stock of pollutants, appealing to the responsibility of countries for the global environment. Accordingly, the countries responsible for the largest accumulated pollutants would have to pay the highest price. Industrial countries would therefore bear the largest burden of emission reduction.

Ability-to-Pay Per Head

Whereas these approaches are very much influenced by the interpretation of the use of global media as an allocation problem, the ability-to-pay approach addresses the issue of global environmental use from the point of view of income distribution. In this case, countries with a higher income per capita carry a larger burden. Traditionally, the ability-to-pay criterion is used to justify progressive income taxation within a nation state. Consequently, this principle lies at the heart of national sovereignty, requiring the democratic legitimacy of national governments ("no taxation without representation"). Under these conditions, the government of a high-income country, while enjoying democratic legitimacy when negotiating the burden of that specific country, does not have an unlimited authority to apply the "ability-to-pay approach" internationally and to cede sovereignty accordingly. Even in the European Union where a sizable part of sovereignty has shifted to the European level, the power to tax remains with the nation state. Accordingly, the willingness to apply a taxation-underpinned ability-to-pay approach is limited internationally. This does not mean that some type of income transfer or technology diffusion cannot be agreed upon, as in the case of international aid.

Another proposal is that emission rights are allocated per head, according to each country's population. The motivation for this egalitarian approach is that the endowment of the planet Earth with given atmospheric conditions and a given climate is considered an entitlement for humankind. It is conceived as a global public good. From this statement, one can reach the conclusion that the capacity to absorb CO_2 emissions is also an entitlement for humankind. Then, each country would receive emissions rights according to the size of its population, and population-rich countries such as China, India, and countries in Africa would have an excess supply of emission rights which they could sell to the developed world. Such an allocation of emission rights per head of the population represents an immense transfer of rents in favor of the developing countries and to the disadvantage of developed countries. Its effect is comparable to the shift of property rights for crude oil in the 1970s. The problem with this approach is the dual nature of the environment. Whereas the world's atmosphere undoubtedly represents a global good, this property does not refer to the capacity to absorb CO_2 emissions since this entity can be organized as a private good, and since in the last forty years markets have already been introduced in industrialized countries to signal environmental scarcity. Therefore, the world is not in a position as if it introduced property rights as a completely new institutional arrangement for an issue that will only become relevant in the future. Consequently, one can argue that the new institutional arrangement should instead develop starting from the given situation. Along these lines, the world's absorptive capacity of CO_2

would be interpreted as an input to production processes, i.e., as a factor of production, and to human activity in general, such as housing and transportation. A possible criterion is then CO_2 emissions per unit of GDP. Admittedly, this argument is very much in line with the current economic and political reality. Moreover, care must be taken that a new global institutional arrangement does not reduce the incentives to avoid and reduce emissions. This could indeed occur if developing countries were to enjoy an excess supply of emission rights. This could lead to negligence in the prevention of CO_2 emissions.

New Technology

In light of the difficulties in reaching an agreement, new abatement technologies and technology transfer are bound to play a major role. An example is the search for new technologies for capturing and storing CO_2. Another important issue is reducing dependency on fossil fuels. Apparently, new technology could increase the willingness of countries to accept emission reduction as an important goal and to enter a new global institutional arrangement to prevent climate change. However, under the Alternative Policy Scenario of the International Energy Agency (2006), all currently installed and planned capture and storage capacity will only be able to save up to 0.2% of coal-fired power generation emissions in 2015. One problem is that companies will only invest in research and development if they believe in the increasing demand for solutions for reducing CO_2 emissions or substitutes with lower CO_2 emissions. In order to avoid risky research and development costs, industry might even discourage national governments from reducing CO_2 emissions.

A Globally Uniform Emission Tax

An alternative to the cap-and-trade approach with allocation of emission rights is to use a uniform carbon tax, i.e., a tax per unit of CO_2 (Nordhaus 2006). Such a tax would generate tax income for states, and therefore might prove more easily acceptable than emission rights. However, it would be extremely difficult to agree on a uniform emission tax worldwide. Besides, a uniform emission tax does not guarantee CO_2 reductions, as it does not constrain the volume of emissions. In a long-run global solution, all countries would have to pay the same tax per unit of CO_2. Consequently, a tax also influences the distribution of reduction costs and rents. In order to entice the developing countries into joining such a system, side payments would be needed. Countries would have to cede their sovereignty of taxation to a multilateral arrangement. This might prove more difficult than joining a cap-and-trade system. In principle, it is possible to find a uniform global tax under static conditions with identical situations in all countries, as it would be necessary for the tax to produce the same results as a cap-and-trade approach. This, however, would only hold under very specific conditions. Thus, the equivalence no longer applies when economic conditions are different in countries and when they change over time (Peterson and Klepper 2007).

Phasing in the Introduction of New Emission Entitlements

Global warming due to anthropogenic causes can be seen as a relatively new phenomenon in the Earth's history. Consequently, it is unrealistic to advocate an abrupt solution. The introduction of new property rights for CO_2 emissions is more acceptable if it is phased in. However, according to many scientists, the world may not have enough time for such a gradual adjustment. Moreover, the accumulation of a carbon stock in the Earth's system has long-lasting effects. Similarly, a reduction of CO_2 emissions takes time.

As an additional issue, the coming decades will experience an enormous geographical shift in industrial production and an increase in the developing countries' share of global emissions to more than 50% by 2030. In order to include these countries into a global emission reduction scheme, a redistribution of the costs and benefits of emission reduction will play an important role. In the contraction-and-convergence proposal of the Global Commons Institute (1996) all countries have to agree on a safe level of greenhouse gases, for instance no more than 450 parts per million by volume (ppmv) by 2100, and on a convergence date by which the per capita emissions of all countries should converge to a common level, be it 2050 or 2100. This approach leads to welfare redistribution from industrialized countries toward developing countries, particularly to China, India, and Sub-Saharan Africa (Peterson and Klepper 2007).

The multi-stage approach, which was first developed by Gupta (1998) and adapted by Den Elzen (2002), includes a gradual increase in the number of countries that are part of binding agreements to reduce CO_2 emissions. More specifically, countries with diverse economic and environmental contexts are clustered into different groups with diverse levels and types of emission reduction commitments. In the first stage, countries do not have any commitments for CO_2 emissions reduction. In the second stage countries have to limit emissions, while in the third stage they must reduce emissions in absolute terms. Countries agree on mechanisms for the transition from one stage to the next. For the participation in stages two and three, den Elzen uses an index of capability, measured in terms of real GDP per capita, and responsibility, measured by the level of emissions per capita.

Institutional Failure

Two major issues have to be recognized with respect to environmental treaties, free-rider behavior and reneging on a contract.

The Free-Rider Problem

After an agreement has been reached, the issue arises as to whether and to what extent such an agreement will be upheld. Countries only enjoy an indirect benefit from an improved world climate. Much depends on whether the country is prepared to impute its indirect net national benefit from the global improvement. Although countries can improve their indirect benefit relative to a noncooperative solution, a country may be tempted to behave as a free rider, i.e., to enjoy the benefits of a better global environmental quality without carrying the costs for it, simply disregarding the agreement. Countries have different economic and environmental conditions with respect to their stage of development and they have different preferences vis-à-vis environmental degradation, varying levels of willingness to pay, and different attitudes and commitments to multilateral approaches. Consequently, countries might be tempted to play the game of enjoying the public good without carrying the cost for it. Then, countries are tempted by the shortcut of noncooperative behavior and they may not be able to find a cooperative solution, as happens in the prisoner's dilemma affecting international trade. Only if the free rider is not essential for the solution, or if a coalition of countries is willing to prepare the way for a solution in the future, as in the Kyoto Protocol, can a solution be implemented. One may take some consolation from the experience that, quite often, a country may not want to be stigmatized as an environmental polluter in an environment while other states are more caring about the world's heritage. In terms of reputation, a country hardly wants to be called the "dirty man of the world."

Reneging on a Contract

Another problem is that a country may walk away from an international agreement later on. An important condition to prevent countries from reneging on an international environmental contract is that they have a net benefit from the arrangement. Unlike the case of international trade, where the benefits are likely to increase over time with the expansion of trade and world growth, this condition is difficult to satisfy in the case of environmental protection. Again, we can look at China's huge coal reserves (see above). Assume the situation is such that energy becomes a limiting factor in China's growth. In this case, it would become tempting to walk away from the contract if China cannot use its coal deposits. Apparently, the contract must have sufficient incentive to prevent such an outcome.

A more fortunate case is when the instruments used, for instance in reducing CO_2 emissions, also allow the country to improve its national environment. Again, we can take China as an example, where reaching the national goal of better air quality would contribute to improving the world climate. Another case is side payments (see below). In all other instances, the benefits accrue to the world and the costs are borne by the country. Not only is the benefit of an improved world climate to the country merely an indirect one, but this benefit is also unlikely to increase over time. Prevention costs tend to rise progressively together with the quantity of emissions abated, assuming a given technology. It then becomes increasingly costly to prevent CO_2 emissions. Emission abatement is therefore unlikely to bring a country increasing benefits as is the case in international trade, unless a country conceives the reduced risk of climate change as an improved benefit per se. Nevertheless, some conditions can reduce this problem. One is that prevention should be phased in so that impact of costs is felt less strongly thanks to an increase in economic development. Another is that the allocation of costs does not shift asymmetrically between countries over time, turning to the disfavor of a country.

Institutional Mechanisms Stabilizing a CO_2 Agreement

A set of institutional mechanisms can help to find and stabilize rules for the global environment. A review of these institutional mechanisms shows how different they are when compared with procedures already established in the WTO.

Commitment

An important prerequisite for multilateral arrangements is that countries commit themselves to the international contract (see chapter IV). Commitment is especially important in treaties in which, unlike the WTO, countries do not have direct and increasing benefits but where cost-sharing is an essential aspect of providing an international public good, such as preventing global warming (Barrett 2005). Commitments can encompass a duty to contribute to financing an agreement in order to make side payments possible, to emission reduction obligations and to rules that recognize emission reductions in other countries if undertaken by domestic firms.

Reputation

Free-rider behavior may be reduced if the agreement can be interpreted as a repeated game played over many periods. Then, a free rider will have to balance the benefits that he can reap from free riding in a specific period against potential costs that he will incur from the reactions of the other players in the future. Reputation matters and this may induce a potential free rider to adhere to the agreement. Reputation is especially relevant if more than one layer of interdependencies exist but interdependencies other than in the case of global environmental media are present as well. Then, the benefits in other fields may offer compensation against free-rider behavior in pollutants.

Mutual Affection

Another reason why agreements to cooperate survive over time is that people care about the other parties affected by the agreement. Dasgupta (2002) calls this "mutual affection"—a phenomenon we know from a family. A similar idea is expressed by Sen (1990), where an action can be understood to be "better for the respective goals of all of us." My concept of a utility function, including argument variables in other countries, contains a similar idea.

Self-Enforcing Contracts

In contrast to a national setting, where sanctions exist, international sanctions are usually lacking, and international agreements can seldom be enforced. As a solution, the idea of a self-enforcing contract has been developed (Barrett 1994a,b, 2005). According to this approach, the incentive structure of a multilateral arrangement must be such that it is in the interest of a country to behave as every country would like it to behave. Following Barrett (2005, p. 196) an equilibrium is self-enforcing if "no signatory can gain by withdrawing unilaterally from the IEA [International Environmental Agreement] and no nonsignatory can gain by acceding to it, given the terms of the treaty and the participation decisions of other countries."

One approach is that countries agree to sanctions and bind themselves in this way in an international contract. For instance, they can create credible sanctions for the members of the group if a member deviates. Barrett (1992) discusses a mechanism by which countries link their abatement activity to those of other countries. If a country reduces its abatement activity, not abiding by the agreement any more, other countries can lower their emission reduction as well, thereby inflicting damage on the deviating country. Chandler and Tulkens (1997) describe an agreement in which, if one or more countries deviate from the agreement, the other signatories can discontinue the agreement (Barrett 2005, p. 213). This threat is believed to prevent deviating behavior. However, these forms of sanction do not make too much sense, taking into account the environmental goal. Unfortunately, to use the threat of lowering abatement efforts or of termination to deter the breaching of contract may well be a destabilizing strategy from an environmental point of view, since the whole institutional arrangement is put into question.

Instead of such a negative mechanism of linking policy instruments in a desta-bilizing way, a positive mechanism can be introduced: a country will abate more if another country abates more. Also, reducing additional emissions by a certain percentage when a new country joins an agreement represents a positive external-ity making a coalition attractive. Moreover, countries may agree on a minimum participation level that individual countries can surpass. This may make it more attractive for countries to join the agreement. Furthermore, countries may agree on a fine system, so that the polluter who deviates from the agreed-upon standards must pay. The countries joining the agreement may commit themselves by means of an initial lump-sum investment in the project similar to a club entrance fee. If they walk away from the club, they lose the initial lump sum payment. Alternatively, the funds provided can be used to finance side payments as an incentive to abate emissions. All this should help in discouraging the potential free rider. Such commitments have some similarity to the commitment in the form of bound tariffs. They are self-enforcing insofar as they are conceived as fair. Apparently, the more demanding an agreement is, the fewer willing participants it will find. A whole array of proposals for stabilizing institutional arrangements for the environment can be found in Heister (1997).

Changing the Rules of the Game

A situation in which countries find themselves in a prisoner's dilemma can be transformed into a game with a different equilibrium if a different treaty is written, i.e., when the properties of the game are changed. Thus, the principal task of a treaty is to change the incentive structure for its participants: "by changing the rules of the game—by writing a treaty that specifies how each signatory should behave, conditional on the number of signatories—the equilibrium of the underlying dilemma game can be transformed" (Barrett 2005, p. 205).

Conditions to Sustain a Treaty

Several conditions make a treaty more likely: common preferences of the members, attaching, for instance, a similar value to the environment; increasing benefits for members or decreasing costs over time; flexibility in the rules if new scientific evidence arises; supporting mechanisms such as compliance and participation enforcement; a low number of participants working to the advantage of the strength of the arrangement, however, at the expense of its breadth (see below); and a commons problem that is limited in space, for instance affecting only some countries.

Strategic Choices

Several aspects of a treaty represent a strategic choice affecting the incentive structure of the treaty (Barrett 2005, pp. 355–57). These decisions involve side payments, the choice of the instruments by which a treaty tries to change its signatories' behavior, the linkage of different instruments, the minimum participation level, and the strength of the agreement (see below).

Depth versus Breadth of Arrangements

A trade-off exists between the depth and the breadth of an institutional arrangement. Different outcomes are conceivable. A deep and narrow treaty attempts to reach ambitious goals. Such an approach may be successful in reaching an ambitious goal and it usually includes the use of specific instruments to be applied. However, depth (goal achievement and intensity of instruments) comes at the cost of breadth (participation). If successful, such an approach may attract other participants over time, but it may also appear as an elitist club and thereby lose its attractiveness. Exclusiveness may then be perpetuated and the deep treaty may end up not succeeding in being extended to a larger group. A broad but shallow treaty has the advantage of large participation, but the goals to be reached are not high-powered and the instruments applied tend to be less specific with respect to high-powered goals. Broad-but-shallow agreements may make it easier for countries to join, since the costs of joining are low. In both scenarios, it is conceivable that the treaties remain stuck to their initial concepts with a rather specific path dependency. In the ideal case, the treaty may succeed in becoming deeper over time, changing its objectives and intensifying the instruments to be used.

Coalitions

In contrast to a wide multilateral agreement with many states, countries with a special interest in environmental problems may form a coalition. Then the issue arises as to whether an agreement can be made attractive for potential members who are still outside, i.e., whether each potential member enjoys a benefit if he joins. Another question is under what conditions a country may develop an interest in joining. A small coalition may eventually extend to a more comprehensive international agreement. An example is the Montreal Protocol, which expanded from the initial 26 members to the current 181. An example from a completely different field is the European Union, which has succeeded in attracting new members over the past fifty years. A major question in this context is whether the abatement level should be chosen depending on the number of signatories and to what extent the abatement level of the coalition can increase over time.

Thus, conditions can exist which make it interesting for a potential member to opt into the agreement instead of remaining outside (Heal 1992). Several reasons can be put forward. First, consider the case where abatement functions are characterized by fixed costs: if a country reduces pollutants unilaterally, the costs of abatement are probably larger than the benefit for the country, unless the country is very large and fixed costs are less of a problem. Thus, a country may be able to reduce the role of its fixed costs if it joins the "club." Second, other complementarities between the abatement functions, i.e., positive externalities, are an additional incentive to become part of a group. Positive spillovers may exist, for instance due to technology transfers, when the technology of the coalition is offered to the newcomer. Especially if no hegemon exists, countries of more or less equal size may form a coalition in order to exploit complementarities. Third, the interdependencies of countries may prevail in other fields as well, thereby increasing the relevance of reputation in the long run. Fourth, countries may introduce a mechanism which effectively creates sanctions. Heal (1992) defines a minimum critical coalition as the smallest coalition, where all members can gain from an abatement agreement. Without side payments, indirect benefits must be at least equal to costs for each country taken separately. With side payments, indirect benefits plus side payments must be equal to costs.

Management Associations

Even though completely local, the water associations in the Ruhr area—the first of which was established in the first decade of the nineteenth century (Kneese and Bower 1968; Siebert 2008b)—contain mechanisms that could possibly be used in international treaties. The water associations in the Ruhr area (Ruhr, Emscher, Lippe, Wupper, Niers, Erft, Left Lower Rhine, and Ruhr Water Dam Association) represent organizations in which membership is mandatory for every polluter. The general assembly of the association determines the water quality standards. When the required environmental quality level is specified, the association can determine the amount of capital equipment and investment to be put in place and the operating costs that it has to spend to attain these standards. Thus, the total costs of abatement are specified. The problem then consists of allocating these costs to the individual polluters. Costs are attributed in such a way that the costs falling upon the individual polluter are related to the quantity (and quality) of pollution he produces. This creates an incentive to abate pollutants. The water associations can be interpreted as an institutional arrangement for cost sharing, in which a quality target is internalized into individual behavior through a mechanism which shares the costs of reaching the targets and simultaneously develops an incentive system.

The water associations exhibit some interesting institutional features. Voting rights vary with the volume of effluent charges paid and consequently with the volume of pollution produced; thus, the largest polluter has the greatest number of votes. In spite of this rule, analysis shows that the decisions of the associations seem to have been reasonable. Klevorick and Kramer (1973) have demonstrated that most environmental concerns have been taken care of by the associations. One reason for this success is that institutional safeguards have been introduced. For instance, in the Niers Association, the downstream polluters received 75 votes before the remaining 225 votes were distributed according to the paid effluent charges. In the Lippe Association, coal mines could not have more than 40% of the votes. Moreover, municipalities—also present in the associations—were interested in the quality of drinking water. This approach is obviously only local, but similar concepts can be adopted in multilateral solutions.

Compliance

A precondition for the effectiveness of international treaties is compliance. This requires commitment, for instance due to homogeneity of preferences. Arbitration and dispute settlement mechanisms are helpful. In contrast to rules for trade, enforcement of environmental treaties is difficult since they deal with a public good (Yang 2006). An important aspect is therefore the transformation of identity and interest.

Sanctions

Unlike sanctions in other international institutional arrangements such as the WTO, sanctions in the international environmental area are as yet fairly undeveloped. One reason is that in the last fifty years, introducing environmental scarcity into institutional arrangements has been mainly a concern of national policy. Another factor is that the United States, as the hegemon of the postwar era, had no interest in international environmental matters. Environmental sanctions must therefore rely on international law, for instance countermeasures, that are allowed by international law such as retorsions, i.e., unfriendly-yet-lawful acts (Yang 2006). Where environmental treaties exist, treaty-based individual or collective sanctions can be applied, including reciprocal action and reprisals and even membership sanction.

Credibility of Sanctions

Threats must be credible. If a threat, for instance the threat of a sanction, is not backed up by facts, such a threat is unlikely to influence the behavior of other countries. This is also the case if a threat is simply infeasible in the eyes of agents, or if it hurts the nation announcing the threat. A threat is also hard to believe if it contradicts a pattern of behavior in the past and if a political economy analysis reveals that it is unlikely to be implemented. Experience with threats is sketchy; unilateral U.S. sanctions with respect to whaling against Japan and Norway have been ineffective (Yang 2006, p. 7). Economic embargoes have often been ineffective (Hufbauer et al. 2007).

The Kyoto Protocol and Its Possible Successor

In the context of the United Nations' Framework Convention on Climate Change, adopted in 1992, the Kyoto Protocol—basically a cap-and-trade system—came into force in February 2005, after it was ratified by Russia in 2004. As of January 2008, the Kyoto Protocol has been ratified by 176 countries plus the European Union, accounting for 61.6% of 1990 CO_2 emissions. The United States, which was responsible for 17.4% of global 1990 CO_2 emissions, has not ratified the Protocol; it withdrew from it in 2001. In getting the Kyoto process started, a particular procedure was chosen to set the Protocol into force. It decided that the Protocol would have entered into effect when at least 55 countries, responsible for at least 55% of the 1990 CO_2 emissions of industrialized countries (the Annex I countries), had ratified the Protocol.

Table VII.2.   World CO_2 emissions in millions of tons, 2004[a,b].

	Emissions	%
EU27	4,237	15.3
France	417	1.5
Germany	886	3.2
Italy	490	1.8
United Kingdom	562	2.0
Australia	382	1.4
Canada	593	2.1
Japan	1,286	4.6
Russia	1,618	5.9
South Korea	466	1.7
United States	5,987	21.6
Brazil	332	1.2
China (including Hong Kong)	5,050	18.2
India	1,343	4.9
Asia[c]	2,220	8.1
Mexico	438	1.6
South Africa	437	1.6
Others	5,538	20.0
World	27,667	100

[a]Excluding Taiwan. [b]For non-Annex I countries, data are from estimates of CO_2 emissions made available by the Carbon Dioxide Information Analysis Center (CDIAC). [c]Excluding China, Japan, India, South Korea, and Russia.

Source: United Nations Statistics Division, Millennium Development Goals Indicator database 2007.

The total global volume of CO_2 emissions amounted to 28 billion tons in 2004 (table VII.2). The United States accounted for 21.6%, the European Union (EU27) for 15.3%, the OECD countries for 49.1%, and China for 18.2%. The issue is how these emissions can be reduced.

The reference scenario of the International Energy Agency (2007) indicates that China, whose emission of greenhouse gases surpassed that of the United States in 2006, will be the largest emitter of CO_2 in 2030 with 11.5 billion tons, more than the United States with 6.9 billion tons and the EU27 with 4.2 billion tons (table VII.3). Note that the "Other OECD" data are slightly understated as they were calculated by subtracting the CO_2 emissions of the United States and the EU27 from the total OECD emissions. Note also that some smaller countries, such as the Baltic States, though part of the EU25, were not part of the OECD at the time of the IEA report in 2007.

The Kyoto Protocol specifies legally binding limits on greenhouse gas emissions in industrialized countries, the Annex I countries. It takes 1990 emissions as a starting

Table VII.3.   IEA reference scenario, in millions of tons of CO_2 emissions.

	1990	2005	2015	2030
United States	4,832	5,789	6,392	6,891
EU27	4,084	3,944	4,011	4,176
China	2,244	5,101	8,632	11,448
India	587	1,147	1,804	3,314
Other OECD	2,137	3,105	3,651	4,000
Other non-OECD	6,804	7,534	9,581	12,076

Source: International Energy Agency (2007).

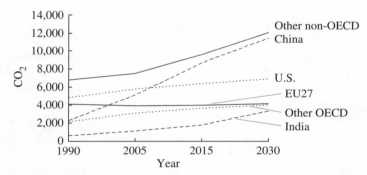

Figure VII.3.   Reference scenario for CO_2 emissions 1990–2030.

point. The "commitment period" for the reductions is between 2008 and 2012, allowing for fluctuations to be averaged out. Commitments are 5.2% on average for industrialized countries relative to their 1990 CO_2 emissions. They vary between countries, with, for instance, -12.5% for the United Kingdom and -8% for the European Union. As of 2007, the signatories have not succeeded in reaching their committed targets. For 2010, the European Environment Agency (2007, figure 4.4) estimates that the EU15 will meet its Kyoto targets if member states make use of carbon sinks, for instance afforestation, and implement additional measures quickly and fully. If not, the EU15 is projected to reduce greenhouse gas emissions by 4.0% instead of 8% compared with 1990. China, India, and Brazil have approved the Kyoto Protocol, but they are non-Annex I countries.

The Kyoto approach contains several flexible mechanisms. According to the Joint Implementation Mechanism, emissions can be traded among Annex I countries. Countries that reduce emissions more than agreed upon can sell their emissions credits to other countries. Emission reductions can also be "banked," i.e., kept over time. The Clean Development Mechanism applies to projects in developing countries that have no targets under the Kyoto Protocol. Firms in developed countries can treat abatement activities in developing countries as if they were undertaken in the developed countries; this may only apply to a certain percentage of abatement. The reasoning is that since the Earth's atmosphere is a global environmental medium, the specific geographical location of emissions reduction is inconsequential. The hope is also that joint implementation will encourage the transfer of environmentally sound technology to developing countries. In the Kyoto framework, a twenty-member Compliance Committee is in charge of handling noncompliance issues. A critical point is which sanctions will be sufficient to change the states' behavior (Yang 2006, p. 40).

The first stage of the Kyoto Protocol, including the reduction commitments, will expire in 2012. Subsequent arrangements are being discussed. Negotiations will take place in the 2009 Climate Change Dialogue among the "G8 plus 5" (United States, United Kingdom, Canada, France, Germany, Italy, Japan, and Russia as the G8 plus Brazil, China, India, Mexico, and South Africa as the "5"). An agreement for such negotiations to take place was reached in Washington in 2007. The participants acknowledged the effects of greenhouse gas emissions on climate change and the responsibility of both developed and developing countries to reduce these emissions. It is intended to establish a global carbon market for CO_2 emissions. In Bali, representatives of 180 countries, including the United States, agreed in 2007 on the Bali Roadmap to complete negotiations for a post-Kyoto treaty until 2009, in order to have sufficient time to ratify and implement the treaty before the Kyoto commitment period ends in 2012.

Meanwhile, in 2006, the United States has launched a counter-agreement in response to the Kyoto Protocol, the "Asia–Pacific Partnership on Clean Development and Climate," including Australia, China, India, Japan, South Korea, and the United States, of which only Australia, Canada, and Japan also have legal obligations under the Kyoto Protocol. The member countries account for around 50% of the world's greenhouse gas emissions. The United States did not want to commit itself to Kyoto, denouncing scientific ambiguity about climate change and fearing strain on its economy, given that its main future rival, China, does not participate. The United States' idea is to have a looser institutional arrangement does not include a mandatory enforcement mechanism. Emission reduction targets are set individually for the member countries. The partnership describes the intent to reduce greenhouse gases in general terms, i.e., to develop, deploy, and transfer existing and emerging clean technology, meet increased energy needs, explore ways to reduce greenhouse gases without hurting the economies and seek ways to engage the private sector. Such a voluntary approach should not be ruled out right away. We have seen examples of "highly-motivated partnerships" (Schelling 2002) such as NATO, where burden-sharing is a central and crucial mechanism, in spite of debates on the allocation of the burden. This presupposes that the major countries of the world agree on the goal of reducing greenhouse gas emissions. In such an approach, technology transfers and income transfers to developing countries to introduce emission-preventing technologies would have to play a large role.

At this stage, it is difficult to see which solution will come out of the post-Bali negotiations and the Copenhagen meeting in 2009. Countries are unlikely to repeal the precedent-setting commitment of all Annex I countries to abate emissions, as the Kyoto Protocol mandated. This means that a continuation of the Kyoto Protocol is a baseline for the future. Most likely, this coalition of countries will intensify its efforts to reduce CO_2 emissions. Unfortunately, this alone would not represent major progress. A preferable solution would be a rule system in which all the signatories of the Kyoto Protocol and all OECD countries, including the United States, agree to reduce emissions relative to a base year. The new U.S. administration will probably be open to such a solution, independent of party affiliation. However, for a new agreement to be successful, it is necessary to make major emerging countries such as Brazil, India, and China part of the agreement, with commitments accepted to reduce emissions. Such commitments could be phased in for these countries, for instance by planning increasing emission reductions over time, possibly two decades. These reductions would be instrumental in improving domestic air quality, for instance in China, and they would therefore be in the countries' own interest. A major issue in such an arrangement is the problem of determining the relative emission reduction obligations of emerging countries. For instance, emission reduction could be specified in terms of CO_2 emissions per unit of GDP. For 2005, the coefficients are 0.2904 kg CO_2 per US\$1 GDP of the EU27; 0.4662 kg per US\$1 GDP of the United States; and 2.2830 kg per US\$1 GDP of China. Apparently, the United States could produce less CO_2 per unit of GDP if it used European technology and the European approach to environmental policy. By the same token, China could improve its own situation by applying U.S. technology. Such a method introduces a best practice approach to a long-run solution. In this approach, the phasing-in could take a longer period for emerging countries—perhaps up to fifty years. Incentives for technology transfer, such as the Development Mechanism, should play a major role. Again, a highly motivated partnership cannot be completely ruled out as a solution; it could represent a solution space including the Kyoto process for a smaller coalition.

EU Emissions Trading

The most significant efforts toward implementing the Kyoto Protocol have taken place in Europe. The EU has committed itself to an overall reduction of 8% of its 1990 emissions; this goal was ratified in May 2002 by the EU and by all its member states. Additionally, the ten new member countries which have joined the EU in 2004 all ratified the Protocol and have set their own reduction targets between 6 and 8%. In 2007, the EU set a 20% reduction target for CO_2 emissions by 2020. It has offered a reduction of 30% if other countries follow, in spite of the fact that the EU has not reached its own targets.

Emissions trading in the EU began in 2005 between member states, each of which had established a national allocation plan. In its first phase (2005–7), the system only covered CO_2 emissions and initially only included certain industries: power generation, oil refining, cement production, iron and steel manufacturing, glass, ceramics, and paper and pulp. The second period (2008–12) will address all greenhouse gases but it is as yet undecided whether aviation emissions will be covered. In 2008, all relevant installations must be included (European Commission 2007). Emissions trading will use one ton of CO_2 as the allowance currency, and fines per excess unit will amount to 40 euros until 2007 and to 100 euros thereafter. It is estimated that between 12,000 and 15,000 installations will be covered by the emissions trading system.

The initial distribution of allowances, as envisioned in the national allocation plans, is one of the most significant determinants of the effects of emissions trading. The European Commission left it to the member states to allocate their emission rights to different domestic sources, and has offered three different approaches to allocate the rights: the historic approach using the emissions of a base year as a frame of reference, the forecasting approach, and the least-cost approach. In the historical emissions model, companies were given permits at a rate matching their current emissions. The forecasting approach was similar, but corrected for expectations about which sectors will grow or contract in the economy in the future. The least-cost approach attempted to equalize abatement costs both within the emissions trading sectors (something which would happen in any event) and abatement costs in other sectors, and consequently allocated fewer permits to the trading sectors. It was heavily debated, for instance in Germany, how past reduction efforts were to fit into this scheme and how the total amount of emissions of these sources related (and still relates) to other emission sources. As for the new EU-member countries, not only do they have lower abatement costs than western Europe, but they are also in many cases already below their Kyoto targets, due to the economic restructuring following the collapse of the communist system. This enables them to sell excess permits. Progressively tightening caps are foreseen for each new period, forcing overall reductions in emissions.

With 764 million tons of CO_2 trade in the first three quarters of 2006, EU emissions trading represented about 75% of the global carbon market in terms of volume traded (table VII.4). Carbon exchanges have developed in different locations, for instance EEX in Germany, APX in the United Kingdom, Powernet in France, and CXX in Chicago. Some of these exchanges also trade futures. Moreover, voluntary pools have emerged (for example North Pool for Scandinavia). The starting price per unit allowance was about ten euros. It passed the 30 euros mark in April 2006 but later dropped back to below one euro. The reason was an excess supply of allowances coming from national allocation plans. A further reason was that the allowance expired at the end of 2007, and new permits were required for the next phase. In 2007, futures for 2008 demanded a higher price. In November 2007, the average

Table VII.4. World carbon market, first three quarters of 2006.

	Volume (in millions of tons)	Value (in billions US$)
Allowances		
EU Emissions Trading Scheme	763.9	18.8
New South Wales Greenhouse Gas Abatement Scheme	16.2	0.2
Chicago Climate Exchange	8.25	0.03
UK Emissions Trading Scheme	2.3	0.01
Subtotal	790.65	19.04
Project-based transactions		
Clean Development Mechanism	214.3	2.3
Joint Implementation	11.9	0.09
Other compliance	7.9	0.06
Subtotal	234.1	2.45
Total	1,024.75	21.49

Source: International Emissions Trading Association (IETA) (2006).

future price for a 2008 European Emission Allowance (EUA) was 22.62 euros at the European Energy Exchange (EEX). In principle, one can rate EU emissions trading as successful.

Multilateral Arrangements to Protect Fauna and Flora

Biodiversity is the richness of species of animals and plants in the ecosystem. It is a good or a resource with strong positive externalities: it enhances the productivity of the ecosystem; it represents a form of insurance, for instance by having a pool of plants being resistant to a virus. It is a source of genetic knowledge and of "keystone species," crucial in defining the property of complex ecosystems and ecoservices. A case in point is the equatorial rainforest in Brazil and other countries having a positive value in absorbing CO_2, producing oxygen, and allowing biodiversity. The valuation of biodiversity varies with the different functions assigned to it. Other more specific, but related value categories may be distinguished, such as genetic diversity and species diversity, natural-areas and landscape diversity, ecosystem functions, and the existence value (Nunes and van den Bergh 2001). Conversely, cutting down the rainforest would reduce these forms of value related to biodiversity. It would reduce the option value or existence value (Heal 2000; Deke 2007) and represent a negative externality for other countries (Barbier and Burgess 2001). Biodiversity

Table VII.5. Selected core multilateral environmental agreements.

Agreement type and name	Date of final agreement	Date of entry into force	Members	Secretariat
Atmosphere conventions:				
United Nations Framework Convention on Climate Change (UNFCCC)	05/1992	03/1994	192	UN
Kyoto Protocol to the United Nations Framework Convention on Climate Change	12/1997	02/2005	176	UN
Vienna Convention for the Protection of the Ozone Layer	03/1985	09/1988	191	UNEP
Montreal Protocol on Substances that Deplete the Ozone Layer	09/1987	01/1989	191	UNEP
Convention on Long-Range Transboundary Pollution	11/1979	03/1983		UNECE
Biodiversity-related conventions:				
United Nations International Treaty on Plant Genetic Resources for Food and Agriculture	2004 11/2001	06/2004	169	UN
Convention on Biological Diversity	06/1992	12/1993	190	UNEP
Cartagena Protocol on Biosafety to the Convention on Biological Diversity	01/2000	09/2003	143	UNEP
Convention on International Trade in Endangered Species (CITES)	1973 03/1973	07/1975	172	UNEP

Source: UN Environment Programme (2007).

loss has been measured through species extinction and through proxies such as the loss of diversified habitats. In recent years, environmental analysts have measured significant declines in biodiversity. The World Wildlife Foundation (2002) asserts that global biodiversity has decreased by one-third since 1970.

 For some of the uses of biodiversity, private property rights can be established, for instance for the role of biodiversity in enhancing the productivity of natural systems such as agricultural land. The price for a unit of land would then implicitly contain the value of the ecosystem existing on this piece of land. Another example related

Table VII.5. *Continued.*

Agreement type and name	Date of final agreement	Date of entry into force	Members	Secretariat
Chemicals and hazardous wastes conventions:				
Basel Convention on the Control of Transboundary Movements of Hazardous Wastes and Their Disposal	05/1992		170	UNEP
Regional seas conventions and related agreements (examples):				
The Convention for Cooperation in the Protection and Sustainable Development of the Marine and Coastal Environment of the Northeast Pacific (Antigua Convention)	2002		5	UNEP
Convention on the Conservation and Management of Fishery Resources in the South-East Atlantic Ocean	04/2001	04/2003	4	UNEP
Global Programme of Action for the Protection of the Marine Environment from Land-Based Activities	11/1995		109	UNEP
Convention for the Protection of the Mediterranean Sea against Pollution (Barcelona)	02/1976	02/1978	22	UNEP

Source: UN Environment Programme (2007).

to land (or water) is bioprospecting rights. In these cases, the competing use of land can be made explicit and the willingness to pay can be expressed by markets. New intellectual property rights are another recent development, as in the case of crop developers patenting genes or pharmaceutical firms patenting natural substances for biomedicine. Such rights establish incentives to preserve certain plants if they provide the necessary input for a marketable product.

However, at a given moment in time, not all potential applications of genes and substances can be known. Thus, property rights and markets cannot be established for all potential future uses. For some of these ecoservices, there is simply no actual demand. Consequently, biodiversity cannot be preserved by markets alone. An alternative approach becomes necessary. The task is to determine the option value or existence value for ecosystems and then to find institutional approaches to preserve them. A possible path is to define an ecosystem that must be preserved in the hope that this system contains a sufficient number of species that may be of value in the future. This can be achieved through a policy of spatial separation. Countries that have ecosystems such as rainforests may be induced to preserve them by international compensation. Similarly, as side payments are required in a solution to reduce cross-border pollution, one can argue for side payments to the countries housing a rainforest in order to encourage them not to destroy the forest. For the bargaining, however, one must stress an important difference with the case of cross-border pollution: it might very well be that it is in the long-run interest of the rainforest countries to maintain their forest for their own advantages (such as tourism) in the future, and that the country has not been aware of its own interests.

A major issue is monitoring and enforcement. An international agreement on the protection of the rainforest can be interpreted as a principal–agent problem, where the international community represents the principal and the rainforest country represents the agent. It is difficult for the international community to monitor whether the rainforest country plays by the agreed-upon rules, for instance when it receives transfers in order to protect the forest.

International agreements to save specific species, such as the whale, represent yet another approach. To date, there have been two major international agreements that attempt to deal with biodiversity loss, though both of them regulate the issue as a legal matter without recourse to economic instruments. The first is the Convention on International Trade in Endangered Species of Flora and Fauna (CITES), which was signed in 1973 and came into force in 1975. CITES was conceived as an international agreement to prevent the overexploitation of species, and 172 nations are signatory to it. It classifies species in three categories, allowing export permits for two types and regulating entirely the trade in the most endangered type (Finus 2003). So far, no species listed on CITES has become extinct. The second treaty, the United Nations International Treaty on Plant Genetic Resources for Food and Agriculture, came into force on June 29, 2004. The Treaty institutes a multilateral system of facilitated access and benefit-sharing for the crops and forages most important for food security. Scientists, international research centers, and plant breeders from public and private organizations benefit from enhanced access to genetic biodiversity. The multilateral system also ensures the fair sharing of the benefits derived from the use of genetic resources, in particular for farmers in developing countries that have contributed for centuries to the conservation of genetic resources.

Existing Multilateral Arrangements

Table VII.5 summarizes the most important international environmental conventions in the fields of the atmosphere, biodiversity, hazardous wastes, and regional seas. It indicates the date of final agreement, the date when the convention came into force, the number of members, and the UN Secretariat in charge. Seventeen conventions exist extending to 140 countries which share common bodies of water and the associated environmental problems. For a more detailed list of conventions, see Barrett (2005).

VIII
Preventing Financial Instability

In the monetary and financial area of the world economy, rules are necessary because money is not neutral. If money were simply a veil that only hides the real side of the economy, the veil could be lifted, and then the real side of the economy, untouched by money, would become visible. Since money is more than a veil, the real economy is affected by such monetary phenomena as inflation, hyperinflation, and deflation as well as by financial and currency crises and, of course, by the malfunctioning of the financial system and bank runs. Consequently, the correct institutional arrangement for the monetary–financial system is a major issue. Such a framework for financial stability has relevance for a market economy similar to the institutional arrangement for competition against endogenous tendencies to monopolies, if they remain uncontrolled. This is the concept of the German Freiburg School whose representatives were ordoliberals looking for an economic order, and not neoliberals as they are sometimes interpreted today.

The national aspect of the nonneutrality of money has to be dealt with by national institutional arrangements. Avoiding inflation requires a sound monetary policy and the independence of the central bank. These conditions are also necessary in order to avoid asset price inflation, i.e., financial bubbles. To prevent a meltdown of assets, a liquidity squeeze and a bank run in a country requires rules of soundness for banks and other financial institutions and makes national supervision necessary. Institutional safeguards are also needed to avoid sovereign default. If national policy does not establish the correct rules or if mistakes are made, the negative impact on the real side of the economy is first of all felt by the country in question, but it may, of course, also spread to other countries.

In a globalized economy, the nonneutrality of money has an international dimension through links between national phenomena of monetary and financial disturbances and a systemic crisis for the world's financial system: national inflationary movements in the price levels affect world inflation and real allocation; monetary policy may cause asset price inflation; likewise, a national deflation may have international repercussions; abrupt changes in the exchange rate as the price of national monies impinge on the international division of labor; exchange rate crises spread from one country to another and threaten to develop into an international systemic crisis; financial crises move from the financial center in one country to that of another; bank runs extend from one country to another; this also applies to liquidity evaporation occurring in the balance sheets of several banks. The cross-border links operate through many mechanisms, among them risk allocation across banking products, contagion as a psychological factor or as a consequence of budget restraints of economic agents. In order to reduce the risk of a systemic crisis for the world's financial system, global rules for the international monetary–financial system become necessary.

Note that these rules for international financial stability are additional to the rules for real capital flows, discussed in chapter VI. There we have argued that a pecking order exists between trade and the movement of factors of production, especially between real capital flows and labor migration. If we choose to interpret "capital" as real capital plus portfolio capital, there is also a pecking order of these two types of capital flows if we use volatility, or more precisely capital flow reversals, as a criterion. In this hierarchy, viewed for instance from the vulnerability of an emerging economy, foreign direct investment is the least volatile. Capital flow reversals are less likely if investors have invested in a firm, even though capital outflows remain possible. Capital flow reversals are more likely for portfolio capital, which can leave a country instantaneously. With respect to such flows, we can differentiate between equity, bonds, and short-term credits which are the most volatile.

Severe Impact of Financial Crises on the Real Side of the Economy

Monetary–financial crises have caused severe hardship in the past. In the Great Depression of 1929–33, the United States lost one-third of its GDP, industrial production halved, and unemployment jumped from 1.8% of the workforce in 1926 to 24.9% in 1933. Stock prices collapsed from an index above 350 in 1929 to 70 in 1932. Consumer prices fell by 20%, thus indicating deflation. The Great Depression represented a major shock to the world economy. World trade declined to about one-third of its 1929 level and the depression spread to the European countries. The global financial system fell into disarray. In a more recent financial crisis, Argentina lost 20% of its GDP in 2001–2. Economically speaking, the country shrank. Real wages fell by a similar percentage. Such calamities with a massive impact on the real economy usually go hand in hand with a political crisis. Other recent crises were the Swedish crisis in 1992; the Mexican peso crisis in 1994; the Asian currency crisis in 1997 in Thailand, Indonesia, Korea, and other Asian economies; the Brazilian crisis in 1999; and the Turkish crisis in 2001. In these currency crises, the nominal exchange rates changed abruptly with devaluations of 50% and more. GDP growth rates became negative. Over the course of history, we have seen many other financial crises (Kindleberger 1989), among them the tulip mania in Holland in the seventeenth century (Siebert 2007e).

Not all monetary–financial crises spread to other countries. An example is the negative impact of the bursting of the Japanese bubble in December 1989, showing up in a poor Japanese growth performance and increased unemployment in the 1990s, but remaining limited to Japan. In the period 1992–2003, the Japanese economy has been nearly stagnant (with the exception of 1996), the average annual GDP growth rate standing at 1.2%. Japan slid into a severe recession in 1998–99. Japan's accumulated GDP loss for the period 1992–2004 amounted to US$13 trillion (in constant 2000 prices), if one assumes that Japan would have continued to expand at its average GDP growth rate of 3.94% from the 1980s for the period between 1992 and 2004. This loss constitutes three times Japan's 1990 GDP (Siebert 2007e). Apparently, the negative impact of the Japanese bubble had indirect second-round effects on other countries in Asia and on the world economy since the demand stimulus coming from Japan was reduced. However, the Japanese financial crisis did not directly affect other countries.

Some years ago it was fashionable to argue that financial markets had become more efficient and were able to deal with risk much better than previously. However, while the technology of risk management of financial institutions may have improved, new risks have emerged, for instance in the derivative market. As the collapse of the hedge fund Long-Term Capital Management (LTMC) in 1998 showed, masterly expertise may not be sufficient to anticipate all possible outcomes. Furthermore, the subprime crisis and the ensuing liquidity crisis with the loss of confidence among banks in the years 2007–9 indicate that risk is far from having disappeared. The impact is massive, affecting the United States and Europe (Schmidt et al. 2008): the collapse of the German Industrie Kreditbank in August 2007; losses at some German state banks; Bear Stearns going under in 2008; the sale of Merrill Lynch to the Bank of America; the bankruptcy of Lehman Brothers and of more than ten U.S. banks; the disappearance of the concept of investment banks in the United States; the nationalization of Fannie Mae and Freddie Mac; the U.S. government taking over the American Insurance Group; the US$700 billion U.S. bailout plan intended to take out bad loans from the system; the nationalization of Northern Rock, the mortgage bank Bradford & Bingley, and other banks in the United Kingdom; the support package for Hypo Real Estate by government and the banking industry in Germany; and the support of Fortis by the Benelux countries and additional capital to Dexia being provided by the French and Belgian government. Governments have given additional guarantees for deposits; for instance, Ireland has introduced a state guarantee for all deposits and debt for its six major banks until September 2010. Iceland nationalized the banking sector. The list is not closed as of mid November 2008. Apparently, new endogenous risks of the banking industry have come to the fore. Moreover, quite a few risks for the financial markets consist of changes of government, which may completely alter the economic environment of the financial industry. Also, business cycles still create uncertainty. It would not be wise to base monetary policy and the financial order on the premise that financial crises and currency crises will be gone for good. Older publications on the emergence of financial instability (Minsky 1986) and reports on former crashes (Kindleberger 1989) should have been a warning.

As far as we know as of November 2008, the financial crisis of the years 2007–8 entailed four different aspects: it had its root cause in the burst real estate bubble of the U.S. housing market, an artificial overconsumption not supported by real savings. The failed mortgage products then led to an evaporation of assets, with financial institutions losing financial assets of about US$1.4 trillion internationally (IMF 2008b). This implied a liquidity crisis, a solvency crisis in which the assets of quite a few banks no longer covered their liabilities and a loss of confidence among banks (Snower 2008). As a consequence, a credit crunch developed so that the real sector was cut off from credit. Moreover, consumers and investors lost confidence in their deposits, uncertainty spread, and they held off consumption and investment, again affecting the real economy. The crisis intensified the slowdown in the U.S. economy, which was under way for other reasons, and also contributed to the deceleration in European economies.

In the following, we distinguish between rules averting an unstable money, those preventing financial instability, for instance the collapse of banks, and arrangements to avoid currency crises, although all three types of disturbances can be interrelated. Note that such rules have the property of a public good: the financial stability they provide is consumed in equal parts by all. Taking stock of the existing rules in these three areas, the rules for monetary stability are national, or in the case of the ECB, multinational; international monetary equilibrium is based on an implicit fragile understanding of the major central banks. International rules on financial soundness are evolving only slowly in a trial-and-error process, with national regulations still playing a major role. For the prevention of currency crises we do indeed have an explicit international rule system in the form of the IMF, but it is somewhat ironic that several countries are no longer in need of the services of the IMF, putting the IMF's mission into question. I will deal with currency crises in the next chapter.

Which Rules for Monetary Policy?

Preventing monetary and financial crises requires a solid and robust financial architecture. It is the role of central banks to provide liquidity as a lubricant for a growing economy without causing inflation, including asset price inflation, and to keep the financial system functioning. Inflation and hyperinflation can be avoided by adequate institutional arrangements for the central bank and by an adequate monetary policy. The independence of the central bank is of utmost importance. A basic rule is that public budget deficits must not be financed by printing money. This condition has been repeatedly violated in Latin American countries in the past. Moreover, an excessive credit expansion endangers monetary stability. In industrial economies, the interrelations between politics and the central bank are more intricate. The position of the central bank must be strong enough to resist political pressure for an easy money policy and for providing means for the public budget. Governments with high debt will push for low interest rates to reduce their debt burden. This also often holds for governments which want to stimulate investment when facing an election and to governments in distress. A central bank giving in to this pressure jeopardizes price-level stability. It loses credibility, which is a crucial precondition for stable money.

Taking these national institutional conditions as a starting point, an international monetary equilibrium can be understood as being the result of an implicit agreement between the major central banks, the Fed, the ECB, the Bank of Japan, and the Bank of England. Central banks usually follow a stability target. While in principle the major central banks have a choice between price-level stability and the nominal exchange rate, only smaller countries can choose to fix their exchange rate, normally to an anchor currency. In setting their monetary policies, larger countries or regions do not usually follow the policy of the anchor country. For instance, if the Fed applies an expansionary strategy, a constant exchange rate would force the ECB to tag along with the Fed's policy, allowing the price level to rise. The ECB then would contravene its target of price-level stability and lose its independence.

Among the central banks, the Fed has a special position, since the U.S. dollar is the dominating currency, with the euro—newly established in 1999—coming in second place. A leading currency or an anchor currency emerges if a country has a high share of world output, trade, and capital flows. Another important condition is that the currency is stable. Such a currency has the prospect of being accepted in many countries (dollar standard, dollarization). Of the total transactions in the international currency markets in April 2007, 86% have the U.S. dollar on one side of the transaction and 37% have the euro, where the sum of the percentage shares of the individual currencies totals 200% since two currencies are involved in each transaction. The yen and the sterling follow with 17% and 15%, respectively. The daily average turnover on the foreign exchange market amounts to US$3.2 trillion. This figure is adjusted for double counting. By far the most traded currency pair was the dollar/euro, amounting to 27% of global turnover; the dollar/yen accounted for 13% and the dollar/sterling for 12% (Bank for International Settlements 2007). Of the total reserve holdings of all central banks in April 2007 that can be allocated to a currency (identified reserves), 64.8% were held in U.S. dollars, 25.6% in euros, 2.8% in Japanese yen, and 4.7% in British pounds. Total reserves including unaccountable reserves total US$5.7 trillion. Euro holdings only amount to a value of US$936 billion (IMF 2007d).

The anchor country enjoys several advantages: it has lower transaction costs because many transactions are made in its currency. It also has the advantage of seigniorage since foreign central banks and market participants hold its currency.

Moreover, the country's financial industry benefits from the currency position. Finally, an anchor country does not have to worry about its exchange rate in the same way that other countries have to. Thus, the United States can follow a strategy of benign neglect ("The dollar is your problem and our currency"). This means that the United States does not have to intervene in the foreign exchange market to keep a specific value of its exchange rate. It can, within limits, use its monetary policy for internal goals without worrying about its balance-of-payments deficit (or its exchange rate) and it does not bear the burden of financing its balance of payments. It may be tempting to play strategically with the external value of its currency, for instance by riding out of international debt through depreciation.

Following this line, however, the United States risks losing its role of anchor, since the U.S. dollar would drop in value and the United States would not be able to attract foreign capital in the future. This, in turn, would reduce the option to finance the United States current account deficit in the long run. Nevertheless, the anchor country may take recourse to this way out in special circumstances. This may happen when the central bank uses the interest rate as a temporary stimulus to counter slipping into a national recession or alleviating a sector problem without taking into account the medium-run risk of generating a financial bubble and having the bubble burst. Also witness the United States giving up its role as monetary anchor after the Vietnam War, which then led to the termination of the Bretton Woods system. A similar case could arise if the United States loses part of its strong economic position with the ascent of China, possibly by not scaling down its military expenditures to its new position and financing the deficit through outside money. Apparently, this would put extreme pressure on other central banks, for instance the ECB, to stand to their price-level targets. As an indication, look at the Fed's lowering of the interest rate in 2007 and 2008 while the ECB did not follow.

Such extreme cases in which the anchor currency loses its role show that the international monetary equilibrium among major central banks is rather fragile. Explicit institutional rules for restraining the behavior of the central bank of the anchor currency do not exist. Since an explicit understanding on the goal of price-level stability and other goals such as preventing asset price inflation is not present, the situation among central banks can be viewed as a game: the central banks are checked by each other's behavior; the threat consists in each central bank following a completely independent strategy. As we know, using this threat may not always be strong enough to yield an equilibrium in which price-level stability prevails (on the role of central banks as a lender of last resort see chapter IX).

In addition to the lenient monetary policy in the United States in the recent past, the increase in the world's money supply is nowadays also influenced by monetary expansion in China; such an expansion, however, is not completely insulated by the devaluation of the renminbi. A situation with international reserves being ploughed back into the system will lead to a low international real interest rate which partly makes U.S. monetary policy ineffective; admittedly, such a low inter-est rate is supported by an international savings glut. This point of wrong incentives and constraints from the international monetary system was discussed at several instances in the past, for instance by Rueff (1972). However, a return to the gold standard is not feasible. Attempts for a reference zone system (Williamson 1993) or a universal currency (Mundell 2003) are not very promising.

Rules for Financial Soundness

Whereas in the area of monetary policy we may interpret the institutional arrange-ment as a fragile implicit understanding between central banks, only some elements of an international institutional arrangement exist that are needed to prevent or min-imize disruptions that can arise in the financial system (Siebert 2007e). Such an institutional design refers to the rules banks set for themselves for their own behav-ior, rules that are agreed upon by the banking industry, laws, and regulation. A core question is how different national institutional arrangements have to be conceived, not only to prevent national disruptions, but also to reduce systemic risks for the world financial system. The approaches "stability for the individual institution" and "stability begins at home" are necessary but not sufficient conditions. Due to the many cross-border links between countries and also between firms, standards have to prevent spillovers, especially contagion. Since financial crises can have a whole set of origins, an efficient institutional arrangement should provide an answer as to how *all* potential origins of financial disruptions can be ruled out. From history we know that a lot of origins can come into play. Often, many of them are forgotten so that pathological learning is typical.

   In order to study rules for the soundness of the financial system, one needs to look at the functions that the financial system has to perform: allocating savings to invest-ment; financing transactions, investment, and infrastructure; transferring, reducing, and managing risks; performing maturity transformation within reasonable limits; and sending reliable signals through prices. These functions should be performed without causing the financial disturbances discussed. Here are some crucial aspects.

Monetary Stability

Since an overexpansion of the money supply, detrimental credit extension, and exces-sive inflation can cause serious disturbances, a reliable, stability-oriented monetary policy is a precondition to preventing financial instability (see above). When this condition is not met and when economic fundamentals are not solid, inflationary expectations and expectations of currency depreciation start to develop. This, for instance, is the lesson that we can draw from the 1997 currency crises in the Asian countries.

Avoiding International Risk Exposure

Argentina in the 1980s is evidence that institutional arrangements which allow provinces to go into international debt may put a country at risk and may lead to sovereign default. This issue also played a role in the ignition of the Brazilian exchange rate crisis in 1989 when the governor of Minas Gerais declared that the province would not pay its foreign debt (Siebert 2005a). Apparently, the lessons are quickly forgotten, as the cases of Iceland and Hungary in 2008 show. Moreover, the exposure to foreign debt can aggravate a crisis, as we know from the Korean crisis in 1997, when the *chaebols* had accumulated debt in yen.

Balance Sheet Truth

The Enron case in the United States in 2001 has made it clear that stock markets cannot successfully intermediate between savings and investment if the balance sheets of firms are forged. Under such conditions, share prices are distorted; when the fraud is revealed, stocks are depreciated, in the case of Enron falling from US$90 to about 50 cents within a year. Stock owners are betrayed and reputation and credibility of the financial market is destroyed—a crucial precondition for market economies. Financial markets cannot function correctly if they do not provide reliable information. Consequently, balance sheet truth is essential; accounting does not permit compromises. The U.S. Sarbanes–Oxley Act of 2002 attempted to lay down a new corporate governance procedure. Auditing firms have to certify dependable data. The International Financial Reporting Standards have to assure that balance sheets, especially of capital market-oriented enterprises, contain reliable information. The subprime crisis has amply demonstrated that balance sheet truth also applies to the banking sector. Bank balances should reflect risks adequately. Risks should not be put off the balance sheet (see below).

A Solid Banking System and the Responsibility of Banks

The financial system of a country must be sound and robust. It has to be organized such that a financial crisis is unlikely to start or to be reinforced. Thus, the crisis in 2008 has shown that a universal banking system is more robust than the investment banking approach; but it may well be premature to declare the end of history for investment banks. Without soundness of the banking system, bank runs may occur and other financial crises such as the evaporation of liquidity may happen. To prevent this requires standards for commercial banks and other financial institutions (including investment banks) to be set so that an economy is not easily affected by external shocks; nor should endogenous shocks be possible. The correct expression of risks in the balance sheets of banks, and reliable accounting and auditing are relevant issues.

It is in the individual bank's self-interest and it has a responsibility to set incentives for its managers and establish norms of behavior that prevent its failure, assuming that the bank cannot implicitly play a strategic game against the central bank and the government that it will be bailed out somehow when the worst case comes to pass. Established banking principles should not be easily thrown overboard. One such principle is that caution is required when long-term tasks are financed with short-term means. Leverage between borrowed capital and equity should not endanger the bank's existence; a leverage of more than 20:1, as used by investment banks, proved to be a disaster. An incentive system that generates high short-run-oriented commissions for bankers so that they have an interest in developing new financial products and inflating the bank's balance sheet is hardly sustainable; it increases the risk of insolvency. Incentive systems of banks should not honor short-term profits and should not favor the accumulation of risks; they should take into account the long-run risk position of a bank, including the risk position over the business cycle. In a recession, some loans become nonperforming and assets in the bank balance tend to lose value. The risk position also varies with what is happening to other banks and the whole industry. This has been labeled the aggregation problem by Scholes (2008) or the problem of interconnectedness by Stiglitz (2008), who somewhat loosely also uses the term "pecuniary externalities." We may also simply state that there is a potential for mistakes to be correlated across banks (Geithner 2008). With such interdependencies, financial markets may not be efficient in providing correct price signals. If assets lose value, a bank only has the option of raising additional equity or selling assets in order to maintain its risk position. Then a bank is severely constrained in its behavior. Witness the situation in 2007 and 2008. De-leveraging by one bank affected the others and the whole industry. Consequently, the bank's risk management has to anticipate how the bank's environment will change, including the probability distribution. A bank has to be aware of risks in the tails of a probability distribution with low probability, but large damage—the "black swans." A bank has to steer its reserves accordingly to prevent getting into an untenable situation. Moreover, in a financial bubble, when the herd is running those in charge have to stay outside the turmoil and remind everyone of the equilibrium that will be sustainable in the long run, so to say the intertemporal "fix point" or the transversality condition known from intertemporal optimization models. Such an intertemporal fix point would have prevented bubbles such as tulip mania in Holland in the seventeenth century; and it could avoid other financial exuberance (Shiller 2005). Whereas we may look for a better institutional infrastructure to deal with the issue of the interconnectedness of risks, it is the bank's own responsibility to be informed on the changing environment.

The necessity of including long-run aspects in a bank's risk management reduces the possibility of increasing profits through technological product innovation. But if a bank does not want to find itself in a position of liquidity shortage, and being forced to ask for fresh capital or to sell its assets and thus to lose its decision freedom, it has to include long-run risks in its calculus, especially if it wants to prevent insolvency.

Similarly, it is in the self-interest of the banking industry to come up with international institutional arrangements that prevent bank failures. If false incentives for the behavior of banks are set, if moral hazard prevails, and if price signals are misleading, the risk of the banking industry is endogenous.

However, experience shows that it is difficult to obtain voluntary instability-preventing institutional arrangements. One reason is that banks have a strong interest in financial innovation. By developing new financial products, banks can make a profit relative to their competitors. Consequently, they tend to outbid themselves in new products, with the industry thus exhibiting herding behavior. This creates the need for regulation. Financial innovation is likely to increase the demand for institutional infrastructure. Self-regulation by banks does not represent a viable solution. However, what an efficient institutional design—comprising rules that are self-set by individual banks, those that are agreed upon by the banking industry, laws, and regulatory mechanisms—for the financial sector should look like is an unresolved problem. The design must be such that the financial sector is robust.

Regulation and Banking Supervision

For the reasons discussed, prudent supervision represents an important aspect of preventing bank failures and financial crises. When a bank run occurs, and when customers lose confidence in the reputation of a bank and withdraw their deposits as quickly as possible in order not to lose their funds (as in the case of Northern Rock in the United Kingdom in 2007), it is too late. This also applies when liquidity is withheld as in the case of Bear Stearns. Regulation of the financial markets includes a broad spectrum of policy instruments, ranging from capital adequacy requirements, margin requirements, and bank reserve requirements to forms of deposit insurance, restrictions on financial products, oversight of market practices (also outside the narrow banking sector), observation of the maturity structure and risk transformation, price controls, and governmental fees (Geithner 2008). Regulations intend to improve information for the investor, to assure the stability of the system over time and to prevent financial crises.

National regulators compete with each other, since financial institutions and investors can avoid a regulatory regime by making their transactions in another country. In this case, regulation may drive the financial industry or a financial product out of a country. One response to this phenomenon of regulatory arbitrage is to agree internationally on standards. For instance, the industry can concur on best practices (Institute of International Finance 2008). Another approach is used by the Financial Stability Forum, hosted by the Bank for International Settlements in Basel, in bringing together senior representatives of national financial authorities—central banks, supervisory authorities and treasury departments, international financial institutions, international regulatory and supervisory groupings, committees of central bank experts, and the European Central Bank. It seeks to coordinate the efforts of these various bodies in order to promote international financial stability, improve the functioning of financial markets, and reduce systemic risk.

The implementation of standards of financial soundness in national institutional arrangements can help to reduce financial disturbances in countries and to limit international repercussions. This holds, for instance, for the Financial Soundness Indicators of the IMF (IMF 2008a), although these only represent recommendations. The Basel II Framework of the Basel Committee on Banking Supervision, agreed upon in 2004 as a consequence of the Asian currency crisis, has established capital adequacy requirements for banks. Banks have to back their claims on the nonbank private sector by an overall limit of 8% for capital endowment (a bank's capital in terms of shareholders' equity or retained earnings as a percentage of its risk weighted credit exposure), permitting a differentiation between different risk categories of claims. External ratings and standardized internal control mechanisms are used to assess credit risks. National supervisory authorities are now implementing these rules through domestic rule-making and adoption procedures. The Basel Committee has addressed the home–host information sharing requirements in a 2006 paper that are necessary for the implementation of Basel II (Basel Committee on Banking Supervision 2006).

While the Basel II adequacy requirements have some merit, they alert banks to risks in their balance sheets, they also point out how difficult it is to establish clear standards for financial soundness: unfortunately, the risks vary with the business cycle. Therefore, the capital adequacy requirements should "breathe" with the economic situation. Possibly, such requirements should be not be defined with respect to the levels of risk-weighted assets but to their rates of growth (Goodhart 2008). Moreover, they do not resolve the aggregation problem or the problem of interconnectedness, i.e., that the risk position of a bank varies with the risk position of other banks. Consequently, Basel II is far from representing a faultless protection against financial crises. Unfortunately, it did not prevent excessive risk-taking and may be considered a regulatory failure (Meltzer 2008).

Some Lessons from the Subprime Crisis

It is amazing that banks have circumvented the Basel II rules by shifting risky business off their balance sheets. This is astonishing because the Basel II rules were agreed upon internationally in 2004 so that good business practice would imply that banks follow these recommendations even if they only came into effect in some countries as of 2008. Instead, banks invented offshore structured investment vehicles, or conduits, as independent subsidiaries that were established with a negligible capital endowment, specializing in securitization (Borio 2008; Brunnermeier, forthcoming). For instance, the conduit bought up mortgages (or other papers), bundled them up, "securitized" them, and offered them on the market to investors as asset-backed securities. It issued short-term commercial paper to finance long-term investment, a maturity transformation that can violate another traditional banking principle. The conduit received funds from investors, because the bank sponsoring the conduit granted a credit line to the conduit. In this way, the bank took the conduit off its balance sheet, as the collapse of the German Industrie Kreditbank (IKB) in August 2007 has shown.[1] Investment banks were also involved in securitizing low-value mortgages. As a consequence, banks often no longer actually know how much credit risk they have hidden in their books. Nor are markets informed on the risk collected in the banking system. Even without the Basel II rules, banks should have respected the principles of decent behavior, and not camouflaged the risk they were exposed to.

The behavior of the banks described above, including their "originate and distribute" business model, occurred during a period of aggressive risk-taking. When some of the risks materialized with the end of the U.S. housing bubble in the fall of 2005, assets melted away and the liquidity of the banking system evaporated (Borio 2008). Some mechanisms intensified the liquidity spiral, for instance the need for de-leveraging (Brunnermeier, forthcoming). One recommendation is that banks must be aware of their risks; risks must be transparent. Regulation should convince banks to hold stronger cushions of capital and liquidity, which is in their self-interest (Geithner 2008). Adequate capital requirements must be enforced. It should also be absolutely clear that balance sheets of banks have to be consolidated and must include all risks that a bank is exposed to. There is no question that financial supervision has to strengthen the rules for the consolidation of off-balance-sheet vehicles and of the risks associated with them. We need to know which part of the credit remains with the sponsor bank and which part is taken over by the vehicle company, or by secondary or tertiary banks to which the assets have been sold; the original sponsor should take over part of the risk (Franke and Krahnen 2007). In any case, the conditions under which risks can be shifted through securitization should be evaluated. Furthermore, in their own interests, banks have to improve transparency. Rating agencies must see their role as one of reducing uncertainty in the financial markets. They have to improve their ratings and should give up consulting. A rating at any given moment in time cannot be sold as remaining constant under all conditions. Consequently, the role of ratings in the regulatory framework such as Basel II has to be revised; regulation cannot rely on ratings automatically. The conflict of

---

[1] It is difficult to determine the risk allocation between the credit guarantor, i.e., the sponsor, and the vehicle company. In the case of IKB, it is reported that the risk allocation is found in a sentence on p. 92 of a 400-page contract, worded in such a way that it is difficult even for legal experts to understand what is meant.

interest of rating agencies being paid by the issuers of the securities they actually rate has to be resolved without introducing new conflicts of interest, for instance being paid by investors (Davies 2008b). Financial supervision should compare the quality of ratings *ex post*, for instance relating statistical ratings to subsequent defaults (Issing Committee 2008). It also has to improve its own efficiency. More specifically, prudent supervision has to make sure that systemic risks do not accumulate in the financial industry; regulation needs instruments to prevent an increase in these risks. In addition, banks have to set the incentives for bank managers such that they are not biased in favor of high risk exposure and that managers are accountable. Prudent supervision should keep an eye on distorted incentives for bank managers, observe market practices and focus attention on the maturity transformation taking place outside the banking system, also through hedge funds and other derivatives. As the actual crisis shows, there is a price to pay if some financial institutions such as investment banks are allowed to remain outside the regulatory framework. This also applies to other parts of shadow banking, for instance of the transparency of systemic risks of these systems such as hedge funds (Snower 2008).

Unfortunately, the subprime crisis had many more origins, exemplifying the difficulty of guaranteeing financial stability. The low interest rate of 1% during some years—a result of the Fed's expansionary policy, and accordingly the expectation of rising interest rates—represented a stark incentive to take out mortgages. The housing bubble led people to expect that the mortgage could be financed through the increases in wealth from rising house prices. This was similar to the herding behavior in previous bubbles, for instance the Dutch tulip mania in the seventeenth century. Mortgage banks and other lenders gave up the principle that a certain percentage of equity, say 20%, was needed to obtain a mortgage when buying a house. Overconsumption in the United States in constructing new homes did not have a foundation in savings; in that sense, it was artificial. Of course, politicians liked that their voters could live up to the American dream of owning their home. In a way, people were lured into taking out mortgages; predatory lending prevailed. Self-control of the banking industry did not exist, nor were standards controlled by regulatory authorities. The industry did not provide mortgage products with which mortgage-takers could live once the housing bubble died down. These false incentives were exacerbated by Fannie Mae and Freddie Mac, government-sponsored organizations, who bought mortgages from mortgage bankers and other lenders, bundled them up and placed them on the international market. This improved the liquidity position of mortgage banks, enabling them to hand out even more mortgages. Thus, some risks were passed on to these quasi-governmental institutions. The regulatory regime for Fannie Mae and Freddie Mac, established by Congress, namely the Office of the Federal Housing Enterprise Oversight, proved to be inefficient; it represented a signal to the market of an implied governmental guarantee. The institutional arrangement for Fannie Mae and Freddie Mac was flawed from its beginning in 1968; their accounting scandals in 2003 and 2004 were covered up by Congress (Wallison and Calomoris 2008). Meanwhile, the government has completely taken over both institutions. Dividends to shareholders were cut; the taxpayer has to step in. The securitization and the repackaging of bad mortgage loans was one channel through which the U.S. mortgage crisis spilled over into Europe. This is how the United States was able to keep its bubble, which had no support in real savings, afloat—similar to the current account deficit finances consumption without savings. Another origin of the actual financial crisis was a 2004 decision by the U.S. Securities and Exchange Commission to grant an exemption of its thirty-year long-standing rule limiting broker dealers' debt-to-net-capital to a ratio of 12:1. It granted the exemption to Goldman Sachs, Merrill Lynch, Lehman Brothers, Bear Stearns, and Morgan Stanley, allowing them to lever up to 30 or 40 to 1—firms that all got into trouble (Ritholz 2008). To sum up: the financial crisis in 2007–8 was not the result of exogenous forces that hit the banking industry; it was an endogenous crisis that developed within the financial system. It was also a result of regulation failure in the United States and in Europe, where regulators did not recognize the problems that were endangering their banking systems. Nor did the IMF make out the structural flaws of the international financial system and the origin of the crisis.

Other Failures of Regulation

The subprime crisis shows that regulation per se, for instance Basel II or semigovernmental institutions such as Fannie Mae and Freddie Mac, is not a guarantee that financial crises will be prevented. On the contrary: since regulations set incentives, they may well set the wrong incentives and cause moral hazard. Another example is the failure of the 747 savings and loan associations in the United States in the 1980s and 1990s; the origin was a government regulation providing special protection to risky loans of these institutions. This was an incentive to go into more risky lending. The failure of U.S. regulators to detect the fraud at Enron is a further case (Meltzer 2008). The failure of regulation in Germany to notice the problems at Industrie Kreditbank and Hypo Real Estate and to act accordingly is another example. Yet another aspect is that the regulation of the financial sector depends on other policy instruments. Thus, the financial crises in Sweden in 1992 and in Thailand in 1997 illustrate that a financial crisis is likely to arise if the capital account is liberalized and if, at the same time, the banking sector is not robust and not adequately regulated with respect to prudential standards; then an overexpansion of credit may result. It has now been accepted that there is a sequencing problem in liberalizing the banking sector and the capital account. The liberalization of the capital account should be preceded by an appropriate prudent regulation of the banking sector. For China, for example, this means that the capital account can only be liberalized after the fragile banking system has been made sufficiently robust (Siebert 2007a).

One major reason why regulation often fails is that the regulator does not have the appropriate information. This is the issue of asymmetric information at a given moment of time, and it is also the Hayekian problem that the regulator cannot possibly have all the necessary information on future economic conditions; most specifically, he cannot have all the information on the product innovation of the industry. Another major reason for regulation failure is capture, i.e., that the interest of the regulated seizes the institutional arrangements and dominates the interest of the public. Asymmetric information is one reason why the expertise of those concerned is needed who then use their influence. Most importantly, regulation may also be captured by the political process, as, for example, the history of Fannie Mae and Freddie Mac demonstrates. That is why I am skeptical about the Stiglitz proposal (2008) to include those affected by financial products into a regulatory body. The body then may well be captured by its members and by politics. After all, we should not forget the good experiences we have with de-politicizing institutional arrangements, for instance in the realm of central banks. New regulations, introduced with the best of intentions, may have hidden incentive effects which may represent new moral hazards so that the institutional arrangement is not improved (Davies 2008b). Moreover, time inconsistency of political decision making with shifting preferences is an important factor affecting the regulatory framework and causing its instability.

Regulations may be able to make a financial system more stable. But since they may also set the wrong incentives, they can only be justified if net gains exist. Stability of the banking system is part of efficiency in a long-run interpretation (Geithner 2008). All this requires complex analysis of the impact of regulations. Since regulation failure cannot be excluded, an institutional arrangement also has to make use of the self-interest of financial institutions, their responsibility, and the strengthening of market discipline.

Crisis Management

Another aspect of a correct institutional design is crisis management, i.e., how authorities should respond to a financial crisis. A distinction must be made between national crises, i.e., those contained in a country such as the deposit run on Northern Rock, and cross-border crises (Goodhart 2008). In the case of nationally contained crises, a major question is whether the central bank or the government has to step in. Although explicit cross-border bank runs have not occurred lately, the 2007–8 meltdown of assets and the liquidity evaporation clearly implied cross-border spillovers. While in cross-border spillovers burden-sharing between countries or some form of cooperation becomes an issue, in the 2007–8 financial crisis losses of banks largely remained the problem of the individual bank, the national safety nets, and of national authorities, i.e., central banks (the Fed in the case of Bear Stearns and the American Insurance Group), or the national public budget (ultimately the taxpayer in the case of Fannie Mae and Freddie Mac as well as in the U.S. bailout deal for bad loans and in Germany for Industrie Kreditbank, Hypo Real Estate, and the rescue plan of 500 billion euros). The United States and European countries have arranged for deposit guaranties, credit guaranties, and capital to be injected into their banks of roughly 3 trillion euros.

Crisis management has followed several paths: in a first response, central banks reacted to the liquidity crisis of the banking system by large-scale exceptional injections of liquidity, for instance €95 billion by the ECB and US$38 billion by the Fed on a single day: August 9, 2007. Massive further injections followed, often undertaken in a coordinated manner. These injections represented short-run overnight liquidity or liquidity for two weeks or even months in which the central banks accept securities against liquidity (repurchase agreement). Along the same lines, central banks lowered the interest rate, for instance in a concerted action on October 8, 2008. In a second response, the Fed reacted by providing credit (see below). In a third reaction, governments increased the guarantee for deposits. They came up with bail-out plans for individual banks, providing a guarantee or supplying fresh capital, and with rescue plans for the entire banking sector, taking out bad loans from the banks' balance sheets and offering to buy preferential shares of banks, partly nationalizing them. All these measures failed to address the crisis in the U.S. housing market and overconsumption, the origin of the crisis. The mark-to-market accounting rules were changed somewhat by the Securities and Exchange Commission and by the European Commission in the fall of 2008. While mark-to-market accounting does indeed make it more difficult for banks to withstand the crisis, the change in accounting rules may invite accountants to hide problems, even if their methods of evaluation have to be communicated to the regulatory authorities.

A way out of the crisis comes if housing prices, the value of bad loans, or other asset prices have fallen so low that it becomes a bargain to buy; then the market will reverse itself. As the case of Wachovia shows, the government-orchestrated solution of selling the bank to Citigroup for US$2.2 billion was inferior to the US$11.7 billion takeover through Wells Fargo, representing a market solution. Other factors would be that an economic upswing, population growth, and immigration will increase the demand for housing and ease the U.S. housing crisis. In addition, the hope for a solution is that the actual loss of confidence is irrational. Thus the Ted-Spread, a measure of the probability of default, was so high at the end of September that "AAA-rated 10 year bonds were priced as if the probability of default of the bluest of blue chips was 39%" (Hassett 2008). This is unrealistic. Consequently, the intertemporal fix point should tell investors that the time for a bargain has come.

Crisis Management in the United States

In addition to providing liquidity, the Fed has started to extend credits. This happened when it gave a credit of US$29 billion to JPMorgan to acquire Bear Stearns, and when it introduced a two-year credit line of US$85 billion to the insurer American Insurance Group, receiving equity participation notes amounting to 79.9% of the firm's capital. The insurer was taken over by the government. In October 2008, the Fed added a second credit line of US$37.8 billion. It was involved in the bailout of US$326 billion for City Bank in November 2008. Moreover, Morgan Stanley and Goldman Sachs now have access to the Fed's support after they have given up their special investment bank status. The Fed has also set up a 28-day Treasury Security Lending Facility, which offers Treasury general collateral to the Federal Reserve Bank of New York's primary dealers in exchange for other program-eligible collateral, including mortgage-backed securities and investment-grade corporate securities. This facility may be used in connection with the US$200 billion package for Fannie Mae and Freddie Mac, although as yet it is only reaching much smaller volumes. In addition, the Fed will directly lend to corporations for a limited time, and not only to banks; this has happened for the first time since the Great Depression. It will also buy up companies' short-term debt; the power to do so was bestowed on the Fed during the Great Depression as part of the Federal Reserve Act. The Fed's balance sheet enlarged considerably in 2008 relative to 2007, with the asset and liability side nearly doubling.

It has to be seen which moral hazards will follow for the financial system in the future from the large liquidity injections and from the Fed's extension of credits. In principal, there is a goal conflict for central banks between price-level stability and guaranteeing the functioning of the financial system. This especially applies to the credits provided by the Fed, since they come close to the Fed providing money to the governmental budget; the Fed's credits substitute tax money. Lending directly to firms endangers the Fed's own exposure. It remains open as to how these unusual interventions, intended to restore confidence among banks, will affect inflationary expectations, possibly leading to a loss of confidence of the public toward the monetary authorities. It also has to be seen to what extent they will be the seed for a new crisis in which confidence in the Fed, and possibly the U.S. dollar, will weaken. Amazingly, this has not happened as of November 2008.

The main argument for the measures brought in by the Fed was that the damage would have been much larger, had the financial system collapsed. This argument is also used for the interventions of the U.S. government, nationalizing Fannie Mae and Freddie Mac, taking over the American International Group, and introducing a bailout arrangement that will take out bad loans from the system in the magnitude of US$700 billion; the program is spread over three stages. Following the United Kingdom's example (see below) and the Swedish experience of 1992 (Ergunor 2007), the U.S. government will buy preferred shares from financial institutions, thus partly nationalizing the banking industry. The premise is that the market will not be able to find its own way out of the crisis and that bankruptcies would aggravate the problem (for the opposite opinion, see Miron (2008)).

The US$700 billion bailout approach is similar to the Resolution Trust Company, which took over bad loans in the savings and loan crisis at the end of the 1980s. Its key element consists of the government buying up bad loans which it will later sell. A process has to be set up for buying up toxic assets, such as mortgage-backed securities from financial institutions, most likely through reversed auctions in which the lowest-valued securities will be bought up. The design of such auctions is complicated because the financial institutions having the bad loans can play strategically against the government. How to take nonperforming loans out of a banking system is a complex matter as the Japanese experience shows (Nakaso 2001). The US$700 billion measure was sweetened by extending bank deposit insurance up to US$250,000 (which may imply emergency lending to the Federal Deposit Insurance Corporation) and by adding new tax breaks. In addition, federal resources will be used to help homeowners at the risk of foreclosure. Whereas there is no alternative to the bailout, it represents a consequence of the housing bubble and institutional failure, especially of the setup of Fannie Mae and Freddie Mac, whose institutional flaws are covered up by the bailout. Also note that the U.S. bailout plan only addresses the liquidity squeeze and the solvency problem for some banks, but does not solve the housing crisis.

The funds to buy up the bad loans and to buy preferential shares in banks will come from government bonds, but in the end, the American taxpayer will have to foot most of the bill, unless the stakes taken in U.S. financial institutions by the government regain value. To finance the program through bonds is doable as long as the American state remains credible; but the future maneuvering space of government will be restricted. It is still up in the air as to whether the US$200 billion support announced for Fannie Mae and Freddie Mac will be sufficient; the debt of Fannie Mae and Freddie Mac is estimated at US$5 trillion, partly supported by real value. If this was the relevant figure, the share of U.S. debt in GDP would rise by 36 percentage points to 100% when OECD data are used. Through the bailout arrangement of US$700 billion, the share will increase by another 5 percentage points. The condition for success of the bailout arrangement is that all uncertainty disappears.

In crisis management, one has to be aware that short-run measures may change the characteristics of the institutional arrangement with a long-run impact on the incentive system and adverse moral hazards. A case in point is the impact of the generous liquidity support, necessary in the short run to reintroduce confidence in the Fed's exposure and the possible impact on inflation. The question arises as to what extent the Fed's policy and the U.S. bailout plan actually keep the bubble going without requiring a fundamental correction of the artificial overconsumption in the U.S. housing market. Moreover, as we know from the savings and loan crisis in the United States, strengthening deposit protection will present a new moral hazard for the behavior of banks, in the actual case by introducing a bias in favor of savings and against investment in the long run. In Europe, deposit protection represents a distortion to the benefit of those institutions that are close to the government, such as semi-public savings banks. Strengthening capital requirements, of course, comes at higher costs for the public (Davies 2008a).

In looking at the way out of the financial crisis, it should not be forgotten that other disturbances of the financial system may occur. Thus, American households may find themselves in a trap in their leasing finance of gasoline-intensive cars which they may have to give up when energy prices rise and when environmental policy mandates the internalization of environmental costs. Adjustment of this situation may have an impact on the automobile industry. Prepaying consumption through credit cards is another story. Moreover, it cannot be ruled out that somewhere in the world a currency crisis will erupt or that the fragile Chinese banking system will create new problems.

Crisis Management in the EU

In Europe, exposed to a liquidity crisis and also a solvency problem of its banking industry, but not to a housing crisis like the United States, the response to the crisis was overwhelmingly national except for liquidity provided by the ECB in the euro area. The ECB balance sheet enlarged from 2007 to 2008, not quite as significantly as that of the Fed. Thus, Ireland has given a state guarantee for all deposits and debt for its six major banks until September 2010. Other countries followed. The Benelux countries injected capital into their Fortis bank, and Belgium and France provided capital for Dexia. The United Kingdom nationalized Northern Rock and took over the mortgage bank Bradford & Bingley which was then partly sold. The United Kingdom also came up with a three-pronged rescue plan, the basis of which is to raise the low capital endowment of U.K. banks. The government offers to take a stake in the banks, up to £75 billion, providing capital by buying preferred shares that pay a fixed interest or underwriting issues of ordinary shares. This means partly nationalizing the banks if they are unable to raise the required capital themselves. Banks participating have to lower their dividends and managers' salaries. In addition, banks that meet the capital thresholds are offered government guarantees amounting to as much as £250 billion, allowing them to renew their bonds when they mature. Furthermore, the government will add £100 billion to the Bank of England short- and medium-term loan scheme, in which banks can obtain short-term liquidity.

The German government sold Industrie Kreditbank with a loss of about €9 billion and arranged financial support of €50 billion together with the private sector for Hypo Real Estate in October 2008.[2] Hypo Real Estate ceded assets amounting to €42 billion to the federal government. The government's guarantee will be implemented through a special purpose vehicle set up by the German Bundesbank. Incidentally, the Bundesbank has created a liquidity facility, accepting securities of Hypo Real

---

[2] The Saxony state bank was sold requiring a guarantee of €2.75 billion from the state of Saxony.

Estate up to €20 billion, similar to the liquidity window introduced by the Fed. The German government also gave a political guarantee for deposits, promising a full guarantee without putting it into law.

In addition, Germany came up with a rescue plan similar to that of the United Kingdom with a volume of €500 billion, about the same amount as the U.S. bailout plan of US$700 billion. It contains €80 billion for the capitalization of banks according to which the government offers to buy preferential shares in financial institutions if they need capital. The government will also give credit guarantees of up to €400 billion for which banks pay interest. All this will be done on a case-by-case basis. The funds are available until December 2009. The government will establish a special fund which will administer the program and can give the guaranties. It is independent, but receives support from the Bundesbank. The government will impose conditions on the behavior of banks participating in the program. These limit manager income to €500,000 per year and forbid bonuses and dividends. Supposedly, the finance minister can intervene in the bank's business model, requiring for instance that credits are given to small- and medium-sized enterprises. The special fund will be financed by bonds. It is reminiscent of the German Unity Fund which was eventually integrated into the state's budget. The upper estimate for the costs to the budget lies at €20 billion. These costs will be split between the federal government and the Länder. The law was passed on October 17 by the Bundestag and the Bundesrat.

In light of the fact that representatives of the German government were represented in the supervisory boards of the failed banks and that financial supervision did not recognize the coming crisis of some German banks, it is somewhat surprising that the government is confident that it can avoid policy and regulatory failure in the administration and operation of the special fund. So far, it was not the expertise of government to run banks. Moreover, the nitty-gritty case-by-case discretionary decisions of the special fund may prove to be prone to mistakes and to be bureaucratic. Also, it is uncertain whether the upper limit of budget costs will be upheld. It is fair to say that the governmental rescue plan was used overwhelmingly by the German state banks, the *Landesbanken*. Amazingly, the government's rescue plan helped the government's banks. Governors of state banks have considered it a matter of prestige to keep their state bank solvent. Finally, the rescue plan presupposes that the general public does not lose confidence in what the government is doing.

National responses create difficulties in the EU's single market, representing a distortion for the financial sector going against the spirit of integration. One country's solution represents another country's problem. For instance, the deposit guarantee of Ireland was an incentive for British depositors to move their accounts to Ireland so that the United Kingdom had to follow with its own guarantee. Through such spillovers, national solutions are interlinked. This is why EU finance ministers have agreed on the guideline that national governments in the EU27 should provide deposit guarantees of up to €50,000. Apparently, this guideline does not cover the different approaches of EU members. Moreover, other approaches of crisis management in the EU are not uniform. Thus, liquidity injections by the ECB positively affect only the euro-area banks. The main reason that, in spite of the spillovers, EU crisis management has remained national (within agreed-upon guidelines) lies in the fact that any bailout of the banking sector must be supported by the national capacity to tax. Due to the EU's federal structure and the condition that direct taxation is national being subject to the EU anonymity rule, any bailout can only be supported nationally. Therefore, an EU rescue plan with burden-sharing would encounter the problem that it would open the road to the EU level deciding on the spending of national tax revenues. Counties are not ready to cede sovereignty in this realm. One would rather not see a major border-crossing financial crisis in the European Union or even in the euro area. It would be difficult to imagine how burden-sharing could be arranged in such a situation and what role fiscal cooperation and the ECB would play. In principle, in the euro area with cross-border banking groups, the Lamfalussy framework attempts to provide a regulatory and supervisory setup to ensure financial stability (ECB 2008); it can be viewed as representing a survey of issues in a nutshell that may arise internationally. However, the European supervisory framework seems insufficiently equipped to deal with a major financial crisis and shield the euro (Issing Committee 2008).

Crisis management in Europe has had political consequences. Take Germany. In view of a rescue package of €500 billion for the banking sector, antirecession programs or subsidies for specific sectors are easily accepted by public opinion, in spite of their failure in the past. It remains open as to what impact the antirecession program will eventually have on public debt. Sarkozy has proposed national bailout plans for European industry. This is not far from the destabilizing actions that are known from the 1930s. It would involve high costs if the world economy now returned to protectionism and if the established rule system for the international division of labor on the world's product market became endangered.

Drawing Up a New Financial Architecture

For crisis management, it is essential to know how the rule system will look in the long run. Drawing up a new financial order can be analyzed with principal–agent theory in which the principal sets the rules and incentives but cannot observe the behavior of the agents, including their efforts and their options to avoid following the rules. The politician is the principal defining the rules for financial institutions—the agents. As we know from principal–agent theory, it is a complicated task to write the rules.

It is open on which basic elements of a rule system the countries of the world, among them the G8 plus Brazil, India, China, and others can agree upon in the financial summits. Countries assign different roles to their financial industry and to financial innovation in their economic strategies. In the past, countries have used quite different approaches to the institutional arrangement of their financial industry and in financial supervision. In addition, the economic situation and structural conditions vary between countries. In any case, a major problem in drawing up a rule system for the financial industry is preventing countries from taking recourse to protectionism and repeating the mistakes of the 1930s when the world economy disintegrated. Instead, the conclusion of the Doha Round is a promising avenue.

In spite of different approaches to the financial industry, it is conceivable that the experience of the financial crisis will prove to be a sufficient impetus to agree on a new set of rules in which countries can find some general principles and concur on some technical points for financial systems, as discussed above: balance sheet truth must hold. Financial institutions should not be allowed to take risks off the balance sheet. Capital adequacy requirements, i.e., a bank's capital in terms of shareholders' equity and retained earnings as a percentage of its risk weighted credit exposure, must take into account the long-run sustainability of a financial institution; a value of 10% seems appropriate. Such capital adequacy requirements have to adjust to adverse situations in the business cycle and in the interconnectedness of risk positions within the industry. They also have to be set higher for more risky activities. Thus, bank credits to hedge funds represent a higher systemic risk and therefore require higher ratios. Levers between debt and the bank's own equity should be limited: they should not exceed 12:1, a ratio in force in the United States before 2004. It is most likely that to rely solely on aggregate ratios will not be sufficient to avoid financial instability. Besides looking at these ratios and interpreting them in a changing environment, regulators have to step in when they observe excessive increases in debt and credits (Smith and Walter 2008). In securitization, the originator of a loan should retain part of the original risk, say 10 or 20%. It should be disclosed to the market who takes the first loss in securitization transactions and to what degree (Issing Committee 2008). Incentive systems for bank managers should be oriented at the long-run sustainability of a financial institution, i.e., its solvency. Prudent supervision has to become more effective. It must be put into a position to prevent systemic risk; it must have the instruments to avert systemic risks, for instance through stress tests. As an example, prudent supervision has to prevent a situation in which a country accumulates too much foreign debt (see Iceland and Hungary in 2008) or in which a country's banking industry accumulates too much risk exposure through loans to other countries.[3] In the insurance industry, the EU has introduced Solvency II, establishing rules for capital requirements and reinsurance solutions of insurers within the EU. This is likely to lead to more convergence in supervisory approaches. Ratings have to be improved (see above). At the same time, regulators should not rely automatically on ratings. All financial institutions that have systemic importance should be subject to

---

[3] For instance, BIZ data indicate that in the summer of 2008 German banks had claims of €21.3 billion on Icelandic banks, €769 billion on British customers, and €310.6 billion against Spanish customers.

supervision. This also applies to investment funds operating inside banks, financial divisions of insurance companies, and partly to hedge funds, i.e., the shadow banks. All financial institutions should disclose their risk; supervisors have to define risk disclosure requirements. The risk going together with new financial products should be made explicit. Transparency for derivatives has to be established. A clearing mechanism for derivatives and hedge funds has to be created, possibly by an industry agreement (Draghi 2008). Offshore markets not participating in the rules exhibit larger risks. Additional proposals include a credit register so that financial authorities are informed on the credits in the system; a world risk map is recommended so that it can be easily detected where risks accumulate. These two instruments require international cooperation (Issing Committee 2008). It is a matter of debate which new financial products regulators should ban, for instance selling short in which sectors. Certification of new financial products may prove a bureaucratic approach. All in all, the financial sector should not distance itself too much from the real economy.

A fundamental systemic problem for an institutional arrangement is that in the long run a bankruptcy procedure for financial institutions must be introduced in which the government credibly commits itself not to bail them out in a worst-case scenario. An important element of such a rule is that in the case of failure the owners of the bank will lose their capital and that its managers will be replaced by the regulator. Due to the pervasive impact of a bank failure on the general public, it would be extremely difficult to give credibility to such a no-bail-out rule. Without such a credible rule, however, banks can expect to be bailed out. Then the actual financial crisis will soon be forgotten and a cycle of pathological learning will recommence. Thus, in ten or twenty years from now, governments will be in the same position as they found themselves when the financial crisis erupted in 2008. In any case, central banks and governments should be aware that without such a credible no-bail-out rule, commercial banks can view the massive injections of liquidity and the immense fiscal support packages by national governments as a strategic game in which they can determine the responses with which they can make the best out of the crisis. In order to prevent such a cat-and-mouse game, the governments must have the ability to write a sustainable principal–agent contract.

Another issue of an international rule system consists in preventing national rule systems from being captured by the national political process, i.e., the financial system being used for political goals. Last but not least, international rules for the financial sector should prevent that a bubble arises if the rules allow an artificial financing of overspending (overconsumption, overinvestment) and if the bubble has no basis in real savings (as in the case of the U.S. housing market); the U.S. credit card sector may represent another example.

Yet another important aspect of a financial rule system is that international spillovers are typical for the financial industry. In order to prevent one country's solution becoming another country's problem, some type of cooperation is needed. This does not only apply to the European Union; it also holds internationally. Coordination among national regulatory authorities is needed similarly as among competition authorities (see chapter V). This can be done under the umbrella of the Financial Stability Forum, which should attempt to open membership to emerging countries to ensure that the Financial Stability Forum does not appear as a rich men's club (Draghi 2008). Cross-border banks especially require some form of cooperation among regulators, for instance within regulatory colleges. The Bank for International Settlements can play the role of standard-setter. Standards should refer to the economic situation and the structure of the banking industry. They do not have to be completely uniform across countries.

The Role of the IMF for Financial Stability

Along another avenue, there is demand for an increased role for the IMF in preventing financial instability. This Bretton Woods institution indeed represents an international forum where finance ministers and central bankers meet and where they can exchange views, for instance on crisis management. There is no question that the IMF can help those countries that experience balance-of-payments or currency problems as a consequence of financial crises, for instance if emerging countries are affected and need credit (see the following chapter). Moreover, the IMF's surveillance can monitor financial stability and the situation of the financial sector, needing data support from national supervisors and authorities and from the Financial Stability Forum. The IMF's Financial Sector Assessment Program, voluntary up to 2008, should become mandatory for its members (Issing Committee 2008). It is conceivable that the IMF would write a joint report with the Financial Stability Forum on the status of the financial industry, pointing out potential problems (Draghi 2008). In its International Monetary and Financial Committee, it has the appropriate institutional forum where the expertise of the Financial Stability Forum can be brought to bear. The IMF can alert the public and hope that national supervisors will intervene.

However, the IMF has no sanctions at its disposal to stop national banking systems from running into trouble. To cede sovereignty in the area of prudential supervision, including concrete sanctions, to an international body is unlikely to happen. It would mean taking a crucial policy instrument out of the nation's hand. As I discuss in the following chapter, countries are reluctant to cede sovereignty to the IMF in light of the IMF's approach to the Asian currency crisis. Moreover, the IMF is not in a position to apply the polluter-pays principle when a country starts a financial bubble that artificially leads to national overconsumption and overinvestment. In that case, the IMF would need strong sanctions against the financial "polluter." However, no sovereign state is prepared to hand over such sanctions to the IMF. Another crucial aspect is that any bailout would have to be backed by national tax money; states are unwilling to cede sovereignty in this realm. The French proposal to endow the IMF with more instruments and to turn it into an economic policy machine or an "economic government" meets the counterargument that the IMF has been a political institution, having been under U.S. influence in the past. Political capture by other states would not represent an institutional improvement, although the French are politically adept and have a preference for such approaches. The objections against an "economic government" in the euro area also apply to the IMF. Thus, the IMF cannot play the role of the world economy's chief regulator. For the same reason, it cannot be the world's central bank; countries would rather not cede monetary authority to the IMF. In contrast, the IMF can be the world's monitor or watchdog.

In the bonanza of national political rescue plans and the ensuing enthusiasm for antirecession programs in the autumn of 2008 and early 2009, central banks must be vigilant that these activities do not erode their position of independence which they have gained from politics in the past. It would indeed be a historic irony of rule-setting if the financial crisis served to again politicize the money-supply process.

The Systemic Risk of Hedge Funds and Derivatives

It is up in the air how hedge funds and other derivatives will fare in the actual financial crisis, especially after new rules have been introduced, for instance if the systemic costs for credits granted by banks to hedge funds are internalized, and when several options of hedge funds like selling short are being limited.[4]

The term hedge fund denotes institutions that specialize in financial arbitrage, exploiting unused financial market opportunities. This includes, among other things, currency arbitrage, arbitrage in time (long and short positions), between locations (seeking assets that are mispriced relative to global alternatives), between products (a convertible bond and equity, buy and sell undervalued securities), and between securities that have deviated from some statistically estimated relationship. Derivatives, i.e., financial contracts whose value is derived from other contracts using leverage, play an important role. Hedge funds used unusually high levers; they often depend on credits extended by banks. Besides derivatives, currency arbitrage is another field. For instance, hedge funds take credits in yen at an extremely low interest rate, swap yen against U.S. dollars and euros with higher interest rates and exchange these back into yen ("carry trade"). This depresses the yen and fuels the other currencies. Hedge funds are only lightly regulated; they receive their capital from wealthy individuals and institutional investors such as foundations, endowments, and pension funds.

Sometimes the term hedge fund is used to include private equity funds which collect financial capital in order to buy up enterprises. Indeed, hedge funds have some similarity to equity funds when they are involved in merger arbitrage, i.e.,

---

[4] When this manuscript was finished, it was unknown as to whether problems were hidden in the hedge funds' balance sheets.

in arbitrage between an acquiring public company and a target public company. Nevertheless, equity funds should be considered as representing real capital flows (see chapter VI).

Hedge funds play an important role. In specific market segments, for instance in trade with credit derivatives, they supply risk capital and allow the limiting of credit risks for individual investors, for instance when a discount certificate introduces a floor in the stock market index, thereby providing some certainty for individual investors. In this way, they permit a more efficient risk allocation. They can lower market risk by spreading it across more shoulders. They make financial markets more liquid and ease price formation, providing information on risk-taking behavior of individuals. For institutional investors, as with pension funds and insurance companies who have invested in hedge funds, they represent an interesting opportunity, albeit a risky one. Also, banks provide capital to hedge funds in the form of credits. The number of hedge funds worldwide is estimated at some 10,000. Their assets are put at US$1.7 trillion.

In contrast to improving risk allocation, hedge funds can represent a systemic risk for the stability of financial markets. This is the case when the risk positions taken show up to be unsustainable, i.e., in the case of a misjudgment by the hedge fund. This, for instance, happens if the statistically estimated relationship that is used to determine the deviation of the value of securities proves to be wrong. Such a situation arises when market trends change and when the change is not incorporated into the econometric models. A case in point is Long-Term Capital Management, which lost US$4.6 billion in a few months in 1998, and had to be bailed out by the Fed. In 2006, Amaranth, speculating on natural gas prices, burnt US$6.6 billion within a week. Hedge funds are said to have unusually high returns. However, it should be noted that quite a few hedge funds have short lifetimes. If returns only reflect hedge funds that have survived, the performance of the industry is definitively overestimated. Hedge fund managers' remuneration is heavily weighted toward performance incentives; they are paid on the basis of annual results. In contrast, unusual events—black swan events—usually happen every five or ten years. Consequently, hedge funds managers have high incomes, while the investors often take the loss.

Market risk increases when hedge funds with wrong estimates move in the same direction. Then a financial crisis will be amplified. The financial market is also affected when hedge funds fail; this applies for banks which have extended credits. Under these conditions, it no longer holds that market risk is reduced through hedge funds. This is the issue of systemic risk for the global financial system caused by hedge funds. Accordingly, the ECB (2006, p. 142) warns that

> the increasingly similar positioning of individual hedge funds within broad hedge fund investment strategies is another major risk for financial stability which warrants close monitoring despite the essential lack of any possible remedies. This risk is further magnified by evidence that broad hedge fund investment strategies

have also become increasingly correlated, thereby further increasing the potential adverse effects of disorderly exits from crowded trades.

Hedge funds cater for market participants who are willing to take on high risks if they get high returns. Whereas the typical public investment company in the United States, for instance a mutual fund, is required to be registered with the Securities and Exchange Commission (SEC) and underlies a set of limitations, hedge funds are open to accredited investors only. Until 2008, they were exempt from any direct regulation by regulatory bodies. Moreover, hedge funds flock to regulatory havens, such as the Cayman Islands, Dublin, Luxembourg, the Channel Islands, the British Virgin Islands, and Bermuda. The Cayman Islands are estimated to be home to about 75% of the world's hedge funds, with nearly half the industry's assets under management.

Given these conditions, policy measures to reduce the systemic risk arising from hedge funds are difficult to come by. One approach is to require hedge funds to register in a country; if they then go offshore, it signals to the customer that a higher risk is involved and that these funds will not be bailed out in a crisis. Another approach is to make national banking systems, including all financial intermediaries, more robust. Accordingly, credits given to hedge funds and derivatives should be adequately reflected in the risk evaluation of banks and their balance sheets. This means an indirect supervision of hedge funds via their regulated creditors (Issing Committee 2008). A dialogue with the hedge funds industry, possibly with the largest 100 funds, should lead to a code of conduct for hedge funds. The global hedge fund industry should review and enhance existing sound practice benchmarks for hedge fund managers in the light of expectations for improved practices set out by the official and private sectors. Part of such a code of conduct can be a self-commitment of the industry to submit to an external rating. More systematic and consistent data on core intermediaries' consolidated counterparty exposures to hedge funds including clearing mechanisms should be developed as an effective complement to existing supervisory efforts (Financial Stability Forum 2008). If the industry is not capable of finding a code of conduct and establishing a clearing mechanism, regulation has to step in to prevent systemic risks.

IX
Avoiding Currency Crises

A specific aspect of the instability of the international financial system is exchange rate crises. With the abrupt fall in the external value of a currency, they can cause major damage to the individual country affected by the crisis and they involve the risk of contagion of other economies and endanger the stability of the global financial system with systemic risk. Consequently, rules and institutional arrangements are necessary to reduce the likelihood of such currency crises. It is apparent that national arrangements in favor of a solid and robust banking system and in favor of the solidity of public finances are important preconditions for avoiding currency crises. Therefore all the conditions discussed under the heading of financial stability at home are relevant in preventing currency crises (chapter VIII). These national conditions, however, are not sufficient on an international scale. After all, a currency crisis caused by one country can be thought of as a border-crossing negative externality, doing damage to another country, so to say representing a monetary–financial acid rain. It is necessary to prevent such negative spillovers and keep them from developing into a systemic crisis. Moreover, using the same analogy, once a crisis has broken out, it is not too helpful to call upon the polluter-pays principle. The international community must stand by to support the nation affected, just as a doctor must help a patient even if the patient himself has caused his illness.

The IMF's Mission

The core goal of a global rule system for financial stability consists in preventing the start and development of such crises, and, once a crisis has begun, to stop it from escalating into a systemic financial crisis of the global economy. Fending off currency crises has become the main mission of the International Monetary Fund (IMF) since the introduction of flexible exchange rates in 1973 that went along with the increased importance of portfolio capital flows. In a world where exchange rates in the short and medium term are determined not only by the trade in goods but also by volatile and rapidly reversing flows of capital, fighting currency crises is the IMF's top priority, consistent with its main purpose of fostering the stability of the international monetary system and, thus, enabling good conditions for successful economic development.[1] Additionally, the IMF provides an institutional framework for discussions of international currency problems. Originally, when the IMF was founded in 1944, its role after World War II was to assist countries that were in temporary balance of payments difficulties by providing bridging loans to them. In this manner, the exchange rates could be kept more or less stable in the Bretton Woods exchange rate system.

The IMF would be misguided in its mission to base its operations on the assumption that there will be no currency crises for a long time. It is the characteristic nature of currency crises that they occur unexpectedly. We realistically have to assume that in spite of all efforts made, there will be currency crises in the future (Siebert 2007d,e).

The Orientation Crisis of the IMF

As an organization, the IMF, representing the only explicit international institutional arrangement in the monetary–financial domain, finds itself in an orientation crisis, facing four dilemmas.[2] A first core issue is that most of the IMF facilities— Stand-by Arrangements, Extended Fund Facility, Supplemental Reserve Facility, Compensatory Financing Facility, Emergency Assistance, and Exogenous Shocks Facility—are only applied after a currency crisis has broken out, notwithstanding some precautionary interventions.[3] The typical pattern is that capital markets no longer provide liquidity to a country in crisis, since the country is unable to meet its payment obligations (debt service, repayment of loans). There is a moratorium, and negotiations with creditors are started which result in the creditors losing part of their loans. To enable recovery from the crisis, fresh capital is the priority need; it is provided by the IMF in the form of liquidity assistance. This is the IMF's firefighting function. IMF loans bear interest, some with a surcharge, and are to be repaid. The existing financing instruments limit the amount which can be drawn as loans to 100% of the quota on an annual basis and to a cumulative total of 300%, net, with consideration being given to negotiated repayments. In exceptional cases these limits may be exceeded.

Ex post assistance has serious shortcomings. It always has a negative incentive effect for the future behavior of borrowing countries and lenders. If generous assistance is granted *ex post*, governments are unlikely to make great efforts to avoid a

---

[1] To throw sand into the international portfolio flows by introducing the heavily discussed Tobin tax (Tobin 1978) is no longer a serious proposal to avoid currency crises (Siebert 2007e).

[2] There is far-reaching agreement by now that in case of a currency crisis it is not advisable to defend at all costs a nonsustainable exchange rate that is not supported by economic fundamentals. Instead, devaluation is one of the instruments with which to exit from the crisis and to avoid distortions in exchange rates, the correction of which would ultimately be enforced by the markets through a currency crisis.

[3] For instance, the attempt to insulate Brazil and Uruguay against the Argentinean default in 2001.

currency crisis ("moral hazard"). Creditors will act with less prudence in granting loans. Governments, political parties, and also creditors such as banks and other lenders can rely on having a currency crisis become less serious because the IMF will be offering assistance. Accordingly, efforts to avoid a currency crisis will be less vigorous. The willingness to enforce institutional rules, for example, in the area of financial surveillance or limitation of public debt, is lessened. Thus, *ex post* assistance can increase the probability of currency crises. Although currency crises are a short-term phenomenon, they always have causes that have evolved over a long period.

A second major dilemma for the IMF consists in the characteristics required by the *ex post* approach, namely "conditionality." Since in the case of a currency crisis, the IMF cannot simply give money to a country without a change in the country's policy, the loans entail conditions for the borrowing country. It is not possible to control a currency crisis in a crisis country without conditions that reverse absorption. However, conditionality has been thought of as too harsh in the Korean crisis. Ironically, this has been expressed in the fact that, as in the Asian currency crisis, an IMF country team consisting of only a few people flies into the crisis country and sets conditions to a country's government, and often a democratically elected one. Governments do not want the IMF to be their taskmaster.

A third dilemma is that governments walked away from the IMF, at least prior to the 2008 financial crisis. This is the fallout of the IMF's approach in the Asian currency crisis. Countries have paid back their loans earlier than scheduled, for instance Argentina in 2005, and they rely on accumulating international reserves in order to avoid abiding by international rules. Cases in point are China and other Asian economies. Total accumulated reserves were estimated at US$6.5 trillion at year end 2007 (Morgan Stanley 2007). These sums are quite different from those we have seen in the past when reserves have melted away quickly as soon as a currency gets under attack. Moreover, countries are more cautious in liberalizing their capital account. The IMF is without customers (Lerrick 2007). Its legitimacy is at stake. For the IMF, this has had the consequence that its income from interest payments has declined; it receives interest for the outstanding loans by the countries affected by a currency crisis. Consequently, the IMF has less revenue to cover its operating expenditures. As of July 31, 2007, total outstanding loans stood at US$11.2 billion (7,355 million SDRs) in contrast to US$91.3 billion in 2003. The lowest lending volume in twenty-five years has resulted in one of the lowest incomes in the Fund's history. In 2007, only Turkey still paid loan interest de facto. Accordingly, interest income amounted to only US$1.0 billion in 2007, whereas it had been US$3.2 billion in 2003. This picture has changed somewhat in the financial crisis of 2008, when countries started to come back to the IMF for credits (Hungary $12.5 billion; $2.1 billion to Iceland; Pakistan $7.6 billion; Ukraine $16.4 billion).

The Fund primarily finances its operations from the difference between interest received from countries who have taken out loans and interest on SDR holdings minus remunerations (table IX.1). The main sources for operational income are interests and charges for outstanding credits. The IMF levies periodic charges on members' use of outstanding credits. The basic rate of charge is set at the beginning of each financial year as the SDR interest rate plus a margin expressed in basis points determined by the Executive Board. The SDR interest rate is determined weekly by reference to a combined market interest rate, which is a weighted average of yields on short-term instruments in the capital markets of the euro area, Japan, the United Kingdom, and the United States. In addition, the IMF earns interest on its SDR holdings. Although SDRs are not allocated to the IMF, the IMF may acquire, hold, and dispose of SDRs. The IMF receives SDRs from members in the settlement of their financial obligations to the IMF and uses SDRs in transactions and operations with members. Operational income is obtained from investment as well. With nearly US$300 million the position "net income from investment" represents the second largest income source of the IMF.[4]

The largest portion of Fund expenditures are personnel costs, which, at about US$700 million in 2007, amount to almost three-fourths of the Fund's administrative expenses. Administrative costs also include about US$50 million for capital investments in buildings and information technology. The IMF pays interest, referred to as remuneration, on a member's reserve tranche position. A member's reserve tranche is equivalent to its total quota minus its subscription payment to the IMF. A member's reserve tranche is considered part of its external reserves and a liquid claim against the IMF.

In 2007, the operating loss stood at US$100 million. Costs have been rising on the expenditure side, while income has steadily declined since 2002. The practice until now has been to set the basic IMF interest rate level in such a way that interest income at least covers IMF expenditures. For its budget, the IMF has reserves in the region of about US$9 billion. But the actual financing situation can hardly be called sustainable if the current trend of declining lending volumes is to continue. The near doubling of expenditures and the doubling of personnel in the last ten years will necessarily have to be corrected.

A fourth dilemma is that the IMF cannot get out of this predicament by looking for new tasks which are not covered by its core mission, for instance playing a greater role in developing countries. While monitoring, advising, and giving financial assistance during balance-of-payments problems belong to the traditional IMF mission in these countries, the approaches pursued in recent times have gone far beyond the core IMF mission. This applies especially to debt relief for the poorest developing countries, which has been provided jointly with the World Bank. It is

---

[4] These investments are held in the Investment Account (US$9,531 million at April 30, 2007) and MDRI-I Trust (US$459 million at April 30, 2007) of the balance sheet and are managed by external investment managers. The IMF invests in fixed-term deposits; short-term investments and fixed income investments, which include domestic government bonds of the euro area, Japan, the United Kingdom, and the United States; and medium-term instruments issued by the Bank for International Settlements.

Table IX.1. IMF consolidated budget, fiscal year ending
April 30, 2007, in Mio U.S. dollars.

Operational expenses		Operational income	
Remuneration	738	Interest and charges	1,047
Administrative expenses	928	Interest on SDR holdings	190
		Net income from investments	295
		Other charges and income	25
		Operational loss	109
Total	1,665	Total	1,665

Source: IMF (2007b).

true that by using this instrument, the IMF can silence criticism of some NGOs; and the argument is valid that the situation of developing countries and their balance-of-payments problems can be improved by loans. But the IMF mission does not include general lending in advance; this blurs the division of labor between the IMF and the World Bank. As welcome as such an initiative may be and as much as debt forgiveness improves the financial constraints of the poorest countries, this is no measure to prevent a currency crisis. Therefore it is not part of the IMF mission and should be left to the World Bank or a coalition of industrialized countries. Assuring currency stability is such a central mission for the world economy that the IMF, as the institution responsible for it, should not be overburdened with other tasks, and its mission should not be diluted. Otherwise the IMF loses its focus. Another important aspect is that these new peripheral tasks use a considerable number of staff and make expenditure containment more difficult.

Refocusing the IMF

To avoid this dilemma, it is necessary to refocus the IMF. It should stick to its mission of fighting currency crises. In order to lose the image of being a disciplinarian of countries, it should clearly give preference to *ex ante* prevention and to creating conditions *ex ante* that preclude the occurrence of a currency crisis rather than relying on *ex post* measures, especially liquidity assistance. *Ex ante* measures embrace financial monitoring by national supervising authorities and central banks; international coordination of financial oversight and its standards within the scope of activities of the Bank for International Settlements and the Financial Stability Forum (all of these are not explicitly IMF missions) and an IMF early-warning system. In early warning, the IMF instruments comprise monitoring economic development and advising national governments (article IV consultations), usually called "surveillance." This incorporates analysis and assessment of currency risks and signaling an impending currency crisis. Information has to be given to the markets. It should include data on the balance-of-payments situation; capital flows and their structure; foreign exchange reserves of a country and their special characteristics (are they "swapped" as they were in the case of Thailand?); foreign debt and its type (direct investments, bonds, bank loans); national public debt and indebtedness of the private sector; maturity structure of such debt; composition of debt with respect to currencies, explicit and implicit indebtedness, including hidden future liabilities; the consolidated annual statements of the financial sector; its most important segments and the largest enterprises; and "off-balance-sheet liabilities." One crucial aspect of transparency is the information about the extent to which international banking rules and financial supervision rules are observed, and whether a national deposit insurance fund exists. The IMF's Financial Sector Assessment Programs are supposed to detect faults in a country's financial system; it is supposed to become mandatory for the IMF's members if the new G20 rules are implemented.

It is necessary to sound the alarm before an incident has occurred. And it is preferable to accept a minor crisis if one can avoid a major crisis in this way. Under no circumstances may the IMF withhold information. It must resist the interests of national governments for whom the news of an impending crisis may be inopportune. There is much to be said for regular publication of data, including statistics (for example "country financial sector fact sheets"), without any consideration being given to national political calendars, such as election cycles. Admittedly, this early warning function is not easy to perform since financial markets may overreact. Care must be taken to ensure that trivial news items do not grow into a major crisis.

With its publications—the World Economic Outlook, the Global Financial Stability Report (IMF 2008b), and the Country Reports under article IV—the IMF contributes to an analysis of the global economy and currency risks. It makes sense for the IMF leadership to include financial market data in the article IV reports and to pay attention to the possible effects of large national economies (IMF 2006a). The request to publish the results of country consultations has to be seen in this light. At this time, however, about 15% of the member nations reject such publication, even 30% in the Western Hemisphere (IMF 2007d). More recent information indicates that reports are published in only nine out of ten cases (IMF 2008f).

As an additional approach to avoid the predicament of *ex post* measures would be to reward adherence to *ex ante* standards in determining access to loan facilities in case of a currency crisis by offering more favorable conditions, either with respect to loan amounts or interest rates. In this way, the IMF can cause nations to create preconditions for a stable currency system. In order to reach this goal, it is advisable to follow the Meltzer Commission's proposal (IFIAC 2000, Meltzer Report), according to which the IMF may give loans only to those countries which have established adequate conditions for stability, among them organized banking supervision and financial market regulation as well as the regular publication of the country's debt structure (see above). No further conditions would have to be required; conditionality could be eliminated. Nations not accepting this condition would not receive any loans. This would be the case even when there is the risk of contagion for other economies. An alternative to this proposal would be to provide more favorable loan access to those countries which meet certain conditions of good fiscal management. Thus, the Council on Foreign Relations (1999) speaks of a club of good economic governance ("good housekeeping club"), whose members get better conditions. The IMF has also proposed preferential access to loans in cases of good economic governance (IMF 2006a).

Furthermore, it has proven necessary to improve the allocation of risk. It is recommendable to specify in advance for bank loans and bonds which creditor majorities will be required to change a loan agreement with a sovereign debtor in case of a crisis, and to approve any losses of lender capital (so called "sharing clauses" or "collective action clauses," rules on collective representation, British-style trustee deed bonds instead of American style bonds). Unquestionably, this raises the risks for lenders and therefore reduces their willingness to offer loans. Hence, loan costs increase for borrowing countries. But at the same time risks are internalized in advance and the probability of currency crises is reduced. All of these rules are designed to replace discretionary decisions (preferred by the United States) by automatic actions (preferred by the Europeans). Farther-reaching proposals to create an insolvency law for sovereign debtors and to establish a type of global bankruptcy trustee in the form of the IMF have not gained acceptance so far. This applies to the concepts suggested by the IMF itself. The reason for rejection is that there is no bankruptcy law for sovereign debtor nations because sovereign nations are not willing to submit to arrangements that would allow the IMF to play the role of bankruptcy trustee and be able to declare a nation illiquid. Equally, lenders do not find it acceptable to have the IMF play a role in which it, analogous to a bankruptcy trustee, could decide the creditors' loss ratio during the illiquidity (or even insolvency) of a sovereign debtor. There is resistance to such a concept even if the crisis country itself could declare a moratorium; by acting as loan monopolist, the IMF in the final analysis would gain considerable direct power over sovereign nations. In contrast, institutional arrangements of collective decision making offer the lenders the advantage that they correspond more to decentralized market-type processes. After Argentina's default, collective action clauses have become more common.

The much-needed refocusing of the IMF mission described here makes clear that the "Poverty Reduction and Growth Facility," introduced in 1999, should be abolished. It is not unusual that facilities become terminated. For example the "Contingent Credit Line," which had also been introduced in 1999, ended in 2003. This facility had been designed to protect member nations from contagion. But it was not accepted by members because those countries that might have signed up for it were afraid to send a signal to the markets that a crisis was to be expected. The instrument acted as a stigmatization. The other facilities, the "Stand-by Arrangements,"[5] "Extended Fund Facility"[6] and "Supplemental Reserve Facility,"[7] "Compensatory Financing Facility,"[8] "Emergency Assistance,"[9] and the "Exogenous Shocks Facility"[10] should be continued in principle except for the reorientation discussed in this study.

The insurance facility proposed by IMF staff is to provide automatic access to IMF funds for emerging countries with a sound economic policy in case there is a financial crisis. But this instrument seems to be rather similar to the abolished "Contingent Credit Line." Negative signaling effects in the markets are likely. Moreover, IMF funds would have to be committed which would then be unavailable during a currency crisis. Thus, this instrument runs counter to a refocusing of the IMF mission.

Any reorientation of the IMF has considerable impact on the staff. Insiders refer to the fact that IMF staff can prove themselves in the use of *ex post* instruments, especially if they have participated in *ex post* crisis control. This is how they advance their career. There is little glory to be gained with *ex ante* instruments. Consequently, the entire organization will face a hard-to-control incentive problem with bias for *ex post* instruments. Insiders talk about a bloated bureaucracy. The mission and expenditure structures have to take into account that the IMF as an institution is moving away from crisis management toward crisis prevention, and that this results in a sizable decline in lending volume.

Although a partial sale of gold reserves as considered by the Crocket Commission (Committee to Study the Sustainable Long-Term Financing of the IMF 2007) was accepted by the Executive Board in April 2008 (with the go-ahead of the U.S.

---

[5] Created as the first facility, the "Stand-by Arrangement" serves to bridge temporary balance-of-payments imbalances. Member countries may draw on up to 100% of their quota within a limited period of time, usually 12–18 months, sometimes up to 3 years. The loan must be repaid in $2\frac{1}{4}$ to 4 years.

[6] The "Extended Fund Facility," established in 1974, is designed for structural balance-of-payments deficits that require a longer adjustment period. It contains greater liquidity assistance than the "Stand-by Arrangements." Repayment must be made within $4\frac{1}{2}$ to 7 years. Surcharges are applied in case of high loan amounts.

[7] The "Supplemental Reserve Facility," created in 1997, is designed for large short-term financing problems and exceptional balance-of-payments problems such as during the Mexican and Asian crises. Repayment is to occur within 2 to $2\frac{1}{2}$ years. The interest rate starts at 3 percentage points above the IMF borrowing rate and rises over time. This facility was created in response to the new type of currency crisis characterized by a reversal of capital flows.

[8] The "Compensatory Financing Facility," introduced in 1963, provides liquidity to countries which experience a sudden collapse of their export prices or an increase in their import prices for grain due to fluctuations in global market prices. The conditions of the "Stand-by Agreement" are applicable.

[9] The "Emergency Assistance Facility" provides funds to countries affected by natural disasters. The interest rate here is the IMF borrowing rate. Exceptions are made for countries that qualify for the "Poverty Reduction and Growth Facility." Repayment is within $3\frac{1}{2}$ to 5 years.

[10] The "Exogenous Shocks Facility" provides low-income countries confronted with an exogenous shock with economic policy and financial support. It is available to countries who also qualify for the "Poverty and Shock Facility." Financing conditions correspond to those of the "Poverty and Shock Facility" program.

Congress still pending in November 2008), the relief provided on the income side will only be temporary. For some time, the need for reform will lose its urgency. Besides, it is difficult to ring-fence this approach in order to prevent future "sins." Reinvestment of profits, a "better" lending strategy and the introduction of an investment fund for existing fund reserves are potential strategies. It does not seem advisable to pursue the idea that the IMF should charge service fees for economic policy analysis in member countries (Country Reports). The IMF would find little favor among its members because its advice is often not welcomed. Thus, the IMF would quickly face a catch-22 situation of buying acceptance by giving positive assessments. Moreover, the IMF does not have a monopoly on these analyses; it competes, for instance with the International Bank for Settlements, the World Bank, the OECD, and the Rating Agencies. Other than by reducing expenditures, the IMF's financing problem could only be resolved for the long term by an increase in capital. It is doubtful, however, whether the shareholders are willing to do so since they rightly fear this option getting out of hand. It is therefore necessary to drastically reduce expenditure, to end noncore missions, and to reduce staff accordingly, in order to assure the IMF's financing for the long term. In 2008, the IMF has responded to this necessity by partly downsizing its expenditures until May 2009.

In delineating the mission and IMF's options when fending off a currency crisis, it should be remembered that the IMF only has a limited capability to fight a currency crisis. The IMF cannot be a "lender of last resort." Here we need to differentiate between a lender of "last liquidity" (who provides liquidity) and the ultimate bearer of costs (who in effect bears the costs of the currency crisis in terms of income losses and taxation—usually the population of a crisis country). The IMF is neither of the two. It does not have sufficient financial funds to prevent a systemic crisis; its one-year forward commitment capacity amounts to US$190 billion, with total usable resources standing at about US$250 billion. During a systemic currency crisis the three most important central banks, the Fed, the ECB, and the Bank of Japan must act in concert to provide liquidity (as they did when the attack on the World Trade Center occurred on September 11, 2001 and in the financial crisis in 2007 and 2008). The rules for this function are preferably not specified and published *ex ante*; this would permit speculators to play against the central banks. But during national currency crises the IMF may provide liquidity without assuming the costs of such a crisis. The real burden of a currency crisis is borne by the citizens of the crisis country, for instance in losses of real income. Thus, somewhat like a pawn in a game of royal chess, the IMF acts in the pre-field of the central banks as lender of last liquidity, thereby, if successful, preventing a national currency crisis from escalating into a systemic crisis.

The IMF needs to be clearly differentiated from national or regional central banks, such as the Fed and the ECB, by the nature of its mission. The objective of central banks is to keep the value of money stable, i.e., to have a stable level of prices; that of the IMF is currency stability, i.e., controlling currency crises. The stability of the value of a currency and currency stability are closely linked, because a loss in the value of a currency always goes hand in hand with a currency devaluation (if the rate of domestic inflation is higher than abroad), and analogously, a stable exchange rate requires a stable currency. If we understand currency neutrality to mean that a currency does not have a negative impact on the real economy of a country, then the IMF is responsible only for one aspect of such currency neutrality, namely currency stability. The other aspect, the stability of the value of money is the responsibility of the central banks.

Rules for Preventing Currency Distortions

A new aspect of its mission was introduced by the IMF in its 2007 Decision on Bilateral Surveillance (June 26). In this subtly worded document replacing the 1977 Decision, the IMF develops a new approach to exchange rates. The concept of "external stability" is at the center of the Decision. "External stability" refers to a balance-of-payments position that does not, and is not likely to give rise to disruptive exchange-rate movements. Each IMF member collaborates with the IMF and other members to promote stable exchange rates (which the IMF calls "systemic stability"). This is achieved by the member countries adopting policies that promote their own "external stability"—that is, policies that are consistent with members' obligations. In its concept of dialogue and persuasion and its approach to bilateral surveillance, the IMF "will clearly and candidly assess relevant economic developments, prospects, and policies of the member in question, and advise on these. Such assessments and advice are intended to assist that member in making policy choices, and to enable other members to discuss these policy choices with that member." External stability then serves as a guideline to determine misalignments. Four principles support this approach: a member (A) "shall avoid manipulating exchange rates...," (B) "should intervene in the exchange market if necessary to counter disorderly conditions...," (C) "should take into account in their intervention policies the interests of other members...," and (D) "should avoid exchange-rate policies that result in external instability...." This represents a considerable change of the IMF mission. It includes monitoring exchange rates.

Bilateral surveillance with the sequence "systemic stability–external stability–misalignment" will prove to be an extremely tricky task for the IMF, which does not have any sanctions available against misaligned exchange rates. Politically, it seems to come at a point where an undervalued Chinese renminbi is a bone of international contention. The IMF will inevitably fail if it promotes itself as the referee of exchange rates and attempts to set "reference rates" for the most important currencies. This strategy, favored by concepts as developed by John Williamson (1993, 2006) and supported by the ideas of Fred Bergsten (1988), can lead the IMF astray. The Fund does not have the necessary information for it; *ex ante* it cannot take on the role of market processes in determining exchange rates. Setting reference rates also presupposes that equilibrium exchange rates are determined and that the lines of monetary policy, fiscal policy, wage policy (in countries in which wages are set by labor and management), and of the entire economic policy are specified in detail (Siebert 2007e, chapter 6). This would be arrogance of knowledge, as addressed by Hayek. Moreover, it seems that economists do not have a model on which they agree in determining the exchange rate. In any case, if there are disequilibria in the balance of payments, it is the real exchange rate that counts. Furthermore, the real interest rate is relevant. As Corden has pointed out, if the Chinese current account surplus is at the heart of the issue, a lower Chinese surplus would increase the world's real interest rate, with unpleasant effects for many countries including the United States (Corden 2007). This approach to determining the equilibrium (real) exchange rate all too easily yields to the temptation of passing the buck to individual countries to bear the burden of adjustment. And often there is no political agreement on the economic paradigm to be used as basis. Finally, the experiences of the Louvre Accord and Plaza Agreement in the 1980s and their impact on the development of the Japanese bubble in 1989 suggest that great caution is necessary.

Similar reasons lead to the conclusion that the IMF cannot be an international coordination agency for national economic policies. The idea of having international macroeconomic coordination is based on quite a bit of naivete. All macro-policies would have to be coordinated, including monetary policy, fiscal policy, and wage policy. What has been unachievable in a regional integration such as the European Union, i.e., harmonization of economic and fiscal policies within the euro zone, would work even less in a global organization. Moreover, this would move the IMF close to being an international economic government. However, the IMF does not have any legitimacy for this function; it would take the place of parliaments and democratically elected governments (compare chapter VIII).

However, no objection exists to having a barometric coordination, in which governments exchange their views during multilateral consultations on the economic situation and on technical policy actions planned by them. This includes the analysis of interdependencies of economic policy actions. Also, there is nothing wrong with having the IMF promoting suitable institutional conditions in the member countries which prevent the development of a currency crisis. The IMF can also focus its instruments on promoting the establishment of such institutional measures. With respect to shaping national economic policy, the IMF has the role of explaining the consequences of national decisions for currency crises to politicians, the public, and the markets. This also applies to excessive current account deficits of individual countries (such as the United States in 2007) if they can lead to crisis-like adjustment processes. In such a case, the IMF has the role of a trusted adviser. In any case, there is a very thin line between barometric coordination and acting as the umpire on exchange rates.

Adjusting the Bretton Woods Quotas to New International Conditions

Quotas of member countries should reflect the changes in the world economy and a new quota formula should be developed. Quotas determine the rights and obligations of the 185 IMF member countries. They specify the capital subscribed by a country, its voting power, its access limits to financing, with arrangements for exceptional situations, and its share of Special Drawing Rights, which represent a reserve currency created in 1969 when the two other reserve currencies, gold and the U.S. dollar, were in short supply. Quotas also represent the weight of the voting power of members when decisions in the IMF are taken by the Board of Governors, which meets twice a year. Each member nation appoints a Governor and an Alternate (in most cases the Minister of Finance, the Secretary of the Treasury, or the Head of the Central Bank). Each country receives 250 basic votes plus one vote for every 100,000 Special Drawing Rights in its quota. The day-to-day business is managed by the Board of Executive Directors, which consists of twenty-four directors. The United States, Japan, Germany, Great Britain, and France appoint one director each; the remaining nineteen are nominated by groups of countries.

Country quotas are determined in accordance with the Bretton Woods Formula and its variations, five formulas in total, comprising five factors, i.e., gross domestic product, currency reserves, current account balance transactions, one factor measuring the variability of current revenues, and the ratio of current revenues to gross domestic product. Although this formula has repeatedly been adjusted, it is not transparent and is too closely tied to the Bretton Woods System. An external commission, appointed by the IMF for the first time, the Quota Formula Review Group (IMF 2000), of which I was a member, therefore proposed a single simple linear formula to determine the quota, namely Quota $= aY + bV$, where Y is the gross domestic product, V is a measure for the external variability of current revenue, and a and b are relative weights. Gross domestic product is an expression of the efficiency of an economy in financing the IMF and is to have twice the weight of variability ($\frac{2}{3}$ and $\frac{1}{3}$). Variability of current revenue, which characterizes the vulnerability of an economy, is to include the variability of long-term net capital flows. Both criteria also express the substantive interest of nations in having an effective international institution. Economies with a high GDP might lose much in absolute terms in currency crises, but the vulnerability factor is also an indicator for the interest of nations in having an effective IMF.

If gross domestic product were measured in purchasing power parities, the nontradable goods sector would be overvalued because purchasing power parities give this sector a greater weight. GDP should therefore be computed in market prices by calculating three-year averages in constant prices. In principle, a country's global market share might be used as a possible criterion in the Bretton Woods Formula. However, market share values fluctuate strongly with exchange rates even if averages over several years are used; an upward revaluation of the U.S. dollar leads to a mathematical increase of U.S. market share and reduces market shares of other countries before the higher U.S. dollar reduces U.S. exports over the longer term in a second-round effect. Moreover, if the focus was only on global market share, no consideration would be given to the total productive capacity of a country's economy; the entire area of nontradable goods would not be covered by the formula. It should also be noted that gross domestic product or global market share cannot represent the sole criteria and that other aspects are relevant, such as vulnerability.

Currency reserves are not a useful criterion for calculating quotas. The experience with currency crises has shown that reserves melt like snow in the spring sun during a reversal of capital flows and that any decline in reserves that becomes public knowledge worsens the situation as in a vicious circle. In addition, large currency reserves are of little use if they represent insurance for a fragile banking system (like in China); reserves would therefore have to be corrected for the stability of the banking system and other factors. Using population figures as an alternative criterion for gross domestic product would express neither the financial effectiveness nor the vulnerability of an economy. Moreover, the principle of "one country, one vote," as applied in the WTO, e.g., would not meet the material interests of member countries and would therefore jeopardize the financing of the IMF.

The current quota allocation no longer corresponds to the actual conditions in the world economy. It does not reflect the growth of important emerging countries and their welcome integration into the world economy. On the basis of the most recent data, China, for instance, has become the third largest economy in the world as measured by its gross domestic product at market prices (in 2005 its share in global economic output amounted to 5%); but it has an IMF quota of only 3.72% (table IX.2). In Asia, China, Japan, and Korea are underrepresented in their quotas if the 2005 gross domestic product in current prices is used as a basis. The current quota allocation prevents underrepresented members from developing an interest in the IMF as an institution, especially when they expect to have strong growth. Over the long term this weakens the IMF's raison d'être, i.e., its acceptance. Consequently, the quotas have to change, and they have to accommodate the rising share of developing countries in world GDP in the future.

Quota allocation is always a zero-sum game: an increase for some countries necessarily results in a decrease for others. On the basis of the gross domestic product criterion, it is especially the smaller countries of the European Union that are overrepresented, such as Belgium, the Netherlands, Sweden, and Switzerland; Spain is underrepresented. The quota of the European Union actually corresponds to its production share. This also holds for the European Monetary Union. Europe provides the Managing Director who heads the IMF and is chairman of the Executive Board, which includes the Deputy Managing Director and the twenty-four Executive Directors. The United States has a quota of 17.09% with a share of global economic output of 28.05% (2005). If gross domestic product is used as criterion, North America, and in particular the United States, is underrepresented. However, the

United States has the advantage that the IMF is headquartered in Washington and that the United States provides the Deputy Director. Moreover, the "peer group" of American economists (it is often desirable for staff to have a Ph.D. from an American university) exerts a not inconsiderable influence on the IMF's direction. In Latin America, when measuring shares of global gross domestic product, Brazil and Mexico have a slightly low quota, while Venezuela has a quota that is too high. Africa's quota is markedly higher than its share in production output. The quota of Asia, excluding Japan, is higher than its production share. Other countries, such as Saudi Arabia and Russia, also have large quotas relative to their shares in production.

A quota is not perfectly identical to the weighted voting power. For example, Germany's pre-2008 reform quota was 5.99; its share of votes is 5.88. For the United States the comparable figures are 17.09 and 16.77 (January 4, 2008). These differences are caused, among other things, by the fact that basic shares are independent of quotas. Each IMF member has 250 basic votes plus one additional vote for each SDR100,000 of the quota (on new basic shares see below). Accordingly, the United States has 371,743 votes (16.79% of the total), and Palau has 281 votes (0.01% of the total).

During the Singapore meeting of the IMF in September 2006, the quotas of China, Korea, Mexico, and Turkey were adjusted in a first step; they were increased by 1.8 percentage points. The quotas of the other countries were proportionally reduced. China's quota was increased by less than one percentage point to 3.719 (IMF 2006d). As a second step, the Board of Governors approved a quota reform on April 29, 2008 (IMF 2008c), proposed by the Executive Committee (IMF 2008d). To become effective, this requires the formal approval of at least three-fifths of the IMF members representing 85% of the total voting power; in most countries the approval of the legislature is needed. The quota formula has been changed, now containing four variables: GDP (weighted with 60% market exchange rates and 40% purchasing power parity), openness, variability, and reserves. The weights for the four variables are 50% (GDP), 30%, 15%, and 5%, respectively. It seems that the formula is moving into the direction as proposed above.

With the new formula, quotas were increased ad hoc in a second round after the Singapore increase. Underrepresented countries saw their quotas enlarged, while overrepresented countries experienced a downward adjustment. Table IX.3 shows the first five top positive and negative changes in the quotas. Several underrepresented countries—Germany, Ireland, Italy, Japan, Luxembourg, and the United States—have agreed to forgo part of the quota increases for which they are eligible. Among the countries that have increased their quotas are Mexico, the United States (both 0.29 percentage points), Spain, Singapore, and Turkey. The Netherlands (−0.29 percentage points), Belgium, Switzerland, Australia, and Venezuela have had their quotas reduced.

Table IX.2. Current IMF quotas, quotas according to the shares in global economic output, in world trade and in a combined indicator.

	Current quota 2007[a]	Calculated quota[b]	Share of global GDP 2005[c]	Share of global trade 2005[d]	Combined indicator 2005[e]
G7	**45.27**	**45.90**	**60.87**	**40.73**	**53.99**
United States	17.09	16.28	28.05	10.19	22.02
Japan	6.13	7.01	10.24	5.40	8.60
Germany	5.99	6.85	6.31	8.99	7.19
United Kingdom	4.94	5.24	4.97	4.60	4.83
France	4.94	4.13	4.80	4.45	4.67
Italy	3.25	3.32	3.98	3.72	3.88
Canada	2.93	3.07	2.52	3.38	2.80
European Union (EU 27)	**32.30**	**37.77**	**31.65**	**40.12**	**34.11**
Eurozone (15)	**23.04**	**27.62**	**23.47**	**30.09**	**25.68**
North America (exc. Mexico)	**20.02**	**19.35**	**30.56**	**13.57**	**24.82**
Asian countries (exc. Japan)	**18.91**	**20.81**	**13.71**	**25.24**	**16.50**
China	3.72	6.14	5.04	6.71	5.59
Korea	1.35	2.51	1.78	2.68	2.08
Transformation countries					
Russian Federation	2.74	1.70	1.73	2.15	1.86
Middle East					
Saudi Arabia	3.21	1.03	0.70	1.51	0.97
Turkey	0.55	0.75	0.82	0.70	0.78
Latin America	**7.62**	**5.15**	**5.50**	**5.16**	**5.37**
Brazil	1.40	1.07	1.80	1.07	1.55
Mexico	1.45	1.84	1.74	1.84	1.77
Venezuela	1.22	0.43	0.32	0.46	0.36
Africa	**5.84**	**2.65**	**1.90**	**2.40**	**2.06**

[a]January 4, 2008. [b]July 11, 2007 (IMF 2007e, table A 5). [c]GDP in current prices. *Source:* World Bank, World Development Indicators, 2007. [d]Trade in goods including services in current prices. *Source:* World Bank, World Development Indicators, 2007. IMF, Balance of Payments Statistics, January 2008. [e]Weighted indicator: 2/3 share of global economic output and 1/3 share of global trade.

A Single Quota for the Euro Area?

There is no agreement on whether the European Monetary Union should have a common representative in the IMF. This would ultimately mean that Germany and France would not be represented by their own directors, and neither would the United Kingdom if it were to join the euro area. Moreover, the other seven of the fifteen Euro Member Countries (2008) would not head their respective constituencies. The IMF statutes stipulate that only nations can become members of the IMF. The arguments in favor of a joint representative of the euro area are the common monetary

Table IX.3.   Changes in quota shares.

Positive changes from pre-Singapore			Negative changes from pre-Singapore		
Country	Percentage point change from pre-Singapore	Post-second round quota in percent	Country	Percentage point change from pre-Singapore	Post-second round quota in percent
China	1.02	4.00	U.K.	−0.52	4.51
Korea	0.65	1.41	France	−0.52	4.51
India	0.50	2.44	Saudi Arabia	−0.34	2.93
Brazil	0.36	1.78	Canada	−0.31	2.67
Japan	0.33	6.56	Russia	−0.29	2.49

Source: IMF (2008d).

policy, increasing harmonization in banking supervision, and the essentially coherent economic area. A currency crisis of the euro would affect the countries' common currency. It is also hypothesized that a single representation of the monetary union could allow Europe to play a pivotal role and swing the votes in the Executive Council (Smaghi 2006) and to give Europe more say. Moreover, it is pointed out that some coordination of European countries is already taking place inside the IMF through the SCIMF, the subcommittee on IMF-related issues in the Economic and Financial Committee, preparing work for ECOFIN, and through EURIMF, the informal committee of EU members represented in the IMF (Ahearne and Eichengreen 2007). However, this last argument is hardly significant.

Arguments against such a move are that the commitment of capital provided to the IMF has to be made by individual countries; the capital is paid from national tax revenue; balance of payments as a macroeconomic budgetary and financial restriction has remained a national function; and balance of payments problems have to be resolved on the national level. Even a currency crisis of the euro could ultimately not be controlled by the European Central Bank; it does not have the policy instruments for it, for example in fiscal policy, including taxation. Instead, the member countries of the European Monetary Union would have to use these national policy instruments and bear the costs of such a crisis by using tax revenues to control the crisis. In case of liquidity assistance by the IMF, any potential conditionality would have to be directed at national governments. This applies in particular to the tax and budget policies of member countries. Large areas of economic policy have remained national responsibilities in the European Monetary Union. Last but not least, European countries are reluctant to delegate sovereignty in this area to the European Union, since it also impacts on their authority to tax. These are the reasons why the European Union is not represented in the IMF as a single member. This is different from the WTO where the EU has harmonized important instruments of trade policy, such as tariffs and the negotiation of trade treaties.

Within Europe, there are diverging views. A common representative would undoubtedly add pressure toward further European integration, including toward creating a unified economic government in the European Monetary Union. But it is doubted whether this argument, which has been raised especially by French economists, would represent a desirable development within the European Monetary Union where the French concept of economic government is controversial. There is, however, no doubt that the European countries have to play according to the rule that the weighting of directors has to follow the economic relevance of countries and that a reorganization of the Executive Board itself is not taboo (see below). But it is a different question whether the EU will in the future be faced with demands that it eliminates its intra-EU trade from its calculation of global trade. In this case, a quota for the EU would be considerably lower.[11]

Institutional Rules for Decision Making

In addition to the orientation of the IMF and an adjustment of quotas, there is also a debate about changes in the institutional rules for decision-making processes. Increasing the basic shares of 250 basic votes, which apply to all member countries, and correspondingly reducing all shares above the basic votes that depend on the quota has been discussed. The Board of Executive Directors has, for example, proposed to raise the basic voting rights to a minimum of 500 in order to give low-income countries a bigger share (IMF 2006b,c). In 2008, the Board of Governors agreed to triple the basic votes (IMF 2008d). The total of basic votes of the 185 members will rise from 2.1% of total votes (amounting to 2,216,193 votes) prior to the 2008 reform to 5.5% of total votes. The aggregate shift for the fifty-four countries that gained votes is 4.9 percentage points. This strengthens the representation of small countries, the majority of which are poor developing countries, many of them in Africa. Taken to the extreme, increasing the role of basic votes would result in each country having the same basic vote and all members having the same voice ("one country, one vote").[12]

However, in contrast to other international institutions, the IMF is an institution whose special nature requires it to have sufficient capital at its disposal to prevent currency crises. Moreover, it is an institution that must make rapid decisions when a currency crisis is developing. The IMF mission and its capacity to react quickly would be restricted if basic voting shares were greatly expanded. Countries would have little interest in contributing to the financing of the IMF. The institution would become less attractive; its ability to perform would suffer. So there are some good arguments for keeping the current approach for determining quotas. Hence, an increase in basic voting shares is possible to a limited extent only.

---

[11] Based on the Foreign Trade Statistics for 2004, this would mean a decline of 66% for the EU25 in the world trade indicator.

[12] Also see internal proposals of the Independent Evaluation Office (IMF 2008f).

The procedure for appointing the twenty-four Executive Directors changes when quotas are adjusted to the new weightings in the global economy. This also applies to the possibility of establishing groups of countries (constituencies). Members with a voting share of more than 4.17% (i.e., 100/24 directors) would have the right to appoint a director to the twenty-four Director positions if the Executive Board continued to have twenty-four Directors. A comparison with the current Board seat distribution confirms that the United States, Japan, Germany, France, and Great Britain could continue to appoint one executive director, each in accordance with table IX.2. This would change if the country's weight fell below 4.17% of the votes. In addition, China, which already has an executive director, would have that right. But neither Russia nor Saudi Arabia would be able to form a constituency by themselves any longer.

In the remaining sixteen constituencies with more than one IMF member country, these countries may appoint an executive director from within their country group if they are able to organize an appropriate voting share by forming coalitions. In principle, the procedure of forming coalitions makes sense. Various groups use different methods for it, rotation procedures are applied and also regular elections are also used. There evidently is one difficulty in that some countries are not willing to form coalitions for political reasons and insist on their own seat in spite of having a low share of votes, for instance Saudi Arabia. Moreover, it is noticeable in the current allocation of Board seats (pre-2008 reform) that the country with the largest voting share among its constituency provided the Executive Director or his Alternate in eleven of the sixteen constituencies. Since these were often the smaller European countries, such as Belgium, the Netherlands, or Switzerland, these nations had an above average influence on appointing the Executive Director. The voting power of an Executive Director on the Executive Board is weighted according to the voting power of the country or constituency he represents. Hence, the U.S. Executive Director had 17.77% of the votes on the Executive Board (pre-2008 reform), whereas the small African constituency has an Executive Director on the Board with a voting share of less than 2%.

A characteristic of the IMF is that IMF management and the interests of member countries are closely intertwined. This can be interpreted in a positive way insofar as the nations must ultimately provide a guarantee with their capital shares and that they gain benefits from the IMF's successful crisis management in other countries for their own foreign trade and capital transactions. This holds for important exporters, importers, their banking industries, and other parts of their economies, and even for growth and employment. To this extent, the interest of member countries in the IMF's work is legitimate; it is also consistent with the basic principle of quota determination. It would be unrealistic to demand that countries all of which have a strong interest in a positive development of the global economy could not combine to form coalitions; even if this results in a situation where the G7 hold almost half the votes. It is a completely different matter if the IMF is used for the foreign policy purposes of a single member country, such as the United States. In the framework of the existing quota system this can be thwarted only by an appropriate resistance by the other member countries, such as the European Union. On balance, these arguments lead to the conclusion to stay with the institution of Executive Directors, although the number of twenty-four is not untouchable.[13]

It is still unclear whether regional IMFs might form in parallel to the disintegration of institutional arrangements within the WTO due to bilateralism and regionalism, as the efforts in Asia seem to suggest. As far as security networks against financial crises are concerned, a hierarchy of such security networks in national systems, for instance safety nets for savings and loans, is recommendable. But with respect to networks for regions of the world such as Asia it is difficult to design such a network in a way that is consistent with the IMF's structure. Furthermore, currency crises by their nature are not limited to a region but are interdependent through multiple mechanisms (Siebert 2007e). Unfortunately, the exchange rate, which is at the core of the IMF's activity, is considered to be a political tool. Any regionalization of institutions must necessarily result in a further fragmentation of the world economy.

The proposals to fundamentally change the decision-making process and to make IMF management more independent are more far-reaching. The proposal made by the Governor of the Bank of England, Mervyn King (2006), returns to some Keynesian ideas: accordingly, the IMF is to be managed by a managing director with a markedly strengthened role who would be responsible for the IMF's proper functioning. The Executive Board would be eliminated or would lose substantially in importance; this would resolve or defuse the problem of how the twenty-four Executive Directors are appointed. The Managing Director would be supervised by the Board of Governors whose national members would meet in Washington more frequently than now, for example six to eight times a year. The Board of Governors would be composed of representatives of the national ministries of finance or central banks, and thus would not reside at headquarters. King pointed out that the lines of authority in the Fund are not clearly discernible in the current structure. Moreover, he makes the point that Executive Directors have a workload (300 pages of documents per working day) which makes them dependent on their national experts.

A major criticism raised against the King proposal is that the individual countries would have to cede important decision-making authority to the Managing Director. For example, they would have to be willing to support his decisions on loans even if this might mean a financial liability for them. In case of a currency crisis, the Managing Director would probably have to be granted far-reaching authority to enable

---

[13] In principle, there is no systemic reason why the Executive Board is to consist of exactly twenty-four directors. It is also possible to imagine an Executive Board composed of less than ten members. Then the position of the U.S. appointed director would approximate the U.S. capital shareholding. Such a proposal would again cause the question of limiting the representation of the European Monetary Union nations to one representative to be raised. But then the ties between individual member countries and the IMF would be weakened, and the interest of countries in the institution would be less strong.

prompt decisions. With a nonresident Board of Governors it might be difficult to supervise the Managing Director. On the whole, supervision becomes more complicated if the current resident Executive Board is replaced by a nonresident Board of Governors. Furthermore, the United States would gain greater influence because of its presence at headquarters.

To avoid the problem of a nonresident Board of Governors, Eichengreen (2006) suggested appointing an independent committee, perhaps consisting of five persons who would be the decision-makers. The Managing Director would be an equal among equals ("chairman of the board"). Similarly to a central bank board, the members would vote on important issues. They would be appointed for a six-year term; the decisive criterion would be their qualification. The number "five" is derived from the five major regions of the world: Europe, North America, Latin America, Africa, and Asia. However, members would not be selected by their regions of origin. Under this proposal, Europe would lose the prerogative to appoint the Managing Director; the United States would lose the prerogative to select the Deputy. The quota system would be suppressed in this IMF decision-making process. This structure, based on the model of a central bank board, such as the central banks with federal elements like the Federal Reserve Bank or the ECB, would represent a marked shift of the decision-making authority from shareholders to the IMF.

While the decisive argument for establishing an independent Central Bank, i.e., the depoliticizing of the money creation process, is that politicians may abuse the control over money for their own purposes (like Hitler in financing military expenditures during rearmament for World War II or governments trying to maximize the votes they get) so that monetary stability suffers, there is no similarly strong argument for an IMF institution to be completely independent of its shareholders. The proposal implies a considerable relinquishing of sovereignty by major national economies which depend on global trade and global capital flows, but also by medium-sized and smaller open economies which derive their wealth from global trade and global capital flows. It is possible to imagine regulatory mechanisms, similar to those of the European Monetary Union, which would obligate countries to contribute capital while they would simultaneously be protected from excessive domination by IMF management. Such regulatory mechanisms would be similar in quality to the Growth and Stability Pact but would be much more complex and would have to regulate both the relinquishing of sovereignty by member countries, for example during contributions of additional capital, and also IMF oversight within an international treaty. It is hard to imagine a pragmatic solution here. King's and Eichengreen's proposals, which aim at strengthening and depoliticizing the IMF, have little chance of being implemented. The IMF is, after all, the resultant force in a force field of member countries with extremely different fields of interest.

X

Ethical Norms, Human Rights, Fairness, and Legitimacy: Restraints for the International Rule System

To be put in place, international rules evolving in a bottom-up process need acceptance. Lowering transaction costs and preventing hardship, as stressed here, are decisive aspects that are likely to bolster the acceptance of rules in the long run. However, these rules must also prove acceptable at a given moment in time under the political conditions then prevailing. Countries find themselves involved in political cycles, and political topics follow waves of fashion. Apparently, in disastrous situations, such as the condition existing in pretransformation economies in Central and Eastern Europe, people are more willing to accept new rules. The acceptability of rules also depends on whether they are consistent with ethical norms shared by many people. Such ethical norms can be viewed as a restraint for the rule system that we observe. This is the line I follow here.

An alternative approach would be normative. It would consist of starting axiomatically from philosophical principles, such as fairness, and deriving international rules from these principles. This is quite different from voluntary rules undertaken for mutual advantage in the world that we know. It would mean mean looking at something like an archetypical Platonic ruler, handing down precepts from on high.

Acceptance of rule systems is a rather broad concept, as it encompasses the approval of public opinion and governments. From this viewpoint, acceptance represents one aspect of legitimacy (see below). When rules are crystallized in international organizations, the legitimacy of these organizations is an important aspect of the acceptance of rules.

Ethical Norms

Human activity is based on ethical norms. We can take this statement as a historical observation, albeit with some exceptions, as ethical norms were sullied severely in the past. Humans normally follow ethical norms, and so does society. Thus, ethical norms serve as a guide to action. Most specifically, they exclude certain actions as unethical. Norms find their basis in values and are acquired in socialization. Instead of interpreting ethical norms through empirical observation, we can understand them normatively as a duty that an individual has to follow. Ethical norms then represent an internal gyroscope for individuals, groups, and nations. Important examples are the natural law, the incest taboo known in nearly all societies, the Ten Commandments, and the norms of other religions. The golden rule (see the section below on fairness) is another example. Here we do not delve into the philosophical debate on whether ethics should focus on the wrongness or rightness of actions themselves (deontological ethics) or whether it should rather focus on the wrongness or rightness of the consequences these actions entail (consequentionalist ethics). In any case, our approach for motivating rules and institutional arrangements is in line with the consequentialist way of thinking. Since Adam Smith's first major book on "moral sentiments" (1759), economists have been aware that economic behavior and economic decisions need an ethical foundation.

With respect to ethical norms, Max Weber (1919) first drew an important distinction between an "ethics of conviction" (*"Gesinnungsethik"*) and an "ethics of responsibility" (*"Verantwortungsethik"*). "Ethics of conviction" relates to a person's beliefs, attitudes, passions, and fervors. It defines the moral behavior of an individual who does not necessarily pay the costs of his convictions and the price of his certainties. He may just act regardless of the consequences of his actions, or even free ride by demanding that others follow specific norms without committing himself. "Ethics of responsibility" refers instead to the situation of an individual carrying the burden of his decisions and looking at the long-run impact of his beliefs for himself and for others. This happens whenever the individual factors his liability vis-à-vis others into his ethical choices, when he is accountable for such choices and takes the blame for his decision. This distinction has been used for politics. While the statesman supposedly stands up to the long-run implications of his decision making, even if they are unpleasant, the politician only looks at the next election. The distinction may also be applied to members of social groups such as the NGOs, where sometimes good-doers follow an ethics of conviction, not considering the implications that their convictions entail for others.

Norms may be informal. An example is the convention of exchanging gifts in archaic societies, as studied by Marcel Mauss (1923/24). In these societies, gifts should be made, gifts should be accepted, and gifts should be reciprocated. Norms may also be established formally in the form of international conventions or lead to international organizations. Today, ethical norms have to encompass the increasingly global and complex implications of economic decisions made by individuals. They therefore have to recognize the increased degree of interdependence permeating the global economy. Moral responsibility thus extends to a larger space. In terms of economics, this means that the utility function of individuals embraces a larger geographical spatial dimension than the nation. A good example of broader utility functions has been the reaction of the citizens of industrialized countries to the tsunami which struck Southeast Asia in 2004; by promptly sending aid to the countries hit by such a tragedy, they showed how much they cared for what was happening far away. Note, however, that introducing phenomena in other countries in the utility function of Western citizens does not entail the right for wealthier people to impose their preferences on poor people living in developing countries. If the rich industrialized countries are really concerned with the economic situation of the developing world, they should rather open their product markets to the goods produced in developing countries and abolish the distortions created by their subsidies. If they really care, they may even give up part of their income and wealth. A different matter is when interventions are justified for moral reasons (see human rights below; environmental issues in chapter IX).

Human Rights

Whereas in a normative interpretation ethical norms describe what man should or should not do, human rights represent the basic rights to which all humans are entitled. Human rights can therefore be understood as being a complement to or the other side of ethical norms, namely an indispensable prerogative protecting the individual. They define the entitlement to be treated as a human being. The UN Universal Declaration of Human Rights states: "All human beings are born free and equal in dignity and rights." Only indirectly do human rights express an obligation, calling implicitly for the respect of these entitlements.

Human rights include the right to life and security of the person, liberty, freedom of thought and freedom of expression or speech, freedom of religion, and equality before the law (Steiner et al. 2007). Freedom of movement, freedom of assembly, and due process under the rule of law are also considered integral elements of human rights. Human rights are universal: they hold for all human beings. Nevertheless, their interpretation differs according to history and cultural traditions. The more specific their definition, the greater the influence of culture in their interpretation. The basic tenets of their definition should hold regardless of any cultural specification.

Human rights protect individuals against the arbitrariness and eagerness for power of governments and other entities, including other citizens. The basics of human rights represent entitlements that a government or a private entity should never attempt to deny. These usually inalienable rights are fixed in the constitution of countries. In the American interpretation, they are negative rights that the state cannot take away. Internationally, they should hold irrespective of the form of government. An example is liberty, whose constitutional recognition stems from a long tradition in the Anglo-Saxon world, but also represents a basic element of constitutions in Europe. Many consider the Principle of Liberty—expressed as "Each person should enjoy the maximum degree of liberty compatible with the same degree for all others"—as an important element of human rights.

Human rights also represent an expression of the principle of equality: "Each person should be shown the respect and consideration of which any moral being is worthy." Equality before the law and due process under the rule of law are important expressions of this principle, mandating equal judicial treatment. Nondiscrimination is yet another aspect (see below). The interpretation of nondiscrimination is subject to given concrete situations. Thus, equal treatment is usually defined within the borders of the nation state: this is the case when a policy instrument, be it a tax rate or a transfer or a judicial procedure, is required to apply equally to all individuals for the same problem.

In this interpretation, human rights refer to civic and political rights. In their quality of negative rights, they differ from positive rights. An example of the latter is the state's obligation to provide social protection to its citizens. This public duty is especially engrained in the European concept of the state as a caretaker, springing from a secular Rousseauian tradition. Positive rights define a wide range of economic, social, and cultural entitlements. Examples are social protection and the access to schools and health services. In a related interpretation, human rights come to include a positive component. One interpretation of such rights, for instance, emphasizes the material prerequisites without which freedom would lose its actual significance (Sen 2001). In this view, the value of freedom itself is small if a person does not have the material means to enjoy it. From a pragmatic point of view, such positive entitlements are first of all defined within the nation state and its cultural environment. When the nation state is understood as a "resource machine" (see chapter I), it is its duty to provide the resources making the implementation of positive human rights possible. By the same token, national policymakers must also include in their decision-making process the opportunity costs of a given choice in terms of forgone policy targets. These costs include lower growth performance, economic erosion, and, as the continental European experience shows, the discrimination of the unemployed due to high unemployment rates. Since all countries face different endowments and preferences, and since their GDP and GDP per capita differ widely, positive entitlements will necessarily diverge among nations.

As human rights expressed in terms of entitlements can be considered the other side of ethical norms, these norms also penetrate the core of individual ethics thanks to the process of socialization and due to their internalization. Thus, human rights come to represent a component of the individuals' ethics of responsibility. Human rights are also implemented by laws, mandating a certain behavior or excluding it, and by the actions of government. Both result in certain things not being done (negative obligation) or (other) things being done (positive obligation).

A major issue is what the world can effectively do if basic human rights are violated as in the case of Darfur (Barrett 2007) or in the case of the cyclone in Myanmar in 2008 when the military junta did not allow international aid in. These are cases when national governments violate human rights or when they are incapable of protecting their citizens. A related question is when human rights are not respected due to military action as under Milosevic in former Yugoslavia. In such cases, humanitarian interventions as backed by the UN Charter are asked for (Benedict XVI 2008). However, the responsibility to protect often cannot be implemented since the votes in the UN Security Council necessary for action cannot be found, as Darfur exemplifies.

International Human Rights Courts

Internationally, the last decades have witnessed the establishment of courts dealing with the most severe violations of human rights. These courts set a limit to the principle of territoriality, which loses its primacy when "natural" law and human rights are violated. Whereas the International Court of Justice, the main legal organ of the UN, tries to settle disputes between countries (see chapter IV), the International Criminal Court, also based in The Hague, deals with the gravest crimes of international concern; namely genocide, crimes against humanity, and war crimes. The International Criminal Court will not act if a case is investigated or prosecuted by a national judicial system. Then, the case is deemed inadmissible according to the principle of "complementarity." However, a case may be admissible if a state proves unwilling or unable to genuinely carry out the investigation or prosecution. For example, a case is admissible if national proceedings are undertaken only in order to simply shield the investigated person from criminal responsibility. The Court's jurisdiction is further limited to events which have occurred since July 1, 2002, when the related international treaty—the Rome Statute—came into force. In fact, only on that date did the states recognizing its validity reach the threshold number of sixty. So far, 105 countries have joined. In addition, for states joining the court after July 1, 2002, the Court only has jurisdiction over crimes perpetrated after the entry date. Moreover, the Court can exercise its jurisdiction only over nationals of states that are party to the Statute. Exceptions are possible if a state otherwise accepts the jurisdiction of the Court; if the crime took place on the territory of a state party; or if the United Nations Security Council has referred the situation to the prosecutor, irrespective of the nationality of the accused or the location of the crime. Participating countries meet in the Assembly of States Parties, which is the management oversight and legislative body of the court.

So far, four cases have been referred to the Prosecutor. Three state parties (Uganda, Democratic Republic of the Congo, and Central African Republic) have brought to the Court situations occurring on their territories, and the Security Council, acting under chapter VII of the United Nations Charter, has referred a situation on the territory of a nonstate Party (Darfur, Sudan).

Unlike the International Criminal Court, which is the product of a multilateral treaty, the Tribunals for the former Yugoslavia and Rwanda were created by the United Nations Security Council in response to specific situations.

The European Court of Human Rights deals with the complaints of states involved in interstate disputes and with applications submitted by single individuals. Its origin dates back to the Convention for the Protection of Human Rights and Fundamental Freedoms drawn up by the Council of Europe, taking as its starting point the 1948 UN Universal Declaration of Human Rights. The actual Strasbourg court is based on Protocol No. 11 of the Convention which came into force in 1988. Protocol No. 14 has not been ratified yet. The Convention has been ratified by forty-seven European countries, including not only the twenty-seven EU member states, but also countries such as Azerbaijan, Georgia, Turkey, and Russia. All the members of the Council of Europe must ratify the authority of the European Court of Human Rights.

Prominent examples of interstate applications are the case brought to the court by Ireland against the United Kingdom in the 1970s, involving security measures in Northern Ireland, and several cases taken by Cyprus against Turkey over the situation in northern Cyprus. The right of individual complaint, today one of the essential features of the system, was originally an option that contracting states could recognize at their discretion. When the convention came into force, only three of the original ten contracting states recognized this right. When Protocol No. 11 took effect in 1998, the recognition of the right of individual petition became compulsory.

A Committee of Ministers supervises the enforcement of the judgments by the European Court of Human Rights at six regular meetings every year. Documentation for these meetings takes the form of the Annotated Agenda and Order of Business. These documents are made public, as are, in general, all decisions taken in each case. The Committee of Ministers' essential function is to ensure that member states comply with the judgments of the European Court of Human Rights. The committee drafts a final resolution at the end of each case. The control exerted by the committee ensures that individual measures are taken, where necessary, in order to ensure that the injured party be put, as far as possible, into the same situation as before the violation of the convention: these measures may consist, for example, in reopening proceedings at the national level, in granting of a resident permit, and in striking out criminal records. When necessary, the committee takes general measures in order to avoid new violations of the convention; these measures may include constitutional, legislative or regulatory amendments, a change in administrative practice or in case law, and publication and dissemination of the court's judgment.

Criteria of Fairness

Criteria of fairness serve to judge whether concrete rules are just and acceptable. We can interpret them as an expression of ethical norms, representing some type of meta-rules; in some cases they are equivalent to ethical norms. These criteria have to be applied to specific economic situations and also to rule systems. They relate to individuals, groups, and countries. In the approach I follow here, criteria of fairness can be viewed as a restraint for the rule system. I will also look at the alternative of a normative approach in which implications are drawn from axiomatically set criteria of fairness.

One of the most basic criteria for fairness, representing an ethical norm, is the so-called golden rule. In its version as the Kantian categorical imperative it says: "Act as so that the maxim of your will can be valid at the same time as a principle of universal legislation." This principle is rooted in nearly all major religions. The most commonly known version in the Western world is the golden rule of Christianity, often expressed as "Do onto others as you would wish them do onto you" or as "Therefore all things whatsoever ye would that men should do to you, do ye even so to them" (Christianity: Matthew 7:12). This represents a positive version of the golden rule. Compare the Greek philosophers "May I do to others as I would that they should do unto me" (Plato) and "Do not do to others that which would anger you if others did it to you" (Socrates), where we have both a positive and a negative version. Similar principles can be found in other religions, for instance "This is the sum of duty: Do naught unto others which would cause you pain if done to you" (Brahmanism: Mahabharata, 5:1517); ". . . a state that is not pleasing or delightful to me, how could I inflict that upon another?" (Buddhism: Samyutta Nikaya v. 353); "Do not do to others what you do not want them to do to you" (Confucianism: Analects 15:23); and "What is hateful to you, do not to your fellow man. This is the law: all the rest is commentary" (Judaism: Talmud, Shabbat 31a); "Not one of you truly believes, until you wish for others what you wish for yourself" (Islam: thirteenth of the forty Hadiths of Nawawi).

The Rawls criterion of fairness goes beyond the golden rule. Rawls's argument (1971) moves from the assumption of a veil of ignorance: individuals do not know into which situation they are born and under this condition they have to decide which rule is acceptable. This means that you do not know whether you are born poor or rich; whether you have an excellent brain or whether you are handicapped; whether you are born in Bellagio, Italy, or Chendu, China; or whether you are born today or tomorrow. The condition of uncertainty influences or even determines the resulting rule system. Rawls looks for a rule that is generally acceptable under the conditions of this thought experiment. In other words, such a system tends to maximize the lowest payoff, applying a maximin strategy. Unlike the golden rule, this criterion does not start from a given situation in which people exist and live. It uses a thought experiment, representing an "as if" approach under hypothetical conditions.

As an implication, Rawls concludes that social and economic inequalities should be arranged in such a way as to ensure the greatest benefit to the least advantaged person. Consequently, offices and positions should be open to all under conditions of equal opportunity, subject to conditions expressed by the difference principle: a society may undertake projects that give some persons more power, income, and status than others—for instance entrepreneurs who are in charge of combining factors of production and producing—provided that certain conditions are met: the project should make life easier for persons who are now worse off (see the section "Is the human condition improved?" below) and access to privileged positions is not blocked by discrimination. Apparently, Rawls's argument is compatible to some degree with the concept of efficiency.

As a thought experiment, the Rawls criterion stresses the normative role of solidarity. It invites people to put themselves into other people's shoes. As such, it can be applied to more specific issues involving solidarity concerns. An example is when judgment is needed on how to organize a health insurance system in a society. For that issue, the veil of ignorance has relevance in the sense that we do not know which illnesses we might contract one day. Therefore, people in Europe are prepared to accept a health insurance setting in which the risks of becoming ill are spread according to the principle of solidarity. (In addition to the sharing of health risk, most European countries have introduced distribution into the contribution rates for the health system, making them depend on income from work.) Another case to which the Rawls experiment can apply is the trade-off between the income levels of different generations. In this sense, the Rawls criterion sharpens our thinking.

Since the Rawls criterion is a criterion of solidarity, its implications conflict with solutions following other principles and criteria. To put it differently, the Rawls approach represents a tabula rasa, allowing us to evaluate practical solutions. For instance, to grant everyone a basic income without requiring that he or she work, as was discussed in Germany in 2007, would have a negative effect on the incentive to work (Siebert 2007c). Labor supply will then practically shrink. Work ethics, usually the cultural result of a society's shared experience, will be lesser. Unless a country is blessed by nature, as in the case of large oil fields, a society may not be able to sustain itself above an extremely low level of income if such an approach of providing a basic income without work is implemented. Similarly, it is questionable whether the application of the Rawls criterion in practice will necessarily hamper the accumulation of physical and human capital, since the driving forces behind these phenomena are individual motives rather than judgments of solidarity. For these matters, the Rawls criterion would require an ideal man, endowed with deep empathy for his fellows and caring sincerely for the future of mankind. Needless to say, historical experience has done enough to shatter this idealization, except perhaps in the Kibbutzim and in early Christianity. As for communist societies, the reality definitively stood poles apart from the ideal.

If we apply the Rawls criterion on a global scale, a substantial redistribution of income would be recommended because someone born in a high-income country may, given the veil of ignorance, think of himself as born in a low-income country. Consequently, he would accept rules that favor more equal production possibilities worldwide. Thanks to this ideal orientation, a more equal income distribution may follow, albeit on a lower per capita income level worldwide. Similarly, we would have different migration laws as people under the veil of ignorance would tend to give every person more rights to live in the country of his or her choice. In the extreme, every person would have the right to live in the country of his choice. This, however, is simply impossible: in such a setting, the acceptance of property rights as they exist today would be unlikely, especially for land; actual property rights would presumably disappear. Only some limited, maybe temporary, property rights would be tolerated. The positive effects of property rights would therefore be lost, weakening the incentive system that promotes production, investment, and innovation. Debates on property rights would be likely. The disappearance of most of these rights would deprive societies of a sound method for preventing quarrels, clashes, and wars. Likewise, it might prove extremely difficult to agree on the principle of territoriality as a procedure for reducing conflict. It is possible that mankind would enter a state of permanent confrontation. In all these cases, the impracticality of the Rawls criterion becomes apparent.

The Rawls concept of fairness represents a normative approach, in which a Platonic ruler derives implications from an axiom and hands down precepts from on high in a Panglossian world. Of course, if the decisions of individuals come to the same conclusions, the implications of the Rawls criterion become a negative constraint in the sense of the approach used here. Otherwise it does not have this property.

This assessment also holds for approaches other than Rawls that look at the issue of fairness under more specific aspects and apply this criterion to detailed situations. Thus, one can ask the question of whether a specific arrangement should be considered unfair, or whether it is inconsistent in itself. For instance, if one accepts the international division of labor as an agreed-upon approach, subsidizing exports is unfair. In fact, these subsidies establish distortions and destroy exporting options for other countries, especially the developing countries. Along similar lines, the principle of free trade requires the provision of free-market access to all countries. Obstacles to trade should be abolished. As a special form of this general principle, Stiglitz and Charlton (2005) propose to apply it preferentially for developing countries with low income: "all WTO members should commit themselves to providing free-market access to all developing countries poorer and smaller than themselves" (p. 94). This would imply that all developing countries could enjoy free access to markets with a larger GDP and a larger GDP per capita. In turn, developing countries with a higher per capita income would also open up to other developing countries.

In trade disputes, developed countries are in a better bargaining position. The costs of bringing a claim in the WTO against a developed country are often too high for a developing country. The options for a small country to impose sanctions on the United States are small, whereas sanctions imposed by the United States tend to have a strong impact. Therefore, Stiglitz and Charlton (2005) propose (p. 68): "Any agreement should be assessed in terms of impact on developing countries." They also make the point that impact assessment should be done in terms of applied general-equilibrium models.

Besides this interpretation of fairness in terms of content, procedural fairness in terms of openness and transparency of the negotiation process is equally important. This corresponds to the rule of law in national rule systems. Any international agreement should be fairly arrived at.

Social Standards

We have claimed that positive entitlements, or positive human rights, will necessarily have to differ across countries, whereas negative human rights, i.e., civic and political human rights, should be universal. However, the issue arises as to whether some minimum positive human rights should hold universally. This is a hotly debated topic under the heading of social standards.

For instance, quite a few NGOs have recently intensified their calls to equalize social standards between countries. Some invoke the same level of entitlements worldwide or even, occasionally, the same or a similar real wage across countries. A major issue behind this claim is how social standards should be defined. In the Western world, some standards upon which the members of the International Labor Organization agreed, for instance the right to establish trade unions, are generally accepted as minimum human rights, or more precisely as civil and political rights. Moreover, improving the level of schooling and advancing the quality of education should be in the self-interest of all developing countries since human capital is an important precondition for good economic performance and for an increase in per capita income. The same applies to the access to health service.

However, identical levels of social protection and similar real wage levels are something completely different. It would also be bizarre to request the accomplishment of such entitlements by means of trade policy measures, by denying the access to foreign markets to countries which do not employ these standards. Furthermore, demands for the harmonization of social standards may even prove harmful. By harmonizing social standards, the developing countries would indeed be negatively affected: because of their lower labor productivity (per head or per hour), these countries would be unable to pay the same wage that industrialized countries pay. For similar reasons, they cannot be expected to adopt the industrialized countries' labor standards or social norms, because these standards increase the cost of production in the same way as higher wages do. In addition, the industrialized nations have no ethical right to impose the implementation of their own social standards on the developing countries. In conclusion, harmonizing social standards would not be a promising strategy for the rich countries against the problem of globalization. By the same token, the rich countries do not have the ethical right to impose their environmental standards on poor countries. Note that, in any case, social standards do not represent a public good in our definition of the term. Note that social standards meet the same potential problems as the Rawls criterion.

Equality of Results versus Equality of Starting Conditions

In the public discussion of Western countries, fairness is sometimes interpreted by some as a desirable equality of outcome; for instance, Socialists, Marxists, and other observers tend to interpret fairness in this way. However, this interpretation is not appropriate for economic processes. One reason for this is that economic situations are specific and different across countries. Therefore, internationally equal results are not possible. The other reason is that the goal of equality of outcome for each individual, irrespective of talent and effort, would give the wrong incentives to the agents of the economic system. Each person would be encouraged to free ride on others, relying on their efforts to improve the general outcome.

Unlike equality of outcome, equality of starting conditions in a person's life and the principle of equal opportunity are widely accepted principles, leading, for instance, to the approach of the World Bank. The goal is a situation in which a person's economic, social, or political success is not predetermined by conditions of birth, race, or gender, as such success should rather reflect his or her efforts and talents (World Bank 2005b, p. 18). Access to health care and education, the quality of the services available and, more generally, the openness of institutions as well as vertical social and income mobility are seen as major factors in determining to what extent a society can ensure equal opportunity. An open society characterized by vertical income mobility and social mobility can be seen as a precondition to implement equal opportunity. The principle of equal opportunity helps maximize the use of all talents in a society and bring into play all the potential effort available. It should therefore have a positive impact on economic growth.

Admittedly, inequality traps exist. Often, discretionary decisions on the access to services controlled by groups are at the root of these traps. An example is university education in some European countries, where students whose parents have an academic background de facto enjoy preferential access due to governmental rationing and other reasons. In contrast, markets, where allocation decisions are made respecting the agents' anonymity, allow free entry. Equal opportunity is a principle that applies, first of all, to a society. In an international context, free-market access is an important expression of this principle as applied to countries.

Is the Human Condition Improved?

A major aspect in the discussion of fairness (in a wider interpretation) is the question of whether the human condition is actually improved by a given system of rules. A system that worsens the general human condition barely deserves to be called fair.

As a possible guideline economists have proposed the Pareto criterion. It can be applied to changes in the economic situation, in our context with respect to rules. A new rule or a change in rules is Pareto-superior if at least one person is better off and no one is worse off. Practically, this means that an improvement may extend to many and no one loses. This criterion may be extended by the principle that the winners should compensate those who lose due to a change in the system (Kaldor criterion). Rawls's difference principle is also a possible answer to our issue. Much simpler and more limited is the Koopmans criterion, which defines improvement as an increased production of at least one good, the production of other goods remaining constant. These criteria stand in the consequentialist tradition.

Institutionally, an essential precondition for applying the Pareto criterion is not given if individuals or groups have a privileged access to the use of resources, goods, or positions. One way of contravening this condition is the segmentation of markets, be they factor markets—such as labor markets and resources markets—or product markets. Often, even informal markets are segmented along differences in social and cultural origins, clan, or tribal membership, and economic factors such as a lack of risk evaluation in infant financial markets. Consequently, some groups are excluded from market processes. Human resources are therefore left idle. On the political stage, privileged positions of incumbents give rise to the risk of coups against governments as a surrogate of a duly accepted democratic process with its periodical change of governments. This increases economic uncertainty and reduces capital formation. Privileges may also include exclusive access to life resources such as water. This hampers the health of people and lowers a country's growth potential. For all these reasons it is important to abolish market segmentation and privileged access.

An unresolved question in using the Pareto criterion is whether individuals are satisfied with absolute improvements, or whether they only accept changes insofar as they do not impinge on their relative income position. As recent neuropsychological analyses have shown, the neuroprocesses in the brain of a human being do not only depend on the remuneration he receives after having solved a task, but also on the remunerations others obtain (Fliessbach et al. 2007). Changes in relative income therefore seem to play a crucial role. These results may also apply to nation states. As put forward in chapter I, some countries may derive a larger gain than others from a rule system. An important condition for the stability of rules is also that the gains for each country be sizable. If the benefits of a rule system are visibly one-sided, or if they diverge strongly, the stability of a rule system is likely to be put into question.

In spite of distributional aspects, rationality tells us that an absolute improvement in the human condition is an important aspect of evaluating a rule system. In no case should equity or fairness be interpreted at a given moment of time only, but it should include the change in income over time. Rising income over time and vertical income mobility of individuals in a society should be important factors in defining fairness. The rationale for stressing the time dimension of a rise in income—for instance, over the life cycle of people and in the process of economic growth, instead of looking at its distribution at a given moment in time—is that the income increase represents an open-ended process whose effects can hardly be known *ex ante*. Hayek's information problem focuses exactly on this: if the emphasis is on the distribution of income at a given moment of time only, it is impossible to know all the potential options and to evaluate the options forgone.

Since the rule system relates to many aspects, goal conflicts between different criteria are possible. Thus, economic conditions may be in conflict with other criteria. Take, for instance, liberty: the economic condition may be improved while liberty is lost. Along these lines, the world knows and will see different forms of government in the future. Nondemocratic approaches—or approaches quite different from those of Western democracies—may perform well in the future from an economic point of view. This will force Western democracies to perform equally well. Usually, observers argue that nondemocratic regimes entail the need for the economic elites to support the political elites and the bureaucracy (as well as often the military), and that this leads to inefficiencies in the long run, eroding the system (Acemoglu et al. 2006). Moreover, with a higher standard of living, the demand for freedom and democracy increases (Lipset 1959; Barro 1999). The economic agents behind the economic success of a country also want to have a say in the rules according to which they have to act, as is likely to happen in China. Nevertheless, at some time in the future, this type of institutional competition will not be easy for Western democracies, especially if their voters are lured by the good performance of illiberal countries.

Keeping in mind the goal of general economic improvement, a core question in the context of equity and growth is how much welfare some groups have to forgo at the present moment in order to encourage growth in the future. Facing the context of an intergenerational trade-off, the parent generation may be willing to make sacrifices in order to ensure a better life for the generation of their children. Such an interpretation of the institutional change necessary for growth does not satisfy the Pareto criterion that no person (or no group) should lose. For instance, in the transition from communism to a free society in Central and Eastern Europe, the old power elite had to go. People in transformation countries had to suffer a severe temporary decline in their GDP per capita in order to enjoy improved economic conditions in the future. Similarly, the civil rights movement in the United States had to tear down the privileges of other groups. Overthrowing apartheid in South Africa meant that the old elites had to give up their positions as incumbents.

A case of general dissatisfaction is voiced by some NGOs and by the radical left, as showed by their heated protests against the WTO in Seattle in 1999 and against the G8 summit in Genoa in 2001. But let us remind ourselves for a second how the WTO started. It was founded after World War II. Europe was in a shambles. Still open were also the wounds left by the disintegration of the 1930s and by the Great Depression, a period of human misery vividly described by John Steinbeck in *The Grapes of Wrath*. This was the background for the General Agreement on Tariffs and Trade, the forerunner of the WTO, founded in 1948 by twenty-three countries. After World War II, the goal was to create a stable framework for international trade in order to provide the necessary preconditions for growth and prosperity. Quite frankly, judged against this background, it is my opinion that the concept of GATT and the WTO stands up well vis-à-vis the targets of today's NGOs.

Taking a broader historical perspective in our discussion on whether the human condition has improved, it is clear that the nineteenth century proposal by Karl Marx to abolish private ownership and to expropriate the capital owners—an attempt to give a political answer to the issue of poverty and deprivation—failed. Eventually, the communist countries were not able adequately to provide their citizens with goods. In the developing world of the 1960s and 1970s, communist ideas were attractive to the intellectuals, young and old alike; they also provided a guiding orientation for economic policy as in India and represented the ideological power base of rulers, quite a few of them dictators, as in Africa. And eventually, the ideas of communism lost appeal when it became apparent that their implementation did not perform in the Soviet Union itself. It also failed in the other COMECON countries. In the industrialized countries, the process of growth was fostered by democracy, which, as an institution, helped the society open up and adjust though progressive institutional reforms to changes in the economic, social, and political environment. In the United States more than in Europe, new entrants to the market, including minorities, and technological change redefined the position of the group of incumbents in an automatic process (for instance the position of landowners and capital owners relative to workers in Europe). Historically, a specific phenomenon was the flow of immigrants to the United States in the nineteenth and twentieth century. In this interpretation, the decentralized market approach of democracy proved successful.

Admittedly, the existing institutions were unable to prevent two world wars, Nazism in Germany and Fascism in Italy. Nor could they prevent the occurrence of crises more closely related to economics, such as the Great Depression in the early 1930s and—at the actual rim—the excessive welfare state with its shockingly high unemployment rate in some European countries. In spite of these political failures, growth continues to be the way out of poverty and low income, especially for the developing countries. The best proof of this is the economic success of China, where real wage income has grown by some 8% per year in the last decade, and where more than 400 million people have been lifted out of poverty in the last twenty years (Siebert 2007a,b). Looking at the period 1975–2004, nearly all developing countries have improved their situation in absolute constant purchasing power terms and many have reduced their relative distance to the United States. The exception is countries in sub-Saharan Africa, which have experienced internal wars and turmoil (Siebert 2007e, figure 10.4).

Is a Rule System Sustainable?

The assessment of the role played by rule systems in improving human conditions must pair with an evaluation of their sustainability. If the human condition is not improved, i.e., if a situation deteriorates over time, a rule system is unlikely to survive. This trend becomes most evident if a rule system finds itself in institutional competition and if it is driven out by a system with a better performance. Here, different answers are possible: a rule system cannot survive if it sets false incentives for resolving the most important issues of a society. Similarly, a system cannot last if it does not satisfy the condition of long-run equilibrium. In economics, a long-run equilibrium is a situation which evolves after all the market participants, consumers, producers, and investors have responded to changes in economic policy instruments. We can speak of an economic law. Politicians, however, often follow a short-term orientation, being more concerned with winning the next election than with long-run considerations—a point of reference being defined by national conditions and nation-specific political cycles. It is therefore difficult for politic makers to establish rule systems that represent restraints for the political process. Thus, a conflict arises between the sustainability of a national rule system and political considerations. This conflict applies foremost to national rule systems, but it also limits the political willingness to cede sovereignty internationally.

. Rule systems should also be able to respond to shifts in economic conditions, such as increasing global resource scarcity or the advancement of developing countries. This means that rule systems should be flexible enough to accommodate new phenomena, especially unexpected states of nature. This requirement is similar to, but stronger than the "force majeure" clause, known from private contracts, which implies that temporary aberrations from a long-run equilibrium must be allowed, that room must be made for new economic trends and that major unexpected events must be taken care of.

The issue of sustainability reminds us that when looking at fairness, one should not forget whether rules are efficient, i.e., whether they are successful in reducing hardship and transaction costs and in allowing benefits. Apparently, there can be a conflict between the goal of fairness and the goal of efficiency. The difficulty encountered in finding an agreement between these two goals becomes clear if we look at the European Union, where the willingness to cooperate is more pronounced than in multilateral arrangements. Take the case of tax competition in the EU. An equity-oriented approach would tend to harmonize tax laws, for instance business taxes. However, the new EU members from Central and Eastern Europe that want to attract capital rightly view the harmonization of corporate taxes as a way of reducing locational competition through the establishment of a cartel of governments.

Legitimacy

The acceptance of rule systems is important. This raises the issue of legitimacy of the rule systems and of the international organizations representing these rules. In a general interpretation, legitimacy is interpreted as the approval of an institutional arrangement, a government, a government system, or an international organization. An institution is perceived as legitimate if its approval is general. Legitimacy is thus linked to consent, be it implicit or explicit. In this interpretation, legitimacy is a rather broad concept related to the general support for a regime. Rules need legitimacy. Legitimacy has been likened to a reservoir (Dahl 1971); as long as it remains at a certain level, stability can be maintained; if it falls below this level, then stability is endangered. It is apparent that the concept of legitimacy is vague and open to interpretation. Therefore, this general concept of legitimacy seldom answers questions concerning the quality of a rule system.

Rulers generally search for consent and support, but this is possible under different conditions. A populist leader looks for the support of the population, be it a populist in Latin America or a brutal leader such as Hitler under Nazism. In the past, communist leaders in East Germany have also sought out support, if necessary by crushing the opposition of the construction workers (as in the uprising of 1953) and by walling in their people as in the period 1961–89. In communism, the state acquired legitimacy through the promise of establishing economic equality in society even though communist regimes eventually had to resort to totalitarian methods as they failed to achieve the goals of social and economic equality. Unpopular regimes have survived by means of brutal force or because they were considered legitimate by a small but powerful national elite. In other cases, religious leaders have succeeded in winning legitimacy vis-à-vis followers thanks to their charisma.

How wide the spectrum of legitimacy is becomes apparent when derived from Weber's (1922) classification of authority into three categories: charismatic authority (e.g., a religious leader such as Khomeini), traditional authority with a government based on popular customs and usages (e.g., a monarchy), and rational authority. In rational or functional legitimacy, authority is based on the concept that a government's powers are derived from set procedures, principles, and laws, complex and written down as part of the constitution, or are part of well-respected conventions, upheld by the judiciary within the state. Examples are direct and representative democracies. Reviewing this wide spectrum of legitimacy, it becomes apparent that legitimacy depends on the paradigm used to define it. The term "legitimacy" is indeed vague, empty, and meaningless if it is interpreted in this generality. Following this interpretation, even the North Korean communist regime might be held as legitimate.

The alternative is to give legitimacy a more substantial interpretation. Thus, a constitutional foundation of legitimacy accentuates the need for a political order governed by basic rules that cannot be changed at all or that can only be altered with an overwhelming parliamentary majority. The rules limit the power of government, render it accountable and protect the liberties of the individuals. Governments change through regular democratic procedures. Constitutionalism divides powers and provides a system of effective restraints upon governmental action (Locke 1689; Montesquieu 1748; Buchanan 1975; Brennan and Buchanan 1985). In democracies, legitimacy is based on the existence of regular free and fairly contested elections to which political parties participate without any fear or pressure. Liberal democracies can be remarkably stable because the legitimacy of the state is not tied to an individual ruler or ruling party. Note that legitimacy is not identical to legality. An action can be legal without being legitimate (a law can be conceived as immoral). By the same token, an action can be legitimate without being legal (as in the case of the ousting of a dictator).

The legitimacy of global rules and global institutions has to be evaluated within this context. Beside ethical founding elements, legitimacy can be interpreted as the formal justification of international rule systems and organizations. In this interpretation, the legitimacy of the rule systems is derived from the existence of multilateral agreements. These contracts are agreed upon by national governments or even ratified in parliaments or through other domestic legislative processes. Quite a few of these governments have come into office through democratic elections, others through other national procedures. Thus, international rule systems and international organizations rest on a form of derived legitimacy. In a similar way, the European Council, i.e., the assembly of the Heads of State or of the respective ministers, and the European Commission derive their legitimacy through the European treaty.

Some have questioned the legitimacy of international rules. In this debate, transparency of rules and of organizations is a self-explanatory approach to increase the legitimacy of rules and organizations. Moreover, the dialogue with NGOs can help improve the acceptance of international organizations and the rule systems they represent. Admittedly, the NGOs' impact on public opinion plays a role in bolstering such legitimacy. Their influence on international organizations depends on their sway with the media. However, since international organizations derive their legitimacy from national governments, the involvement of NGOs in a direct discussion with international organizations can only be limited. As a matter of principle, NGOs should rather deal with the donors of legitimacy, namely the national governments. For instance, the WTO cannot affect its dependence from and responsibility toward the nation states by negotiating with the NGOs (WTO 2004b). This also applies to other international organizations and conventions. In addition, an international organization faces the problem of selecting the NGOs with whom it wants to discuss its policies. Last but not least, NGOs represent the aggregated value judgments of their members, reflecting the opinions and preferences of people close to them. As such, NGOs are not legitimized in the same way as democratic governments, since they do not represent all people as democratically elected governments do. They have to accept that their narrower legitimacy directly competes with the legitimacy of national democratic governments. In conclusion, they cannot claim to have the same level of legitimacy as national governments and international organizations. Looking at the history of thought on social movements (see, for instance, Michels 1915), the democratic legitimacy of social movements is far from guaranteed. Sometimes it would be good to remember this caveat.

The decision-making and voting rules applying to international organizations and international conventions are a relevant aspect of legitimacy (see chapters IV, V, and VII). Thus, the "one country, one vote" principle used within the WTO and the World Bank and in many other conventions enhances legitimacy. When consensus is required, or when major decisions require unanimity, the "one country, one vote" principle protects smaller countries from being outvoted or dominated by large players, or being forced to abide by rules that they do not support. The "one country, one vote" principle also applies to the General Assembly of the UN and for nearly all of the specialized UN agencies. In the IMF, where the provision of capital is crucial in order to bail countries out of a currency crisis, the "one country, one vote" rule cannot be applied. Moreover, in a currency crisis, it is vital that decisions be taken quickly in order to prevent a crisis from getting out of hand. In other cases of international arrangements, it is necessary to concentrate power in order to reach decisions that are underpinned with some credibility of being enforced. An important example is the UN Security Council, which has five permanent members, each of which can exercise veto power; the nine votes of the fifteen members are not sufficient if a veto is used. Only in procedural matters does the veto not apply and is the support of nine votes sufficient. In the International Labour Organization, a specialized agency of the UN, trade unions and the employers' associations have equal weight. The European Council of Heads of States takes several decisions with qualified majority, while fundamental decisions require unanimity (Siebert 2005c, chapter 13). From 2014 onward, qualified majority will come to mean double majority (assuming problems with the Irish "no" in 2008 can be overcome): any decision will require the approval of 55% of states, representing at least 65% of the EU population supporting a decision. (This assumes that the Irish "no" is resolved.)

Interdependence of Orders, Structure of the Rule System, and Institutional Fit

The institutional arrangement for the world economy represents an international economic order in which nation states have ceded different degrees of sovereignty in specific areas of economic policy. The reason behind this move is that states expect welfare gains from shifting some decision-making authority to multilateral institutions. These expected gains would come either as direct benefits for their countries, or as general improvements of given international conditions. By giving up policy instruments, nations bind their future actions to the respect of internationally agreed-upon rules. The international rule system is a complex institutional arrangement which sets incentives and restraints for nation-states and allocates benefits and costs to them.

Suborders within an Order and Their Goal Relations

An order can be conceived as a set of several existing suborders (Eucken 1940). The institutional arrangements for different spheres of human life—economic, political, educational, cultural, and religious—are partially separate. Similarly, the suborders within the economic order, the topic of this chapter, are also partially separate. The main areas covered by institutional arrangements are the decentralization of decisions through markets, the trade of goods and services, border-crossing factor flows—capital movements, the diffusion of technology and migration, the allocation of global environmental media, financial stability, and the implementation of human rights as well as equity considerations.

An important aspect of suborders already stressed by Eucken is their interdependence. This is a difficult issue since in a Hayekian view rules should "emerge" spontaneously from a seemingly complex network of interaction among agents with limited information and knowledge. Indeed, rules are necessarily so complex that it is impossible for any individual to know all the facts relevant to their functioning. *Ex ante*, when rules are conceived and introduced, it is difficult to forecast how a rule system will perform. This depends on how agents respond to rules and even on how they anticipate rules. Agents form expectations on how rules will function and, if possible, they will try to avoid their negative effects. Thus, they use rational expectations to predict how rules will affect their lives. Moreover, rule systems find themselves in institutional competition. All these arguments suggest that interdependence among rules only tends to become apparent over time.

As for the types of interdependence that exists between rules, a threefold theoretical classification is possible according to the relationships between goals: goal harmony (line I in figure XI.2) defines a kind of interdependence where the achievement of one goal (z_1) also helps to reach another (z_2); goal conflict or trade-off (line II) takes place when the objectives oppose each other, i.e., when reaching one goal leads away from the other goal; finally, goal neutrality (line III) exists, when reaching one goal is indifferent to the achievement of the other goal.[1] An example of goal harmony is a flexible exchange rate system that both establishes an equilibrium in the balance of payments and contributes to the reduction of inflationary pressure. Another example is the case of a double dividend when internalizing an environmental distortion which not only improves environmental quality, but also eliminates other distortions in the economy—a hypothesis which has only weak empirical support (Siebert 2008b, chapter 7). An example of goal conflict is the arrangement for the labor market in many continental European countries, where rules attempting to increase employment and rules for social protection may conflict, as the latter may actually reduce employment. A goal conflict also exists in the short run, between NAIRU, the nonaccelerating inflation rate of unemployment, and price-level stability, if one accepts the downward sloping Phillips curve as the underlying model. An example of goal neutrality is the neutrality of money with respect to the real economy, at least insofar as one adheres to the theory of classical economists—a theory that is no longer accepted today. Yet another example of goal neutrality is improving the environmental quality of completely separated systems, for instance of river systems in different continents—although on closer inspection it might well be that some linkages exist.

With respect to the use of policy instruments, we can either have a substitutive or a complementary relationship between instruments (and consequently between goals). Thus, for instance, trade can substitute for the migration of people (see chapter V). This also applies to capital flows when they replace the movement of people. In these cases, the institutional arrangements can be interpreted as being substitutes to each other. In other cases, instruments can be complements to each other, for instance when addressing a major policy issue requires the use of several

---

[1] This classification used to be standard in German university economics some forty years ago, when the subject "Economic Policy" was one of the three areas included in the final exam for the four-year economics curriculum, besides "Economic Theory" and "Public Finance." Since then, the economics curriculum has been reformulated due to American influence. "Economic Policy" ceased to exist as a distinct subject, now being integrated as applied economics into "Economic Theory" in most German universities.

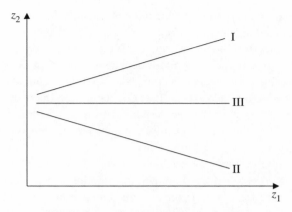

Figure XI.1. Goal relations for rule systems.

policy instruments at the same time. Consider the case of transforming countries in Central and Eastern Europe, whose transition from a planned economy required many instruments, such as commercializing state-owned firms legally, privatizing these firms, changing their product set, investing and innovating, allowing free prices and introducing markets, mopping up a monetary overhang, setting up a new banking system, and stabilizing the country's macro-economy. Another example comes from countries that had to be rebuilt after World War I.

Among the categories classifying relations according to their goals, another important category is goal dominance, when one goal enjoys supremacy over the others. This refers both to the way of organizing rule systems efficiently and to normative aspects. If we have different layers in a rule system, with one layer governing the other, a goal hierarchy exists. An example is fiscal federalism, itself reflecting the concept of a multilateral order, albeit within a much less formal structure. According to this concept, the basic rule is the one relating to the local level, at which local preferences can be expressed, local conditions are taken into consideration, and local information is processed. Issues related to a larger spatial dimension fall under a broader level, moving to the provincial and eventually to the national level-dimension along the principle of subsidiarity. Problems entailed by the extension of institutional arrangements beyond the nation state apply to regional integrations, to multilateral, and even global solutions. As explained in chapter I, the local-to-global dynamics of the subsidiarity approach is also in line with the transaction-costs approach.

In terms of substance, the dominance of one order over another raises important issues. A major question is whether the political order dominates the economic order or whether it is the other way around. As an empirical example, one can refer to the centrally planned economies in which communism as an ideology dominated the economic incentive system. Ruling out private ownership of capital implied that these systems could not rely on the price mechanism for transmitting the necessary informational signals on scarcity, restraints, risks, options, and promising economic opportunities. The rule system lacked a reliable steering mechanism for the economy. Eventually, the economic system deteriorated. An example of a value-oriented relationship is German unification, where political rationality, pursuing the overriding goal of unifying West and East Germany, took the lead over economic rationality. This approach overlooked the potentially negative impact of some policy instruments, such as the establishment of a one-to-one exchange rate for the East German mark against the West German mark.

In this context of rule dominance, a fascinating issue is whether economic freedom necessarily leads to political freedom, i.e., to some form of democracy—an issue of great importance for China. Economic freedom can be viewed as a necessary condition for strong economic growth, as the Deng Xiaoping reforms have shown. Whereas democracy tends to imply economic freedom (Friedman 1962; Schumpeter 1942), it is an open question as to whether this causal relationship also runs the other way around, i.e., whether the introduction of economic freedom starts a process leading to widespread demand for political freedom. The main argument supporting this interdependence is that economic agents will develop an interest in setting by themselves the rules according to which they have to operate, or at least in influencing the rule-setting process. Market capitalism allows economic power; it also allows the separation of economic power and political power. Whether this separation of the economic power from the political power will eventually make its way into China is an unresolved dilemma. In the Chinese case, the explanation has been offered that the Chinese people may be satisfied with becoming rich insofar as the Party lets it happen, and if it manages to adjust smoothly to the preferences of the economic elite without losing the support of other important constituencies, such as the military and the bureaucracy. However, it is likely that the Chinese GDP growth rate will come down, and that the period of positive surprises for the population will end. Moreover, unlike the current "old" generation, the younger generation is more likely to take high growth rates for granted, so that political leaders can no longer assume that the people will continue to be pleasantly surprised. Declining growth rates may lead to disappointment (Siebert 2007a,b).

For the international rule system, goal relations play a role in the aggregation of preferences. If a goal dominates the rank order of national goals in the different countries, it is more likely that the international rule system will also rank this goal highly. If, as is most often the case, preferences and the constraints under which they can be expressed differ widely, then a common hierarchy of goals is difficult to develop. But even when goals are similar, nation states have to be aware that their own goals and constraints can change over time. This will make them more cautious when ceding sovereignty.

Among the many trade-offs, the conflict between stable and flexible rules is an important one. As a principle, institutional arrangements must be stable. The reason

is that major economic decisions have an intertemporal dimension, requiring reliability and constancy of the rule system. This applies to the important decisions of
firms, concerning investment, innovation, and the hiring of personnel, and also to
the decisions of households, as in the case of savings and human capital formation.
Whereas stable rules can easily coexist with stable trends, temporary crises, shifting
economic conditions, and unexpected events represent a major challenge to the stability of the rule system (see chapter XII). Safety valves can serve to accommodate
these temporary irregularities. In addition to safety valves, the system also needs
some flexibility in order to accommodate unexpected events.

As a result of these considerations, the rule system represents a complex multi-
dimensional matrix. It has a vertical structure with different dimensions in space:
we can distinguish between local rules, regional rules within a nation state, national
rules, rules in cross-border regional integrations, multilateral approaches, and global
rules (figure XI.2). We can speak of a hierarchy of rules. This is in line with the
subsidiarity principle. At the same time, there exists horizontal interdependence
between different walks of life. With respect to the realm of economics, this relates
to product markets, factor markets, the environment, and monetary and financial
conditions. Beyond the realm of economics, rule systems encompass additional
aspects of human life. Moreover, the matrix contains both goals and a rich set of
policy instruments. In addition, some rules such as ethical norms and natural law are
more or less universal. These universal rules cut through the network of hierarchical
rules. Thus, the rule system encloses many dimensions: it is defined over space; with
space it has a vertical structure; it applies to different walks of life, and also having
a spatial dimension; and it contains universal rules.

Another important aspect in the goal relations between rule systems is whether
suborders contradict each other. Clearly, they must be mutually consistent: one
suborder must not lead to behavior on the part of economic agents which contradicts
and undermines another suborder. As a consequence, suborders must share the same
or similar objectives and philosophies. An important example of this consistency
issue is the relationship between the world trade order and the world environmental
order (see below).

A further issue is to what extent the withdrawal of benefits from one suborder
can be used as a threat or sanction enforcing the compliance to the rules of another
suborder. In a game theory approach, threatening the withdrawal of benefits from
one rule system may be interpreted as an inducement to join and to respect another
rule system. Thus, some propose to use the withdrawal of membership from the
WTO or other trade policy instruments to enforce human rights. However, this
approach makes one suborder contingent on another suborder. If one institutional
system falls, the other falls too. This would lead to a built-in institutional domino
effect threatening the overall rule system. Therefore, the advantage of using the
withdrawal of benefits of one suborder as a threat must be weighed against the risk
of destroying the overall rule system.

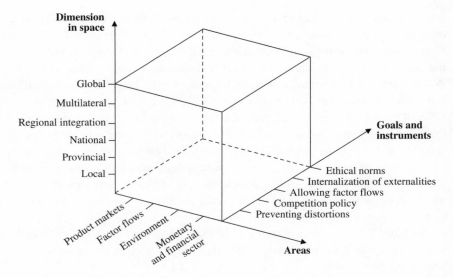

Figure XI.2.   Structure of rules.

One possible way of approaching the contingency problem is to explicitly distinguish between two different stages, namely between when an existing institutional arrangement is implemented and when it is created. Once an institutional arrangement is established, the validity of one suborder should not be contingent on the functioning of some other suborder. Such decoupling would prevent institutional domino effects. This means that the instrumental levels should remain clearly separated. As a rule, economic policy instruments available to an international organization should be limited to the specific suborders that they are a part of. Trade policy instruments, for instance, should—as a principle—not be employed for environmental policy purposes. The instrumental level should thus be subdivided into different, clearly demarcated modules. When a new institutional framework is established, it may be tempting from a game-theoretic viewpoint to withhold benefits to nonmembers from another subsystem as a sanction that is positive for establishing the new order. However, this involves a similar risk of a domino effect, for instance when benefits from the trade order are withheld for those countries that do not want to join in a new environmental arrangement. Besides, it is very often impractical to define the withdrawal of benefits.

This consideration also relates to the concept of single undertaking: the "offsetting" of the advantages of suborders should not be carried too far. If, in the course of time, the advantages of countries shift asymmetrically within the individual suborders, a fragile structure of acceptance could collapse like a house of cards. To avoid domino effects, the suborders should basically legitimize themselves on their own and their acceptance should not be conditional.

Consistency between the International Environmental Order and the International Trade Order

In the past, the international frameworks for environmental issues and for the world trade order have developed side by side, with an arrangement for the environment starting to evolve slowly as the trade order was already well established. The consistency of these two frameworks will become increasingly important.

Environmental policy aims at protecting the natural conditions of living; it deals with environmental scarcity. An institutional order for the international division of labor tries to allow an increase in the prosperity of all countries through exchange, i.e., by exploiting differences in factor endowments; this order also embraces scarcity. Both orders attempt to eliminate distortions and represent institutional frameworks having allocation at their core. In principle, therefore, the aims are not contradictory, since economic scarcity must be defined by taking the natural conditions of living into account. The more successfully the environment as a scarce good is integrated into the economic order of individual countries, i.e., the better affluence is defined by taking the environment into account, the sooner the congruence of targets will be achieved between the two orders.

Following this way of thinking, inconsistency between the two rule systems can be mitigated if both systems are able to provide signals for scarcity by relying on the same policy instruments. Compared with the administrative approach in applying regulations, the market economy approach to environmental policy, by using scarcity-signaling prices, provides more consistency between the two sets of rules. Prices expressing environmental scarcity can easily be integrated into the world trade order, based on the principle of comparative price advantage. This would, of course, hold for the "polluter-pays" principle, if all countries accepted it as a general guideline for their national environmental policies. For global goods, however, the implementation of the polluter-pays principle requires overcoming the difficulties discussed in chapter VII, such as the differences in preferences, in willingness to pay, and free-rider behavior. Instead of the polluter-pays principle, a consensus has to be reached for global goods on the necessary abatement levels and on the conditions under which compensations should take place. Once these conditions are satisfied, prices for emission rights can be used. This is consistent with both orders.

As explained in chapter VII, if prices are not (or cannot be) applied for national environmental allocation and if other measures such as administrative approaches, emission norms, or product standards are employed, the consistency between both orders becomes more complicated, as such measures represent an obstacle to trade. In principle, the policy instruments specific to each order—for instance, tariffs being specific to the trade order and environmental regulation to the environmental order— should be kept separate. As a rule, trade policy instruments should not be employed for environmental policy purposes. However, the trade order allows a country to protect its citizens' health and life and to preserve natural resources (Article XX of the GATT Treaty).

As a specific requirement, these environmental measures must be nondiscriminatory. Nondiscrimination necessitates that in the case of market entry restrictions, regulations through production permits, facility permits, and product norms must not give preference to domestic producers and domestic goods. Thus, it is not be permissible, for instance, with the aim of reducing health hazards, to restrict the import of goods or to tax them unless the same measures are simultaneously applied to similar domestic goods. A relevant example is the Thai cigarette case (1990). Nondiscrimination should also satisfy the condition that policy instruments should respect the proportionality principle. Accordingly, measures must be necessary in the sense that otherwise environmental policy aims or the protection of natural resources could not be achieved.

A more specific question is whether countries should have the right to apply their environmental policy outside their own territory. Since countries are differently endowed with environmental resources and also have different environmental preferences, those with stronger environmental preferences should not be entitled to impose their environmental preferences on other countries by means of trade-restricting measures (Siebert 1996b). The thesis that the country-of-origin principle should enjoy fundamental recognition for national environments can be generalized. Harmful effects appearing outside a country's territorial area, if they are not caused by the country and if they do not affect a country's territory, i.e., if there are no cross-border externalities, should not give countries the right to use trade policy in order to influence the production methods of another country. The country-of-origin rule should apply. The protective clauses for health, life, and exhaustible resources found in Article XX should, in the case of national environmental goods, apply only within a country's own territorial area. Thus, countries should not have the right to employ unilateral measures to protect the environment in other countries. This statement is consistent with the tuna–dolphin case (1991). However, it is not consistent with the shrimp–turtle case, unless it is accepted that the environmental goal to be achieved is more or less universal.

Transfrontier pollution, however, is a different issue. In this case, a Coasian solution has to be found.

Global warming requires, first of all, an agreement on the targets to be reached, i.e., the tolerable level of climate change or the total emission reduction. Ideally, such an agreement also includes an understanding on policy instruments to be used. Even in the case of global public goods, in principle, a country should not impose its environmental standards extraterritorially to other countries. This also holds for its imports. From a practical point of view, however, countries may apply different environmental policy instruments and they may be tempted to apply their environmental standards to their imports as well in order to avoid a loss of competitiveness of their import-competing sectors. This means that Article XX of GATT is not only interpreted as protecting the health of a country's citizens and a country's environment. In order to prevent a mishmash of diverging environmental standards being applied to imports, Hufbauer and Kim (2008) propose a code specifying under which conditions standards can be applied to imports, introducing a "green space" into the WTO. This is supposed to represent a bridge between the trade order and environmental policy. Unfortunately, this proposal will raise many issues: it requires establishing comparability of environmental approaches, most specifically of the way to produce carbon-intensive products; it means accepting that a country can impose its standards on other countries; and it implies introducing another waiver into the WTO. Moreover, it is open as to how such an approach would fit into a new Kyoto-like environmental agreement which might be reached and which would define what individual countries have to do in terms of emission reductions. Then, to apply national performance standards in a green space would mean dealing with global warming twice. This becomes apparent if emission certificates are used, since then the prices for certificates express environmental scarcity of a specific country, as agreed upon internationally. By international agreement, the global public good has been transformed into a national endowment.

It appears ill-advised to create a temporary waiver for the environment as an exception to the world trade order. One reason is that the previously created exemption for agriculture has become resistant to change and has led to a permanent infringement of the most-favored-nation principle. If an exceptional regulation is questionable even in the case of a very specific and internationally declining sector like agriculture, then a similar procedure appears much less desirable for an area like the environment, which encompasses nearly all sectors of the economy and is bound to become increasingly important in the future.

Even if the international environmental order and the international trade order have consistent aims in principle, the rules of the two orders should not be contingent upon each other. Making the rules mutually conditional would cause considerable uncertainty, not only in the international division of labor, but also in the production of environmental goods. In general, as we saw above, institutional orders should not be conditional upon each other. A mechanism similar to the WTO dispute settlement system should be developed for the environmental domain.

Ideally, the countries signing international environmental agreements should not be too divergent from those who are members of the WTO.

The Institutional Setup for the World Economy

The institutional arrangement for the world economy varies with the type of interdependence among countries. Trade policy rules for the world product markets have been intended to facilitate the international trade of merchandise and services. These rules—such as the most-favored-nation clause and the principle of national

Table XI.1. Elements of an institutional order for the world economy.

Rule system	Goal	Distortions	Rules	Major unresolved problems
Trade order	Allowing benefits from the international division of labor (trade of goods, services, multilateralism)	Trade: protectionist trade policy (tariffs, strategic trade policy, antidumping, subsidies, product standards)	Trade rules, above all against new forms of protectionist trade policy; most-favored-nation clause; national treatment; country-of-origin principle for product norms	Market access to developed countries for developing countries, especially for agricultural products; market access to developing countries for industrial products
		Services: discrimination against foreign suppliers	National treatment	Market access for services
		Open question: the role of bilateral agreements in a multilateral order		
International competition policy	Preventing monopolistic practices	Market power of firms; damage to consumers	Competition rules. Free access to markets; effects doctrine; cooperation between competition authorities	Only rudimentary rules in place

treatment—play the role of preventing protectionist trade policies, including tariffs, strategic trade policy, antidumping, subsidies, and trade-distorting product standards (table XI.1). Among these rules, the role of bilateral and regional arrangements as opposed to multilateral arrangements is open to debate. Another important institutional arrangement relating to the product market is competition policy. Norms for the mobility of production factors—technology, physical capital, and labor—refer to the factor markets. Since factor flows can be interpreted as substitutes to trade, such arrangements can be considered part of the rules for the international division of labor. Norms for the use of the global environment will acquire greater significance in the future. They are different from the rules for trade and for the international division of labor. All these arrangements relate to the real side of the international economy. Preventing financial crises and currency crises deals with the monetary side, which obviously has repercussions on the real economies. Ethical norms and human rights extend to all aspects of interdependence.

The multilateral order contains a large set of international treaties or conventions in which states are contracting partners (table XI.2). These agreements define rules for

Table XI.1. *Continued.*

Rule system	Goal	Distortions	Rules	Major unresolved problems
Cross-border factor flows (capital flows, technology flows, migration)	Permitting gains from factor flows	Capital flows: risk of expropriation of foreign investments	Free capital movements as a substitute for labor migration; restraints on expropriating foreign direct investment	No international rule system in place
		Technology flows: low incentives for technological progress, due to property rights not respected internationally	Property rights which protect new knowledge but permit gradual diffusion	Reliable intellectual property rights
		Migration of labor: abrupt mass migrations	A right to emigrate (right of exit); openness in immigration policy; not achievable: a universal right of immigration	How to make migration unnecessary in a pecking order of commodity and factor flows
Global environmental media	Preventing misallocation of global environmental public goods, for instance global warming	Cross-border pollution, free-riding of individual countries with regard to global environmental problems	Some conventions on global environmental issues (e.g., Montreal Protocol) in place; EU emissions trading on CO_2; separation between environmental policy and trade policy	Kyoto Protocol, ending in 2012
International financial system	Preventing financial instability and currency crises	Inflation, deflation, bank runs	Each country must keep the value of its money stable	Arrangements under attack from politics; markets preempting regulators
		Currency crises	Rules of the IMF	Currency crises are likely to be with us
Human rights	Ethical behavior, respecting the dignity of man	Disrespect of norms and human rights	Ethical norms and human rights	

Table XI.2.   Examples of important multilateral treaties.

	Role	Established in year	Number of countries	Decision body/ decision rule
International Competition Network	Informal multilateral cooperation framework	2001	More than 80 jurisdictions	None, cooperation on a voluntary basis
European Patent Convention	Simplifying the application for a patent	1973	34	Administrative Council
International Court of Justice	Solving disputes between states	1945	65 states accept the jurisdiction of the court as compulsory; 192 are parties to the court	The Court is composed of 15 judges, who are elected by the United Nations General Assembly and the Security Council
Kyoto Protocol	Environmental protection through the reduction of greenhouse gases	2005	40 and the EU; Annex-I countries 4	Convention of the Parties
Convention on International Trade in Endangered Species of Flora and Fauna (CITES)	Preventing the over-exploitation of endangered species	1995	172	Consensus
World Trade Organization[a]	Liberalizing trade	1947	153	Consensus, unanimity
International Labor Organization[a]	Promotion of dignified working conditions throughout the world	1919	181	Governing Body, composed of 28 government members: 14 employer members and 14 worker members

[a]This is an organization, not a convention.

specific areas, as in the case of the International Competition Network (see chapter V) and of the European Patent Convention (see chapter V). Such conventions specify which decision rights the supervisory bodies of the conventions have, determining how much sovereignty is actually ceded. A convention is not to be confused with international organizations, of which states are members rather than contracting partners. Important conventions crystallize in international organization such as the WTO, the IMF, and the World Bank.

In yet another organizational layer of the world order, we find international political forums and the most important international organizations (table XI.3).

Institutional Fit

Can the existing institutional arrangement of the world economy be improved? An answer to this question must consider two different issues: one is the division of labor between international rule systems, and more specifically between international organizations; the other is how much sovereignty should be ceded.

In the division of labor between international organizations, the trade of goods and services is clearly the domain of the WTO. Improving structural conditions for long-run growth in developing countries and thus making it possible for them to participate in the international division of labor is instead the task of the World Bank. Competition policy remains in the hands of national authorities and of the EU as a regional authority with some degree of cooperation between them. With respect to rules for factor flows, we have to distinguish between the types of factors. Conventions on patents ease applications internationally; WTO rules on trade-related intellectual property rights (TRIPS) bolster the certainty of such rights. Rules for capital flows are put into bilateral agreements; rules for migration are in the hands of national governments, who control immigration. In Europe, some EU rules for the mobility of factors have taken precedence over national rules. Institutional arrangements for the global environment are developing slowly, with a new agreement needed by 2012, the expiry date of the Kyoto Protocol. In the monetary area, rules for a stable money are laid down in the institutional arrangements of national central banks and—as an attempt at regional integration—the ECB. Due to international financial markets, the major central banks are interdependent in their monetary policy; a lax monetary policy of one central bank affects the exchange rate and may make it more difficult for another central bank to keep money stable. Regulations for the banking industry are national, with some attempts to introduce internationally accepted standards. The Bank for International Settlements (BIS) in Basel is in charge of securing the functioning of the payment system. The IMF has the role of preventing a systemic financial crisis, to avoid national currency crises, and to provide assistance with credits once currency crises erupt.

As for the assignment problem, a crucial question is which tasks should be assigned to which rule system and to which organization. A first answer is that the rule systems and organizations are separate with different tasks being allocated to them. As already pointed out and discussed for the trade order and the environmental order, the incentives set by these arrangements should not contradict each other. A second answer is that the assignment of tasks to different rule systems or organizations should satisfy optimality conditions. As a principle, a task should be assigned to the institution that is best equipped to deal with that task. This way of allocating responsibilities is similar to the idea that transactions would take place within firms if transaction costs were lower than in the markets; in markets if they are more efficient than firms; or within the political process if this is the most efficient realm. A third answer is that the assignment of tasks is path-dependent in its

Table XI.3.   Global political forums, regional integrations, and international organizations.

	Role	Number of members	GDP 2005[a]	Population 2005[b]	Decision rule
G7-G8[c]	Meetings of heads of states	7 (8)	26.95 (27.71)	718.7 (861.8)	No formal rule
G20[d]	Forum for cooperation, G8 plus developing countries	20	39.90	4,248	No formal rule
BRIC[e]	Forum for the exchange of ideas among population-rich countries (expected powers)	4	4.59	1,673	No formal rule
EU27	Single market with four freedoms: freedom of the movement of people, goods, services, and capital	27	13.58[f]	501.4[f]	Complex decision-making rules with unanimity, qualified majority and national sovereignty
OECD	Governments compare policy experiences in economic, environmental, and social issues	30	34.85	1,167.1	OECD Council made up of one representative of each country plus EU; decisions and recommendations by mutual agreement of all members
IEA	Energy security and environmental protection	27	33.76	1,025.6	Part of the OECD

development and that nations are often only prepared to opt for a new approach after a major disaster; witness the creation of the three Bretton Woods institutions and European integration after World War II. Finally, the institutional design of the world economy is in a process of continuous development, with new questions such as climate change and other environmental issues coming to the fore, requiring rule systems that deal with them.

An international organization, just like a national organization, will naturally seek to pursue its own interests, and attempt to increase its power, by including new issues under its umbrella. In this respect, international organizations are no better than national ones. Therefore, it is necessary to put in place appropriate mechanisms to monitor the international organization's expenditure and budget. Also, international organizations have their own constituencies in their scuffle for more influence and power. These include, most importantly, their employees, but also their supporters in international social movements and NGOs. Some individuals rank global concerns extraordinarily high in their utility function; they have been described as do-gooders with elevated moral aspirations that they want to be realized in all or most of the countries of the world. Of course, it is the privilege of the young generation to look

Table XI.3. *Continued.*

	Role	Number of members	GDP 2005[a]	Population 2005[b]	Decision rule
WTO	Liberalizing trade	153	42.57	5,704.2	Consensus, unanimity
World Bank	Reducing poverty in developing countries; loans to developing countries	184	43.52	6,305.6	Voting according to capital share; president is elected by the United States; the United States is the only country which has enough votes to unilaterally veto decisions
IMF[g]	Oversees the global financial system and provides support in exchange rate crises	184	43.52	6,305.6	Voting according to capital share; president is elected by Europe; the United States is the only country who has enough votes to unilaterally veto decisions
Kyoto Protocol[h]	Environmental protection through the reduction of greenhouse gases	40 and the EU; Annex-I countries	34.42	1,258.6	Is embedded in the UN Framework Convention on Climate Change
UN	International law, security, economic development, social progress, human rights	192	43.56	6,365.5	Veto right in the security council of permanent members; each member has one vote in the general assembly; two-thirds majority and majority voting

[a]In current market prices and trillions of US$. [b]In millions. [c]Canada, France, Germany, Japan, Italy, U.S., and U.K.; G8 includes Russia. [d]G8 plus EU and Argentina, Australia, Brazil, China, India, Indonesia, Mexico, Saudi Arabia, South Africa, Turkey, and South Korea. [e]Brazil, Russia, India, and China. [f]Data for EU25. [g]Identical membership to IMF. [h]A treaty, not an organization.
Source: World Bank, World Development Indicators Online.

for new solutions and to dream about new answers without looking too sharply at restraints. Last but not least, it is an open question as to whether and how international organizations can legitimize themselves democratically.

Besides the problem of allocating tasks and responsibilities, another issue is how much sovereignty the nation states should cede to multilateral arrangements. In his still readable book *An International Economy*, Myrdal (1956) discusses in chapter IV the relationship between national integration and international integration: "I am more convinced than ever that ... national economic progress and integration can only reach the highest possible level in a well integrated world" (Myrdal 1956, p. 33). While this statement can be better understood under the conditions prevailing after World War II, it would be naive to hope that nation states would simply recognize the authority of a world government. With this book, I have no intention to justify such a world government. Values are too diverse, cultures too dissimilar, religions too far apart, preferences too different, ways of life too diverging, and historic conditions too varied. This variety can be an advantage for mankind in solving its problems. For these reasons, a world government is not a choice that can seriously be considered (see Barrett 2005, p. 71). It is inconceivable that an efficient multilateral arrangement could be found in which citizens could express their preferences. The same criticism relates to the idea of a world parliament and a cosmopolitan democracy; this is unrealistic (Archibugi 2008). In spite of the utility function extending to include phenomena beyond the national border, the experience of the European Union teaches us that even a rather close regional integration is far from creating a new multilateral identity, or, in the case of the EU, a European identity. Capture by interest groups of such a global institutional arrangement would have disastrous effects, since the plurality of solutions and democracy would be lost. The power accruing to those in power would be an incredible temptation for the decision-makers; and they would quickly develop an interest in extending their power. Rules can be used to imprison the freedom of decision making and close society, as the communist experience has shown. It is impossible to legitimize such a world government.

I therefore provide a different answer to the question of the optimality of ceding sovereignty, noting that it is justified to cede sovereignty if transaction costs are reduced and if benefits can be obtained. I have pleaded in favor of the subsidiarity principle and of fiscal federalism, interpreted for a global economy. In this approach, we rely on the fact that preferences of different individuals in the countries of the world are different, that factor endowments are diverse, and that production conditions and technologies as well as many other factors are dissimilar. Integration is not a goal per se; it does not legitimize itself. It must serve to reduce transaction costs and to prevent hardship.

XII

Major Challenges to the Rule System in the Future

Within the world economy, continuous change is a normal feature. In this concluding chapter, I look at how the forces of change impact on the rule system and how rules have to adjust to accommodate the change.

In the past, we have seen trends in which important variables change at a more or less steady pace. Such trends include population growth; urbanization; the reduction of transaction costs through the removal of market segmentation; the integration of developing countries into the international division of labor; a rising awareness of environmental deterioration, especially in the industrialized countries; the increasing expansion of major regional integrations; and, possibly, a shift in the leading currency. For these trends, information on their past patterns allows us to infer—under normal conditions—how they will evolve in the future.

While we may be able to forecast some of these future trends with some certainty, a trend may break, so that a pattern observed in the past may no longer hold. Examples of such discontinuities are changes determined by new scientific and technological breakthroughs in the form of new machinery, such as the steam engine in the early stages of industrialization, making traditional modes of production and transportation obsolete. Further examples come from the impact of new technologies, as in the case of the IT revolution. Moreover, we may observe shifts in the paradigms adopted by the scientific community (Kuhn 1962), including new concepts in economics, for instance, the introduction of new property rights for networks that were once considered natural monopolies. In all these cases, the experience of the past centuries shows that the shift to a new technology or concept does not take place quickly, but needs time, as technological diffusion processes often require a decade and even more to bring about change.

In contrast to more or less steady trends, other phenomena appear abruptly and unexpectedly: the oil price shock in the 1970s; the fall of the iron curtain in 1989–90; September 11, 2001 and the sudden emergence of international terrorism as a primary threat; currency crises such as the Asian crisis in 1997 and the Brazilian crisis in 1999; the subprime and liquidity crisis that hit the banking industry in 2007–8; and political revolutions in the institutional setup of a country, as in the case of the French and the Russian revolutions. It is in the very nature of unexpected events that it is impossible to forecast such uncertain events in the future. In addition, the impact of unforeseen changes is also unknown; it is terra incognita, unknown territory. One of the reasons for the impossibility of forecasting these events is that economic and political conditions are subject to changes in human behavior, expectations, and preferences. Moreover, behavior and expectations change when new information becomes available on the public's radar screen, for instance on the discovery of new resource deposits or on the depletion of a resource stock.

Attitudes and behavior also change when new cohorts of the population, and new generations, become voters and decision-makers. Another reason is that future technological breakthroughs may occur that positively affect the underlying production conditions of an economy or of the world as a whole. On the contrary, supply shocks such as the oil crisis in the 1970s affect the production conditions negatively. Consequently, what we can say about future challenges is subject to the caveat that the future is indeed highly uncertain.

In the following analysis, we will draw a distinction between observable trends and uncertain events. We will then discuss how the existing international system of rules will be affected, for instance when trends weaken existing rule systems or make them obsolete, and how rules should respond to geopolitical shifts. We will also discuss how rules should be conceived in order to accommodate such uncertainty.

Trends in the World Economy

Normal trends that we have observed in the past are likely to continue into the future. The main characteristic of such trends is that change does not occur abruptly, but rather slowly, following a more or less steady path.

Population Growth

The world population, 2.5 billion people in 1950, had doubled by 1990 and will triple by 2020. It is expected to reach 9 billion by 2050 (United Nations 2008). Such an increase will require additional supplies in many areas: food and other consumption goods; investment goods; water; energy; housing; and infrastructure. More natural resources will be needed in production; land use will intensify. In 2000, about 38% of the world's population lived in 335 major urban centers with more than one million people each. In 2015, it will be more than 40% in 460 urban centers (UN Human Settlements Program 2008, table A2). All this will put further pressure on the environment.

An important precondition for dealing with these pressures is the existence of an efficient and acceptable rule system. Population growth is a decentralized process, taking place within the existing multilateral institutional arrangements that limit conflicts. Such arrangements encompass the principle of territoriality, property rights, and markets. Whereas the principle of territoriality and the recognition of property rights—especially for land—represent instruments backing the decentralized nature of population growth, other mechanisms can have an equilibrating function if population growth between regions is too diverse and if, consequently, pressure between regions becomes too strong: among such mechanisms are trade, capital flows, and also migration. Trade enables population-rich countries to earn income through exports and to support a much larger population than would be possible in a "closed" economy (on migration, see below). Besides the equilibrating role of markets, a major issue for the world as a whole is whether the existing rules will stimulate sufficient technological progress and organizational innovation to accommodate these pressures, for instance by providing more food, adequate housing, and satisfactory infrastructure. It is therefore paramount that the proper incentives for superior technological solutions are at the core of the institutional arrangements.

Aging Society

A specific trend, even though temporary in mankind's history, is the expected aging of population in Europe, Japan, the United States, and even in China. With respect to the institutional arrangement, the old-age pension systems that can accommodate an aging population will have to be national. In fact, retirement schemes must be financed through the income generated in the productive processes, namely from a country's GDP or from accumulated savings, themselves stemming from a country's GDP. Many public pension systems in the developed world are conceived as pay-as-you-go systems, where the young, productive generation pays in its contributions, which then are immediately handed out to the retired. In such systems, which present severe adjustment problems to population aging, there is no capital stock. In capital-funded systems, on the contrary, countries that face an aging problem can invest savings abroad which are used later as capital inflows for the retired. As with population growth, the capital markets can play an equilibrating role between "old" and "young" countries.

With respect to the institutional setup, the national arrangements have to be improved, for instance by giving special protection to savings for old age in the case of bankruptcy. Such an approach seems less feasible for the worldwide capital markets. A major prerequisite for retirement savings is that the value of money is stable, since inflation, hyperinflation and currency crises entail a degree of uncertainty hampering the accumulation of savings over a long time horizon; the absence of inflationary expectations is necessary so that people can save for old age. Consequently, it is essential that the central banks steer the money supply to ensure a stable price level. It is also important that the rule system prevents financial instability.

234 XII. Major Challenges to the Rule System in the Future

Emerging Markets

The international division of labor allows emerging countries to enjoy gains from trade and to increase their standards of living. This option is open to all developing countries, provided that they are able to create the institutional preconditions to let their economy grow. These preconditions include stability in the institutional framework (more specifically, the absence of internal turmoil and civil war), reliability, and a certain degree of constancy in economic policy, together with assurances about property rights, the rule of law, and due process. These requirements are clearly an essential precondition for the national institutional arrangements. If these conditions are not satisfied, a country is unlikely to benefit from the international division of labor. It is therefore not surprising that those sub-Saharan countries that were characterized by internal turmoil and civil wars did not manage to improve their income per capita in the period 1975–2004, but rather fell back (Siebert 2007e, table 10.4). In contrast to this deplorable experience, the world trade order enables countries to enjoy an increase in their well-being whenever the necessary institutional conditions are satisfied. In this case, all countries can gain.

The improved integration of developing countries brings a decline in the share of world GDP generated by the industrial countries. This trend, by itself, is not a matter of economic concern insofar as the developed countries experience an absolute increase in their welfare (on the aspect of geopolitical shifts, see below). However, enjoying benefits necessitates structural adjustments in which some sectors in the developed countries must decline, as the standard Heckscher–Ohlin trade model predicts. The burden of structural adjustment is borne by capital and labor, but it weighs more heavily on labor, since capital enjoys an exit option. Workers have to invest in human capital in order to improve their employability and their income. If the advance in human capital does not succeed, job security deteriorates. Then, political parties and the whole political process may find themselves under pressure to indulge in protectionist policies. This tendency entails the risk of forgetting the positive experience of the rule system for the international division of labor put in place since 1945, with consequent erosion of such rules.

Rule systems in the main areas of trade and balance of payments and the prevention of currency crises have come into existence after World War II, initiated by the then-hegemon, the United States, and supported by the Western countries, which, in terms of numbers, represented a small group of the world economy. The rule system has to adjust to the changes which have taken place since then. One aspect is that emerging markets need a voice, a problem most apparent in the quota calculation of the IMF. Moreover, in principle, a different group of countries may draw the rules differently. Here, however, path dependency works in favor of the initial setup. Furthermore, it is wise to gain experience with given international rules and to continuously adjust the rules in light of this experience. In addition, new problems have to be addressed, such as the increasing role of portfolio flows and financial markets relative to commodity exchange after the Bretton Woods period.

Energy Scarcity

The growth of the world population, the further industrialization of developing countries, and the increase in real per capita income in nearly all countries will exercise demand pressure on energy and other natural resources, including food. This means that the scarcity of energy and other natural resources will increase.

Historically, resource scarcity has often been a matter of confrontation and conflict between countries. However, instead of dashing each other's heads over the scarce energy, we have a normal mechanism at our disposal to get to grips with the phenomenon of increasing scarcity, namely the market mechanism. It is the role of the markets to allocate the scarce resource "energy" to the competing users. Rising real prices signal scarcity and represent a peaceful way to accommodate additional demand. Rising energy prices have several functions. They serve as an incentive to use energy more parsimoniously. They are also an enticement to look for additional and alternative energy sources, most importantly to find a backstop.

In the past, price forecasts have often proven to be off the mark. Thus, Bergsten (2004) foresaw a climb of oil prices to $60–70 per barrel in one or two years (relative to 2004); contrary to this forecast, the price had nearly doubled by mid 2008. In the interim, it has fallen to the $50 range. Apparently, forecasters have their difficulties in predicting price increases for future periods, since such forecasts seem to be irresponsibly high in a given situation, so that the public and the markets may understand them as aggravating the energy problem.

Admittedly, rising prices drive out the demand with a lower willingness to pay or a lower capability to pay. However, as energy use is a long-run problem, temporary price supports in energy-importing countries are unlikely to help resolve the problem. This applies especially if the world faces rising prices in the long run.

Unfortunately, the allocation problem is complicated by several other factors: subsidies, export taxes, the intertemporal time path of extraction and energy use, and the existence of monopolies, oligopolies, and cartels. In principle, energy should be treated in the same way as other goods in the world trade order. Energy-importing countries should not be allowed to apply import subsidies in order to lure demand away from other countries. Similarly, energy exporters should not be allowed to introduce an export tax. Unfortunately, the WTO has no explicit rules for the trade of the good "energy." The solution becomes even more complex given the fact that energy policy has an intertemporal aspect. With respect to the time path of resource use, each resource-importing country is free to apply the taxes it wants, for instance by setting an incentive to use energy parsimoniously in the future. This is different from the requirement not to use an import tax; a general tax on energy does not discriminate between domestic products and imports. Similarly, the resource country is free to determine its intertemporal time path for extraction. While the extraction schedule over time will influence export prices, its choice does not discriminate between exports and domestic use as an export tax does. The intertemporal aspects of extraction and resource use encompass another issue: overshooting expectations. If an increase in scarcity is expected, energy prices rise; speculation may then exacerbate the price signals of the market relative to what is justified in a long-run equilibrium.

A further problem is the existence of dominating market positions and cartels such as OPEC. Resource countries may be tempted to charge a higher price than justified by the real scarcity conditions at any given moment in time, which, admittedly, has to take into account the scarcity of future periods. Similarly to what happens for trade in the energy sector, where no specific trade rules exist, no international rules against monopolistic or cartel behavior regulate the energy market. An international competition policy does not exist. The alternative to facing a resource cartel by establishing a monopsony of importing countries does not seem too promising. In fact, the demand side in different countries has diverging interests which are extremely difficult to organize as a single countervailing power.

Given this situation, to demand fairness from the part of resource-exporting countries is rather unrealistic. Indeed, such an approach does not constitute the core of the international division of labor that rather relies on exploiting differences in factor abundance, technology, and preferences between countries. A more promising answer is to establish mutual interests: mutual foreign direct investment in the energy area and in natural resources can deepen the relationship between energy suppliers and energy importers: let intensive energy users invest in the upstream activities of energy-rich countries and let energy-rich countries invest in the downstream activities of energy-importing countries, i.e., in their distribution systems. Mutual interests also grow tighter when resource exporters invest their trade surpluses in resource-importing countries through foreign direct investment, i.e., when they practice petro-dollar recycling. Admittedly, this puts limits on the option of countries that intend to restrain sovereign wealth funds (see chapter VI).

A further way of tackling increasing energy scarcity is for resource-importing countries to search for and find a backstop technology, representing a ceiling to the energy price. Then, the energy issue would lose prominence. Indeed, each resource country has to face an intertemporal calculation as high energy prices represent an incentive for energy saving and for actively searching for a backstop technology in energy-importing countries. If successful, these dynamics can, in turn, reduce the future value of the resource country's deposits.

Rising Food Prices

Population growth, rising income per capita, and higher energy costs also lead to an increase in the demand for food. Additionally, the problem of rising food prices is influenced by a variety of factors, as the doubling of prices for wheat and rice in 2007–8 has shown: poor harvests, speculation, and higher energy costs. There are further long-run false incentives. For instance, agricultural protection in the industrialized countries—especially the EU, the United States, and Japan—destroys economic opportunities for the agricultural sector of developing countries. In order to resolve this problem, agricultural protection—mostly in the form of subsidies and consumer-paid transfers—must be discontinued. In terms of fairness, this is the crucial requirement for the agricultural sector. Unfortunately, all attempts at dismantling agricultural subsidies have failed so far. So has the conclusion of the Doha Development Round, whose mission was exactly to open up the agricultural markets of industrialized countries. Despite this setback, the long-run task of the WTO and also of international policy mandates to discontinue agricultural subsidies. A related desideratum is that food-producing countries do not use export taxes, as they distort the international division of labor and violate WTO rules.

Furthermore, "bio"-fuel subsidies drive out traditional agricultural production (Siebert 2008a). These subsidies should be removed. Clearly, their opportunity costs in terms of higher food prices should be factored in when subsidies are praised for preventing CO_2 emissions. However, to specify land-use rules to favor food production instead of biofuel production, as some politicians in Germany and in Europe suggest, will create a bureaucratic chaos already at the national level. At the international level, worldwide regulation is simply naive. The same applies to the idea of introducing WTO product standards for biofuel production and then to ban from international trade biofuels that do not satisfy these standards. To harmonize such standards would prove infeasible. Note also that product standards and trade bans are not appropriate when it comes to preventing the destruction of the rainforest. This requires other incentives (see chapter VII). As in the case of energy, it does not seem promising to take recourse to fairness criteria in order to resolve the problem of rising food prices. The first step is to reduce agricultural protection in the developed countries and to open up the markets for the developing countries. Fortunately, the problem of rising food prices can be made less severe if additional land can be put into cultivation in the long run and agricultural productivity can be increased. If the productivity increase is larger than the increase in demand, food prices need not rise.

Global Warming

A further trend in the last forty years has been the increased awareness concerning environmental issues. As explained in chapter VII, an institutional arrangement for the global environment, for instance the global atmosphere, is far more difficult to reach than for trade. The reason is that the environment as a resource has two different and competing functions: it provides the climate we enjoy; as such it represents a public good that must be consumed in equal amounts by all. But it also serves as a sink for pollutants, for instance CO_2 emissions, and as such it is similar to a private good for which rules can be formulated and prices set.

The public good of reduced global warming is often conceived as generating no direct national benefits, so that nations may be tempted to behave as free riders. In contrast, to push back the environment's role as a sink for emissions requires abatement activities, which in turn involve abatement costs accruing to the nation state, for instance its industry. In conclusion, different conditions apply to this rule area compared with the world trade order, so that we have to rely on other approaches: side payments to join an agreement, technology transfer, rather complex self-enforcing multilateral contracts, and burden-sharing. Given the scientific data on global warming and the predictions of climate models, it is paramount to find a successor to the Kyoto Protocol (see chapter VII). It is possible that we will witness the birth of a new international organization in this area (Hufbauer 2008).

Whereas global warming can be treated as a trend, it has been pointed out that an increase in the world climate's temperature by more than 5% would push the world into unknown territory (Stern 2007). In this case, we might well have to classify global warming as an uncertain event.

The Increasing Role of Regional Integrations

In the future, regional interests may come to play a larger role. In the trade area, regional free-trade associations and, as in Europe, economic and semi-political unions can exploit gains from trade between neighboring countries; this is even possible among distinct economies, sharing mutual interests. In such a setting, the European Union, NAFTA with the United States as its chief member, and, possibly, a stronger evolution of the Asian Free Trade Association pivoting around China will be the major players as super-regional free-trade areas in the next twenty to thirty years. These regional integrations will not only favor the flow of goods and services; they will also allow a deeper integration of the capital market, leading to a mutual expansion of foreign direct investment. Whereas asylum migration and migration of highly qualified labor will take place within some regional integrations, free migration is unlikely to be part of such regional arrangements, for instance in the EU with respect to Turkey and North Africa.

If the trend toward deeper regional integration continues, the WTO will lose importance and may end up providing a mere institutional superstructure for regional integrations and bilateral agreements, with the task of mediating between them and setting some common standards. In the finance and currency area, countries may cooperate to some extent in order to protect themselves against financial crises. However, they dislike depending on the IMF as an international taskmaster and are likely to look for regional approaches, such as an Asian IMF, possibly around China. Again, an international rule system would lose its importance. In the monetary–financial area, a regional approach is likely to fail as soon as financial crises are systemic rather than regionally contained. In contrast to these two areas, regional cooperation in global environmental issues appears more promising. Such cooperation is needed in order to implement global goals. A case in point for such cooperation is Europe. From a global point of view, the issue in the area of an environmental agreement will be to what extent a multilateral approach including two layers—namely, agreeing on targets for the global environment and implementing the targets in regional integrations—can be viable.

Changes in the World's Leading Currency

In the very long run, the world may witness a shift in the leading currency, which until now remains undoubtedly the U.S. dollar. With the relative decline in the U.S. shares of world output and world trade, the U.S. dollar becomes less attractive. Other currencies—for instance, the euro or, possibly, an Asian currency—may fill the void in the next century. In the next three decades, the euro has a good chance of being fully adopted as one of the major international currencies. The euro will then be an equal to the U.S. dollar. Accordingly, the ECB is likely to become as influential as the Fed, being one of the two dominant central banks on the global stage, and its decisions, together with those of the Fed, will determine the pulse of the world economy. Together with regional free-trade agreements, regional currency areas may arise. However, it usually takes between fifty years and a century before a leading currency is driven out by a newcomer, as shown by the substitution of the British pound by the U.S. dollar.

Unexpected Events

In contrast to such trends, unexpected events come as a surprise, not having been present in the calculations of economic agents and also of policymakers. Let me look briefly at three such unexpected events: financial crises, border-crossing mass migration, and terrorism.

Financial Crises

If this book had been written two and a half years ago, financial crises might not have been mentioned under the heading of unexpected events. Back then, the general mood was that the Asian currency crisis of 1997 would have been the last financial disturbance with global repercussions. The Brazilian currency crisis of 1999, Argentina's collapse in 2001–2, and the Turkish crisis of 2001 all appeared as localized and contained issues.

With Basel II, the international financial system was considered to have done its homework to make the banking system more robust and less prone to risk exposure. Modern theory appeared to suggest that thanks to innovations, the financial industry was much better at handling risks, and that all could enjoy the benefits of an improved risk management. Some even went as far as raising the issue whether the IMF was needed after all, since currency crises seemed to belong to the past.

Surprisingly, it has faded from memory that financial crises, including currency crises and bank runs, can have a severe impact on the real side of the economy. In the Great Depression in 1929–33, the United States lost one-third of its GDP; Japan—a dynamic economy in the 1980s—was weakened considerably due to its bubble, remaining mired in stagnation for over a decade; Argentina's GDP shrunk by 20% in 2001–2; and the countries affected by the Asian currency crisis in 1997 have all had negative growth several years in a row.

The crisis that hit the international banking industry in the years 2007 and 2008 reminds us that financial crises are here to stay. Its causes were manifold: a strong increase in liquidity due to the Fed's monetary policy under Greenspan, adopting ever lower interest rates; predatory lending in the U.S. housing market; the mood that mortgages could be financed through the bubble as in the Dutch tulip mania, without requiring real savings; flawed institutional quasigovernmental arrangements such as Fannie Mae and Freddie Mac aggravating the crisis; financial innovations such as the securitization of bad loans, for instance house mortgages from the housing market; the international diffusion of bad loans from the United States to Europe, similar to a disease like SARS; dwindling information on the kind of risks bundled in asset-backed securities; hedge funds using extremely high levers of own equity to credits of up to one to thirty; and finally, putting risks simply off the balance sheets. In some of these developments, such as taking risks off the balance sheets, the banking industry violated its own long-established standards, thereby contravening what is professionally sound and required. Meanwhile, regulators were not able to keep up with the innovations of the financial industry. All of the above factors can have the implication that even a small disturbance is enough for banks to lose confidence in each other. Heavy write-offs and a credit crunch are the consequence; bank failures followed.

The answer to these issues requires national and international solutions. Nationally, monetary policy must make sure that inflationary expectations are kept low; that the price level remains stable; that the central bank is independent; that the banking sector is robust; that banks do not set incentives for their employees to increase risks artificially; that prudent supervision does its job and provides real-time information; that regulators are not outsmarted by the financial industry; that balance sheets are true; and that the financial markets have a reliable intertemporal fix point as a protection against financial bubbles. Internationally, countries must be economically viable in order to withstand contagion; they must also adopt appropriate standards for their banking system and financial supervision, in order to prevent a financial and currency crisis; the International Financial Stability Forum should make sure that national regulatory and supervisory authorities do not apply inconsistent standards; the IMF's task is to prevent a systemic currency crisis from arising; central banks will have to step in as lenders of last resort in a worst-case scenario.

As a lesson from the financial crisis, international rules for the financial sector should prevent a bubble from arising. Consequently, in the long run the rules for the financial system have to change. Since international spillovers are typical for the financial industry, an international agreement on common standards is needed. In the past, however, countries have used quite different approaches in the institutional arrangement of their financial industry and in financial supervision. They have attached different importance to the role of the financial industry in their economic policy, and also to financial innovation. A crucial reason why it is difficult to agree on policy instruments lies in the fact that in the future, any bailout will have to be backed by national tax revenues, and ceding sovereignty in this area is unlikely, even in the European Union. Last but not least, international rules have to prevent an artificial overspending as we have seen in the U.S. housing market that has no basis in real savings. The financial sector should not distance itself too much from the real economy. In terms of institutional arrangements, the IMF may play a role in supervision in order to recognize when things go wrong. However, it is unrealistic for the reasons mentioned that the IMF or another international institution will be endowed with the instrument of sanctions. The IMF taskmaster role in the Asian crisis is not forgotten; Asian countries and emerging economies are reluctant to bestow powers on the IMF.

Border-Crossing Mass Migration

With diverging per capita income between countries and different living conditions, in the past, people have simply moved to other more promising regions, completely disregarding territoriality and property rights in a Hobbesian way. We have seen signs of this phenomenon recently when Africans crossed the Sahara desert and climbed the barbed fences in the Spanish enclaves of Ceuta and Melilla in order to get into the European Union. We cannot be sure that this will not occur on a wider scale. Luckily enough, income per capita has been improving in many developing countries in the world, in particular in China and India (Siebert 2007b). In the future, obstacles to trade that restrain developing countries in building up their export sectors should be abolished; the WTO should be strengthened. Trade makes the migration of people less necessary. In fact, we have a "pecking order" between migration, trade, and capital flows. When products between countries are traded, people do not have to move. Instead of moving, they can sell the goods they can produce best in foreign countries. In addition, it is better to bring capital and jobs to the people than to move people to capital. By and large, immigration policy is likely to remain in the hands of nation states and—partly—of regional integrations, as in the case of the EU. A GATT-like agreement for immigration in which rules for immigrants are established is instead unlikely (Hufbauer 2003).

Terrorism

Terrorism represents a phenomenon in which a group of people is prepared to do harm and kill other people. Terrorist groups are violently opposed to the way of life of other people or social groups, not accepting their practices, routine, behavior, principles, and religion, upon which terrorists are ready to wreak havoc. They may have a national outreach, such as the Red Army Faction in Germany and the Brigate Rosse in Italy, or they may operate internationally, as in the case of Al-Qaeda.[1] In the international arena, deep cultural and religious clashes—the clash of civilizations—are at the root of the issue. Under such conditions, it is impossible to find and establish global rules and to avoid a Hobbesian perspective where human life would be "poore, nasty, brutish and short."

The solution to terrorism requires complex answers. One answer consists in eradicating the very reasons for terrorism: poverty, illiteracy, poor education; a low level of development, among other factors. This is a promising approach that can also be applied to avoid mass migration. Poor integration and alienation within their new society may have been at the root of the attackers' action in London and Madrid. However, some of the most destabilizing terrorist actions in the past years—in particular, the September 11 attacks—were carried out by fairly wealthy and educated people. Instead, a second answer is a change in attitudes, developing mutual respect for the way of life of others. This is a matter of education, including that of religious leaders. Yet, from an optimistic point of view, the strongest weapon against terrorism is rationality based on human experience, including the development and spread of natural science, knowledge, open access to information and know-how. This is the kind of rationality which the Western world has experienced in the age of Enlightenment. Before coming to Europe with the Renaissance, rationality existed already in the Arab world (Serageldin 2008). Rationality will most likely be able to put irrational beliefs, illogical attitudes, and unfounded viewpoints to a test. Rationality may also be capable of transforming identities and interests.

Risks for the World Economy

The list of unexpected events mentioned at the beginning of this chapter is inevitably incomplete since, by their very nature, such events cannot be forecasted. Other challenges come to mind, such as nuclear proliferation, major diseases, for instance a bubonic plague, the Ebola virus, SARS (severe acute respiratory syndrome), and avian flu. Further unexpected events are discussed in exploratory publications, including outer space, killer asteroids, and terrorism on the seas (Barrett 2007; Hufbauer and Kim 2008).

---

[1] The terms "terrorism" and "revolution" are not identical. Revolutions use force and violence, but are accepted afterwards.

Together with trends that break, unexpected events represent risks for the institutional arrangement of the world economy. A case in point would be a major change in economic fundamentals, inducing countries to give up cooperative behavior and to switch to opportunistic or strategic actions defined by their national interest, for instance if the loss of jobs in import-competing sectors leads the political process to become more protectionist. Similarly, rising food prices tempt food-exporting countries to restrict their exports by means of export taxes, thereby crippling the international division of labor. No doubt, the different risks can reinforce each other.

Uncertain events and breaking trends require an international rule system flexible enough to accommodate shifts and changes in the world economy, robust enough to withstand blows, made credible by the fact of being underpinned by the commitments of nation states, and sustainable, namely able to digest major changes in the fundamentals of the world economy. What must be prevented is a phenomenon similar to the one involving the Earth's crust: tectonic plates move against each other and lock themselves so that an earthquake is the only way to unload the pressure that has built up in the system. "Economic earthquakes," often arising when the necessary institutional adjustments are endlessly postponed, must be prevented.

Unfortunately, when we mention this requirement, we cannot forget that in the past, rule systems have often broken down, for instance in wars. Regrettably, we have no guarantee that an international order will endure. Sometimes men seem to be only one generation away from a beastly state (see chapter I).

Competing for a Better Institutional Concept

Countries and regions of the world have different historical roots, follow distinct ways of life, adhere to different philosophies and consequently develop diverging institutional arrangements. Thus, countries and regions find themselves in locational competition on the issue of which institutional model performs best (Siebert 2006a). In the last sixty years, the Asian model has performed much better than the Latin American model. Some twenty years ago, the capitalist market economies won a nearly century-long contest over the Soviet-type central planning which went down with the fall of the Iron Curtain. In 2008, Wall Street and its financial system, being exposed to its own bank failures and also spreading the risk of a credit crunch to other parts of the world, especially Europe, has lost international attractiveness because it had to be bailed out by government. It is open as to which basic elements of an international financial rule system the world can agree on and which role the Anglo-Saxon model, the European approach, and some fundamental laws of economics will play in conceiving a new order.

In the future, a similar horse race is likely to take place between democracy and authoritarianism. Democratic systems have the advantage that individuals can express their preferences, that governments are accountable, that they change according to the preferences of voters, and that no absolute power can be established. Liberty, the protection of individual rights, and the rule of law are constitutive elements of democracies. This allows flexibility in the adaptation of solutions and also the development of entirely new solutions. However, decision making in a democratic system is time consuming. In contrast, authoritarian systems, such as those in China or Singapore, are usually based on one party exercising strong control on the government; the press is managed; such systems lack political liberty as we mean it along the Anglo-Saxon and European interpretation; they seldom respect individual rights; often, the rule of law is not respected; the judiciary is not independent, and the political process is not restrained by a constitutional framework, for instance, political decisions are not subject to decisions of a constitutional court. However, their advantage is that economic decisions can be taken quickly and that a consistent concept can be pursued in an autocratic fashion over a long time horizon, as in the case of China or Singapore. Note, however, that a long-run concept can be a false concept, as the Soviet system has shown.

A major issue is which system will have the better economic performance. We cannot exclude the possibility that, at some time in the future, autocratic systems, not allowing liberty, may have a better economic performance than market economies in terms of temporarily higher growth rates. Even if this may not hold in the long run, it may well be true at a certain moment in time. Institutional competition may then put Western democracies on the defensive if their voters are lured by a good economic performance toward the adoption of more autocratic systems, and if voters are willing to forgo liberty in exchange for a higher income per capita. Note, however, that the income per capita in China and in the Western market economies is still miles apart. Also, it is in no way certain that autocracy is a viable form of government in the long run (see chapter XI).

Other forms of government that also participate in the worldwide institutional competition are autocracies based on theocracy, as in Iran, or based on oil, as in Saudi Arabia and the Gulf states (Hufbauer 2003).

Geopolitical Shift in Power

A major risk for the future is a geopolitical one: the economic option for developing countries to participate in the international division of labor means an increase in the developing countries' share of world GDP. This implies a decline in the relative output share of the industrialized countries. Looking at the United States and China, the United States' output stood at 27.4% of world GDP in 2006, China's at 5.5%; these shares are calculated on the basis of market prices and actual exchange rates. In another thirty years, the shares of outputs are likely to be 24% for the United States and 10% for China. The underlying assumption is that China's real growth rate in the years to come will be 5% per year instead of 10%, as many factors work toward a lower growth rate (Siebert 2007a). The United States' average growth rate is set at 2.5% per year; note that this is a high value if one considers that growth takes place through booms and busts. The world's GDP rate is set at 3%.

Admittedly, such calculations are subject to many qualifications, such as the assumptions about the growth rates of the United States and China as well as for the world economy as a whole. Moreover, appreciations and depreciations of currencies will impact on the shares, since the 2006 output values are calculated in actual prices and with actual exchange rates. An appreciation of the renminbi vis-à-vis the U.S. dollar by 15% will increase China's share to above 11%; the share of the United States will fall to 20%. With a 30% appreciation of the renminbi, the shares would be 13% for China and 17% for the United States. Depending on the assumptions underlying such forecasts, it is no wonder that another approach comes to the conclusion that China's GDP will overtake that of the United States in 2039 (Wilson and Purushothaman 2003). Forecasts for the shares of other countries are also available (O'Neill 2008).

Instead of working with such simplified assumptions, we would need a structural model, including several equations, explaining the growth rates of the different regions of the world, and also encompassing the fluctuations in the exchange rates. Note that, in such a model, changes in the exchange rate would be linked to production conditions, among other factors. As we know, reliable exchange rate forecasts are impossible, even for shorter periods of time. Even a more refined forecasting model could not include structural breaks, i.e., new patterns that are completely different from the past.

Looking solely at the share of world output, possibly enriched by other economic variables such as the share of world trade (Siebert 2007e), hides many other considerations such as areas of poverty in the world economy, the security context, as well as oil and culture (Hufbauer 2003, 2008). Also, more vivid descriptions of how the world might look can be found in geopolitical publications (Khana 2008). In any case, the economic shift in shares of world output can be interpreted as a geopolitical power shift.

Equilibrium or Conflict between the "Big Three"?

A fascinating, but open question is whether institutional competition between locations will eventually lead to an equilibrium in the world economy, whether a single universal equilibrium will exist, whether multiple different national or regional equilibria are possible, coexisting with each other, or whether the world will tumble again into conflict. These questions leave open the choice between an optimistic outlook and a pessimistic one.

From an economic point of view, the argument in favor of several different equilibria vis-à-vis the mobility of factors and residents is that conditions in the different regions of the world are markedly diverse, while historical experience suggests that different institutional solutions can coexist exactly because people's preferences and the fundamental economic conditions of countries differ. Apparently, a condition making several national equilibria possible is their sustainability in the long run. Locations must be able to attract and keep both factors of production and inhabitants. If factors and people exit a given location, this process must at least come to a halt at some level that is sustainable. Otherwise, several national equilibria will not be possible.

Multiple economic equilibria are consistent with a multipolar world featuring three major players: the United States, the EU, and China (Hufbauer 2003; Khana 2008). Other powers such as Japan, Russia, India, and Brazil may also play a role, but remaining outside the big three power circle. Quite predictably, regional integrations will be further enlarged, among them the EU.

The United States is no longer an omnipotent superpower; the Pax Americana with the United States as the sole hegemon has ended, after having brought an era of progressively free trade similar to the Pax Britannica, which drew to a close in 1914. We may even see signs of imperial overstretch from the part of the United States, for instance in the large current account deficits due to military interventions. From an optimistic point of view, the early twenty-first century may resemble the Concert of Europe following the Congress of Vienna of 1815. The three global powers would then agree on basic security principles to avoid confrontation (Hufbauer 2003). They may develop an interest in acting together in order to discipline rogue states and terrorist movements, although the evidence so far is not too convincing, as they seem more concerned about their "own" terrorists (Hufbauer 2008). However, this setting does not rule out wars between secondary powers and worldwide terrorist attacks. Admittedly, we cannot rule out the appearance of new dictators. The communist as well as the Nazi experience warns us that rules, even when agreed upon, may not be stable.

In contrast to such a cheerful outlook, the other perspective is much less comforting. History tells us that geopolitical shifts in the balance of power are often accompanied by struggles and wars between the incumbent hegemon and the newcomer. Witness the birth and the rise of Germany in the second half of the nineteenth century relative to the already industrialized Great Britain. Since then, Europe and the world have seen two world wars. Similarly, the emergence of Japan on the world scene can be cited as an example. We cannot claim that a law exists according to which a war is the unavoidable implication of a shift in the balance of power, but we can postulate that such shifts increase the likelihood of a war. A conflict can be ignited by a tiny spark, seemingly small from a global perspective, for example, a skirmish over Taiwan or Tibet spawning a Sino-American conflict. This could trigger World War III.

For these reasons, it is necessary to have appropriate international forums and procedures of intermediation in which potential conflicts can be discussed and which serve to channel quarrels. Examples are the UN Security Council, the G9 (G7 plus Russia and China), the Bretton Woods institutions, and international conventions that reduce conflicts. A major task is to find an institutional arrangement to combat global warming in which China and India will participate. Looking at the potential conflicts ahead, we must ask if the world has adequate institutional arrangements for intermediation to prevent them?

References and Further Reading

Acemoglu, D., D. Ticchi, and A. Vindigni. 2006. Emergence and persistence of inefficient states. Working Paper W12748, National Bureau of Economic Research.

Ahearne, A., and B. Eichengreen. 2007. External monetary and financial policy: a review and a proposal. In *Fragmented Power: Europe and the Global Economy* (ed. A. Sapir), pp. 128–55. Brussels: Bruegel Books.

American Trade Commission. 2008. www.ftc.gov/oia/authorities.shtm.

Archibugi, D. 2008. *The Global Commonwealth of Citizens*. Princeton University Press.

Axelrod, R. 1986. An evolutionary approach to norms. *American Political Science Review* 80:1095–111.

Bagwell, K., and R. W. Staiger. 1998. An economic theory of the GATT. *American Economic Review* 89:215–48.

———. 2002. *The Economics of the World Trading System*. Cambridge, MA: The MIT Press.

Bank for International Settlements. 2007. *Triennial Central Bank Survey of Foreign Exchange and Derivatives Market Activity in 2007*. Basel: Bank for International Settlements.

Barbier, E. B., and J. C. Burgess. 2001. The economics of tropical deforestation. *Journal of Economic Surveys* 15(3):413–32.

Barrett, S. 1991. Side-payments in a global warming treaty. Paper prepared for the Environmental Directorate of the OECD, Paris.

———. 1992. International environmental agreements as games. In *Conflicts and Cooperation in Managing Environmental Resources* (ed. R. Pethig). Springer.

———. 1994a. Self-enforcing international environmental agreements. *Oxford Economic Papers* 46:878–94.

———. 1994b. Strategic environmental policy and international trade. *Journal of Public Economics* 54(3):325–38.

———. 2005. *Environment and Statecraft: The Strategy of Environmental Treaty-Making*, 2nd edn. Oxford University Press.

———. 2007. *Why Cooperate? The Incentive to Supply Global Public Goods*. Oxford University Press.

Barro, R. J. 1986. Recent developments in the theory of rules versus discretion. *Economic Journal* 96(Supplement: Conference Papers):23–37.

———. 1999. Determinants of democracy. *Journal of Political Economy* 107(6):158–83.

Basel Committee on Banking Supervision. 2006. Home–host information sharing for effective Basel II implementation. Available at www.bis.org/publ/bcbs125.pdf.

Benedict XVI. 2008. Address to the General Assembly, United Nations, April 18. Available at www.vatican.va/holy_father/benedict_xvi/speeches/2008/april/documents/hf_ben-xvi_spe_20080418_un-visit_en.html.

Bergsten, C. F. 1988. The case for target zones. In *The International Monetary System: The Next Twenty-Five Years*. Symposium at Basle University to Commemorate Twenty-Five Years of Per Jacobsson Lectures.

———. 2004. The risks ahead for the world economy. *The Economist*, September 9.

Bertrand, O., and M. Ivaldi. 2007. Competition policy: Europe in international markets. In *Fragmented Power: Europe and the Global Economy* (ed. A. Sapir), pp. 156–99. Brussels: Bruegel Books.

Bhagwati, J. 1984. Splintering and disembodiment of services and developing nations. *The World Economy* 7(2):133–44.

———. 1991. *The World Trading System at Risk*. New York: Harvester Wheatsheaf.

———. 1992. Regionalism and multilateralism. *The World Economy* 15(5):535–55.

———. 1995. U.S. trade policy: the infatuation with free trade agreements. In *The Dangerous Drift to Preferential Trade Agreements* (ed. J. Bhagwati and A. O. Krueger), pp. 1–18. AEI Press.

———. 2005. From Seattle to Hong Kong. *Foreign Affairs*, December.

Bhagwati, J., and R. Hudec (eds). 1996. *Fair Trade and Harmonization: Prerequisites for Free Trade?*, volume 1. Cambridge, MA: MIT Press.

Blackhurst, R. 1997. The WTO and the global economy. *The World Economy* 20(5):527–44.

Borio, C. 2008. The financial turmoil of 2007: a preliminary assessment and some policy considerations. Working Paper 251, Bank for International Settlements.

Boss, A., and A. Rosenschon. 2006. Subventionen in Deutschland: eine Bestandsaufnahme. Kiel Working Paper 1267. Kiel, Germany: Institute for World Economy. Available at http://opus.zbw-kiel.de/volltexte/2006/3930/pdf/kap1267.pdf.

Brecher, J., and T. Costello. 1994. *Global Village or Global Pillage*. Cambridge, MA: South End Press.

Brennan, H. G., and J. M. Buchanan. 1985. *The Reason of Rules*. Cambridge University Press.

Brown, D. K., A. Deardorrff, and R. M. Stern. 2003. Multilateral, regional and bilateral trade-policy options for the United States and Japan. *The World Economy* 26(6):803–28.

Brunnermeier, M. K. Forthcoming. Deciphering the 2007–2008 liquidity and credit crunch. *Journal of Economic Perspectives*.

Buchanan, J. M. 1975. *The Limits of Liberty: Between Anarchy and Leviathan*. University of Chicago Press.

Buchanan, J. M., and G. Tullock. 1962. *The Calculus of Consent*. University of Michigan Press.

Calomiris, C. W. 1998. The IMF's imprudent role as a lender of last resort. *Cato Journal* 17: 275–94.

———. 2000. When will economics guide IMF and World Bank reforms? *Cato Journal* 20(1): 85–103.

Calomiris, C., and A. Meltzer. 1998. *Reforming the IMF*. New York: Columbia Business School.

Chandler, P., and H. Tulkens. 1997. The core of an economy with multilateral environmental externalities. *International Journal of Game Theory* 26:379–401.

Coase, R. H. 1937. The nature of the firm. *Economica* 4(16):386–405.

——— 1960. The problem of social cost. *Journal of Law and Economics* 3:1–44.

Coeuré, B., and J. Pisani-Ferry. 2007. The governance of the European Union's international economic relations: how many voices? In *Fragmented Power: Europe and the Global Economy* (ed. A. Sapir), pp. 21–60. Brussels: Bruegel Books.

Cooley, T., H. Siebert, and I. Walter. 2009. Financial polluters need to pay. Preliminary manuscript.

Corden, W. M. 2007. Exchange rate policies and the global imbalances: thinking about China and the IMF. Paper for James Meade Centenary Conference. Bank of England.

Council of Foreign Relations. 1999. *Safeguarding Prosperity in a Global Financial System: The Future International Financial Architecture*. New York, Council of Foreign Relations.

Dahl, R. A. 1971. *Polyarchy.* New Haven, CT: Yale University Press.

Dales, J. H. 1968. *Pollution, Property and Prices.* University of Toronto Press.

Dasgupta, P. 2002. Social capital and economic performance analytics. In *Social Capital: A Reader* (ed. E. Ostrom and Z. K. Ahn). Cheltenham, U.K.: Elgar.

Davies, H. 2008a. New banking rules: tread carefully. *Financial Times*, October 1.

———. 2008b. The future of financial regulation. *World Economics* 9(January):11–34.

Deke, O. 2007. *Environmental Policy Instruments for Conserving Global Biodiversity.* Kiel Studies, volume 339. Springer.

Den Elzen, M. G. J. 2002. Exploring climate regimes for differentiation of future commitments to stabilise greenhouse gas concentrations. *Integrated Assessment* 3(4):343–59.

Diamond, D., and P. Dybvig. 1983. Bank runs, deposit insurance, and liquidity. *Journal of Political Economy* 91(2):401–19.

Dixit, A., and V. Norman. 1980. *Theory of International Trade.* Cambridge University Press.

Draghi, M. 2008. Statement: follow-up report on implementation, October 11. International Monetary and Financial Committee.

ECB. 2006. *Financial Stability Review*, June.

———. 2008. Developments in the EU: arrangements for financial stability. Monthly Bulletin, April.

Eichengreen, B. J. 1999a. Involving the private sector in crisis prevention and resolution. In *IMF Conference on Key Issues in Reform of the International Monetary and Financial Systems, May 28–29.* Washington, DC: IMF.

———. 1999b. *Toward a New International Financial Architecture: A Practical Post-Asia Agenda.* Washington, DC: Institute for International Economics.

———. 2001. *The EMS Crisis in Retrospect.* Discussion Paper 2704, Centre for Economic Policy Research.

———. 2002. Capital account liberalization: what do the cross-country studies tell us? *World Bank Economic Review* 15(3):341–65.

———. 2006. *How to Really Reform the IMF.* Speech held on February 23. Available at www.econ.berkeley.edu/-eichengr/reform.pdf.

———. 2008. Die Parallelen zur Asien-Krise. *Frankfurter Allgemeine Zeitung*, September 27.

Elliott, K. 2006. *Economic Sanctions as a Foreign Policy Tool.* Washington, DC: Institute for International Economics and Center for Global Development.

Elliott, K., and G. C. Hufbauer. 1999. Same song, same refrain? Economic sanctions in the 1990s. *American Economic Review* 89(2):403–8.

Ergunor, O. E. 2007. On the resolution of financial crises: the Swedish experience. Policy Discussion Paper 21, Federal Reserve Bank of Cleveland.

Eucken, W. 1940. *Die Grundlagen der Nationalökonomie.* Jena: Fischer. (English Edition: *The Foundations of Economics: History and Theory in the Analysis of Economic Reality.* Springer.)

European Commission. 2007. *EU Action Against Climate Change: EU Emissions Trading: An Open System Promoting Global Innovation.* Brussels: European Commission.

European Court of Justice. 2007: *The Court of Justice of the European Communities.* Available at http://curia.europa.eu/en/instit/presentationfr/index_cje.htm.

European Environment Agency. 2007. *Greenhouse Gas Emission Trends and Projections in Europe 2007.* Copenhagen: European Environment Agency.

European Patent Convention. 2007. Available at www.epo.org/patents/law/legal-texts/epc.html.

Federal Trade Commission. 2008. Available at www.ftc.gov/oia/authorities.shtm.

Feldstein, M. 1998. Refocusing the IMF. *Foreign Affairs* 77(2):20–33.

Fikentscher, W., and U. Immenga (eds). 1995. *Draft International Antitrust Code: Kommentierter Entwurf eines internationalen Wettbewerbsrechts mit ergänzenden Beiträgen.* Baden-Baden, Germany: Nomos.

Financial Stability Forum. 2008. Report of the Financial Stability Forum on enhancing market and institutional resilience. Available at www.fsforum.org/publications/r_0804.pdf.

Finger, J. M., M. D. Ingco, and U. Reincke. 1996. *The Uruguay Round: Statistics on Tariff Concessions Given and Received.* Washington, DC: World Bank.

Finus, M. 2003. Stability and design of international environmental agreements: the case of transboundary pollution. In *The International Yearbook of Environmental and Resource Economics: A Survey of Current Issues* (ed. T. Tietenberg and H. Folmer), pp. 82–158. Northampton, U.K.: Edward Elgar.

Fischer, S. 1998. IMF and crisis prevention. *Financial Times*, 30 March.

———. 1999. On the need for an international lender of last resort. *Journal of Economic Perspectives* 13(4):85–104.

———. 2000. *On the Need for an International Lender of Last Resort.* Princeton University Press.

———. 2001. Distinguished lecture on economics in government: exchange rate regimes: is the bipolar view correct? *Journal of Economic Perspectives* 15(2):3–24.

Fliessbach, K., et al. 2007. Social comparison affects reward-related brain activity in the human ventral striatum. *Science* 318(23):1305–8.

Franke, G., and J. P. Krahnen. 2007. Finanzmarktkrise: Ursachen und Lehren. *Frankfurter Allgemeine Zeitung*, November 24.

Frankel, J. A. 1997. *Regional Trading Blocs in the World Economic System.* Washington, DC: Institute for International Economics.

Frieden, J. A. 2006. *Global Capitalism: Its Fall and Rise in the Twentieth Century.* New York: W. W. Norton & Company.

Friedman, M. 1962. *Capitalism and Freedom.* University of Chicago Press.

Furubotn, E. B., and S. Pejovich. 1972. Property rights and economic theory. A survey of recent literature. *Journal of Economic Literature* 10:1137.

Geithner, T. F. 2008. Reducing systemic risk in a dynamic financial system. *BIS Review* 74. Bank for International Settlements.

Gilpin, R. 1987. *The Political Economy of International Relations.* Princeton University Press.

Gilpin, R. 2001. *Global Political Economy: Understanding the International Economic Order.* Princeton University Press.

Global Commons Institute. 1996. Draft proposal for a climate change protocol based on contraction and convergence. Available at www.gci.org.uk. Accessed February 13, 2008.

Global Subsidies Initiative. 2007. *Biofuels—At What Costs? Government Support for Ethanol and Biodiesel in Selected OECD Countries.* Prepared by Ronald Steenblik. Geneva: Global Subsidies Initiative.

Goodhart, C. A. E. 2008. The regulatory response to the financial crisis. Working Paper 2257, CESIFO.

Graham, E. M. 1995. Competition policy and the new trade agenda in OECD. *New Dimensions of Market Access in a Globalizing World Economy.* Paris: OECD.

Grossman, G. M., and E. Helpman. 1991. Trade, knowledge spillovers, and growth. *European Economic Review* 35(2/3):517–26.

———. 1995. Trade wars and trade talks. *Journal of Political Economy* 103(4):675–708.

Gupta, J. 1998. Encouraging developing country participation in the climate change regime. Discussion Paper E98-08, Institute for Environmental Studies, Free University of Amsterdam.

Haggard, S., and B. A. Simmons. 1987. Theories of international regimes. *International Organization* 41(3):491–517.

Harris, J., and M. Todaro. 1970. Migration, unemployment and development: a two-sector analysis. *American Economic Review* Papers and Proceedings 60(1):126–42.

Hassett, K. A. 2008. *Sale of the Century*. Washington, DC: American Enterprise Institute for Public Policy.

Hayek, F. A. 1944. *Der Weg zur Knechtschaft* (special edition, 2003). München: Olzog.

——. 1952. *Individualismus und wirtschaftliche Ordnung*. Erlenbach-Zürich: Rentsch.

——. 1968. *Der Wettbewerb als Entdeckungsverfahren*. Kieler Vorträge 56. Kiel, Germany: Institute for World Economy.

——. 1971. *Die Verfassung der Freiheit* (ed. A. Bosch and R. Veit), 4th edn, 2005. Tübingen: Mohr.

——. 1973. *Law, Legislation and Liberty: A New Statement of the Liberal Principles of Justice and Political Economy*, volume I: *Rules and Order*. London: Routledge & Kegan Paul.

——. 1975a. *Die Theorie komplexer Phänomene*. Tübingen: Mohr.

——. 1975b. *Die Irrtümer des Konstruktivismus und die Grundlagen legitimer Kritik gesellschaftlicher Gebilde*. Tübingen: Mohr.

——. 1979a. *Entnationalisierung des Geldes: Eine Analyse der Theorie und Praxis konkurrierender Unternehmen*. Tübingen: Mohr.

——. 1979b. *Die drei Quellen der menschlichen Werte*. Tübingen: Mohr.

——. 1979c. *Liberalismus*. Tübingen: Mohr.

——. 1981a. *Regeln und Ordnung*. München: VMI.

——. 1981b. *Die Illusion der sozialen Gerechtigkeit*. München: VMI.

——. 1981c. *Die Verfassung einer Gesellschaft freier Menschen*. München: VMI.

——. 1996a. *Die Anmaßung von Wissen: Neue Freiburger Studien*. Tübingen: Mohr.

——. 1996b. *Die Verhängnisvolle Anmaßung: Die Irrtümer des Sozialismus*. Tübingen: Mohr.

Heal, G. M. 1992. International negotiations on emission control. *Structural Change and Economic Dynamics* 3:223–40.

——. 2000. Biodiversity as a commodity. In *Encyclopedia of Biodiversity* (ed. S. A. Levin), volume 1. San Diego, CA: Academic Press.

Heister, J. 1997. *Der internationale CO-2-Vertrag: Strategien zur Stabilisierung multilateraler Kooperation zwischen souveränen Staaten*. Kiel Studies 282. Springer.

Herzog, R., and G. Gerken. 2008. Stoppt den Europäischen Gerichtshof. *Frankfurter Allgemeinen Zeitung*, September 8.

Hillman, A. L. 1989. *The Political Economy of Protection*. Chur, Switzerland: Harwood.

——. 1994. The political economy of migration policy. In *Migration: A Challenge to Europe* (ed. H. Siebert). Tübingen: Mohr.

Hirschman, A. O. 1970. *Exit, Voice and Loyalty: Responses to Decline in Firms, Organizations and States*. Cambridge, MA: Harvard University Press.

Hobbes, T. 1651. *Leviathan, or the Matter, Forme and Power of a Common Wealth Ecclesiasticall and Civil* (1946 edition). Oxford, U.K.: Blackwell.

Hoekman, B. M., and M. M. Kostecki. 2001. *The Political Economy of the World Trading System*. Oxford University Press.

Hoekman, B. M., and P. C. Mavroidis. 1994. Competition, competition policy and the GATT. *The World Economy* 17(2):121–50.

——. 2007. *The World Trade Organization. Law, Economics, and Politics*. Abingdon, U.K.: Routledge.

Hoekman, B. M., and P. K. Saggi. 1999. *Multilateral Disciplines for Investment-Related Policies?* Presented at the conference on Global Regionalism, Instituto Affari Internazionali, Rome.

Hoekman, B. M., K. E. Maskus, and K. Saggi. 2005. Transfer of technology to developing countries: unilateral and multilateral policy options. *World Development* 33(10):1587–602.

Hoggarth, G., R. Reis, and V. Saporta. 2002. Costs of banking system instability: some empirical evidence. *Journal of Banking & Finance* 26(5):825–55.

Hufbauer, G. C. 2003. Looking 30 years ahead in global governance. In *Global Governance: An Architecture for the World Economy* (ed. H. Siebert), pp. 245–69. Springer.

——. 2008. Global governance: old and new issues. In *Conference on Global Governance in Honor of Horst Siebert*. Kiel Institute for the World Economy.

Hufbauer, G. C., J. J. Schott, K. A. Elliott, and B. Egg. 2007. *Economic Sanctions Reconsidered*, 3rd edn. Washington, DC: Institute for International Economics.

Hufbauer, G. C., and J. Kim. 2008. Reconciling GHG limits with the global trading system. Draft paper.

Hufbauer, G. C., and S. Stephenson. 2007. Services trade: past liberalization and future challenges. *Journal of International Economic Law* 10:605–30.

Hurrell, A. 2007. *On Global Order: Power, Values, and the Constitution of International Society*. Oxford University Press.

Institute of International Finance. 2008. *Final Report of the IIF Committee on Market Best Practices: Principles of Conduct and Best Practice Recommendations*. Washington, DC: IIF.

International Accounting Standards Board. 2008. International financial reporting standards. Available at www.iasb.org/Home.htm.

International Emissions Trading Association (IETA). 2006. *State and Trends of the Carbon Market 2006: Update*. Washington, DC: World Bank. Available at www.ieta.org/ieta/www/ pages/getfile.php?docID=1929.

International Energy Agency (IEA). 2006. *World Energy Outlook 2006*. Paris: IEA.

——. 2007. *World Energy Outlook 2007—China and India Insights*. Paris: IEA.

International Financial Institution Advisory Commission (IFIAC). 2000. *Meltzer Report*. Washington, DC: IFIAC.

International Monetary Fund (IMF). 1999. *Involving the Private Sector in Forestalling and Resolving Financial Crises*. Washington, DC: IMF.

——. 2000. Quota Formula Review Group. Report to the IMF Executive Board of the Quota Formula Review Group.

——. 2003. Lessons from the Crisis in Argentina. Prepared by the Policy Development and Review Department. Washington, DC: IMF.

——. 2005a. *Annual Report 2005*. Washington, DC: IMF.

——. 2005b. *International Financial Statistics*. Washington, DC: IMF.

——. 2005c. *The Managing Director's Report on the Fund's Medium-Term Strategy*. Washington, DC: IMF.

——. 2006a. Press Release 06/189.

——. 2006b. Press Release 06/205.

——. 2006c. Report of the Executive Board of Governors. Quota and voice reform in the International Monetary Fund.

IMF. 2006d. The Managing Director's report on implementing the Fund's medium-term strategy. Available at www.imf.org/external/np/pp/eng/2006/040506.pdf.

——. 2007a. Crocket Commission (Committee to Study the Sustainable Long-Term Financing of the IMF 2007).

——. 2007b. Financial statement for the years ended April 30, 2007, and 2006.

——. 2007c. International financial statistics.

——. 2007d. Key trends in implementation of the Fund's transparency policy.

——. 2007e. Quotas: updated calculations and data adjustments.

——. 2007f. Statistics department Currency Composition of Official Foreign Exchange Reserves database. Available at www.imf.org/external/np/sta/cofer/eng/index.htm.

——. 2008a. Financial soundness indicators (FSIs) and the IMF. Available at www.imf.org/external/np/sta/fsi/eng/fsi.htm.

——. 2008b. Global financial stability report. Last updated Tuesday October 7, 2008.

——. 2008c. IMF Board of Governors adopts quota and voice reforms by large margin. Press Release 08/93, April 29.

——. 2008d. IMF Executive Board recommends reforms to overhaul quota and voice. Press Release 08/64, March 28.

——. 2008e. Progress report on the activities of the independent evaluation office. Available at www.ieo-imf.org/pub/pdf/IMFC10112008.pdf.

——. 2008f. IMF surveillance: a factsheet.

International Organization for Migration (IOM). 2005. *World Migration 2005: Costs and Benefits of International Migration*. Geneva, Switzerland: IOM.

International Tribunal for the Law of the Sea. 2007. Available at www.itlos.org/start2_en.html.

Internet Corporation for Assigned Names and Numbers (ICANN). 2007. Available at www.icann.org.

Issing Committee. 2008. New financial order. Recommendations by the Issing Committee.

Kant, I. 1795 (1983 reprint). To perpetual peace: a philosophy sketch. In *I. Kant. Perpetual Peace and Other Essays on Politics, History, and Morals* (transl. T. Humphrey). Indianapolis, IN: Hackett.

Kemp, M., and H. J. Wan. 1976. An elementary proposition concerning the formation of customs unions. *Journal of International Economics* 6(1):95.

Khana, P. 2008. Waiving goodbye to hegemony. *New York Times*, January 27.

Kindleberger, C. P. 1973. *The World in Depression 1929–1939*. London: Lane.

——. 1989. *Maniacs, Panics, and Crashes. A History of Financial Crises*. New York: Basic Books.

King, M. 2006. Reform of the International Monetary Fund. New Delhi.

Klevorick, A. K., and G. H. Kramer. 1973. Social choice and pollution management: the Genossenschaften. *Journal of Public Economics* 2:101–46.

Klodt, H. 2005. *Towards a Global Competition Order*. Berlin: Liberal.

Kneese, A. V., and B. T. Bower. 1968. *Managing Water Quality: Economics, Technology and Institutions*. Baltimore, MD: Johns Hopkins Press.

Krueger, A. O. 1996. *The Political Economy of Trade Protection*. University of Chicago Press.

—— (ed.). 1998. *The WTO as an International Organization*. University of Chicago Press.

Krugman, P. R. 1991. *Geography and Trade*. Leuven University Press.

——. 1994. Competitiveness: a dangerous obsession. *Foreign Affairs* 73(2):28–44.

Krugman, P. R., and M. Obstfeld. 2006. *International Economics: Theory and Policy*, 7th edn. Reading, MA: Addison-Wesley.

Kuhn, T. S. 1962. *The Structure of Scientific Revolutions*. Chicago University Press.
Kydland, F. E., and E. C. Prescott. 1977. Rules rather than discretion: the inconsistency of optimal plans. *Journal of Political Economy* 85(3):473–92.
Langewiesche, D. 2007. Die Nation schafft Freiheit. Interview in *Der Spiegel*, February 20.
Langhammer, R. J. 1995. Regional integration in East Asia: from market-driven regionalisation to institutionalised regionalism? *Weltwirtschaftliches Archiv* 131(1):167–201.
Lerrick, A. 2005. A leaf of faith for sovereign debt default: from IMF judgment to automatic incentives. *Cato Journal* 25:25–31.
———. 2007. What's left for the IMF. *Wall Street Journal*, April 13.
Lerrick, A., and A. H. Meltzer. 2002. Sovereign default: the private sector can resolve bankruptcy without a formal court. *Quarterly International Economics Report*. Mimeo, Carnegie Mellon.
———. 2003. Blueprint for an international lender of last resort. *Journal of Monetary Economics* 50:289–303.
Lipset, S. M. 1959. Some social requisites of democracy: economic development and political legitimacy. *American Political Science Review* 53(1):69–105.
Locke, J. 1689. *The Two Treatises of Civil Government*. Quoted according to the edition by Peter Laslett, 1960. Cambridge University Press.
Lorz, O. 1997. *Standortwettbewerb bei internationaler Kapitalmobilität: Eine modelltheoretische Untersuchung*, Kieler Studies 284. Tübingen: Mohr.
———. 1998. Capital mobility, tax competition and lobbying for redistributive capital taxation. *European Journal of Political Economy* 14(2):265–79.
Lucas, R. 1990. Why doesn't capital flow from rich to poor countries? *American Economic Review* 80:92–6.
MacNeil, I. R. 1978. Contracts: adjustment of long-term economic relations under classical, neoclassical, and relational contract law. *Northwestern University Law Review* 72(6):854–905.
Maddison, A. 1982. *Phases of Capitalist Development*. Oxford University Press.
———. 1992. *Dynamic Forces in Capitalist Development*. Oxford University Press.
———. 2001. *The World Economy: A Millennial Perspective*. Paris: Development Centre of OECD.
Mankiw, N. G. 1995. The growth of nations. *Brookings Papers of Economic Activity* 1:275–326.
Marx, K. 1867. *Das Kapital*. Kritik der politischen Oekonomie. Erster Band. Der Produktionsprozess des Kapitals; Band II: Der Zirkulationsprozeß des Kapitals 1885; Band III: Der Gesamtprozeß der kapitalistischen Produktion 1895. Hamburg: Otto Meissner.
Maskus, K. 2000. *Intellectual Property Rights in the Global Economy*. Washington, DC: Institute for International Economics.
Mauss, M. 1923–4. Essai sur le don. Forme et raison de l'échange dans les sociétés archaïques. *Année sociologique*.
———. 2005. *Exchange Rates under the East Asian Dollar Standard: Living with Conflicted Virtue*. Cambridge, MA: MIT Press.
McKinnon, R. I. 1982. Currency substitution and instability in the world dollar standard. *American Economic Review* 72(3):320–33.
Meltzer, A. H. 1998. Asian problems and the IMF. Testimony prepared for the Joint Committee.
———. 2008. Regulatory overkill. *Wall Street Journal*, March 27.
Messerlin, P. A. 2001. *Measuring the Costs of Protection in Europe. European Commercial Policy in the 2000s*. Washington, DC: Institute for International Economics.

Michels, R. 1915 (1962 edn). *Political Parties*. New York: Collier.

Minsky, H. P. 1986. *Stabilizing an Unstable Economy*. New Haven, CT: Yale University Press.

Minton-Beddoes, Z. 1995. Why the IMF needs reform. *Foreign Affairs* 74(3):123–33.

Miron, J. A. 2008. Bankruptcy, not bailout, is the right answer. *CNN International*, October 2.

Montesquieu. 1748. *De l'esprit des lois*. Geneva, Switzerland (published anonymously).

Morgan Stanley. 2007. *G10 Currencies. Tracking the Tectonic Shift in Foreign Reserves and SWFs*. Morgan Stanley Research, March 15.

Mundell, R. A. 1961. A theory of optimum currency areas. *American Economic Review* 51(4): 657–65.

———. 2003. The international monetary system and the case for a world currency. Lecture series. Available at www.tiger.edu.pl/publikacje/dist/mundell2.pdf.

Myrdal, G. 1956. *An International Economy. Problems and Prospects*. New York: Harper & Brothers.

Nakaso, H. 2001. The financial crisis in Japan during the 1990s: how the Bank of Japan responded and the lessons learnt. Paper 6, Bank for International Settlement, BIS.

Neely, C. J. 1999. An introduction to capital controls. *Federal Reserve Bank Review* 81(6): 13–30.

Nicolaides, P. 1994. Towards multilateral rules on competition: the problems in mutual recognition of national rules. *World Competition* 17(3):5–48.

Nordhaus, W. D. 2006. After Kyoto: alternative mechanisms to control global warming. *American Economic Review* 96(2):31–34.

North, D. 1990. *Institutions, Institutional Change and Economic Performance*. Cambridge University Press.

Nunes, P. A. L. D., and J. C. J. M. van den Bergh. 2001. Economic valuation of biodiversity: sense or nonsense? *Ecological Economic* 39:203–22.

OECD. 2005. *Science, Technology and Industry Scoreboard*. Paris: OECD.

———. 2007. *International Trade by Commodities Statistics*, various issues. Paris: OECD.

Olson, M. 1969. The principle of "fiscal equivalence." *American Economic Review* 59:479–87.

———. 1982. *The Rise and Decline of Nations. Economic Growth, Stagflation and Social Rigidities*. New Haven, CT: Yale University Press.

O'Neill, J. 2008. Russia and the world in 2020: Goldman Sachs. Paper presented at the XII St. Petersburg International Economic Forum, June 6–8.

Ostry, S. 1995. New dimensions of market access: challenges for the trading system. In *New Dimensions of Market Access in a Globalizing World Economy*. Paris: OECD.

———. 1997. A new regime of foreign direct investment. Group of Thirty Washington occasional papers 53.

Oxfam. 2006. G8 subsidies contributing to WTO crisis. Press release, July 11.

Panagariya, A. 1999. *TRIPS and the WTO: An Uneasy Marriage*. Mimeo.

Peterson, S., and G. Klepper. 2007. Distribution matters: taxes vs. emissions trading in post Kyoto climate regimes. Kiel Working Paper 1380. Kiel, Germany: Institute for the World Economy.

Pidgirsky, A., and K. Dittmeier. 2007. Foreign investment and national security act of 2007. *Client Alert. Corporate Law Alert*. August 2007. Adams and Reese, LLL.

Plummer, M. R. 2005. Creating an ASEAN economic community: lessons from the EU and reflections on the roadmap. In *Roadmap to an ASEAN Economic Community* (ed. D. Hew). Singapore: ISEAS.

Plummer, M. R. 2006. *The ASEAN Economic Community and the European Experience.* Working Paper on Regional Economic Integration 1, Asian Development Bank.

———. 2007. "Best practices" in regional trading agreements: an application to Asia. *The World Economy* 30(12):1771–905.

Plummer, M. R., and E. Jones. 2005. Global economic regionalism and Asia: the implications of intra- and extra-regional accords. *Journal of Asian Economics* 16(1):1–3.

Pomfret, R. 2007. Is regionalism an increasing feature of the world economy? *The World Economy* 30(6):923–47.

Popper, K. R. 1945. *The Open Society and Its Enemies.* London: Routledge & Kegan Paul. (Quoted according to the 5th edn, 2003.)

Prebisch, R. 1950. *The Economic Development of Latin America and Its Principal Problems. Economic Commission for Latin America.* New York: United Nations Publications.

Rawls, J. 1971. *A Theory of Justice.* Cambridge, MA: Belknap.

Ritholz, B. 2008. How SEC regulatory exemptions helped lead to collapse. *Finance & Markets Monitor.* October 21.

Rodrik, D. 1997. *Has Globalization Gone Too Far?* Washington, DC: Institute of International Economics.

Rodrik, D., A. Subramanian, and F. Trebbi. 2004. Institutions rule: the primacy of institutions over geography and integration in economic development. *Journal of Economic Growth* 9(2):131–65. Available at http://ideas.repec.org/a/kap/jecgro/v9y2004i2p131-165.html.

Rubin, R. E. 1999. Remarks on reform of the international financial architecture to the School of Advanced International Studies. *Treasury News*, April 21.

Rueff, J. 1972. *The Monetary Sin of the West.* New York: Macmillan.

Sachs, J. 1997. Limits of convergence. Nature, nurture and growth. *The Economist*, June 14.

———. 2003. *Institutions Don't Rule: Direct Effects of Geography on Per Capita Income.* Working Paper 9490, National Bureau of Economic Research.

Samuelson, P. A. 1954. The pure theory of public expenditure. *Review of Economic and Statistics* 36(4):387–89.

Sapir, A. 2006. Global governance: an agenda for Europe. *Bruegel Policy Brief*, issue 2006/07. Brussels: Bruegel Books.

———. 2007. *Fragmented Power: Europe and the Global Economy.* Brussels: Bruegel Books.

Schelling, T. C. 2002. What makes greenhouse gas sense? Time to rethink the Kyoto Protocol. *Foreign Affairs* 81(3):1–9.

Scherer, F. M. 1994. *Competition Policies for an Integrated World Economy.* Washington, DC: Brookings Institution.

Schmidt, M. M., R. C. Smith, and I. Walter. 2008. Der globale Finanzsektor im Sturmtief. *Neue Zürcher Zeitung*, September 20–1.

Scholes, M. S. 2008. The role of liquidity and risk transfer services in the economy. Third Lindau Meeting in Economic Sciences. Available at www.lindau-nobel.de/LecturesOnline. AxCMS?ActiveID=1173.

Schulze, G. G., and H. W. Ursprung. 1999. Globalisation of the economy and the nation state. *The World Economy* 22(3):295–352.

Schumpeter, J. A. 1934. *The Theory of Economic Development. An Inquiry into Profits, Capital, Credit, Interest and the Business Cycle.* Cambridge, MA: Harvard University Press.

Schumpeter, J. A. 1942. *Capitalism, Socialism and Democracy.* New York: Harper & Row.

———. 1943. *Capitalism, Socialism and Democracy.* London: Allen & Unwin.

Scitovsky, T. 1954. Two concepts of external economies. *Journal of Political Economics* 62: 143–51.

Seidel, M. 1997. Between unanimity and majority. Towards new rules of decision-making. In *Quo Vadis Europe?* (ed. H. Siebert). Tübingen: Mohr.

Sen, A. K. 1990. Gender and cooperative conflicts. In *Persistent Inequalities: Women and World Development* (ed. I. Tinker). Oxford University Press.

——. 2001. *Development as Freedom.* Oxford University Press.

Serageldin, I. 2008. Science in Muslim countries today. Mimeo.

Servan-Schreiber, J.-J. 1967. *Le défi américain.* Paris: Editions Denoël.

Shiller, R. J. 2005. *Irrational Exuberance.* Princeton University Press.

Siebert, H. 1983. *Ökonomische Theorie natürlicher Ressourcen.* Tübingen: Mohr.

——. 1993. Internationale Wanderungsbewegungen: Erklärungsansätze und Gestaltungsfragen. *Schweizerische Zeitschrift für Volkswirtschaft und Statistik* 129(3):229–55.

——. 1996a. Institutionelle Arrangements für die Zuweisung von Opportunitätskosten. In *Festschrift für Ernst-Joachim Mestmäcker* (ed. U. Immenga, W. Möschel, and D. Reuter), pp. 309–20. Baden-Baden, Germany: Nomos.

——. 1996b. Trade policy and environmental protection. *The World Economy: Global Trade Policy*, pp. 183–94.

——. 1998. An institutional order for a globalizing world economy. In *Trade, Growth, and Economic Policy in Open Economies: Essays in Honour of Hans-Jürgen Vosgerau* (ed. K. Jaeger and K.-J. Koch). Springer.

——. 1999. What does globalization mean for the world trading system? In *From GATT to the WTO: The Multilateral Trading System in the New Millennium* (ed. WTO). The Hague, the Netherlands: Kluwer.

——. 2000. *The Paradigm of Locational Competition.* Discussion Paper 367, Kiel Institute of World Economics.

—— (ed.). 2001. *The World's New Financial Landscape: Challenges for Economic Policy.* Springer.

——. 2002. Europe: quo vadis? Reflections on the future institutional framework of the European Union. *The World Economy* 25(1):1–32.

—— (ed.). 2003a. *Global Governance: An Architecture for the World Economy.* Springer.

——. 2003b. Globalisierung und internationaler Handel: Dimensionen, Ängste und Chancen. *Wirtschaftspolitische Blätter* 50(4):457–71.

——. 2005a. Das Minas-Gerais-Problem des Euros. *Handelsblatt*, February 4.

——. 2005b. TAFTA: a dead horse or an attractive open club. Working Paper 1240, Kiel Institute of World Economics.

——. 2005c. *The German Economy: Beyond the Social Market.* Princeton University Press.

——. 2006a. Locational competition: a neglected paradigm in the international division of labour. *The World Economy* 29 (2):137–59.

——. 2006b. Where do we go after Hong Kong? *International Economics and Economic Policy* 3(1):7–10.

——. 2007a. China: coming to grips with the new global player. *The World Economy* 30(6): 893–922.

——. 2007b. China: opportunities of and constraints on the new global player. *CESifo Forum* 4:52–61.

——. 2007c. Gegen ein bedingungsloses Grundeinkommen. *Frankfurter Allgemeine Zeitung*, June 27.

——. 2007d. Reforming the IMF. *Occasional Paper. Konrad Adenauer Foundation.* Washington, DC, February.

——. 2007e. *The World Economy: A Global Analysis*, 3rd edn. London and New York: Routledge.

Siebert, H. 2008a. Die verfehlte Subvention der Biokraftstoffe. *Frankfurter Allgemeine Zeitung*, May 16.

———. 2008b. *Economics of the Environment. Theory and Policy*, 7th edn. Springer.

———. 2008c. Ein Regelwerk für Finanzmärkte. *Frankfurter Allgemeine Zeitung*, October 25.

Siebert, H., and M. Koop. 1990. Institutional competition: a concept for Europe? *Außenwirtschaft* 45:439–62.

———. 1993. Institutional competition versus centralization: quo vadis Europe? *Oxford Review of Economic Policy* 9(1):15–30.

Singer, H. W. 1950. The distribution of gains between investing and borrowing countries. *American Economic Review* 40(2):473–85.

Smaghi, L. B. 2006. Powerless Europe: why is the euro area still a political dwarf? *International Finance* 9(2):261–79.

Smith, A. 1759. *The Theory of Moral Sentiments*. London. (Facsimile of the original edition.)

———. 1776. *An Inquiry into the Nature and Causes of the Wealth of Nations*. (Reprinted in Penguin English Library 1982.)

Smith, R., and I. Walter. 2008. Kein Ende des agressiven Banking. *Sonntagszeitung*, November 9.

Snower, D. 2008. A long way to go. *Wall Street Journal*, November 12.

SPD. 2008. Eine neue Balance zwischen Markt und Staat: Verkehrsregeln für die internationalen Finanzmärkte. Mimeo, October 27.

Sovereign Wealth Funds Institute. 2008. Available at www.swfinstitute.org.

Srinivasan, T. N. 1998. Regionalism and the WTO: is nondiscrimination passé? In *The WTO as an International Organization* (ed. A. O. Krueger). University of Chicago Press.

Steiner, H. J., P. Alston, and R. Goodman. 2007. *International Human Rights in Context*, 2nd edn. Oxford University Press.

Stern, N. H. 2007. *The Economics of Climate Change: The Stern Review*. Cambridge University Press.

Stiglitz, H. E. 2008. The global financial crisis: lessons for policy and implications for economic theory. Third Lindau Meeting in Economic Sciences. Available at www.lindau-nobel.de/LecturesOnline.AxCMS?ActiveID=1173.

Stiglitz, J. E., and A. Charlton. 2005. *Fair Trade for All. How Trade Can Promote Development*. Oxford University Press.

Stoeckel, A., D. Pearce, and G. Banks. 1990. *Western Trade Blocs: Game, Set or Match for Asia–Pacific and the World Economy?* Canberra: Centre for International Economics.

Summers, L. 2007. Funds that shake capitalist logic. *Wall Street Journal*, July 29.

Tiebout, C. 1956. A pure theory of local expenditures. *Journal of Political Economy* 64(5): 416–24.

Tobin, J. 1978. A proposal for international monetary reform. *Eastern Economic Journal* 4(3/4):153–59.

Triffin, R. 1978. The international role and fate of the dollar. *Foreign Affairs* 57:269–86.

Tumlir, J. 1979a. The new protectionism, cartels and the international order. In *Challenges to a Liberal International Order* (ed. R. Amacher, G. Haberler, and T. Williett). Washington, DC: American Enterprise Institute.

———. 1979b. Weltwirtschaftsordnung: Regeln, Kooperation und Souveränität. *Kieler Vorträge 87*. Kiel, Germany: Institute for the World Economy.

———. 1983. International economic order and democratic constitutionalism. *ORDO* 34:71–83.

UNEP Net. 2007. http://climatechange.unep.net/.

United Nations. 2008. World population prospects: the 2006 revision and world urbanization prospects. Available at http://esa.un.org/unpp.

United Nations Human Settlements Program (UN Habitat). 2006. State of the world's cities 2006–7. Available at www.unhabitat.org/content.asp?typeid=19&catid=555&cid=5359.

United Nations Statistics Division. 2007. Millennium Development Goals indicator database.

Viner, J. 1950. *The Customs Union Issue*. New York: Carnegie Endowment for International Peace.

Wade, R. 1996. Globalization and its limits: reports of the death of national economy are greatly exaggerated. In *National Diversity and Global Capitalism* (ed. S. Berger and R. P. Dore). Ithaca, NY: Cornell University Press.

Wallison, J., and C. W. Calomoris. 2008. The last trillion-dollar commitment. The destruction of Fannie Mae and Freddie Mac. *American Enterprise Institute*, September 30.

Weber, M. 1919. *Politik als Beruf*. (Quoted according to the edition Büchergilde Gutenberg, Frankfurt, 1999.)

———. 1922. *Wirtschaft und Gesellschaft—Grundriss einer verstehenden Soziologie*. (Quoted according to Weber 1958, a translation published posthumously. The three types of legitimate rule. *Berkeley Publications in Society & Institutions* 4(1):1–11.)

Williamson, J. 1993. Exchange rate management. *Economic Journal* 103(416):188–97.

———. 2006. Fred Bergsten and the Institute's work on exchange rate regimes. In *C. Fred Bergsten and the World Economy*. Washington, DC: Petersen Institute for International Economics.

Wilson, B. 2006. *Remedies in WTO Dispute Settlement: Experience to Date (1995–2006)*. Presentation at WTO Appellate Body Conference, Columbia University, April 8, 2006. Available at www.sipa.columbia.edu/wto/pdfs/RemediesInWTODisputeSettlement.pps.

Wilson, D., and R. Purushothaman. 2003. Dreaming with the BRICS: the Path to 2050. Global Economics Paper 99, Goldman Sachs.

World Bank. *Global Development Finance* (previously: World Debt Tables), various issues. Washington, DC: World Bank.

———. *Global Economic Prospects and the Developing Countries*, various issues. Washington, DC: World Bank.

———. *World Data*, various issues. Washington, DC: World Bank.

———. *World Development Indicators*, various issues. Washington, DC: World Bank.

———. *World Development Report*, various issues. Washington, DC: World Bank.

———. 2005a. *Global Development Finance 2005: Mobilizing Finance and Managing Vulnerability*. Washington, DC: World Bank.

———. 2005b. *World Development Indicators 2005*. Washington, DC: World Bank.

———. 2005c. *World Development Report 2006*. Washington, DC: World Bank.

———. 2005d. *World Development Report 2006*. Washington, DC: World Bank.

———. 2006a. China Quarterly Update, February 2006. Available at http://siteresources. worldbank.org/intchina/resources/318862-1121421293578/cqu_feb06.pdf.

World Bank. 2006b. Corruption & Development Assistance. Available at http://web.worldbank.org/wbsite/external/topics/extpublicsectorandgovernance/ extanticorruption/0,,contentmdk:20222111-menupk:1165474-pagepk:148956-pipk: 216618-thesitepk:384455,00.html.

———. 2006c. Global economic prospects: economic implications of remittance and migration. Available at http://wdsbeta.worldbank.org/external/default/WDSContentServer/IW3P/ IB/2005/11/14/000112742_20051114174928/Rendered/PDF/343200GEP02006.pdf.

———. 2007. *World Development Indicators*, various issues. Washington, DC: World Bank. Available at www.worldbank.org.

World Intellectual Property Organization. 2007. Available at www.wipo.int/portal/index.html.en.

———. 1995. *Regionalism and the World Trading System.* Geneva: WTO.

———. 2004a. *International Trade Statistics 2004.* Geneva: WTO.

———. 2004b. *The Future of the WTO.* Report by the Consultative Board to the Director-General Supachai Panitchpakdi, Geneva.

———. 2005. *International Trade Statistics 2005.* Geneva: WTO.

———. 2007a *Annual Report 2007,* various issues. Geneva: World Bank.

———. 2007b. India et al. vs U.S.: "shrimp–turtle." Available at www.wto.org/english/tratop_e/envir_e/edis08_e.htm.

———. 2007c. Regional trade agreements: facts and figures. Available at www.wto.org/english/tratop_e/region_e/summary_e.xls (retrieved July 4, 2007).

———. 2007d. Understanding the WTO: settling disputes. Available at www.wto.org/english/tratop_e/dispu_e/dispu_e.htm#dsb.

World Wildlife Foundation. 2002. Living Planet Report 2002. Available at www.panda.org/downloads/general/LPR_2002.pdf.

Yang, T. 2006. International treaty enforcement as a public good: institutional deterrent sanctions in international environmental agreements. Paper 1136, Bepress Legal Series.

Zanker, B. 2006. *Internationaler Währungsfonds 2015. Reformbedarf und Reformmöglichkeiten.* Berlin: Stiftung Wissenschaft und Politik.

Zhao, Z. 2005. Migration, labor market flexibility and wage determination in China: a review. *Developing Economies* 43(2):285–312.

Index